Polar Eskimo

Alex Hibbert

Polar Eskimo

Photographs © Dark Ice Project, Hans Jensen, or public domain/expired
Original illustrations by Vuk Žugić
Typeset in 10-point Baskerville

ISBN 978-1912821723 (paperback)

First published in 2018 by Tricorn Books
Aspex Gallery, 42 The Vulcan Building
Gunwharf Quays, Portsmouth, PO1 3BF

Printed and bound in the United Kingdom

Amazon UK review average score
4.4/5 correct as of Sept 15th 2020

Polar Eskimo

A young polar traveller's time living
with hunters of the Far North

To Martha,

Best polar wishes!

Alec Hutch

CONTENTS

ABOUT THE AUTHOR

Alex Hibbert was born in 1986 in Hampshire, England. He was educated at Canford School, then went on to study Biological Sciences at the University of Oxford, where his interests included large animal behaviour, language and evolutionary theory. His first major polar expedition, The Long Haul, still holds the world record for the longest unsupported Arctic journey in history. Hibbert is the author of three books prior to *Polar Eskimo*, is a public speaker invited to address audiences in numerous countries, and his photographic collection has been published worldwide.

You can follow Alex Hibbert on Twitter and Instagram:
@alexhibbert

Website:
www.alexhibbert.com

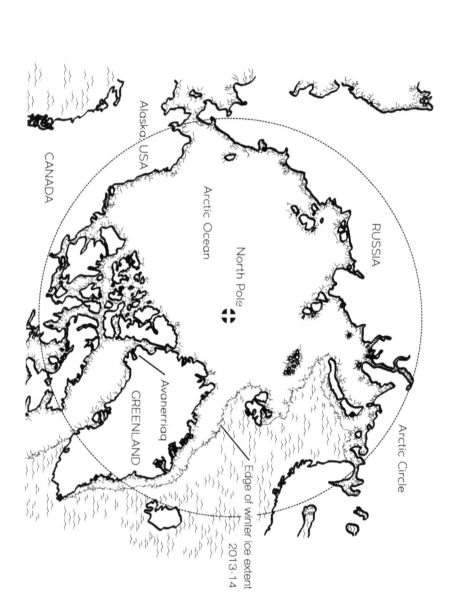

CANADA

Alaska, USA

Arctic Ocean

North Pole

RUSSIA

GREENLAND

Avanerriaq

Arctic Circle

Edge of winter ice extent
2013-14

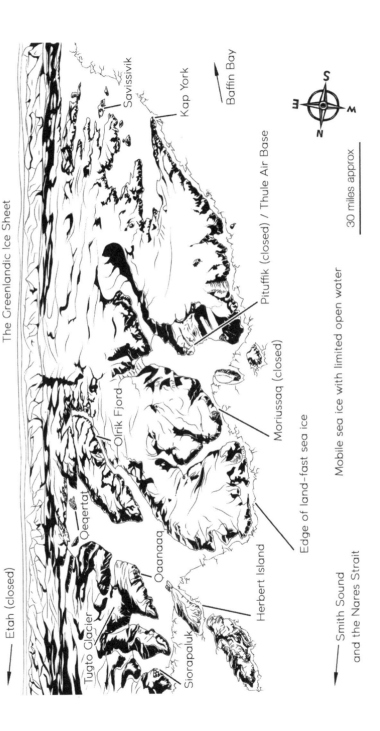

The Greenlandic Ice Sheet

Etah (closed)

Tugto Glacier

Qeqertat

Olrik Fjord

Savissivik

Kap York

Baffin Bay

S
E · W
N

30 miles approx

Pituffik (closed) / Thule Air Base

Moriussaq (closed)

Edge of land-fast sea ice

Mobile sea ice with limited open water

Qaanaaq

Herbert Island

Siorapaluk

Smith Sound
and the Nares Strait

*In memory of four people who via differing
avenues contributed to society's understanding
of the Arctic and Polar Regions,
and our affection for them:*

Finn Hansen, *who epitomised the acceptance of
hard-working people into life in the Far North*

Henry Worsley, *a humble man of immense
ability and champion of the Antarctic*

Philip de Roo *and his teammate* **Marc Cornelissen**, *who
took their risks in the name of science and knowledge*

INTRODUCTION

IN THE EXTREME northern reaches of Greenland, the largest island on the planet, there resides an unlikely band of hardy and ingenious human beings. Their story is one of survival and persistence that can barely be equalled, even amongst pages of fiction.

Their communities are found hundreds of miles north of any other native settlements; sporadically located along shorelines and perched on rocky outcrops. On one side are the dynamic, treacherous icy Arctic waterways. On the other, precipitous cliffs and the almost unimaginably vast Greenland ice sheet, which imprisons four-fifths of the island under its gigatons of bulk.

For more than four months of the year, the extreme latitude plunges all into darkness for long, cold winters. Even as the midsummer brings with it day-round sunlight, its warming effect is feeble and very little vegetation can survive on the few flattened areas of rocky ground.

The people are small in number but have proven to be as inventive with scant resources as civilisations a hundred times as large. They are there by choice, with knowledge of the lands to their west, north and south even in the days before contact with outsiders. With the almost inconceivable strain of living, prospering and raising new generations in one of the most barren places on Earth, they make use of everything available – from a rock to a passing migratory summer bird.

The ancestral settlers of this, the most isolated of any native Arctic territories, travelled across continents unbeknownst to the burgeoning and industrialising civilisations elsewhere across the globe. In the past, our destinies were irrelevant to each other's. The world was a large place. Today, for the first time in history, these people who have harvested local wildlife for food, clothing, fuel, tools and shelter for centuries without major impact on their surroundings are seeing their futures intertwined with us in the south.

This place, Avanerriaq, regardless of goings on elsewhere through the centuries, is the home of the Polar Eskimos.

Clockwise from top left: Hans and Birthe, Lars, Peter and Alex, Rasmus

The new quay off Qaanaaq's beach, 2020

IN CONTEXT

THIS BOOK does not presume to be the first on the subject of the Polar Eskimos. Nor has it been written by a native of the Arctic. As one of the few remaining vestiges of a partially traditional, self-determined way of life, this corner of a widely misunderstood land has attracted curiosity since first 'Contact'. A trickle of linguistic and anthropological studies have resulted; their tone in keeping with their point in history and the agenda of their author. A number manifest as if dryly studying a species with a biological protocol, and the consequent dehumanisation can be hard to reconcile.

There will never be a definitive account and mine is most certainly not an exhaustive history – the truths are too complex and each person's experience will be unique. These are my own memories and my contribution to a discussion – a single moment in the long narrative of the Polar Eskimos. Of those who became friends it is impossible not to write warmly, but I do have a responsibility to remain dispassionate and objective on key issues – not sugar-coating moments when a community must seek its own difficult path.

I have been fortunate to be able to set these tales into the context of around four hundred days of experience in the world's cold regions, all before my thirtieth birthday. More than two thirds of these were spent in Greenland: the east, west, north and on the ice sheet.

Others too will rightly continue to add balance to the broader picture – this should reflect natives, non-natives, scientists, explorers, hunters, artists, linguists and bystanders alike. Particularly, a work such as mine must necessarily sit alongside works, of any format, created now and through history by the people to which these places are home. I have enlisted the assistance and judgement of friends born and resident in the place it aims to portray.

LANGUAGE

THERE ARE VAST collections of urban myths surrounding Inuit, from whether or not they live in igloos, to the number of words they have for snow, all of which are greatly wide of the mark. In fact, there is no generic word for snow as we have. Perhaps the most frequent misconception though is that of their cultural identity and what those on the outside should refer to their people as. It's important to get this out the way early on, or else you will no doubt wonder about the correctness of the words I use. It is worth saying that we are not talking about a single nation of homogeneous people. It would be more accurate to think of the native people of the extreme north as similar to those of a continent. There is a common thread, or a few common threads of ancestry, but variation in other aspects from language to lifestyle.

Firstly on that point of language, or more specifically the language we are commenting on and which one is actually being utilised. This book is clearly written in English, and so I will use English terms or words borrowed and integrated from other tongues. We call Greenland, 'Greenland', yet to the Danes, whose self-governing region it is, call the territory 'Grønland'. Many to whom it is home call it 'Kalaallit Nunaat', which translated to English means simply 'land of the people'. So, these different words for the same entity do not translate directly from language to language. In Western Greenlandic (the dominant native Greenlandic language), a direct translation of Green-land would be *nuna qorsuk*. Because of all this, it is sensible to choose one language as a foundation, allowing for the fact that another person might use a different one to achieve the same end.

Let us cut to the chase then. *What's in a word?* Is the word 'Eskimo' acceptable for a European to use to refer to the people of the Arctic lands? The answer is yes, in certain circumstances.

Conjecture surrounds the origins of the word 'Eskimo', which is an English variation of the French word 'Esquimaux' used by early French traders in what is now Eastern Canada. The most common belief, for which there is remarkably little evidence, is that it means 'eater of raw meat'. This can immediately explain the strong case for its disuse, since although purely descriptive, it could paint a false picture of a 'savage' or primitive human being.

Other theories suggest it could mean 'laces a snowshoe' (from the Montagnais language) or 'speaks another language', but what we must do today is decide whether it is useful or appropriate. It surely depends partly on the self-determination of the people it describes. The Alaskan Yup'ik do not recognise the term Inuit (although some identify as Eskimo), but the main concern is for the large native populations of Canada and Greenland, together numbering around one hundred thousand. Aside from those of First Nations, the native Canadians of Nunavut, the Northwest Territories and neighbouring areas are a proud people and keen to be deemed both Inuit (meaning simply 'the people' or 'human beings' in the dominant languages of Inuktitut and Western Greenlandic) and as modern native Canadians. It is here that the desire is strongest to relegate 'Eskimo' to history and leave behind what to them is a pejorative, demeaning slur that makes them out to be simple barbarian hunters. In Canada, to call Inuit 'Eskimos' would be enough to seed a fierce storm. Perhaps it's equivalent to calling an Englishman a 'tea-sipping, colonial, thatched-cottage dweller'.

A word that has long fallen out of usage is *skræling*, derived from Old Norse and a time when Nordic settlers happened upon the ancestors of today's Inuit. It translates as somewhere between 'barbarian' and 'weakling', depending on whether you look to modern Icelandic or Danish for assistance. In a strange twist, it may also have been the inspiration behind today's Western Greenlandic word 'Kalaallit', adopted to self-describe the largest modern group of Inuit in Greenland and indeed the nation's own local name.

You must candidly ask the people themselves to uncover their feelings. The consistent response, from the many Greenlanders I have met and come to know, is that the Western and Eastern Greenlanders (both with cultures and languages distinct from one another, separated by hundreds of miles), wish to be termed Inuit, Greenlandic or Greenlanders. It's straightforward then that the Canadian and Greenlandic consensus on this has led to the Inuit Circumpolar Council making the word Inuit the official term for self-description. Other dialects, even if their variation on the word differs, share a common source in the Proto-Eskimo *iñuy*. I did, however, sense a great deal less resistance to the word Eskimo in Greenland – they accepted it as a foreign word people use to describe them. Originally, the word Greenlander denoted a person of mixed Danish/Norse and Greenlandic Inuit heritage, not unlike the Métis of Canada. Reports tell of these Danish-speaking people taking on higher-class rankings in early colonial society, but the word is now commonly also used to describe anyone from Greenland.

Do these labels really matter? If we mean no harm from using a word and people know what you mean, can't we just get on with it? We need to use one word or another, after all. I suggest an emphatic 'yes, it does matter'. Words have implications and even if you're ignorant of its pejorative meaning or historical legacy, it doesn't excuse steaming onwards regardless. The power of language can be profound – not pedantic.

Now, to the people of Avanerriaq, the isolated extreme north of Greenland, who self identify in their language (Inuktun/Polar Eskimo) as Inughuit, pronounced in-ohh-hway (some replace the h with another g), similar to Inuit but meaning 'great people'. This is not a reflection of hubris but 'great' in terms of relative numbers, or so they thought prior to contact. Other Greenlanders to the south call them *avanersuarmiut* – 'men from the north parts'. The surprise is that when asked to describe themselves as a group in English or Danish, they are relaxed with Greenlandic, Greenlander, Inuit, Inughuit but equally or even preferentially, Polar Eskimo. This appears to be a secondary adoption and certainly can't date from before the arrival of Europeans, since it is an exonym, a European word. Many of the men and women I got to know well proudly call themselves Eskimo and a handful even adopted an accepting stance over the theory that it means 'eater of raw meat' – wisdom suggests that nutrients do often break down through cooking. Of this they are actually proud, albeit despite the fact much of their food today is cooked. Are they just adopting a foreign word to make life easier communicating with outsiders like me, or do they really wish to take ownership, given the precedent with the origin of the word Kalaallit? I think a mixture of the two. At any rate, in this book, when I refer to the people of extreme North Greenland, I will use Polar Eskimo with the general consent of the very people it describes. The 'Polar' suffix differentiates the umbrella term from the local. At any rate, political correctness has not reached this far-flung outpost, since I was referred to as 'white man' as much as I was 'Englishman'. The result is descriptive, with no offence intended or received.

In Inuktun, *tuluk* means Englishman and *qallunaaq* (or *kadluna*), foreigner. The former is a charming interpretation of the words 'do you' often spoken by the very earliest English-speaking visitors. Descriptions were simple identifiers: whalers *upernaallit* (men of springtime), Norwegians *umittoormiut* (the great beards) and early Danes *kunukormiut* (Knud Rasmussen's men).

Another seemingly uncomplicated word, 'arctic', can itself take on different meanings – above the Arctic Circle, above the 10°C isotherm, north of sixty degrees, or above the tree line. The latter is most useful when dealing with human populations, as the Arctic Circle can be a blunt instrument.

As a side note to this language conundrum, and a final aspect to explain prior to the main narrative, are place names and spellings. Denmark has held Greenland as its territory since the mid-eighteenth century and so as far as the wider world was concerned, the place names were Danish, superseding words used by the native people for centuries. This worked for a time as the words were easier for Westerners to spell and pronounce, and native Inuit had little interest or no knowledge of the perception of their home outside of their bounds. The capital became Godthåb, then a collection of wood and peat cabins and a population of only around a thousand, and a special outpost in the extreme north, Thule. 'Thule' is a much-used, legacy word which has long referred to semi-mythical northern lands. As time passed and Inuit Greenlanders became educated and interested in national identity and self-government, place names began to revert, using usually the standard Western Greenlandic language, or perhaps a local dialect. Godthåb reverted to Nuuk, New Thule to Qaanaaq and Kap Dan to Kulusuk. I will use the modern local place names for consistency when referring to Western or Eastern Greenlandic settlements.

The extreme north is, unsurprisingly, complex as the fluid local language was historically vocal only, not written, and it evolves fast. Those in their seventies speak a noticeably different dialect today to those in their twenties. This oral reliance extended to their sense of their own history too, without written legends as so many others had. Remarkable but vague references to climatic events, 'raining fire', and great monsters may have been interpretations of volcanic eruptions and mastodons in Asia millennia ago. Storytellers are never disbelieved – their recollections are seen as gospel, but began to be lost after first Contact despite attempts by explorers to write them down.

Only decades after their first interactions with southerners were attempts made to write down their language, leading to some major spelling inconsistencies. 'L' can take on a 'dgl' sound and with oft-used letters like 'Q' and 'K' having similar spoken sounds at the end of a word, they're often interchanged and so much of the time, spelling can be a matter of preference. For example, one particular tiny settlement can be Qeqertat, Qikertat or Qekertat. I will use the one that I find most helpful and will defer to the local language where possible. There will always be oddities in the attempts to tell stories in English of places where the English language is of almost no importance, now or before.

Inuktun is not even vaguely phonetic for a European and if that were not enough, words are often used repeatedly in wildly different parts of the vast island, largely because they mean simple, non-specific things. *Uummannaq* means big, heart-shaped mountain and *Kangerlussuaq* means long fjord. These two features are not in short supply... Through all of this, though, I hope it will not be too taxing to keep track of where's where and who it belongs to. Language is not an absolute – it is a human construct, and can be manipulated and misunderstood. This reality we have to live with and so do our best.

CHAPTER 1: Ukioq – Winter

Copenhagen, Denmark – December 2013

THE FIRST of many travel legs was becoming familiar to me; the only feasible route to the western coast of Greenland from Europe is from Copenhagen. Only in the summer are there a few other places from which to start your journey. Air Greenland's sole jet airliner flies infrequently to and from Kangerlussuaq, the hub of Greenland's air travel and the only large runway outside of a US airbase far further north. Our first job though was to pick up Anders, aside from shrink-wrapping our fastidiously weighed cargo. Being our Danish representative and not, as he still maintains in jest, only on the team due to his translation skills, he was to join the three of us Londoners the next morning for our second flight. My normal routine is to get a late arrival flight to minimise the stay in the airport before the 7am check-in the next morning, sleeping on the padded terminal seating and keeping the 24-hour canteen in business – aiding our pre-expedition weight-gain goals. Given there were three to split the bill and with the prospect of seven months without a bed, we opted for the convenient Hilton attached to the airport and settled in for a comfortable night. This was quite the contrast to the experiences of polar travellers, settlers and scientists before the era of scheduled flights. For them, embarking on their own ships, finding space on steamers, or climbing aboard barely airworthy planes, the adventure began long before they saw a single flake of snow. Theirs was a more innocent time – romantic certainly. Courage was demanded just to get to the starting line.

Our international team of twenty-somethings comprised the four of us. James Wheeldon and I were the Brits and in addition to Anders Rasmussen our Dane, Anastasia Kim, a Siberian native now resident in England, joined us. Our aim was simple – to be the first to make a journey from land to the North Pole, without support or resupply, all before the sun rose to signal summer. If successful, it would become the first ever unsupported North Pole winter journey, and be via the final new route – from Greenland. I called it the Dark Ice Project.

Meeting Anders' family for the first time at an ungodly hour the next morning, we gave him time, I wondered if enough, to say goodbye to his family. He admitted, they had mixed opinions about him taking such a big step onto a dangerous project.

Our flight, aboard the brilliantly stark red Air Greenland Airbus, left on time and only a few hours later, peering mournfully out of the window, we witnessed our final glimpse of the sun for, we suspected, over three months. The darkness was always a dominating feature of my Dark Ice concept and it was a poignant moment. No-one pointed it out; we all knew what it meant. For me, it was not a deep sadness for it was of my own making. I didn't expect my mood to be too dependent on the presence of sun or lack thereof. Instead, a moment of 'oh, that's a shame', and then I moved onto more productive thoughts.

The snake of flights it's necessary to make to get from Western Europe to Qaanaaq, our starting point and one of the most northerly airstrips on Earth, had become almost routine over the previous year. Having gone up for a first attempt at laying depots in December 2012 and then spending around a month in the late summer of 2013 doing local logistics, I had made contacts and got some supplies laid by boat to the north. Qaanaaq, a small camp abandoned in the mid-1940s and today the hub of the Polar Eskimos, was recreated artificially in 1953 from the forcible relocation of the groups that had congregated around the location where Danish ships landed. Those settlements were Pituffik and Uummannaq but the Danes and the Americans, who earmarked the area for a military airbase, dubbed it Dundas or Old Thule. This congregation marked a de facto end to the Polar Eskimo habit of maintaining flexible camps. They had, for the first time in their history, a reason to stay put but in a not entirely uncontroversial relationship, much like those Canadian Inuit previously trading with the Hudson Bay Company across the water.

Far from being a touring holiday though up the west coast, we had jobs to do at each stop. We needed shotgun ammunition and a Greenlandic SIM card from Kangerlussuaq, to refuel in Aasiaat, to purchase the correct high calibre rifle bullets in Ilulissat and to refuel yet again in Upernavik. Kangerlussuaq, being only a few dozen miles north of the Arctic Circle, was still benefitting from plenty of natural light as we landed, albeit without the sun actually rising, and it reminded me of exactly a year before – even the weather was the same, a bit cloudy but windless and around -10°C. The hillsides held the same light covering of snow. I watched out of the window of the sole terminal as local Greenlanders cleared snow off the wings of waiting propeller aircraft, a product of the strange mix of modern airport facilities and raw Arctic wilderness you get in these transitional settlements between south and north. I knew modernity was soon to end though and, all tasks completed, we continued our rampage of feasting, first with muskox burgers and then with puddings from the local store.

It was from that point northward that getting a view from the small windows of the Dash planes became essential, especially since the spectacular views of Iceland, the mountainous east coast of Greenland and the descent of the icecap off the crevassed Russell Glacier (both locations playing host to my past journeys) had been obscured by cloud. Every minute the light dropped a little more and the endless views across the frozen fjords wiggling their way amongst the low white hills to the flat icecap beyond became more dramatic. No matter how many times I see it, or those like it, this aerial panorama of my favourite place on Earth retains its magic grip on me. Like a child seeing the ocean for the first time, I stared wide-eyed, not wanting to miss out on one detail. Aasiaat, a small settlement near Ilulissat, is perched on a small island group to the west, far from the icecap, which despite its utter dominance of Greenland, plays little part in the lives of most Greenlanders. Instead of the sea ice which weakly forms in only the narrowest of fjords in the south of the two thousand-mile-long island, these islands were surrounded by strong currents, meaning ice-free sea. The result was a black and white picture, highlighting perfectly the white land against the black sea, more like an abstract map than reality.

In the distance, as the pilot banked the plane firmly to the left in order to approach the small airstrip head on, we spied a handful of twinkling lights against the black. These were hardy Greenlandic fishermen, returning to home in their tiny open boats. From up in the air they looked so vulnerable, and they were. Life even in the relative south of Greenland is tough and conditions are unforgiving.

Given the chaotic smattering of islands that made up that part of the coastline, there was barely a flat spot to land a plane and, from our viewpoint, it seemed like we were still over water just a second or two before we felt the wheels touch down with a bump.

There was barely time for a leg-stretch but the light outside was beautiful, a rich blue from horizon to horizon and the snow reflected the same tones. We wandered halfway down the snow track towards the little village, caught a glimpse and then ran back, our aeroplane clothes not really suitable for the ever-decreasing temperatures and a chilly breeze. Ilulissat it was next, Greenland's 'third town' to Nuuk but still only home to just over four thousand people and with an industry based on fishing and processing the catches. It is also on the doorstep of a highly productive ice fjord, which earned it UNESCO World Heritage Site status. Really, it is the only substantial tourism boost the country has, not made easy by its inaccessibility.

We planned to overnight in Ilulissat, staying in a quiet guesthouse placed between the airstrip and the town itself. A few failed enquiries later, we had found the large quantity of ammunition we required and settled in for the night, again focussed on the consumption of food. The effectiveness of our collective weight-gain, vital for a very long journey based on a necessary daily calorie deficit, had been mixed and so I had put everyone on strict orders to not give up the grand eating contest.

Our early flight the next day, our third and final day of flying, was sweetened by news that the lack of locals wishing to land in Upernavik, and limited cargo, meant we could fly direct to Qaanaaq. This saved an hour or so and my only regret was not getting to enjoy the ferociously committed landing and take-off needed at Upernavik's super-short airstrip, perched on a cliff. To Qaanaaq we were headed, entirely without delays or cancellations – surely a record for Greenlandic air travel.

I looked over the team, proud to have come all the way from meeting in cafes in London less than a year before to being united in taking on a massive journey together. This was Anders' and James' first time, and although by now, far beyond seventy-five degrees North, we could see nothing of the ice, frozen sea, cliffs and mountains beneath in the dark, I remembered the excitement and trepidation of my first arrival here. I reminded myself not to gloss over new experiences too eagerly, for I knew that they wanted to soak it in and get their heads around where they were. Stepping down onto the snow after an expertly smooth landing, (Qaanaaq's airstrip is very long and flat after all), I felt a pang of responsibility, happiness and fear. I had brought these people up there and I must keep them safe. I was glad to be in the environment I love, and I was scared of the sheer enormity of what I had thrust upon myself. For a fraction of the money just I personally had invested into the enterprise, I could have funded a quick and straightforward sixty-mile ski to the North Pole from an ice-base in the most pleasant time of year, ticking the North Pole box and having to the layman, conquered it. That was not my game though and the concept of shortcutting and glory hunting was toxic to me.

A friendly face greeted me as I was the first to enter the little building by the airstrip. Hans Jensen, a Polar Eskimo gentleman with whom I had lodged many times in his small but welcoming guesthouse, beamed at me and we shared a quick hug before I introduced him to the team. Anastasia and he had met two years before and he remembered her, despite her dramatic change of hairstyle – she had cropped hers for practicality, as had James and I. Anastasia, with her mixture of Russian and Korean heritage, immediately found herself being spoken to in the local dialect, her appearance apparently mistaken for being Greenlandic. Hans was dressed in his definitive green parka with fur ruff and chatted in Inuktun to a couple of local friends before ushering us outside. The weekly flight, often not even filling the tiny aircraft, was nonetheless something of a social event with families reunited and people taking the opportunity to exchange local news.

Vehicles are a complicated matter in Qaanaaq. Although snowmobiles and other snow machines were outlawed for hunting and not used for inter-settlement travel anyhow, there is nothing of a road network in the settlement of fewer than six hundred individuals. Instead, rather like forest trails being beaten down and flattened by persistent use, the gaps and natural routes amongst the wooden buildings and dog staking areas serve as makeshift roads – ice and snow in the winter and dirt, thawed dog mess and gravel in the summer. Cars are the preserve of only the few representatives of the government temporarily living in Qaanaaq and the occasional local who had accumulated wealth beyond that which a hunter could reasonably expect. Hans, being the sole recipient of guests to Qaanaaq – from scientists in the summer to travellers like us – was the latter. The logistics of getting things that far north is complex and unsurprisingly, cars were high on the list of 'hard to get'. You can walk from one side of Qaanaaq to the other in less than ten minutes, but for some a car is useful and certainly more effective than using dogs on the hill for moving loads around. The interaction of old, albeit well-made, Japanese pickups and 4x4s and a super-dry, extremely cold and tough climate means that not one of them would be in with a chance of an MOT.

Hans' Toyota had been coughing and spluttering the summer before and had now completely given up. Instead, Finn Hansen, a Danish-born but naturalised Greenlander, would give us and Hans a lift back along the winding snow track into the settlement itself. Finn was a character and would become a central part of our time there.

Only able to take three passengers at a time, especially ones wearing thick clothing, it would take two shuttles and so I awaited the second. I took the twenty minutes or so as an opportunity to wander away from the airstrip building and take advantage of the calmness typical of the region in winter. Although only early afternoon, there was not a glimmer of light in the sky, and I had to look hard to make out anything in the gloom – the lack of moon was not helping. Almost everything along this coastline called Piulerruup Nunaa locally (or Piulip Nuna in Western Greenlandic) is on the beach. As we've seen, the word *nuna* is used when talking about land, earth or a 'place you belong to'. The land in this area is, if not covered by ice, either a dramatic cliff or a rubbly, low beach that rises into a steeper hill a few hundred yards inland. As such, the airstrip was only fifty yards or so from the shoreline and ice tide crack. Beyond, I painted a picture in my head, based on memories from earlier in the year. Then, I was able to see twenty or even thirty miles across the sound to the glaciers, islands and coastline afar. It is probably this mental image that dominated most of what I thought I was seeing, but it gave me a moment to settle – transit flights were now over and we were nearing our start line. I had to focus, yet also relax and make sure no mistakes were made. Once we set off, there was no chance to fix a major mistake or omission; we would have to live with it for months.

The white pickup which, like the handful of others in Qaanaaq, had seen better days, rumbled into view and into the warm artificial light outside the corrugated metal building. I jumped in, comforted by the relative warmth (it was only twenty degrees below zero outside but Finn kept his heater on full blast) and breathed in the familiar fog of cigarette smoke. Anders was riding with us too and for some of the drive, they chatted in Danish – me able to pick up the rough gist of the conversation but unable to contribute, being an untalented linguist. It gave me a chance to watch out of the dirty windscreen as the two headlights painted a cone of light onto the snowy loose gravel and rock ahead on the track, which was no wider than the truck. It wouldn't be until the final half mile that the lights of Qaanaaq would spring into view as we crested a small hillock.

I asked Finn how the winter had been so far, in particular snowfall and sea ice formation. Apart from the poor winter-time satellite data (which obviously can't sense any visible light, since there wasn't any), my only intelligence about the ground condition had been the odd message from Hans, which often contained confused English despite his best efforts. I once tried to email with him in Danish but it ended up confusing the two of us even more!

In Finn's faux-cynical way, he recounted how the winter so far had seen precious little snow, even by the dry standards of Qaanaaq, but that the sea ice was building fairly well in the local area at least. It could take a short while to adjust to Finn's way of seeing the world – what at first could come across as negative and even a little grouchy, was in fact just his brand of humour and he did love to tell stories of gloom and doom, only to get a reaction that he found mischievously satisfying. I had learned to pick out the actual information from what he said and played along with his tricks and elaborate stories.

I smiled as the first lights of Qaanaaq came into view, studying the faces of my team every time they experienced a new sight or sound I was familiar with. It is part of the magic of the 'cold places' for me, and why I love working in teams. The wonder and excitement that drives my own continued thirst for new experiences in my chosen profession is so plain to also see on the faces of others. In context though, we were not at all spoilt. Making our visits in the era we happen to have been born into, we had missed the boat, so to speak. Qaanaaq, which for me represented the gateway to remote Greenland, had sparked a look of horror on the faces of those who returned after years away, having experienced traditional life before towns, even tiny ones, existed there at all. Comparison is subjective and for some, even Qaanaaq has slipped too far towards modernity and is not authentic enough.

Somewhat usefully for a place regularly plunged into darkness for months at a time – *kaperlaq* - the sun setting on 28th October and rising again at the far end of February, the influence of the south brought electric lighting to Qaanaaq some time ago. Being the only non-military location in the entire North (I capitalise here to differentiate the place, the North of Greenland, with cardinal points or more general northern regions) with a population above one hundred, it is also the only one with such facilities. I suppose the effect is, therefore, one of slight surprise for a newcomer expecting a trip into prehistory.

Finn drove us quickly past the first of the brightly coloured but small and wooden homes and then up the hill towards what looked like a red, stretched version of one of the usual pre-fabricated, but attractive, Danish-imported dwellings. I was impressed that on the icy surfaces he was able to drive so surefootedly, but with only a few tracks and decades in which to travel them, I suspected he must know every pothole. Like the vast majority of the Arctic, the ground was barren and treeless, being hundreds of miles north of the tree line. The presence of an Inuktun word for tree, *orpik*, must be a legacy of their ancestors' journey across North America's upper reaches.

We pulled up outside Hans' guesthouse and Birthe, his wife, was beaming with a wide smile in the doorway – this was one of the few places on Earth where a smile retains its honest sincerity. Five-foot nothing and seemingly always in a great mood, her English consisted of as many words as I knew in Inuktun, and so we continued our normal communication of a hug, and pointing and smiling at things.

Anastasia and James were already inside and moving our boxes and bags into the small rooms set aside for guests. The building was essentially a corridor with a few rooms coming off it, plus an office for Hans, a bathroom with standard bucket loos and then a communal area with a small kitchen where Birthe prepared a mixture of local and Danish food.

With only two or three days set aside and budgeted for in Qaanaaq before we needed badly to get moving northward, there was not a great deal of time to sit back and settle in. It was early evening, not that you'd have noticed, and before getting stuck into opening boxes and reacquainting myself with the hundreds of pounds of supplies I'd painstakingly organised up there the past August, I suggested a walk around town to orientate everyone.

Now in our oversize goose-down jackets, all bright yellow like a quartet of giant canaries, I led the way down the hill. From each wooden building a pipe protrudes at waist level, coming from the cooking area of the home. Although some newer homes owned by employed locals have enough space for separate kitchens and bedrooms, a large number are single spaces. This insulated pipe is their drain and everything comes pouring out of it, from washing-up water to the diluted blood following the butchering of a seal, walrus or other animal. This leaves an ice-slick leading from a giant icicle coming out the pipe, on the downhill side of every single home. Some could be twenty feet wide and long, only thawing in the early summer sun and absorbing into the dry, infertile earth. This basically meant that to the unaware or distracted, there were an infinite number of opportunities to end up bum first on the very hard ground.

We first went down to the beach, or at least what we called the beach because in winter and spring it is entirely ice covered. There's a flat section flooded at the highest tide of the month, which regularly renews the flat ice layer as the sea water freezes. Beyond that is the turbulent ice of the tide crack and the sea ice beyond. There was a selection of both new and broken, disused dog sleds parked along the beach, plus small open wooden boats which are used as mother ships in the summer. From these locals could hunt from kayaks and travel to other settlements. Also, there was a curious set of rickety-looking wooden frames set eight feet or so above the ground. These, *ikaat*, are used as places to keep tasty morsels such as seal carcasses and fish away from the ever-keen grasp of loose dogs and on which to dry their catches in the cold, parched air.

Appearing out of the gloom in the warm, dim light of the outdoor lamps that spread across the main parts of Qaanaaq, was the functional hub of this remote outpost. Danish and American funding, now supplemented and controlled by Greenland Self Rule (self-governing but not independent, made official in 1979), had led to a strange dichotomy of simple, tiny huts occupied by elderly Polar Eskimos and then next door, large fuel storage vats, modern piping and power management buildings. Once beyond this area and around the, again, quite smart-looking school and health centre, more little wooden houses, coloured yellow, blue, red and green – a common Scandi-borrowed theme in all Greenlandic settlements and part of their photogenic charm.

We had done a full sweep of the area, showing the team important places and the houses of people I had briefly got to know the last winter and summer. 'This guy knows Inglefield Land well', 'this lady said she had old charts from the 1980s showing safe routes here and there', and it went on. Of major importance to me was to find Dave, my dog. I had bought him the winter before from a supremely experienced hunter, Rasmus, with the help of Hans as translator to ensure my quest for a 'slightly lazy but

9

excellently-trained bear dog' was heeded. We only had a brief adventure due to the medical mishaps of my teammate that winter, but had spent a few weeks together over August and the start of September.

I knew Rasmus moved him around a lot and had been paid to feed him up. We didn't need a super-fit dog; we needed a robust, tubby one who could handle slightly sub-optimal feeding. He would not be hauling a sled – just walking – but regardless, these dogs eat a great deal. I was hoping to find Dave healthy and happy, with a bit of a belly wobble, but did not hold out much hope for him to instantly recognise me – it had only been a few weeks over the summer and Thule Eskimo dogs, numbering in their hundreds even in small settlements, are fickle creatures.

Dave had been picked for a number of reasons, but primarily due to his excellent health, he had not lost any teeth (or had them removed or filed down by hunters to stop them chewing fabric harness and ropes – a practice now outlawed in Greenland) and he seemed to have the right personality. Dave was calm, if a bit lazy, and friendly, but not always in your face and he had a large, strong build.

Throughout the centuries as people migrated east from Siberia to Alaska to Canada to Greenland, the wolves – *amaqqut* – with which they formed a hunting partnership and later domesticated as early Thule Eskimo dogs, were selected and bred to make a better next generation. Clearly without knowledge of genetics or the actual mechanisms of artificial selection, which is how all domestic dogs and animal breeds are created, they nevertheless managed a crude form of it by simply observing the results. Besides, genetics only became partially understood in Europe in the nineteenth century and dogs have been bred for certain traits long, long before then. As well as thick, healthy coats, a willingness to listen, long legs and endurance, it is very common for some of these to be overlooked in deference to a purely 'handsome' dog.

Dave was without doubt one of this latter group, stocky and tall at the shoulder with a thick coat of a quality I had seen in only a few others. He was a black and white dog with an attractive pattern of colouring and a wide, keen face. When sat down, he had a slightly majestic, sphinx-like air about him.

I eventually spotted him far from the main hillside where most teams were staked out, outside Rasmus' small blue home which had a prime position not far from the shoreline. Dave had been staked outside on his own, with a rare luxury of a kennel made from old shipping pallets. He had clearly been put there so that he could be intensively fed up without Rasmus or his family having to walk far. I double-checked we hadn't found a doppelgänger by scanning him with a microchip scanner – thankfully it beeped cheerfully. We had asked Greenland's sole vet to chip and vaccinate Dave in October as she visited, to allow him an EU Passport and potential entry to Svalbard if need-be.

To not overwhelm Dave, the others held back and I approached, stooping down as to not be too intimidating and to let Dave, who was looking a little nervous, have a good sniff of me. He would be unlikely to recognise me visually from summer due to a complete wardrobe change on my part. He gradually came round but I knew it was going to be a slow process. He did not really remember me, apart from deciding I wasn't an immediate threat, and to get him to settle down around all four of us would take time. Inuit generally do not spend too much time patting or giving social attention to their dogs, believing it to soften them, and so those who have even less human contact than most, especially as puppies, will become very timid around new people, or what the locals called 'wild'.

We made the decision to take over feeding duties from Rasmus for the few days until the off and spend as much time as practical socialising him. Rasmus was now moving up the hill to a larger home, house exchange being a remnant of the past, perhaps for the sake of novelty. By slowly drawing in on his metal chain, thereby encouraging him to come to us rather than encroaching on his space, we hoped before long, and with frequent feeding, he would make friends of us. It wasn't a total start from scratch though as every time we came down the hill and as he first glimpsed us in our bright yellow jackets, he bounced around in excitement from foot to foot and across the whole range of his staking chain, only to slightly withdraw as we came near. Every time was an improvement though and was helped inordinately by the arrival of a trio of tearaways in the form of three puppies, perhaps three or four months old.

Given their black and white coats and instant draw to Dave (their mother being staked slightly up the hill), we suspected they were Dave's brood and of course, we instantly took to them. All puppies have free rein of Greenlandic settlements until six months of age, and then have to be staked out in either pairs or small groups, ready for the start of sled training.

They seemed to relax Dave, although they did cheekily begin to steal a fair quantity of the food we were giving him, and we had to keep an eye on the amount of time we wasted with the dogs. After all, we had just three days or so until we had to launch, and had a massive amount of administration and packing to do. Leaving Dave, Gilbert (one of the puppies we named after my amusingly yet intentionally expanding waistline, an affliction usually alien to me) and the other two down the bottom of the hill, it was time to set to work.

The list before the off was daunting. Although all that was feasible was done in advance, in some cases six months beforehand, a few things could only be completed on location. We had to empty gallon after gallon of olive oil into freezeable ice cube packs, paint the rifles with tough yellow paint, unpack and bag up our clothing and food – the list went on. As the only visitors, we spread out across Hans' guesthouse and got to work. Two days later, I had earmarked a day for a 'test haul'; to move our full two sleds' worth each of supplies west and lay a few supplies a short way down the coast. It would have a purpose, to lighten the loads slightly for the main initial launch, but would also allow us to settle, get a feel for the conditions and iron out any little issues we found. Unlike other trips where the insertion is via boat or helicopter and you have to jump in the deep end, starting from Qaanaaq meant we could be more controlled in our approach.

It was very important for us to keep an eye on what was going on north of us on our route ahead. To that end, we had set up the best internet connection we could via the fledgling Greenlandic network and with our UK support team helping out too. Weekly blurred images of the straits came through from RADARSAT feeds, obviously having to use infrared instead of visible light due to the daylong darkness from our latitude, around seventy-eight degrees North, northwards to the Pole.

That, combined with some basic temperature and wind data coming from tiny automated weather stations in Qaanaaq, on Hans Island (a lump of rock in the middle of the Nares Strait with sovereignty contested by Denmark and Canada) and Canada's Alert station at the extreme north of Ellesmere Island, was our full picture of what we could expect to face.

Even though we, apart from the particularly scant layer of snow, known as *aput*, that had accumulated, had pretty much what we expected to find in Qaanaaq's midwinter – calm, clear weather with gradually thickening sea ice and 'pleasant' temperatures between -20°C and -30°C, the realisation grew that not all was well up north. When I say north, I mean north of the region of Greenland we were on, Piulerruup Nunaa and Inglefield Land, and from the Kane Basin to where Greenland gives way to the vastness of the Arctic Ocean in the Lincoln Sea.

We knew that the calm weather had not been replicated in the uppermost area of the strait, and on the third day Hans handed us a basic black and white print out of the sea ice in the Lincoln Sea and wind speed measurements. Hans had long since been far more than just a guesthouse owner; he had been the connection between the community and the handful of expedition teams who had spent time in the outpost, usually of course in the more benign late spring and summer. As such, he was enormously proud of the signed photos on the corridor wall of people who had come through before – some were familiar names and faces – Wally Herbert and family (of whom locals were very fond), Lonnie Dupre, Alain Hubert and other experienced polar travellers.

This time, though, Hans' interest in our plans brought sad news. He said in good English, despite often self-deprecating his linguistic skills, "Not good news Alex. Much wind and broken ice. I am sorry."

We all crowded round one of the small tables in the communal area and looked at the damage. It takes a little experience to interpret infrared images of sea ice, as at first glance the whiteness of thick, reflective ice and snow contrasts with the dull greys of new or thin-ish ice which may be, in fact, still navigable on foot. It does initially look like open water though, so it takes time to pick out where the real open water and leads (water channels between cracked ice pans) are.

Nevertheless, the picture showed that a large storm system had moved across the northern coasts of Canada's Ellesmere Island and Greenland, breaking up the fragile newly forming ice. The area is renowned as turbulent anyhow with the effects of Arctic Ocean drifts and a strong current funnelling down the narrow straits.

We had to be sensible about how we received this news. Sea ice is incredibly dynamic and unpredictable, being simply a thin skim of brittle ice floating on top of the seas, oceans and fjords that are ever in motion. I also had to look ahead; bad news at this moment, early December, could repair itself by the end of January, our predicted arrival time at the Lincoln

Sea. Cold conditions would allow ice reformation if there were no more storms.

There was a compounding factor. As is well known, the straits do not consolidate into immobile '10/10' ice (floes with no open water, confusingly also called 'fast ice') – until later in the winter or even early spring. Historically they did, but a decade or two of data shows only a handful of pre-New Year consolidations. This has many consequences, the major one being that the ice in the straits was not locked shut and could move south with the current. Instead of the broken ice staying put and becoming part of the refreeze, it would move south at quite a pace with nothing fixed in the way to stop it, right out into Baffin Bay south of Smith Sound (the entrance to the strait) and past Qaanaaq.

For those with an eye for detail, a full reasoning for how our thinking progressed is included in Appendix B.

Simply, my conclusion was that the viability of the journey was in question – a tough thing to consider given that the previous year had been immaculate for travel and only two, maybe three, of the last decade's worth of seasons had been unacceptable for travel. I had considered this a perfectly reasonable risk on which to base a project. All of this came on our test day.

Having got our gear sorted, thrown out unnecessary items, let the painted rifles dry and olive oil freeze outside, it was time for testing our systems on a 'dry run'. Finn helped load our eight sleds, totalling more than 1.3 tons, onto his tired but trusty white pickup and trailer, and drove us down from our storage area to the beach and along a little bit, past the airstrip (when not in use only a couple of red lights give away its presence) and as far as he felt it safe. Finn had lived there for over thirty years and had accrued a balance of vast knowledge, caution, and no-nonsense 'get on with it'. He had to return alone and did not have a rifle or satellite phone on him, so apologised, quite unnecessarily of course, for not taking us further.

From there, our plan was to complete a good haul – perhaps six miles – with full six hundred-pound-plus loads and then leave a stock of food and fuel in a derelict corrugated iron shelter down the coast.

It had been a mammoth job to load the hundreds of different items, all having had their necessity and usefulness versus weight agonised over, into sleds and we had actually slightly overflowed. This was despite having a total of nearly ten feet of sled capacity each for food and supplies for seven months.

We moved off and the ice, although in fairly good condition, still had areas of *manüllat* pressure (where ice from either side compresses, cracks and pushes the ice into tall piles of rubble) and was very slippery in other areas where the tidal ice had experienced high tide. The loads were, there's no getting away from it, heavy. I have covered things like sledge weights and how they feel in other writing, for example *Maybe*, so I won't re-tread the same ground, but we moved off slowly, leaning forward with each stride and did not pick up much of a pace. All of us became warm in the -25°C temperatures within minutes and vented our already minimal, breathable clothing.

Critically, though, and allowing for the fact this was not turbulent pack ice, with loads that most would consider ridiculous, we were making good progress. Anastasia was moving well, despite the fact that she had naturally less bodyweight to throw forward and fewer inches in height. After a few hours, we were walking in a standard line, quite elongated given there were four of us and eight sleds in total, and Anders at the front glimpsed a reflection with his head torch. All else around us was dark, although only three in the afternoon.

It was the remains of an old hunting cabin, a hundred yards or so from the tide crack (essentially the shoreline) and up a snowy and gravelly slope. Our steady yet encouraging progress had put me in a good mood. After all, we were not going to be able to replicate the strains back in the UK, so this was our first real test. I was the first to the top of the snowline where it gave way to stones, so I stopped, not wanting to scratch the low-friction runner under the sledges.

I unclipped and enjoyed the few moments of freedom from a heavy sledge where you feel almost like you are falling forwards after the weight releases. Looking down, the three other headtorch beams shone a route up to where I was and I noticed them working hard to get up the slope too. Anastasia was noticeably slower on the rises, and I kept that in mind for how I would route-find for the months ahead.

Around a cabin, which contains food and supplies, the risk of a polar bear scavenging is pretty high, and the rubbish dump – *aktat* – (a sad sight comprised of southern packaging and casually discarded belongings) outside Qaanaaq is a strong attractant for them, as well as the sinister ravens – the sole winter birds. Early in the winter season of 2016, three large adult bears walked via the dump straight into the centre of Qaanaaq – three hunters were subsequently proud owners of new fur clothing. In the same way I'd approach or pass that area with care when back in the settlement, I proceeded with caution alone as the others unclipped and sorted themselves.

Unslinging my rifle, I brought it to my shoulder and loaded a round from the magazine. Then, putting my headtorch onto a long beam, I walked straight for the cabin, not wanting to overdramatise. If a bear was foraging behind the corrugated walls or even inside, going through one side that missed a wall, I would have very little time to react if it was startled and made a charge.

I rounded the corner at a distance to make sure I had as much time and the best view as possible and then the next, clearing the two blind sides of the shelter and then I slowly approached the gap in the wall, hearing nothing and quickly confirming that no-one was home. Giving the surrounding area a quick scan with the strongest beam, I concluded all was well and opened the rickety wooden door to find the place in a real state; a broken shelf on one wall and massive snowdrift the other side of the small structure. It was sad as Finn said he had spent many comfortable nights there whilst hunting and fishing in past years before it began to fall apart. For us though, it would serve perfectly. We needed a reasonably safe place to stow our supplies, already odour-sealed, as well as was practical, and protected in depot barrels. Also, we wanted somewhere easy to spot on our way back through when we started the journey in earnest.

Coming back out of the hut, I saw the others arriving, already with drybags on their shoulders as the 'lift and shift' began. It would take us a good dozen shuttles each to move the hundreds of kilos up, and I brought up Dave to make sure he didn't go hunting for his supper in our sledges whilst our backs were turned.

Dave had done very well; I knew he would as he was picked specifically for the task and had been great the year before, during our brief time on the ice. Used to pulling a dog sled with a tight rope and being in a large team, he took a moment to get the idea but then seemed rather keen on the notion of just ambling along and sniffing at everything that we passed. He was attached to my hip by a long lightweight chain. We had occasionally

16

crossed slippery ice and I couldn't help myself but laugh as considerately as possible when he lost his traction once or twice.

It was time for the return trip, with obviously much lightened sledges, but the full day would actually end up being pretty long, covering over six miles, and I hoped, absurdly given our situation, that we would be back in time for supper cooked by Birthe.

The pace quickened a little and our raw performances became a little more apparent than before when those super-loads had been an effective leveller. Occasionally the front skier, whoever's turn it was, would leave a gap as he sped off, and I would need to remind everyone to moderate their pace. Overenthusiasm can sometimes lead to a team member who is having a hard day losing heart, so as leader it's something I always keep an eye on.

Eventually the warm glow of Qaanaaq returned ahead of us and we pulled up onto the beach by a storage shed. It was quite late and we imagined Birthe had left our food out, so we covered our gear over to protect them from dogs and went up the hill for a well-earned meal and to debrief how we felt it went.

On the whole the team was happy, beyond the tired eyes and slightly red faces. Despite us wanting to rethink some of the orders in which we had loaded the sledges and fiddling with face masks, plus Anastasia having a niggle about her perceived lower pace, we felt it a success. This made the dawning realisation of the satellite imagery all the more galling. I brought the main points to their attention and suggested we should sleep on it. There was little we could achieve with brand new information, sat tired around a table at midnight.

The new morning was the day before I had earmarked our launch of the main journey and we were greeted by another calm, starry-skied cold day – almost as if to taunt us with great conditions as we considered our project's viability.

We went over the images and ice reports again from scratch, spoke to Hans and others from town, such as Rasmus, Otto (who laid my summer depot by boat) and Finn, and tried to make sure nothing had been missed. We didn't want to walk ourselves down an alley in a daft self-fulfilling prophecy of only looking at the negatives.

I asked for opinions, one by one. Anastasia was a little pre-occupied with her hauling ability which to me was a side-issue, Anders was still clearly torn and James said he wanted to give it a go. There was no difference in opinion about the implications of the storm and the ice. It was what we wanted to do about it that was the question. I had from the word go said that my leadership style would be to guide on skills where needed, but only make instructional decisions when there was no natural consensus. These were intelligent and capable outdoor travellers who would not appreciate rigid-style management.

As such I wanted their candid opinions and then would collate them and make a decision best for the team. James was, I think, finding it overtly hardest. I was keeping my inner turmoil quiet and didn't want to ask leading questions or sway people. His commitment to the journey, desire for the sheer hard work and I think very single-minded attitude towards something he had devoted himself to made the concept of giving it up unthinkable.

My own thoughts were those of horror. I was looking at a second early cancellation in as many years. I had to consider the implications of the safety of my team who looked to me as the creator of the whole thing, the financial and career implications of a rescue, the emotional hurt of losing something you want so very badly, and finally the stress of trying to extract true feelings from the team and dealing with them properly.

I wondered if my lack of outward emotion swayed them or made them wonder why I wasn't more obviously troubled. It became a dark day, emotionally as well as literally.

It came to the point, sat around a small table with the dark window to our side and dim lamp contributing to a sombre atmosphere, for me to make a decision. James had been for a walk, I had gone to the room I shared with Anders for some time with my own thoughts, and we had met back with a cup of sweet, fruit-flavoured 'saft' drink sat in front of each of us. Each had our name on it; mine jokingly inscribed 'our dear leader'.

James was still troubled and maintained that he wanted to give it a go, but visibly softened when one of us reiterated the ice charts. He was clutching at straws, we all were, and I could understand why.

What I then said changed the mood almost instantly. "Guys, I don't think Dark Ice can happen now. But, I don't think we should go home. I think we should stay."

There was a look of confusion around the table. What? It was probably all the more stunning because I had for the first time clearly stated that Dark Ice was not happening. It wasn't closure, but certainty can be far more settling than vain hope.

"Well," I explained. "Way back early last year when I was rebuilding Dark Ice and when I had no assurance that I would find the right team for the job, I thought about what I'd do if I wasn't successful and couldn't go. I came up with a Plan B."

Dave

CHAPTER 2: Reset

SAT IN HANS' guesthouse I gradually unveiled an idea which was totally at odds with Dark Ice, and indeed everything I had focussed on to date. I suggested that we buy large teams of dogs, the best in the world, build wooden sleds from scratch and learn the art of driving them. The ultimate aim would be a strong grasp of this ancient skill of native northern people, real albeit brief integration into their way of life, and hundred of miles under our belts. To learn, and not to chase a record. To be immersed in something unique.

Dark Ice was thwarted for a second year, the first through my former teammate's injury and this second time through concerns over the lack of ice. There was, this time, a massive difference though. We were healthy, fit, motivated, and full of frustrated energy. There was no need to retreat entirely. We could adapt.

The new plan was a shock and couldn't be implemented too quickly. I had held it until the end, for fear of steering people's views. We all had to let it sink in. The team had to individually ask themselves why they were here. What did they want? Could they re-motivate?

I may well be wrong if you were to ask them in confidence, but to me they were minded as follows. James was there to develop his experience and complete a supremely physically and technically demanding journey. Anders joined to be part of something exciting, stimulating, and to build on his raw experience. Anastasia was there as a sort of catharsis, for a more singular connection with the wilderness that she found lacking at home. Anastasia did not naturally take to crowds or gregariousness by her own admission, and it was the place that attracted her, not the goal or even the people.

My own motivation was complex. The purity, the environment, the team and the brand new technical hurdles attracted me. But, it was also a career journey. Polar travel is the backbone of my full-time work and so it was important for me, as well as succeeding, to return home with a story to tell. The success though was for me a major influence. As detailed

21

in *Maybe*, some huge targets I had set myself from 2011 to 2013 had not fallen easily, and it was important to achieve some completion.

I think James was least keen on the idea. He said that he found dogs 'fine' but wasn't a 'dog person' as such, and the new alternative was a long way from what he signed up to. Anders confided in me a little later, eventually common knowledge, that he frankly didn't care what the actual task was, as long as it was challenging and in the High Arctic. Dog driving was actually something he found as motivating as man-hauling (hauling a sledge manually), as a longstanding admirer of Knud Rasmussen's Thule Expeditions in the early twentieth century.

Anastasia was particularly receptive, since again, it would involve time in the Arctic environment she loved and would involve working with animals. She re-voiced the concern that her slower hauling pace was swaying us in order to keep the team together, but I quickly nipped that thought in the bud.

It was time to make decisions, partly to alleviate the remains of the Dark Ice despondency, and secondly so we could reset the team and get on with whatever we judged to be best for us. James was pragmatic and said his full enthusiasm would be channelled into a new team focus once the 'mourning' for Dark Ice had passed – this was a sentiment we could all identify with. I motioned, 'ok then, we're all agreed that the evidence points towards a very slim chance of the ice being in condition, that we want to stay, and that this would be a great use of the coming months'. There were three nods around the table, reserved at first but growing in confidence as moments went by.

Like that, the plan for nearly half a year of our lives changed in a flash. We were now to base ourselves in Qaanaaq throughout the dark, cold winter, become locals, train both ourselves and our still hypothetical dogs, and then build up to longer journeys.

How big would these be? We certainly had very little appetite for anything lacking serious endeavour. The truth was that unlike man-hauling or other forms of polar travel that I was so well versed in, there were new blanks in my knowledge. That was exciting, but I did not have the answers to the questions that we all, myself included, now had. How far? How fast? Where? For what purpose? Where are the routes? Are there access points to various regions? We would have to find out.

It made sense for us to have something significant to build up to, and I mused that we might access the icecap from the coast and complete a major journey there. To where, how far, and a number of other things, I did not know, but I had ideas.

Aside from the routine logistics amendments and contract changes with suppliers and operators, I had to contact our myriad of sponsors and supporters. Perhaps more arduous yet, as leader I penned a public message to explain the situation and why we were changing tack.

It wasn't time to abandon our preferred mode of travel though – not just yet. The 21st December, the darkest day of the year – winter solstice or 'Midwinter's Day' – was a few days away. Before we got fully stuck into our dog training and all the things that went along with it, we needed to 'move house' and also get some of that pent-up energy released. Still in Hans' guesthouse, we sought a more long-term solution and a real base for our equipment. Hans was suffering from low occupancy generally, and more so outside of the late spring and summer. It was a trend he mentioned to me the year before; since the airstrip was created and prices for aeroplane tickets rose (the original access method was a heli-shuttle from the Thule Air Base), and visitors went from few to almost none – mostly scientists, the odd sledger and well-funded creatives.

I wish to take a moment to place the people we were now to live amongst in some historical context. If you were to ask an average inquisitive child what an 'Eskimo' is, even from a young age they might conjure an image of a fur-clothed man fishing through a hole in the ice. Whilst this imagined character is wildly simplistic and dated, remarkably for the majority it does not really change into adulthood – simply due to a lack of exposure to this distant world they will probably never see with their own eyes. It is a quaint and romantic image of a past time. But, how much of it is true and how much is something conjured up by fairy tales, children's books and even a colonial indoctrination?

For most, there is an awareness that people still live in the frozen wastelands of the extreme north, and some may be aware that nowadays a partially accurate general term for those native people is Inuit – a word that is the plural of *inuk* – and meaning just 'the people or human beings'. It is not a direct equivalent of the word Eskimo, but I have touched upon that already. There are several distinct communities and traditions across the vast swathe of the world around and above the Arctic Circle and their history is complex. We are concerned here with the Polar Eskimos, a tiny group who are widely considered the hardiest and whom many other Inuit communities revere. But, for clarity, I need to explain how they got there – this nine-hundred-strong population who call their corner of the Arctic home. In two sentences, the Polar Eskimos are the descendants of multiple migrations of Eastern Asian peoples who colonised modern-day Alaska, then Canada, then Greenland, over the past two thousand years. They were bordered to the south by Native Americans, and to the north and east by oceans – these combining to dictate their furthest limits.

Those with a thirst for historical detail may find this quenched in Appendix A where I delve further.

Phoenix

CHAPTER 3: Finding Our Feet

IT WAS TIME to find a home. Our plans were far from concrete. We did not know how feasible acquiring a dog team would be, let alone two, and even then getting them to run for us. We also had no idea whether we would make the necessary progress to make an extended journey away from the region.

We did know, though, that our meagre funds could not withstand a multi-week or even season-long lodging with Hans, despite his concessions and our best intentions. Our training and journeys would involve significant time away from settlements and in the wilderness, either using our tipi tent or one of the tiny hunting shelters built by locals over the decades. However, we needed a headquarters in which to live, work, plan and recuperate amongst the community. A couple of options presented, one a long-abandoned one-room home only a five-minute walk over rock and snow from Hans'. We knew plenty of these were dotted around town, some of them in the sorts of positions you'd expect would command premiums in a European property market – close to amenities and with perfect vantage over the sea. Curiously, though, empty they remained. A tentative question to Hans was parried with a restrained explanation that all house sales had to go via a centralised auction, controlled by the local and then the wider government. Land itself cannot be owned. It was the first in a seemingly never-ending, yet subtle, spiral of evidence that oppression via over-regulation from government was infecting Greenland – even in its most distant settlements.

A few years previously I had stayed in a small hut in Kulusuk, Eastern Greenland, and the situation there seems far more relaxed. Basic shells without facilities or 'extras' could be had for ten thousand Danish kroner, perhaps only a thousand pounds sterling or a little more. I wondered whether the freedom of simple, cheap cash sales and a sensible flow of ownership was now under threat there. Hans' voice sounded tired almost immediately, as if it were a battle the people of Qaanaaq have lost after a long fight. I dropped the topic.

The result of the curious housing situation was that homes were abandoned, and those Greenlanders in employment and therefore with buying power had more spacious and modern dwellings built on the western edge of town. East of Qaanaaq is a *heerahaaq*, a bog, in the summer months, and so cannot be built on. There's a strange ghost-town feel in some areas, with broken windows and a general state of dilapidation. It also seemed that convenient house fires break out every now and again when there is a pressure for a rebuild or a space to be opened up.

After viewing one non-starter, Hans showed us a small house with flaking yellow paint. It was, in fact, quite familiar as it was the first building you'd reach on the track from the airstrip, and almost the nearest to the water, separated only by a steep hill used for staking out dogs.

The key in the lock took some persuasion, but soon the five of us stood inside the dark main room. Locking doors at all is a rare state of affairs – even a sign of distrust. Again, there was no heating, and our breath was visible as we spoke. It is a strange sensation to be standing indoors, yet have the temperature hanging around -25°C. We knew instantly this was for us. Whilst by no means a palace or as cosy as Hans' guesthouse, it was ideal and we were not on holiday – we were not seeking luxury. It needed to be practical, large enough to work and have somewhere to relax after long journeys. It was a definite step up from the earliest houses that a European would recognise as such, initially merely wooden versions of the basic *iglu* layout. All the basics were there: a small washroom with obligatory loo bucket, two small rooms for sleeping and a main room with seating, an oven, sink, cupboards and table. A small area housed a water tank and cold storage zone. We were lucky; most homes still lack baths or showers, although a communal one is available in the centre of Qaanaaq.

It is no slur on the Polar Eskimos to state that the addition of washing facilities developed post-Contact. Prior to then, fresh water was a precious resource, as it mostly required the burning of oil to melt snow or ice. They did not have multiple changes of clothes and mended those that ripped or wore through. Some limited bathing or 'flannel washes' did take place, often using urine or even blubber. It was commonplace for entire families and visitors to strip entirely naked to allow time to delouse their furs; the lice then frequently eaten. I suspected that the tendency to overheat homes as compensation for this is a legacy of that time. In context at the time, of course, bathing was far from a daily ritual even in the world's largest cities. With some resistance, mainly through confusion as to why, the Polar Eskimos did begin to bathe more regularly once ships, especially those with females aboard, landed annually.

Ventilation of a historic *iglu* was taken far more seriously. A gap in the roof let vapour escape so that the air inside could not become stagnant or too humid. A thin, dried skin could be used as a window to let light in. The end of the main entrance tunnel was also protected from blasts of icy wind or the visits of loose dogs by an animal skin.

Anders contacted the owner and soon agreed a fee. The home was ours. Chuffed, as proud new tenants, we thanked Hans and walked back up to his place to remove our belongings and settle up the bill.

Our first evening involved the basics; getting the electricity running and then pumping in some heat. The heating oil burner was slow but reliable and our thermometer crept upwards, the four of us still fully clothed for the outdoors. We closed the doors to the small sleeping rooms so they didn't suck our warmed air from where it was needed. We did occasionally go inside them, though, just for the oddly enjoyable sensation of walking into a deep freezer.

To speed up the process, we switched on the oven and set up a table nearby to take advantage of the warm wafts of air (unwise to try at home). Alas, water would be the real issue.

In the Arctic there are various ways to go about gaining the second most important of resources, after warmth of course, water - *imeq*. In the southern regions or around the larger towns like Nuuk, Iqaluit in Canada or Murmansk in Russia, there are large infrastructures to provide water supplies, sometimes pressurised to avoid freezing in bitter winters.

In more remote communities where facilities are still needed for industries and where sizeable populations number in the hundreds or even thousands, governments often collect ice from icebergs or water from deep lakes to distribute via trucks as liquid water or as large chunks of ice. Qaanaaq had the whole range. More recently-built homes had water tanks installed which could have centrally melted iceberg ice pumped in. Every few days we would see a large truck drive out onto the frozen sea to break off a large freshwater iceberg chunk. Others could purchase a cubic metre of iceberg ice, beautiful azure-blue blocks, from the community for the equivalent of a few pounds. These sat outside their front door to be chipped off as needed.

A final option is *nilagtartoq*, the do-it-yourself method – walk or dog sled out onto the sea ice, be it winter or spring, dark or light, and hack off a few nicely sized pieces of ice with your axe. A sled full of ice will last days and this is the method that the predecessors of today's locals employed for hundreds of years.

Our water tank was a fairly old example, not being part of a recently built dwelling, and the residual water from the last inhabitant we discovered as a single huge block of ice. All of the water in pipes would of course also be frozen and so as we heated the house, we gently allowed the ice to heat. Too fast and joints could crack with the thaw, spelling a watery disaster in our new home.

To give the house a chance to reach -15°C, and then -10°C, then crawl encouragingly towards the magical freezing point and beyond, we took the opportunity to collect some iceberg ice for the coming days. Without a dog team or sled at that point, save our hauling sledges which we didn't want to unpack just yet, three large rucksacks would have to do, along with an axe bought from the local store.

Qaanaaq's limited electric outdoor light helped us pick our way amongst the broken and jagged ice of the tide crack, where the tidal sea ice meets the beach. Initially, the hummocks of ice, some six foot or taller, turned out to be pieces of sea ice lifted up on the rocks beneath the surface, or cracked into ridges by the pressure of ice either side. Obviously, this would be salty and no good. We needed to find a nearby iceberg that had been locked into the sea ice as it formed in the late autumn. Most likely, it would have originated from one of the dozens of calving tidewater glaciers in the fjord.

As a four, we wandered across the flat and at times slippery ice, with only a smattering of snow covering the smooth surface. Three of us carried rucksacks, Anastasia with the axe and Anders carried one of our rifles. We only planned to venture a few hundred yards offshore and still within the illumination of Qaanaaq, but bears are an ever-present threat. Only rarely entering settlements at that time of year, the rubbish dump not far from the settlement is a risky area and it would be Sod's Law that the one day we decide not to bother with protection, it would be the one that makes worldwide headlines.

Our iceberg, chosen from half a dozen or so, wasn't large or particularly impressive; perhaps thirty feet long and twelve feet high. It was raised up on about five feet of pressured sea ice. Its attractive features though were clean, glassy walls of pure ice and overhangs that should be dislodged with a few good strikes.

Taking it in turns to swing our hand axe into the wall of ancient ice, which almost seemed a shame, shards and then blocks came raining down to the ground below, where two of us hurriedly loaded them into bags. A fourth would be slowly wandering around the iceberg, scanning the middle distance with a powerful LED torch to warn us of any unwanted visitors. The work was surprisingly tiring and so five-minute rotations meant that the axe-wielder could strike with necessary vigour without tailing off.

Bags full, childlike-amusement of hitting large things with an axe complete, we turned for home. Although we should have had the water tank thawed in a few days and be able to use Qaanaaq's centrally melted ice, a more efficient option, I was pleased we had done it the old way at least once, and could do so again if need be.

For the first time, warmth greeted our cold faces as we opened our front door. It was only -25°C outside, usual for Avanerriaq's mild winters, but a fifteen degree or so gradient to the indoors was welcome.

We set out our ice to melt slowly in buckets on the counter top and then turned our attentions to the future, our plans, and general housekeeping – we could not live like a student houseshare. Kit needed organising and to be given its place and other space kept clear for work. But, it was dinner time. There was no time to head over to the store with its limited opening hours, hours we'd later find would be rather random, so rehydrating some freeze-dry meal packets it was. Huddled around the table that had been set near the heat, we poured over maps, did distance and cost calculations and planned our diary. It was half-way through the evening that we heard the first creaks and squeaks of life in a couple of pipes carrying water to the main room. Our heating oil boiler was straining at the leash and had been doing a sterling job. A muted cheer went round the table.

We arrived at a plan – settle ourselves into our base and re-sort gear. Buy dogs and build sleds. Learn how to drive dogs properly. Do some serious man-haul journeys. Make friends. All of these sounded great, but the order in which we did them would be critical. It was approaching Christmas-time, a major holiday in the actively Christian Greenlandic society. We knew that dogs nigh on outnumbered people in this region, but dogs were important; bred and then trained at great cost and effort, so would not be let go of easily. There was surplus, Hans assured us, but getting out into the 'marketplace' and buying dogs soon, whilst the need for ready cash for Christmas was at the forefront of hunters' minds would be wise.

Our biggest unknown was in how to establish viable dog teams and this presented a lot of problems, not least that the only person with experience with arctic dogs was me, and that consisted of vaguely assisting hunters in the East.

We needed to choose how many sleds, how large they would be, our planned cargo and distances for the whole season, where materials would come from, if we could afford them, how many dogs per sled, what genders and how many of each, how would we pick the best, how would we mix them. The list went on.

Many answers would come from the locals, so we set up a meeting with Hans and a collection of the most experienced hunters in town, generous with their time, headed by the ever-present Rasmus.

The hunting union is a locally run group that all hunting communities, mostly in the North and East of Greenland, have fashioned to standardise prices and practices. They also keep prices for the day hire of dog teams and boats stable for the short period of the year when a few scientists may visit and need taking from here to there. Before, prices would match budgets, and the Polar Eskimos became adept at predicting a visitor's buying power. Most importantly, surplus catches of fish, seal and other mammals can be collated in a hut near the beach. This service provides cheap unbutchered meat for dogs, a much better and cheaper alternative to bags of kibble. The union is not a modern addition though – its roots go back centuries as a central guardian of property (most of which was considered as belonging to the community, not an individual) and to keep basic order.

Rasmus spoke precious little English, but the little he understood he was keen to show he had mastered. With that, we began probably the most complex and confusing discussion-slash-negotiation-slash-lesson the world may have ever witnessed.

We wanted to do our very best to not force the language towards English, the lazy option, but we needed to speak with details and understand fully what was being said. So, Anders spoke Danish to Hans, whose Danish was superior to his English and found it more comfortable, who would then speak in Inuktun to Rasmus, Mads Ole, another hunter, and the others. Rasmus usually looked directly at Anders or me and began to use as much English as possible before reverting to Inuktun, for Hans to relay in English or Danish via Anders. We tried to pick up as much Inuktun as we possibly could, linking repeated words and sounds to what we found the translation was, and asking what some words meant. An English discussion about what had been said then began between the four of us on the team, and from there the cycle began again. It was quite the game of Chinese Whispers and it was obvious from the start that details and subtleties would be lost. I did get the impression our basic, though unimpressive, efforts to not just demand English, was appreciated. We had to start as we meant to go on if integrating with the people of Avanerriaq could hope to work. I had surprised myself at how much of the Danish I was picking up, but the local dialect was so abstract that it would take time to even scrape the surface of. Those unfamiliar would describe Inuktun as a dialect of sighs and mumbles, but these unrushed, detailed nuances are the natural form their words have forged through time.

An hour or so later, we had advice and more importantly, a deal. Firstly, the dogs. A local radio transmission would alert local hunters to the demand for around twenty dogs. Nineteen to be exact, given we already had Dave. Rasmus also offered to contact family in nearby villages to gauge interest there too. Once we had the dogs secured, at a modest sum of eight hundred kroner (around ninety pounds) per animal, the sleds needed to follow. We wanted to undertake extended journeys and travel in pairs, across two sleds, so settled on the longest sixteen-foot design. It would be quite a monster, we were told, and the amount of timber required needed a serious chat with Kim Petersen, another Dane and the local importer of building supplies.

It was here that things got more confusing. We didn't want to buy two old transit sleds, and at any rate there were none for sale, or pay someone to construct them and hand them over. The skills surrounding sleds and their peripherals are about as central to the pride and knowledge of a true Arctic hunter as any I can think of. This is where we must begin our education and really get stuck in.

Instead, we agreed to compensate Rasmus for his time showing us how to make a single sled. We would speed up the process by taking over the repetitive tasks once shown how it was done. Then, we'd take on the second sled solo. We would have to draw straws to see which pair of us ended up with which! We'd also planned a man-hauling trip, so decided to agree a start date either before or after so that it didn't clash with or limit Rasmus' hunting. A couple of days off the ice could cost him many seals, his dogs' vital food source.

Drawing lots for who would train which sled team, Anders and I paired up and Anastasia and James would head the second team. But, who would our canine engine-houses be? I was undeniably excited about the early days of this great unknown – our very own dog teams in the most special location on Earth to travel so traditionally.

Just the next day, a visitor at the door beckoned surprising and excellent news. Any concerns of a lack of available dogs were unfounded. We were to report to the hunting union shack, a single room around twenty foot by ten foot down on the beachfront, at lunchtime. Perennially dark of course, in midwinter, I wasn't even sure what time we stirred at. As we were warned previously, you can end up with your circadian rhythm of sleep patterns being confused by the lack of visual cues for day and night. Sleeping in was a common result, and I noticed it was nearly 10am. What a lazy bunch he must have thought we were. Our only consolation was that in days before clocks found their way to Avanerriaq with the strict, scheduled lifestyles of Danish settlers, timekeeping was loose. There was some legacy even today, with opening times of the store, for example, being very approximate. I learned that historically, rising in the early afternoon was not uncommon in winter, balanced by early morning activity in the midnight sun of summer.

At noon, in our large yellow goose down jackets, for which we had already generated quite a jovial local reputation, to the hunters' shack we went. A group was gathered inside and out, and dogs tied up here, there and everywhere – to pipes, to wooden beams, to a lighting post. No lack of dogs then.

We had spoken the night before about our 'tactic' when it came to purchases in settlements. Conscious not to underpay a group of people for whom wealth was not abundant, we needed to strike a balance nonetheless. We must start as we meant to go on, and if we were to show a frivolous disregard for money or a lack of savvy, we could end up with every deal from then until the summer being much to our disadvantage.

The risk was that from any either unscrupulous or hard-up hunters, injured, ill, badly treated or just plain bad dogs could be offloaded for more than they were worth. With a good working knowledge of canine behaviour and husbandry, a mental checklist should keep us safe from any disasters.

The best dogs, or at least those we had a shot of making into a decent team animal, should be confident when you approach them. 'Wildness' or hand-shy dogs typically have had a tough upbringing. Perhaps given very little human attention and contact whilst a pup, a dog will be cautious and withdrawn, much like a wild animal, keeping just out of reach. Alternatively, a handful of dog-team owners are rough with their dogs and a dog that flinches at the sight of a moving human hand has likely become used to being struck. Neither are good candidates for sled teams.

Greeting each hunter as they arrived, we went through the standard broken English, broken Inuktun and then reversion to passable Danish via Anders. This palaver typified our early days.

I took the lead with examining the dogs, and Rasmus sat business-like inside the hut with a sheet of paper to write down names of hunters, numbers of dogs and if sales were agreed, the money spent. Taking each dog in turn, I sat down next to them, those that would allow me to anyhow, and went through a routine. First I just said a standard dog 'hello' as you would to your neighbour's pet dog, and scratched it under the chin, a less intimidating and dominant greeting than between the ears. Then I gave each leg a good squeeze and checked the underside for any pain when touched. Finally, I needed to see clear, healthy eyes and then open the mouth to see present, clean teeth with no evidence of pain, filing or knocked teeth. We did not want dogs from a hunter who was cruel to their dogs, even though it would sadden us to not be able to liberate them.

So far, so good. We accepted the first two pairs of dogs, who seemed fit and eager. I was then shown to a lone dog, tied on the opposite corner of the shack. Rusty light brown in colour, most probably what some would call strawberry blonde, he stood tall and confidently but without any of the puppy-like enthusiasm of some. I approached and was met by a low, borderline-inaudible rumble, almost like a cat's purr. It grew into a soft growl by the time I knelt down next to him. He looked straight past me, as opposed to at me, something canine behaviour students call 'averted gaze' and I turned my body to the side, not directly at him, so as not to come across as aggressive. I have to admit, kneeling down and being a foot away from a large, unknown dog's head was slightly concerning. I didn't sense any malice in him though, only concern and perhaps a fragile ego. I had to check him over like the others and every time my hands made contact, the growl grew. He was no doubt a strong dog and I thought, if we took him, he'd either be an excellent alpha (what locals called a king dog or *naalagaq* – an important Inuktun word also applied to men, meaning 'leader' or 'with authority') to keep discipline, or a downright troublemaker. His name was instantly Thor, Norse god of thunder, and another eight hundred kroner was counted out and handed over to a smiling hunter.

Dogs came and men went. It was an opportunity to learn names and mingle a little – to show our faces and make sure people knew why we were in their village and that we were friendly. Having a purpose and not just 'taking' would be key.

A final pair of dogs, we were told, had just arrived outside and were tied to a fuel tank bracket. We were up to fourteen or so in total, with a promise of more the next day from another settlement as Rasmus' brother was due to arrive. The pressure to buy therefore wasn't overwhelming; they had to be right.

I couldn't see any dogs at first. Stooping down in the darkness, we only had a single lamp the other side of the track to see by, I spotted two medium-size dogs. One was light brown with a slightly-built, fox-like appearance. The other was more typical, although a dirty white and ginger mix. Both seemed absolutely determined to stay as far from me as possible and at the same time apart from each other. Ropes were already tangled – like a chaotic hair braid. What a mess.

I picked the fox-like dog first and coaxed him out, mainly by a constant pull on the rope. Reluctantly, he sat beside me, as low to the ground as possible as I did a check. Although clearly underweight, he seemed healthy and was probably only a year or eighteen months old. Lack of food growing up had limited his size, I decided. Thor and this dog couldn't have been more different, one showing every alpha behaviour in the book, and the other a firm omega-type, the opposite end of the spectrum.

Immediately as I let go, the poor animal rushed back to the safety of a niche next to the wall. It was time for the second dog. Let's say it was a battle of wills. Whilst forcing a dog into uncomfortable close proximity is not a path to fostering trust, for now it had to do. I had to work out what was wrong with these dogs and whether they had any potential. He was healthy, better fed than the first and with bright eyes, albeit ones that would not do anything but stare widely anywhere but at me. I worked with James to keep him in place so I could check for injuries.

Some might be surprised, but having chatted amongst ourselves, watched the dogs who clearly didn't get on, and asking indirect questions of the hunter, we bought them. Direct quizzing would usually result in a closed-up vagueness. The ginger dog would every now and again lash out at the younger, who in turn cowered and yelped. The boxes of basic health were ticked and I reasoned that we were to have two teams. One dog was bullying the other, so separation would be vital, and their fear of humans could be worked on. They certainly had to be 'staked out' apart from each other when not supervised.

It was a successful shopping trip – with only a few gaps left to fill and with our very limited pouch of expedition cash depleted we walked our motley crew of dogs along the frozen beach and to a spare area of hillside had been told was free for us to use. It was as we had left the lit, inhabited part of Qaanaaq, and switched on headtorches that Peter Duneq (his local name was Aaqioq) arrived. We all had both hands busy with very energetic dogs on six-foot ropes, so couldn't be introduced properly, but he beckoned over to a flat area in limited but urgent-sounding English.

Peter began to walk from spot to spot, pulling ropes from the snow and pointing to them. He was showing us where the fixed staking points were. In the summer, bolts and spinning metal loops are buried under the temporarily unfrozen ground, mainly gravel, dirt and a few pioneer plants, so that a secure and permanent point can be used year-round for dogs. He was walking in a set pattern, methodically searching out the loops with a triumphant smile and "here" at each one. Having clipped all our groups of dogs out, mostly in pairs or alone in initial caution, we shook hands with Peter and thanked him.

Peter wasn't tall, not unusual for native Arctic people, at around five foot six, with a neat moustache on an olive-skinned face. His ready smile combined with, it had to be said, somewhat mischievous eyes set behind a pair of glasses. Clothed in western-style outdoor clothing, there were numerous small rips and repairs that we had seen with almost all those hunters we'd met thus far. Ready money was not plentiful, but an enviable 'make do and mend' mindset ran through the community.

After making a joke about one of our dogs, the 'puppy' (who was probably around nine months but seemed set to grow to a monstrous size), being extra keen on nuzzling between our legs, Peter said we must come to his home for tea the next day. Whilst we were keen to accept voluntarily, it was clearly an instruction, not an invitation, and we had to assure him we'd come.

The evening heralded great excitement and I was part-relieved, part-delighted, to see my team's motivation back again. I knew James in particular needed time to reset and I felt we were now on that road. As some pasta and tinned vegetables were being cooked to accompany our dried ration packs, I drew up a 'team list'. We knew we had more to come, but having a working idea of which dog goes where could help decisions the next day.

One of the things I said, assuredly, as we changed tack from man-hauling to dogs, was that my bear dog, Dave, would stay with us and become simply one of the dogs. No special treatment. I saw a couple of eyes roll as I first said so. They knew how fond I was of him and they were right. His lack of athletic distinction and ample proportions were also a source of mockery – my final attempts to protest falling flat as two young men wandering past our home at feeding time decreed Dave was fat.

Dave was duly added to the list under Anders' and my name, and Anders made a play for Thor. Some of the dogs were as yet unnamed, so had descriptions only. We couldn't just claim dogs like children in a playground choosing teammates. Logic needed to prevail – each team needed to number the same, be a similar size and speed, with the important characters, a lead dog – *ittuqut* – and a king dog. Dave, whilst a massive fluffball, probably nearly ninety pounds, was a lazy dog, and a bit of a wuss. I didn't want him to tug whilst walking on a chain, so this was why I picked him for Dark Ice duties. Thor was a puller and a strong personality. There was little resistance to us having them. In fact, as days passed, Anders would always be found bonding with Thor at the deference of the others.

To even things up, James and Anastasia would have the next pick of a pair of dogs. Perhaps things would have to change later. Perhaps one team would outpace the other. Perhaps two dogs, strangers right now, would not get on. One thing was for sure, though, the two meek ones would have to be separated by as much distance as possible. Healed wounds on the younger, fox-like one, were undoubtedly from the ginger's attacks. Bullying among dog groups is common when food is involved. Names were starting to develop though. The younger, we all agreed, would come up and live outside our home on a different corner to Dave, for special feeding and to rehabilitate. He needed building up and strengthening if he was to be any use. So, he became Phoenix – somewhat prematurely of course, but we were determined that he would emerge from 'the flames' to be an excellent dog. His tormentor we couldn't warm to easily, whether around other dogs or not, and so he became OJ. You may believe the party line that it's an 'orange juice' reference to his fur colour, or...

We kept an eye out to the west for lights the next day – the headtorches of visitors from Siorapaluk, a small settlement. Rasmus' brother, another Peter (certain Danish-sourced names like Peter and Mikael had become popular and bewilderingly common), would be coming over to see family, and had enough dogs spare to fulfil our shortfall. We weren't quite sure how it would work if we didn't want some of them, awkward perhaps, and also couldn't imagine how he'd get home again, but we went along with the plan nonetheless.

Locals very rarely use headtorches whilst in transit. The long winter months are dark throughout much of the day and in the middle of the season, there is almost zero natural light, save for stars and the moon. When working around the village or tending to dogs on the dark hillsides, of course they take advantage of head lighting – usually ten dollar knockoffs imported from China. Before electricity, they would burn oil-soaked moss or peat on the end of a harpoon. I noticed a fabulous repair and elbowed James to point it out when meeting with the dog sellers the day before. An unusually tall hunter, whose name we never learned, had broken the switch on his low-cost headlamp, so had rewired in a full-size domestic light switch. This was attached proudly to the side of his head. Fantastic.

Out on the ice, though, hunting and moving from settlement to hut to settlement, Polar Eskimo hunters move in darkness, almost silently swishing along. It's a bewitching experience to watch. So calm, so controlled, so comfortable with the environment and a display we admired each day off the shoreline. The moonlight, stars and an encyclopaedic knowledge of the area, plus total confidence in their dogs' instinct, made them quite an act to emulate.

We had a clear line of sight from the window across the hill, towards the dump and the sea, with Herbert Island many miles beyond. The darkness made this view only theoretical of course, and the dogs were out of sight behind a small rise of snow. As Anastasia was tending to something in the worktop area, she saw cones of light sweeping the snow quite a way off.

A group of hunters, Rasmus included, were also wandering slowly towards our home from the other direction. By design this was the typical way we had seen locals walk, originally in order to limit body moisture encroaching into non-breathable furs. We donned jackets, gloves, hats and our dwindling cash pile and headed out into the calm -25°C air.

Peter, dressed in fur trousers and a hand-stitched canvas parka with fur lining, had his hands full. He had three ropes in one hand and four in the other, a dog on the end of each, and he walked with strength that belied his short stature. Peter had done this once or twice before.

The four of us stood back as the hunters grouped together with a muted exchange of smiles, greetings and aloof glances. We exchanged names and were handed the ball of tangled ropes. Using a set of spare staking points that we'd earmarked, we randomly spread them out, both hunters and team. Peter was keen to advise as much as he could about each, his English slightly better than Rasmus' and his smile more easily won.

A trio of dogs, one huge dominant burnt-orange animal, was with a black and white and a slighter white dog. A pair of older, calmer dogs sat patiently and then there were a few more white dogs. We assumed they were related.

Peter pointed at each in turn. "Brothers" he said to two. "Friends" to another pair. "Do not mix" to a couple kept well apart. "They are old, and run well. They you will like."

The numbers added up, there didn't seem to be any basketcases, so we accepted the lot, taking us up to a round twenty dogs. Still unsure as to Peter's plan to get home, we bade farewell and gave all the dogs a good feed. There is no better way to build a canine bond.

The two older dogs, one white and black and the other white and ginger, had a sort of knowing professionalism about them. Not barkers or constantly jumping up at us when we came near, they also seemed very comfortable in each other's company. James turned to me and said, "we'll have those two then?" Deal done.

Over yet another gourmet concoction of rice, sauce and a base of freeze-dried meal, two lists took shape. We had no idea who the leads would be, but first I'll provide a rough notion of how dog teams work.

Dogs are driven all across the various regions of the Arctic. The terrain, materials available and dogs at their disposal will tend to dictate how the technique developed in a combination of isolation and chance meetings, leading to skill exchange, over hundreds of years. Malamutes of Alaska are amongst the heavier-set draught dogs and can haul large loads. Lighter Siberian Huskies, those famous animals now often found down south as pets with their bright, colourful eyes, are ideal for travel in their forested homeland. Once people began to harness dogs and use them to pull along their belongings; selectively breeding them to exaggerate attractive traits like stamina and a keenness to listen, they used sleds to control the whole system and to ride. Trees were scarce in some regions, in particular Greenland, so whale bones and the occasional drift wood log would be prized property. There was always a solution – a way to improvise and overcome.

You may have seen dogs used for tourist rides in Scandinavia or on races like the famed Iditarod in Alaska. They are usually slim, fast animals in a 'gangline' configuration; pairs of dogs in a long line out to a lead dog or lead pair. This is ideal for racing, where maximum power is needed, and where trees need to be avoided. Having two dogs pick one route around a tree and the rest choose another could be very messy if not harnessed correctly.

Greenland, from south to north, east to west, is treeless, even in the small area not covered by permanent ice. Different priorities apply to different dog drivers and chief is the fact that the majority of dog travel is on the frozen sea ice, not overland or over hills. Dogs in the Far North are specialised for long distances, efficiency and flat, but bumpy surfaces. Instead of the 'gangline', the Polar Eskimos and most Greenlanders have adopted a 'fan trace' or a 'fan hitch'. A line for each dog comes from the front of the sled and the dogs run alongside each other. Power is therefore not as focussed to the front, but it means individual dogs can leap and dodge obstacles like ice blocks. The dogs also feel more 'pack-like' and as such feel secure and motivated. Travelling with a fan of dogs ahead of you can be mesmerising. The subtle moves and interactions are dynamic and at its best, the fan can appear somewhat like a dance.

In both systems, and the endless variations that remote communities have tinkered into them over the years, there is a lead dog or lead pair. This dog may not be the king dog, in fact it's better if it isn't, or the strongest or the fastest. The lead dog is however almost always the keenest to run and critically, a listener. Often, a promising sled dog can be let down by its reluctance to listen to its master and follow instructions. With a lead dog out front, most dogs will follow happily in their wake.

Gender is a final major consideration. With most sled dog varieties, females are significantly smaller than males and less suited to hard physical work. In fact, tough though it may be to swallow for those back home with domestic animals, most females are immediately put down at birth, except if a hunter is in need of a new breeding female or whose team would benefit. We ended up with only one female in our new menagerie, and she was chosen due to her close bond with the young but strong ginger dog we had committed to. Although we had no breeding ambitions; quite the opposite, the birth of a litter whilst on an extended journey would be a tragedy as they would not survive, we were told a female in a team could be useful.

In the western fjords of Greenland, there are far more overland, hilly hunting routes than elsewhere on the Arctic giant of an island. As such, dogs bred and trained there have historically been smaller and more nimble; better for hill-climbing in steep passes. In the opposite sense, and in part of what makes the extreme north legendary even amongst other Arctic people, dogs of the Polar Eskimos are different.

As they migrated to Avanerriaq from Canada, the people had excellent breeding stock plus a knowledge and desire to pick the best to breed – the same artificial selection breeders use today. Evidence suggests Inuit ancestors first travelled with dogs well over a thousand years ago. Scant resources may have limited the earliest to a pair of adults per family, increasing over decades to half a dozen and in the modern trading era, a full team of a dozen, plus spares and those 'in training'.

Whenever I asked in detail, either mischievously or as an indirect question, how you 'make' an Avanerriaq dog, it turned out to be almost a local secret, with only vague and mysterious replies. The same species as all other dogs and direct descendants of Canadian sled dogs, and close cousins of the 'standard' southern Greenland dogs, Thule dogs are nonetheless unmistakable. Hugely tall at the shoulder, thick set, with long legs, wide heads and a confident demeanour – you have the rare and very special Thule Eskimo dog or Thule Greenland dog. Curiously, it appeared that there is no local word to differentiate Thule dogs from a typical dog, *qimmeq*. Next to a southern dog though they look like giants, with extraordinary pulling ability and stamina. Rumours persist that wild Arctic wolves were relatively recently bred into the Thule bloodline. Indeed, their long legs could support this theory. However, my university studies and fieldwork with wolves, and experience with wolf-dog crosses, make me sceptical. The problem-solving ability, aloof independence, different walking gait, and indeed the slighter build of white Arctic wolves, are absent in the Thule dog.

What is the secret for their bulk then? Hard training from a young age of six months or so, careful selection for breeding and we, think, walrus meat. Although never confirmed, lots of little hints suggest that this rich, protein-heavy red meat is a reason for strength in both Thule dogs and the disproportionately strong Polar Eskimo people themselves. If there's another unknown ingredient or trick, well, perhaps it should stay a mystery.

Tragically in 1988, long before I first visited Qaanaaq and the surrounding area, viral distemper broke out amongst the Thule dog population, which had outnumbered the people. It had originated in central Arctic Canada and spread rapidly via foxes, wolves and of course, dogs. There is some belief in town today that the infection that left few dogs alive was rabies, not distemper, which is a very different infection and even then widely inoculated against. Decimating the teams of dogs and due to a limited knowledge of disease control, distemper spread fast and even with a later attempt to separate healthy dogs from the infected, some hunters lost their whole team. Hundreds of years of breeding, knowledge and hard work were gone in a few months. Whilst not the only disease to strike polar people – smallpox, measles and tuberculosis were others – this was amongst the most devastating, especially due to their reliance on traditional dog sled travel.

As a heartening example of the attitude shown by the colonial state, Denmark, widespread vaccination was funded to save the remainder around Greenland. Dogs are so intrinsic to the lives of Inuit that without them, much falls apart, beginning with their culture and links to their ancestors. In other northern nations, colonists have actively removed dogs from their people, sometimes in mass slaughters, as a way to undermine their way of life.

The solution after the disease, after concern of a recurrence dissipated, was to restock from Canada and the south on the west coast, where dogs were plentiful but less critical for day-to-day life. It's now very obvious in Qaanaaq whether your team is compromised of these slighter-built Greenland dogs, a mix, or a mammoth pack of Thule dogs. Some of the most successful hunters in Qaanaaq were fiercely proud of their Thule teams, which I would confidently say have no equal anywhere on Earth. Some were so large and stocky they resembled bears.

We had a mix of dog types and that frankly, since we were outsiders who could have been sold the real dregs, was remarkable. We hadn't bought any star performers, but we were optimistic. There was also the added challenge of how our teams came to be – adult dogs plucked from across settlements, few of which had worked together before. This can cause friction and we knew there was potential for the teams to never really mesh at all. Ideally, new dogs are fed into an established team as older puppies, able to learn and grow into the role without upsetting the dynamic or challenging the king dog for control. Dogs over seven or eight years old would be retired as their performance declined, so there was a natural throughput.

For ours though, over the next few days, name suggestions came from all directions – some visual prompts which morphed into names and some entirely down to character, which all the dogs had in bucket loads.

Dave – my original bear alarm dog. Large and with long-coated white and black fur. Most likely a Thule or Thule with a minor southern input. Nervous initially around humans and one to avoid a scrap at all costs. A lazy and fidgety runner.

OJ – the cowardly bully who arrived with Phoenix. Wiry and strong but not tall, with a white and ginger coat. Cripplingly nervous and skittish around people. Needs physical restraint to examine. A work in progress but little optimism.

Crazy (Jack) – a young and hyperactive super-friendly beige dog. Strong Thule characteristics but a slimmer frame. The son of Comedy and known together as the 'comedy pair' due to their initial antics making us laugh. An awkward gait, but seemingly happy with it.

Odin – although unrelated to Thor, his sandy single-colour coat reminded us of him, so Odin seemed fitting. An enormous Thule dog, most likely the largest we had with a square stance and large limbs. Docile and nigh-on 'sedated' around people and when in a team, yet dominant within his trio over food.

BS – named due to being a mostly black-coated dog (with some white) from Siorapaluk. Black-Siorapaluk dog was abbreviated to BS, much to obvious amusement. Very attractive and healthy, but quite shy, slight and submissive in his trio. Frantic when separated from Odin.

DWNN – the dog with no name, in homage to Clint Eastwood's Hollywood Western character. A slim and white-coated dog from the south, although not elegant. Submissive to Odin to the point of sycophancy and uncontrollably frantic when separated from him. Later named John by Anders, a label not universally adopted.

Enrique – a loud and irrepressibly energetic, young but experienced thick-coated dog. With significant Thule content, in excellent condition and named due to his discordant range of vocalisations.

Lyka/Leika – our small, young, black-coated female who came along with Houdini. A handful, although sweet-natured and extremely friendly. Cunning and independent with a penchant for rope and harness chewing.

Thor – the troublemaker. Tall, strong and hardworking, but without the stockiness of a classic Thule. Most likely from an original Qaanaaq bloodline though. Usually the sort to start scraps with other dogs, he whines endlessly when feeling left out but was to become very loyal and friendly with the team.

Garfunkel – another white southern dog. Somewhat shy and with an innocuous personality. A perfectly functional if unremarkable sled dog.

Pinky – part of double trouble. A white southern dog with a similar appearance to his brother, The Brain, but a very clean, pink nose, which helped to differentiate. Enthusiastic and friendly with a gentle temperament.

The Brain – the more confident of the duo and with a darker nose. Friendly and confident with a dominance over Pinky which only really manifested at feeding time after a lean period.

Comedy – along with Dave, he was the old hand of our team at six or seven years old. Calm and friendly with lots of personality, he was without doubt Jack's father with the same stiff running style and beige coat with black markings. A keen runner and with a sort of wisdom about him.

Leon & Jason (the Hitmen) – a calm and 'professional' pair of hard workers. They didn't get involved in childish scraps and only became rowdy when food was in sniffing distance, so we gave them movie assassins' names – the eponymous Leon and Jason (Statham). Not handsome, but mid-sized; Jason white and ginger and Leon black and white.

Houdini – what is there to say? Initially a cocky upstart with no sense of hierarchy or respect for other dogs, this tall, but very young ginger hurricane of energy was an early favourite. No experience, maximum confidence. We all know one of these.

Phoenix – the basket case adoption and the one we could have easily rejected. This submissive and underweight, young dog would need care. A small, wide face with fox-like tufts and light brown fur – most likely a southern import bloodline.

LBD – Little Black Dog. Fairly self-explanatory really. LBD was a slightly built yet highly enthusiastic dog. Obsessive about food, he could food-guard aggressively.

Scar – a dominant white southern dog with a good number of battle scars, hence his name. A serious food-guarder meant that unless supervised, his staking mate Batman would end up foodless.

Batman – a good natured and noisy dog. Another white southern Greenland dog but with a nondescript personality. Often identified in the early days by a process of elimination.

There you have our starting line-up. Far from being a gaggle of homogeneous sled dogs, each looked and behaved with a uniqueness that foretold a serious handful for us as novice dog drivers. Solely based on first impressions, Anders, James, Anastasia and I made two team lists. Thor would control Anders' and mine, and Jason the other. We'd try Crazy as our lead dog due to his enthusiasm, and James and Anastasia earmarked Comedy. Not coincidentally, both these were Peter Duneq's dogs.

Instead of buying up vast bags of imported dry dog kibble to feed their voracious appetites, it was an easy decision to stay traditional and stick to seal meat. Although in the depths of the dark winter, hunting was in full swing. Using cracks and holes near the edge of the sea ice extent, many miles out at sea, the hunters use nets to collect seals as they traverse the ice edge – *qaattaqtuq*. To complement the spring/summer-time tactic of stalking and humanely shooting these staple food-animals of the north whilst basking, netting is vital. Dogs and people alike need feeding year-round, and you can't stockpile enough in wooden huts in the summer for the darkness of October through to February. Nonetheless, any short-term surplus could be sold or exchanged with other families throughout the year, perhaps to *kiffaq*, the term for a non-hunter, derived from a slightly-mocking use of the word for a clerk.

During the summer dogs are not worked, for obvious reasons, and so populate the open areas of settlements and the beaches and hillsides surrounding. The sight, and sound, of literally hundreds of dogs in pairs, trios or alone in rows of staking points is beyond description. It seems tough, and the lack of exercise and attention for those months, combined with only once or twice weekly feeds, could attract criticism. What must be remembered though are the dogs' experiences and expectations – limited to say the least. The standards we in Europe might attach to the emotional needs of a pet dog do not apply to differently trained and bred sled dogs. Studies have even shown that weight loss is lower than might be assumed during the rest season.

I had casually read a great deal about sled dog feeding and nutrition, with no professional application at the time, and so knew there was a lack of clear conclusions on the matter. Research had been limited: with southern commercial sled dogs in Minnesota perhaps, the Greenland dogs historically used by the British Antarctic Survey (until the truly abominable and non-evidenced banning and eviction of dogs from the continent), and finally very limited observational studies of the dogs of other aboriginals.

Dog health, weight gain and loss and various work levels, the type of food – manufactured or natural – and other factors impacted feeding regimes. Some studies claimed they should be fed ten ounces twice a day. Some said five pounds daily. Others insisted on a couple of pounds daily with feed-ups on rest days. No real consensus prevailed, and so we needed to take local advice, especially from those whose dogs we envied, and make an educated guess at what our new teammates needed. Five pounds, every two days, with occasional feed-ups seemed sensible. Why not feed every day? The answer is psychological, Peter explained, as he saw us carrying food through Qaanaaq. When on the ice and hunting, success was not a certainty and days without catches could pass. If a dog team grew used to the routine of daily feeds of good fresh meat, it would expect them. Miss out for a day, two, or even three, and motivation might fall through the floor. A dozen mutinying dogs was a nightmare prospect and besides, they are said to run best on lean days. Random or infrequent feedings therefore build a mental resilience into the animals.

There are reports of these only partly domesticated and most unrefined of working dogs being aggressive, and predatory, towards people. One such tells of a hunter tripping in front of his team whilst on a remote hunting excursion. Alone and with the dogs sensing his vulnerability, a primal instinct was triggered and they set upon him. He survived, saved only by his thick furs and will to fight them off. I do question the story, and also how after such an event he could regain control of a team to travel back to his settlement. In years of spending time with sled dogs of all varieties, I have not once seen a single act of aggression towards an adult. Rarely, there are tragic instances of children injured or killed by a dog, a crime for which they are swiftly put down. This is invariably a starving, stray dog that behaves like most feral animals would, given opportunity for easy prey. They are not typical or healthy members of a dog team.

Our slimmer dogs were due some extra meat during the weeks of training so as to have a chance to recover and bulk up. We weren't hunting ourselves – goodness, we'd not even gone one yard with our dogs, so the union community stock of seal was perfect. Rasmus showed Anders and me the options for purchase one breezy evening, a rarity for the calm weather of Avanerriaq. Prizing a rusty padlock off the bracket and yanking the old wooden door open, we shone our lights inside to see what could be a props room of a slasher-movie. Inside was a pile four feet high of skinned seals, all of which had been sliced perfectly in half across the middle. Hunting had been good. A pile of skins lay to the side, folded like bed linens. It was macabre, but the deep freeze temperatures meant there was precious little 'gore' or mess and not much odour.

We chose enough for a week, around a hundred and thirty pounds, which translated to around one full seal, costing the equivalent of around thirty pounds sterling. Rasmus weighed the meat out with a large scale, having wisely donned large blue rubber gloves, and thumped them out onto the snow for us to bag up and take away. Rather like a tombola stall at a summer fete, he had a small lockable money tin from which to do the transaction. He threw in a few pounds of furry-skin and blubber, which are good for the dogs' teeth and digestion – a sort of sled dog toothbrush. Rasmus beamed one of his smiles at us and with a happy 'ii', Inuktun for yes, (pronounced 'eee') wandered off home. Every dog nearby, none of them ours, was transfixed on every movement, and a few had started to howl and wail in anticipation. Sadly, it was not their turn.

Although the meat, innards and bones were frozen solid, blubber remained greasy, so bin bags and rubber gloves averted an almighty mess. The energy-rich blubber and oils had long been more than a source of dog food for the Polar Eskimos, also being used as a fuel for heating and light.

You will recall one of the unsubstantiated origins of the generic term 'Eskimo' – eater of raw meat – and be of the assumption that since the Polar Eskimos lived a near-Stone Age existence prior to Contact, this was the case. The lack of trees and vegetation for tinder and wood fires might support the theory. In actual fact, the Polar Eskimos had long since mastered fire and boiled a good proportion of their food. The key, was blubber.

Along with the meat and innards of various seal species, mostly ringed seals, to feed both human and dog, the thick layer of greasy, pink insulating fat beneath the seal's skin was indispensable to many Inuit communities. The Polar Eskimos were no exception. After a skilful fashion, sparks from flints could create a small flame with the aid of a tuft of dried moss, and thereafter fuelled by a small reservoir of seal or whale blubber in a soapstone lamp. Much like the whalers who came north to seek great whales for their oils, this was central to heating, lighting and cooking. Early Inuit fire-making varies in technique and depended on resources – the central Canadian Inuit used bow drills to make fire from friction, and the Polar Eskimos a flint with moss or cotton-like plants.

Of course, the luxury of heating, illumination and boiled meat was constrained to life in the *iglu* – or house. As trading began, Primus stoves took their place – cleaner, powerful and more efficient than blubber lamps, which coated both skin and clothing in a black, fatty soot. For centuries though, they represented comfort and even wealth. More steam filling the *iglu* from boiling meat meant more demand for blubber, and copious blubber could only be the result of successful hunting. It was the solemn and respected duty of the 'lady of the house' to tend to and control the lamps – she would become quite expert at the skill of producing enough but not too much heat, and then ensuring it lasted through the night.

When travelling, or even by choice at other times in the *iglu*, meat and fish was eaten raw, either frozen, thawed or fermented. From this came the unique palate of the Polar Eskimo, and an exceptionally strong constitution. Some foods were central to survival – for example *mattaaq*, the raw tail skin and fat of the narwhal. If cooked, the Vitamin C needed to stave off scurvy would be no more, and the Polar Eskimos would have perished. Hans in particular was proud of the tradition of only cooking some meat, and had before offered me prime *mattaaq* to chew on.

Our teams were beside themselves with excitement at feeding time. The butchering was done outside with a combination of an axe and carving knife. Our skills were hopeless and chunks ended up uneven and mangled – we would have to practice to make this routine swift and neat. It didn't get much better as we doled it out. Keeping hold of the slabs of flesh, innards and fat too long, both James and I had our fingers nipped by frantic dogs. Ironically, my crushed nail and blood blister was courtesy of Dave, my trusty hound. Northern dogs eat their food with a manic gusto – never chewing and instead violently jerking their heads back to swallow quickly. Some dominant dogs in groups stole their underlings' rations, making us dig for more in our bucket. Much room for improvement and better tactics.

Meanwhile, with a rough plan with Rasmus for the sled build, we turned our attentions to man-hauling. We needed a transition to allow us to almost grieve for Dark Ice; to burn those calories we so desperately wanted to expel over long, hard, Arctic miles of barren ice.

Anastasia had picked up a cold, presumably from the travel up north, a constant source of bugs and stagnant aircraft air, which was getting progressively worse. The initial assumption was that it was viral, so rest, sleep, water and good food was the treatment, but it was worsening and we feared a chest infection. With only a tiny medical centre, a 1996 update of the original 1950s facility, in Qaanaaq and no doctor at the time, we spoke to our expedition doctor back home and provided a course from our significant stock of antibiotics. We travelled complete with a pharmacy box; enough for a whole team for seven months of who-knows-what ailments.

This meant that a conundrum about finding a dog-sitter for our army of four-legged loudspeakers was no more. Reluctantly, Anastasia would stay and hold the fort whilst us three remaining headed off to get our man-hauling fix.

Leon, Jason and Comedy

CHAPTER 4: Scratching the Itch

M ID-WINTER'S DAY had been and gone. This brought the very darkest conditions, save a tiny glint of a glow on one horizon for a few minutes at midday. We would walk into pitch blackness on sea ice that had not been covered by anyone in some time, so with the ever-present risk of polar bears. Instead of the single alarm dog I had in Dave, and in a way for a sort of bonding experience, James and Anders too chose a dog each to haul with. James chose Enrique and Anders, Odin. Our hope was that they would behave and not tug annoyingly – they were not there to lessen the punishment on our own bodies by pulling weight after all.

With sleds packed with just a week or so of supplies, we assembled on the ice at the bottom of the hill having bidden farewell and 'get well soon' to Anastasia. I think she was looking forward, in between wheezing, to being with the dogs, for whom she already had a deep affection.

Our target was Qeqertat.

A few satellite communities exist around the 'hustle and bustle' of the six-hundred strong Qaanaaq. Each have had a critical part to play in how Avanerriaq's history has moulded the modern place we now see.

Inhabited today are Siorapaluk (Hiorapaluk to an Inughuaq), home to around eighty people and some of our dogs, Qeqertat, a tiny outpost of twenty-five, and Savissivik (locally spelt Havighivik), reducing now at under seventy inhabitants. Older settlements, some of which were just hunting camps or transient, have been abandoned. Most recently were Moriussaq (Moriuhaq) not far from the Thule Air Base at Pituffik (Pitugvik) and Qeqertarsuaq (Qikertarraaq) (meaning large island) on Herbert Island, itself locally given the same name. Past examples were the blizzard-plagued Etah and Anoratok to the north. There is also the Thule Air Base itself with early Cold War origins, but that is a wider issue needing later attention.

Qeqertat, a tiny cluster of wooden buildings, we were told was on a rocky outcrop to the eastern end of the wide Inglefield Fjord of which Qaanaaq sat on the northern opening shore. The word is spelled Qikertat in Inuktun and means 'island'. The sea ice was consolidated in these slower-moving waters, unlike the chaotic mess of broken and mobile ice to the west and north. This meant there should be a feasible route forty miles east to the settlement. This would be our aim.

We walked east along the frozen ice on the beach, passing hunters and other locals, many of whom came over to say hello and ask our plans. After a quick stop at the town store, it was time to go. Anastasia had come to see us off and with an 'air hug' each (we didn't want the lurgy) off home she went.

The beach was a great asset for Qaanaaq and in fact many other settlements in frozen places are chosen by their proximity to one. Tides, especially at the more extreme ends of the lunar cycle, cause the sea underneath the ice to rise up. Offshore, the ice lifts with it and this can cause fractures and raised 'boulders' if the ice grounds on rocks below. Near the shore though, where ice is locked to the land, the water can rise above the ice and flood. Flat areas like the beach, around twenty feet wide and ending as the hillside begins, are flooded too. Give it just an hour or so plus the retreat of the tide, and this freezes like an ice rink. Try and walk without spikes or polar boots and you'll be on your behind in seconds. Rapidly, though, sled runners, a little frost or snowfall honed it into a smooth, fast motorway, potentially stretching for miles down the coast. It's certainly a quick way to avoid the bumpy tracks across Qaanaaq's centre.

With rifles, loaded and slung, dogs on ten-foot lines and sleds pointed eastward, I could sense the pent-up energy and motivation in James and Anders. Hauling, at last – what we came here to do. The darkness too – that thing which set our project apart from the vast majority of polar ventures, past and present, and the thought that both rallied and terrified us.

taaq – the darkness

I led the first session. Fitting into the standard man-haul routine of one hour to seventy-minute hauls with ten-minute breaks (or less rest if it's windy), the first miles spanned a criss-cross of sled tracks, most likely to and from the fishing holes a few miles out. We needed to hug the coastline for a short while and then head straight for Qeqertat. Our new GPS (a device we wished to make minimal use of) had excellent built-in mapping, so I could point directly to a tiny cluster of huts dozens of miles away in the blackness with certainty. What we'd find in the way we had no idea. Pressure ice, leads, open water, bears, maybe all. Maybe a flat, safe route all the way there.

That first hour was different to any of the thousands of others I had previously travelled on foot on ice. We didn't wear skis as the snow was so thin that the ice was easy to walk on with polar boots. Instead of a view to a bleak and empty distant horizon, I saw nothing but the surface a few yards ahead of me. The snow and ice sparkled as the beam of my headtorch reflected back at me like a million little motorway cat's eyes.

It was this scant snow of Avanerriaq that cemented the Inuit decision to not adopt the use of skis. Lack of timber planks aside, their ability to 'float' a person in deep snow had limited application locally, and even in the snowier regions in the Canadian Arctic skis were absent. A few groups developed snowshoes of sorts. For skis, though, even in the twenty-first century, there is scepticism towards their use.

The sleds were under two-hundred pounds in weight and so moved with ease. It's all very well being able to see the ice immediately ahead, so you aren't going to fall over, trip or end up down a hole, but it's beyond that's the issue. Practically, the lack of knowledge we had of the world just beyond the reach of our torch beams was a concern, one I had never had to face before, perhaps apart from in whiteout. There could be a pressure ridge ahead or a lead, completely obvious if there was daylight, and perhaps a flat, easy route to either side. We could just walk straight into it, oblivious. A mile could become unnecessarily arduous purely due to lack of vision. A polar bear could be aware of us – approaching, or worse stalking, from miles off and we'd not know until it was within throwing distance. We had a three-hundred-yard range 'bear torch', but this could only be used at intervals.

Forget the actualities though. They can be allowed for, planned against, mitigated or just plain accepted. What is more immediate and visceral is the blind stare into nothing and the fear that generates. I read a paper by the Russian team who made the first winter North Pole journey, with resupplies, a few years before. It explained through interview how they feared the dark and what was or could have been there. Sheer terror. Imagining things that aren't there – those childish 'monsters under the bed' or 'things that go bump in the night'. Controlling that over-thinking and keeping a grip on reality is tough, yet vital.

The ice remained good and we cleared the last signs of human activity; now beyond the sled tracks or wooden markers in the ice. A hunter had warned us that whilst the ice against the cliffs, which rose up east of Qaanaaq's gentle hillside, was flat, it was then mashed up offshore, and flatter again well away from land. This is normal and can be caused by tides, currents and shallow waters around headlands or other landmarks. It was all very well but again we couldn't see where, and there were no details or distances offered.

Soon, the ice changed. The Danish word for pressure ice, or the other English words you could choose for that phenomenon, is translated as 'screw ice', so was the term we adopted for ease. First, we found a few broken bumps we could avoid or yank sleds over easily, but then we faced large slabs and ice boulders the height of a person. Other areas resembled giant shards of broken glass. Going around the problem was a no-go since the chaos continued left and right as far as we could see. A massive detour would add miles and sounded daft, so we got stuck in.

Dave and the other dogs weren't much help, as they often tugged in an unhelpful direction, then stopped and stared at us as we yanked and heaved our loads over a barrier of ice.

We stopped halfway through the worst of the rubble and had our break for flapjacks and hot tea from a flask. Life was good, the ice was tough but do-able and the windlessness continued. An hour or so later, the flatness returned and we concentrated on distance. The aim was to get to the halfway point to Qeqertat, over twenty miles in a day, and camp before a second leg. It was approaching midday and we were heading offshore, a straighter line than hugging the coast all the way, which was the hunters' route. Dog teams and people on foot often have different criteria.

Sat on the fronts of our sledges for another rest, I took the chance to film some clips as a tiny hint of a glow appeared to the south. It was not enough to illuminate anything, but enough to show the black silhouette of mountains – *qaqqat* - on the southern shores. Anders ruined the shot by standing and answering the call of nature right in front of my carefully set up panning shot, and James began one of many running jokes during our time in the North. "It's kinda just like Scotland!" he said nonchalantly. The philistine!

Miles ticked by. On the left was an iceberg, on the right a pile of rubble. However, we consistently managed to find good ways through.

Scanning for bears was a job we all took to enthusiastically. At the front, whoever was on 'point' would be both navigating and finding good ways through the immediate terrain. A good judgement in this role can go unthanked, but forethought and experience on whether to snake left, right or surge through can stave off deterioration. Naturally, the cone of light from this man's torch would wave left and right to the front, picking up any bears nearby or if eye contact is made, reflecting in the eyes of an unwanted guest further off.

The middle skier (a general term we use, whether we had skis on or not), also scanned to the front more carefully and also checked the sides. It seems like a little thing, but as number two swept left and right with his head, he had to be careful to dip as the light beam crossed the point man. Rather like driving in country lanes at night back home, the glare of lights from behind can be very irritating.

Rear man had the hardest job. As well as controlling his dog, he needed to negotiate the ice surface without tripping, keep pace with those in front, and regularly stop to sweep behind. Bears are intelligent and curious. Using any wind there is and an awareness of direction of travel, from behind would be a likely approach. Preying on the mind of the rear man is always, 'am I turning and checking enough?' Too much is energy-sapping and unnecessary. Too little and it could end very badly.

My watch half took me by surprise as I noticed it was evening, and so we began to search for a good camping spot. There were a lot of small, maybe foot-wide, refrozen leads where pans of ice had cracked apart. Although the risk of a split wasn't high, I used common sense to spot an area that I suspected was thickest and not on a likely fracture zone. It was the first time that the tipi tent, unusual by modern polar expedition standards, had been used in anger (save for Icelandic testing) since my short Dark Ice Project foray in 2012.

Eight ice screws held the canvas down as a single large pole raised the tent aloft. Perhaps trickier to tension and look the part than a tunnel tent, the benefits of standing room and hoarfrost-free, three hundred and sixty-degree protection from the elements were a winner. *Ilu* – hoarfrost, internally frozen moisture from cooking and human habitation, is a real Arctic adversary.

Having gone through that age-old polar routine of staking out and feeding dogs, securing the tent, throwing in tent bags, getting the stove roaring and then checking belongings are safe for the night, we were in. It was our first night together as a team in the darkness of polar winter.

I had made a mistake – a rookie error. As the foremost counter-intuitive fact of polar travel by human power, it's easier to overheat than to get dangerously cold. So what? Too hot means sweat. Sweat means damp clothing. Damp clothing chills down immediately after work stops and ruins the insulation properties of goose down, and even synthetics to a lesser extent. I had been enthusiastically leading the final hauling session and the ice had been bumpy – needing more energy than usual.

James fired up the stove and laid out sleeping mats as I was the last to come inside. A warmth already greeted my cold cheeks, even though most of the stove's energy was directed towards a pan full of fresh snow. Snow on icecaps is deep and fresh; easy to collect and always good to melt and drink. On sea ice the job of selecting water for food or drinks is tougher. Salt from sea ice leaches into snow directly in contact with it, so to avoid a briny surprise, you need to scoop off just the upper layers of fresh snow, or find a deep drift behind an ice block or iceberg. Of course, if you're patient and have an axe, iceberg ice is good too.

As I laid down in my 'area', barely six feet by two feet at the back of the octagonal tipi, I realised I'd made the mistake I teach all novices to avoid. I had skied in too hard on the final session. Not dramatically, but enough for a gentle cloud of vapour to be rising from my salopettes. I've seen far, far worse in the past, but it was silly for someone with hundreds of Arctic tent nights under their belt. The solution is pretty simple, if uncomfortable. The main rule is not to take damp clothes off, except small things like mitts or socks which can be quickly and actively dried with a Nalgene (a robust plastic bottle) full of boiling water or in the sun, if available, another day. Damp clothing, even if synthetic thin fabrics like Pertex, will freeze in seconds into a crusty disaster zone of unpleasantness if removed. Instead, the unlucky skier will have to continue to wear the garment, using body heat to push the moisture out from within. It was a minor case, but a shot across the bows, and I noticed the others weren't innocent either. Only once the vapour stops and the full thickness of fabric layers are dry, can they come off or go inside a sleeping bag. A damp sleeping bag without sun radiation to dry it will mean a world of icy discomfort.

We positioned the three dogs in a protective triangle around us; if a bear approached from the pitch black, attracted by a lingering odour of food, we relied on them to keep one ear up and raise the alarm. The majority of serious injuries and deaths from polar bear attacks are when people have been sleeping and unaware of the threat. Having a gun next to you when you can't use it is useless. Warning is key.

The night was so calm, with not a breath of wind, that the tent canvas barely moved and with the comfort of knowing our guard dogs were outside, three content polar skiers slept a good eight hours in our -25°C home. I was awoken by the infuriatingly irritating high-pitch 'beep, beep' of my cheap watch. A few seconds later, the others' watches chimed in. I don't think there are any less welcome sounds in the world, especially when warm in a cosy sleeping bag. Their chirpy alarm, like that person we all know who's full of beans at ungodly hours on early mornings, can't help but be at that pitch and intensity. Foretelling another cold and icy morning, that noise makes you want to bury it in the snow and be done with it. I've never been an early-morning person.

Something was moving outside. My eyes were still closed, head inside sleeping bag hood, feeling the cold air drawing into my lungs and the fog of condensation exhaling, and I froze still so as to hear properly. Anders was awake and so his snoring had finally ended. Few sounds could compete with him when in full sonorous broadcast. A scratching. Then some footsteps; slow and deliberate. Then silence. Then the same again. It's so easy when on guard to allow your brain to morph anything, any sound, into the worst possible conclusion. Is it a bear about to pounce on the tent? Or is it sea ice settling and groaning on a rising tide? Is it a guy line flapping gently against a ski pole? It was time to get up anyhow so I quietly gestured to James to unzip the bottom of the tent door to have a quick look. I had my hand on a rifle, just in case.

James lifted the zip just a few inches and then peeked outside, no torch on his head and just using the ambient moon and starlight. His body visibly relaxed as he looked at me and laughed.

"Hello Dave!" he exclaimed. Unzipping the door and flapping it open, an even colder pocket of air reached my face in seconds and there he was. Dave sat smartly and patiently in our doorway, as if to greet us 'good morning'. He made no attempt to enter the tent, still slightly shy, but like so many dogs clearly sought proximity to 'his humans'. Behind him was his chain and on the end, lay the ice screw that should have been embedded in the ice where we left him. Imagining it was mostly dumb luck, we chuckled about how Dave had apparently gone in circles around the screw in the same direction so many times that it had unscrewed. His bid for freedom was most likely more a surprise to him than it was to us and with obviously limited ambitions, the extent of Dave's rampage was to walk around and then sleep around fifteen feet from his staking point.

The stove was on, Nalgene bottles were emptied into the pan and the water reheated for breakfast and coffee. We flasked the hot water, melted the night before to allow for a fast start, and checked for temperature. It was job done. It's possible to go from alarm clock to outside and ready to ski in under an hour, but we could afford for a less frantic pace. With around twenty miles to Qeqertat, it would be a long day, but the time we reached the settlement was fairly immaterial.

The dogs were particularly energetic in the first few sessions, pulling left, right and centre. Dave continued his nightly antics and was going forward, stopping, spinning left and doing a full circle before repeating. Without a spinner on his light chain, this wrapped the chain around itself into a knot which I needed to untangle every half hour or so. Clever with a devious sense of humour or with a sort of compulsive disorder, I couldn't decide. Anders and James weren't doing a lot better. Enrique was pulling, but never at helpful moments, and Odin had a habit of walking out front and then stubbornly stopping and staying put until walked into.

Around twelve miles out from where the GPS told us we were aimed, it was still a world of three hundred and sixty degrees of darkness with just our little patch of snow-sprinkled sea ice illuminated by headtorch light. Large flat pans of ice were divided by neat, narrow refrozen leads which presented almost no challenge and actually served as a navigational aid as something to focus on. Little sets of footprints almost always run along the side of the cracks and little piles of ice. Arctic hare had been using them to find their way across the vast expanse of the fjord from hill to hill.

All of a sudden, Dave stopped, stared out to the front left of our column of skiers and sledges, and barked. Then again, and then louder and more frantically. We all stopped. I saw beams of light coming over my shoulder on their 'spot beam' setting for longer reach. Nothing. Dave was still alarmed and so we kept on scanning, more looking for the reflection of eyes than an actual figure yet.

Nothing appeared and Dave seemed to calm. I turned around to face the team and they both shrugged. Onwards we skied and then five minutes later, the same happened again. It makes the hairs on the back of your neck stand straight up and places every sense on high-alert. A combination of surprise, confusion, vigilance and a little fear permeated. Rifles stayed slung over our shoulders; there was no need to overreact, but something was clearly up.

By the fourth time it happened with no sign of trouble, let alone tracks or other signs, I tried to think of another cause for Dave's jumpiness. I went back to basics and thought of his priorities. With a grin to the others, I shovelled out a small pile of dog kibble (more practical than seal for this trip). Problem solved – we didn't hear a peep out of our oddball hound for the rest of the day. A habit though this could not become. Dogs very quickly repeat behaviour they've found directly results in food handouts.

Anders was in the lead on one fairly uneventful session, perhaps five or six hours into our haul, when he stopped, pointed and exclaimed, "I see lights!" We drew up into a line and squinted our eyes to try and make out the dimmest of glows on the horizon. It was certainly something. My eyes were playing tricks on me. The speck of light was in the exact direction we knew Qeqertat to be, but it appeared to move! I asked for confirmation for fear that I was going crazy but affirmation came back. We were baffled as the shapes wafted from left to right, and leaping up and down like we were staring into a log fire.

"Are we sure that's not a really remote fishing spot from a Qeqertat hunter and the movement is his lantern moving about and his dogs jumping around?" Depth perception was impossible in the gloom, so it could be a mile or fifteen miles away and we'd have no idea.

We walked on, hour after hour, but never found ourselves visitors to a lonely fisherman's camp, so Qeqertat it must be. The light grew painfully slowly brighter, yet still moving as we saw it. It was some trick of the light, the cold and our eyes, we resolved. Perhaps it was similar to a heat haze but in reverse.

Smaller, but much sharper and whiter lights began to appear to the front, left and some to the right. Some moved at a pace, some stayed still. Now, these really were hunters and their fishing spots. It seemed so odd to be in the most abstract and sensorily-deprived environment I could imagine, yet find ourselves gradually seeing signs of life.

It's an enormously powerful emotion for those who have spent prolonged time without outside human contact. My longest stint was one hundred and thirteen days in 2008. The waves of comfort the smallest sign of familiarity can generate is very special indeed.

The miles we'd put through our legs were beginning to bite. Although a two-day haul from settlement to settlement is almost negligible in comparison to a full-on extended journey, twenty miles on sea ice with mentally draining navigation and significant sledges is not inconsiderable. Qeqertat was in sight, buoying morale, and then it got even better. A much stronger light than any we had seen before shone straight at us. It blinked a few times and then shut off. A minute later it came back. We were being guided in. Had they seen our lights and done this spontaneously, or had someone from Qaanaaq contacted a friend or relative in Qeqertat to say that newcomers unfamiliar to the region were on their way? We blinked our headtorches in reply and so it continued on and off for hours. The other little lights were blinking back too – a sort of hello and hat tip to fellow travellers in the cold from miles away.

The final hour was tough, there's no doubt. We were all tired, it was 10pm, and Anders had not fed himself enough calories from lunchtime onwards. He had clipped his ski poles to his sledge, an odd thing to do, and was walking along with limp arms and a meandering gait. I skied up alongside James and said we needed to keep an eye out for change, and encouraged Anders to eat some chocolate and drink from his flask, which he duly did.

Qeqertat is perched on a rocky outcrop on a small island group in the furthest corner of the vast fjord. This is unusual, with many Inuit settlements being located on long beaches or low hills near the sea. Our GPS had a rough guess as to the exact location, but when you're talking a cluster of a dozen small buildings, error is amplified. Yes, we could see the now significant glow of a few lights plus our spot-lamp friend. However, it was becoming evident that we couldn't just ski onto an icy beach. Ice was becoming more jagged and tide-ravaged, making route choices more important. To our right, ice was formed into spectacular static waves ten feet from trough to peak, as if a stormy sea had been paused in an instant.

Bizarrely, despite these various lights, I wasn't sure where to lead us. They were high up, or a glow behind rocky hills. I tried right, seeing the end of a low cliff in the dusky half-light. Perhaps around the corner there would be a slope or natural harbour. Nothing. Just more rock and turbulent tidal ice. I stopped and asked for opinions. We either keep motoring on and risk ending up miles away as we follow an island's coast, or we go back and try left from our decision point instead. I didn't get a great deal back, save a vague 'perhaps' this and 'perhaps' that. I can't blame them. We were all confused, and it was dark and hard to make anything out, and we were tired. Slightly curtly, unfair I'd now admit, I said we're going back and trying the other stretch of tidal ice, nearer some other lights.

Retracing our footprints on the lightly snow-dusted ice, the dogs pushed our patience to the precipice edge of failure. Walking directly across our path, then stopping and staring at nothing in particular, then wrapping their chain around one of our ski poles, they simply wouldn't do as they were told. Obedient domestic hounds they were not. Eventually we rounded another corner of rocks which rose high above our heads and were instantly blinded by the brightest of the lights, the one that had lured us in from all those miles away.

About fifteen minutes later, a large barrier of turbulent blue and white ice gave way to show a narrow route towards shadows of man-made structures – wooden drying frames and oil drums. The ice, rocks and slope beyond seemed to be navigable so I asked James to watch the gear and the dogs whilst Anders and I clambered up, almost tripping a few times on the steep, icy ground. You'd never know it, but it was night-time and so the chance of finding a soul awake would be slim. There could be fewer than twenty people in town anyhow. If we found no-one it wasn't a disaster, we'd just camp on the sea and wait for morning.

Our luck was in. A middle-aged man stood on the wooden platform outside his small yellow home, puffing away on a self-rolled cigarette. The home was typical in style of those elsewhere, if a little smaller. A generator buzzed away on the other side of the house that presumably accounted for the lights in and outdoors, unlike others in the distance, which stood as shadows in the darkness.

A modicum surprised, for sure, he saw two lumbering, bearded southerners approach in our bright red smocks and smile, each with a raised arm.

"Alluu!" we both said. Quickly we found that he spoke reasonable Danish, so Anders introduced us and asked if there was a good place to camp. In an extraordinary show of generosity, the man greeted us both warmly with pats on the side of our arms with his strong, weathered hands and said we could sleep in the communal building. He explained that it served as everything for this tiny community; church, school, elder's centre and much more. Then he disappeared for a minute and returned with a plastic container half full of fresh water, a precious resource.

It happened again and again but our appreciation grew for these people who, invariably with very little in terms of worldly goods, welcomed strangers into their world. They knew we were *qallunaat*, foreigners, clearly here for 'sport' and curiosity into their way of life, wealthier than they were purely by luck of birth, but yet they continued to graciously assist without a single demand in return.

We hopped back down the cliff edge, careful not to lose our footing on the ice which was in places glassy hard and slippery, and then often brittle and liable to collapse. Relaying the good news to James, I found him sat on the front of his sledge, resting, and having a chat with the three dogs. I chuckled to myself as just a few weeks before he had said that whilst he found them ok, he wasn't a 'dog person'.

We also shared the news that there was a narrow, twisting path through the tidal ice to a tiny bay, perhaps twenty feet wide. There, repeated use had carved a shallow ramp from the sea ice to the shore. A few heaves later, and working as a team to move sledges and keep dogs under control, and we were in Qeqertat. Our host had walked over from his house and pointed us towards the communal building. On a little wooden sled, like many we had seen in Qaanaaq to move seals and other supplies around town, there was the water container and a can of fuel. Far beyond the welcome we had expected, realistically a safe area to camp and stake out our dogs, he was soon busy firing up an ancient-looking generator outside the sloped roof building and taking fuel inside for what we assumed was a burner for heat.

Each dog was designated a wooden post for their sleeping spot and given a good mound of kibble. For Dave it was his second feed of the day after his barking extravaganza. His reputation as the fat dog would not ebb at all soon.

Walking inside the large single room, smiles spread across all three tired and cold faces as -20°C became +20°C. The sudden change made our cheeks burn a little. A small lightbulb lit the room with a dull glow and two giant burners had begun to churn out an almost oppressive amount of heat. This was our Qeqertat Savoy. For a moment I contrasted what we had there against the continuous desolation of life on an icecap, as during my *Long Haul* and other journeys.

Along the sides of the room were rows of books, mostly for children, for school time. There must have only been half a dozen or fewer pupils but it was remarkably well-stocked. Some were in Greenlandic and others in Danish. A small trolley adorned with Christian icons and paraphernalia, presumably for Sunday services, sat in the corner.

With a mixture of enthusiasm tempered by tiredness – it was now past midnight after a long day of hauling in the draining darkness – with our tent bags of gear and food in, we slept where our sleeping mats fell.

There was no point in visiting Qeqertat, fourth from smallest out of the seventy-four Greenlandic settlements (correct at the time of going to press), if we just turned tail the next day and headed back. Our expedition, our project and our winter and spring, was now as much about learning and experiences as it was about physical endurance and skill. We would sleep well and explore Qeqertat the next day, hopefully meeting some of the residents.

We did not have to wait long. Word had clearly spread across the miniature Qeqertat grapevine and whilst still dozing in our spots on the floor at nine o'clock the next morning, a loud bang at the door made me sit up with a jump. Knocks are a recent Greenlandic habit and permission to enter thereafter isn't sought. The door opened, a blast of icy cold air shot across the lower few feet of the room and in came a man and his wife, probably both in their thirties. One of Han Jensen's brood, we finally had the chance to thank our late-night light signaller with whom we had exchanged lamp flashes for some hours the evening before. Almost as if there were a queue outside to examine the curious newcomers but not overcrowd us, we went on to meet much of the population without so much as having to leave our building.

The three of us headed out to see the dogs and investigate our new surroundings. Dave and Enrique had disappeared underneath the wooden deck, given away by their chains leading from post to hiding place. Only Odin sat out in the open, his expression vacant as ever, rewarded by a good dose of ear scratches and pats, followed by a pile of kibble, that brought the other two out from their secluded spots. Fear of missing a meal is forever the strongest way to motivate a dog.

It was approaching midday and the faintest of deep blue glows hung over the landscape, helping us make out vague shadows of structures and mountains. Qeqertat was a world away from the metropolis of Qaanaaq – no permanent outdoor lighting, and no well-trodden routes between buildings for sleds and vehicles. It was a pedestrian hamlet of the smallest proportions, perched on a low clifftop where there was barely a flat spot to be found. The population had always been small, but now at officially around two dozen when everyone was home (a rare occurrence), most huts were empty. When they become disused, they either end up left to decay, have parts scavenged for new-builds, or are storage areas for those living next door. This leads to a real ghost-town feel, not unhindered by the sinister half-light.

Presumably from the once-a-year sea resupply, near the 'harbour' were row after row of oil and fuel drums. Unable to be flown in, anything heavy or hazardous was stockpiled to keep everyone going through the rest of the year. A couple of small boats for summer travel were pulled up on the shore and buried in snow. Fibreglass boats have mostly replaced the traditional *umiaq*, a larger ferrying boat or mothership for kayaks historically popular in the less icy south, then often paddled by a female crew.

We ventured further up, past a row of three untouched but frozen-solid seals, neatly awaiting use as either dog food or dinner for a family. By this time, we could see a few windows faintly lit with flickering orange light – either from candles or oil lanterns. Our generator had run out of petrol, so we set up a headtorch in the corner of the ceiling to reflect light into the room. Outdoors, though, they were vital. The whole hamlet was steep, with endless things to trip over and avoid on the ground.

We wanted to see as much as possible and get a feel for our location, so aimed for the top of the hill. There we found, beyond a large shipping container that marked the edge of Qeqertat, a mass of staked-out dogs, all bleary-eyed and not as confident as many we'd met before. Near was a large flat expanse, the lake. Unlike many Inuit settlements where icebergs are the main source of freshwater, here they could draw up unfrozen freshwater, *imeq*, from below the ice. Up another rise onto a ridge was an automated weather station, amusingly with a solar panel fixed to it, and four empty oil drums. We surmised this must be the makeshift helipad for the odd summer visit or a medical evacuation.

One of our earlier house-guests mentioned the shop was open from twelve until two, a good time to meet people. It took the form of a small wooden hut with no sign or official designation, and was clearly a locally developed affair, comprising a few shelves of tinned goods – mostly vegetables from Denmark and cake mixes. Greenlanders really, really love making cakes.

Best of all was the cash register, a manual one probably from the 1960s and operated by a large lever next to the circular clock-face style counter. The friendly-looking keeper grinned widely as we made an effort to find something to buy as we felt it rude to wander in, speak to the villagers and leave again. Trying to find something we needed, yet had plenty of stock so that we wouldn't deplete their precious stores, we settled on a can of coke each. Outrageously priced and incredibly out of place given the location, they were a welcome change from water and tea. One man congratulated us as being the first visitors to Qeqertat for some weeks. Attention though moved to the next day and our plan for the home journey.

It would be sensible to haul the outward journey in reverse. There had been no wind to speak of and certainly no fresh snow (we'd not seen a single flake fall since arriving) and so our tracks would be easy to follow. Camping halfway again, but perhaps not using the same spot, we'd be in Qaanaaq after a couple of reasonably tough slogs across the winter sea ice. With that and sledges packed for an early start, we slept, only disturbed by the odd howl from Dave and Enrique.

Our hauling out of Qeqertat began with a surge of enthusiasm. Having bidden farewell with locals who seemed keen to assist in moving our sleds, we promised to meet up again in future weeks either in Qeqertat, Qaanaaq (where most had family) or on the ice. The handful of dull lights, this time a couple of families had their generators running for electric lighting and charging up torches and the like, merged together into one as we moved further away.

I turned around to Anders and James and inquired about whether the pace was ok. With two chirpy responses, consensus was reached and so I inquired, "Guys, we started early and I'm feeling good. If we're all in the same mood, shall we push this? Get back to Qaanaaq in a oner?"

With mischievous smiles and a sense of 'you're thinking what we were thinking', it was settled. Qaanaaq here we come. Accepting that it would be a seriously long day regardless of pace, we didn't hit the gas too hard for fear of burning out. It would take as long as it takes and it's not like we could tell if it was day or night anyhow.

Our tracks led the way and the routine of taking turns at the front allowed the hours to pass by. We felt strong and I was enjoying it. There was no question of using an iPod or another distraction due to the bear threat, but I didn't feel the need. Dave was getting into a real habit of spinning around and snagging his chain, but I tried to channel the 'tut tut' irritation into amusement as my dog showed no signs of regaining sanity.

Ten hours became twelve, then fifteen, and we, according to the GPS, were approaching the long cliffs that lead to Qaanaaq. Vast, but invisible to us. Our pace was holding strong but we were beginning to feel the miles. My lower back and legs were draining and the need to hydrate and eat regularly became more important than ever. I noticed that the amount the three of us chatted during rest stops reduced and the spring with which we stood up again slowed. It hurt.

If I squinted and strained, I could make out the shadow where the ridgeline of the cliffs met the starry sky. Eventually at the left-hand end, the western end, a tiny glow. This wasn't courtesy of the sun far, far below the horizon but the artificial lights of Qaanaaq. We were still a long way away and the torment was about to begin.

When travelling in daylight with landmarks; glaciers, hills, icebergs, it's easier to gauge progress. You see something, you approach it, you pass it, and it disappears slowly behind you. On a large icecap it's tougher, with a three hundred and sixty-degree barren icescape, but small details on the surface are still an aid. In the dark, nothing helps. It's just the ice around your feet and the small cone illuminated as your headtorch scans around. Distant objects like mountains or cliffs might be discernible against the ambient star or moonlight, but the distances involved are huge and you can't judge them.

The final hours, up to twenty hours in, were a succession of almost every barrier to progress imaginable. The snow was so light that we lost our tracks and had to navigate afresh. We ended up in a rubble field with ridges and ice blocks almost constantly, with only the occasional flat mini-pan, and all our dogs were playing up. We couldn't blame them. Walking slowly on chains was alien to them, but that rationality wasn't much help to us. Our bodies ached and felt like they'd aged fifty years.

It took every ounce of discipline to be bothered to eat and drink every hour. The temptation to only sit and rest for ten minutes each time, instead of opening the sledge zip and rustling around for a flapjack and flask, was overwhelming. The glow in the sky, beyond the cliff shadows that never seemed to move, became a source of unimaginable frustration. In a sign of real teamwork that gave me a great deal of pride, we all placed our cards on the table. We all admitted we were spent, and needed to help each other – saying the 'right things' to get us home.

Instead of the theoretical route straight to and from Qeqertat we'd used before, I suggested we might want to either haul aggressively out to sea to get away from the energy-sapping screw ice, or the opposite and try and pick up the land-fast ice next to the cliffs. We settled on the latter and took a dogleg across to the right. We sure as hell weren't stopping and letting that infernal glow beat us, but we needed to exercise our grey matter as well as our muscles.

It paid off. Within ten minutes, we found a real improvement in the cracked surface. According to the GPS, we had just four or five miles to haul. The glow seemed stubbornly stationary but the smallest hints of civilisation boosted morale. A stick in the ice here, an old sled track there. Before long, we had clearly intersected the main hunting and transit route from Qaanaaq and heavy use had resulted in a slick, fast, flat motorway. All we needed to do is ski the final hour strongly and we'd be home.

Still, the glow was unchanged. It was maddening. Why wasn't it brighter? Why couldn't we actually see any lights yet high up on the hill at the northern extent of the settlement? Our answer only came in the final ten minutes of our twenty hour man-haul. A low hill was directly in the way between us and Qaanaaq. Beyond it was the marshy area (in the summer at least) where only the cemetery could stand. It had acted as a blind and was the source of our confusion and frustration. A small hill. No higher than a hundred feet. It didn't affect our distance to haul, but my goodness it had tested us mentally.

Rounding the mound, Qaanaaq revealed itself after only a minute of slow hauling; from nothing to the entire settlement, lights, fuel-containers, buildings and all.

"Wahay!" – the resounding cry. Not far.

Staring ahead at the shoreline, one light split into two, and small details became visible – the Greenlandic flag above the school and dogs littering the beach. Picking a small ramp in between two staking points of dogs which led up to our small shipping container 'lockup', we stopped. The dogs, all previously fast asleep, either eyed us with a certain disdain or stood up in hope of food. We'd skied over forty miles in a single march. It was a single day of effort, not a multi-month expedition or a brand new glacial route. Somehow, though, I was immensely proud. It was different. It was an all-out athletic challenge unrestrained by sustainability.

Having shoved our sleds haphazardly into the lockup, three yellow down jacket-clad zombies walked up the hill. Anyone who's undertaken a serious physical endeavour will know the phenomenal ability the body has to 'ignore' fatigue and keep moving until it's safe to stop. I remember after my 2011 Greenland icecap speed crossing – around three hundred and thirty miles in less than twelve days – that Wilki, my teammate, and I pushed hard to our heli-pickup and then could barely walk after we landed in Kangerlussuaq. Once the pressure is off, weight is taken off your feet and especially when going from weeks of cold into a warm room, the body says 'I've done it. Enough. I give up entirely.' With that, it repays the debt.

Shuffling one foot in front of the other, we took a comically long time to reach the little yellow house. It was the early hours of the morning and we knew our lurgy-stricken teammate, Anastasia, would be fast asleep. We didn't have keys and so had to knock gently, then increasingly louder until we heard movement inside. Utterly bemused and bleary-eyed, she didn't expect us until the next day and actually said she half-considered getting something to defend herself with as she opened the door!

CHAPTER 5: Education

THE NEXT DAY was designated as sleeping and recuperation day; something Anastasia also needed more of as her infection had really wiped her out. We had some visitors around lunchtime and I can only imagine the image they must have come away with. In a small town where gossip ruled supreme, news that the newcomers from the south were still in bed at lunchtime again must have spread like wildfire.

More or less able to function again by the evening, we received some more troubling news. Whilst out to collect some provisions from the store, Anastasia had bumped into Rasmus and relayed a garbled message back to us about the sleds. He was due to work on them with us as agreed but the details had not been fully understood. We had not confirmed a start date and since he seemed far from rushed, we understood that he'd let us know when he wanted to meet and get going. Word that we had gone to Qeqertat had reached him and, keen to get out hunting and not stuck in a workshop throughout good weather, he had started without us.

Concerned, given that we were supposed to watch and assist with the first so we could construct the second, we got dressed and walked briskly to the communal workshop – a heated large space for everyone to work on sleds, kayaks and boats. A handful of hunters surrounded our wooden planks sourced from the yard at the top of the hill belonging to Kim Petersen. Not only had the flat bed and two runners of a sled been completed, but it was obvious not only Rasmus was on the job – a friend was there too. What would this mean? It wasn't what we agreed and budgeted for.

Confused and with lots of shrugging and mumbling going on, we said that they should leave things for the time being and we could meet the following day for coffee and clarification.

Nothing became any clearer as we, Rasmus, his friend and fellow master-builder Tobias, squeezed into our seating area at home the next morning. Coffee, the main diplomatic tool we could all easily lay hands on, was deployed in force. We even broke open some boxes of food that might accompany, but realised that our copious expedition snacks were less than alluring in warm, comfortable surroundings. Biltong it was. The spiced and dried raw beef was a taste that Inuit had no past experience of and the combination of raw meat and new spices proved addictive. We'd have none left if not careful.

It transpired that Rasmus had begun work on the sleds because he was in a rush to get out hunting, and his time with us could extend to three days. He hadn't really shown a great deal of urgency before, but we obviously appreciated this point. Perhaps we should have both penned in a definite date for work, but that sort of exactness seemed to fly in the face of the passive way many deals are done. We didn't want to inflict strict deadlines on people who had no care or need for them. It did seem though a little unbalanced. We had gone along with their relaxed attitude when in fact, more certainty would have helped us, and now apparently caused a problem by the same hand.

More awkward though was the issue of payment. We agreed, days before, a fixed compensation for his time and expertise that seemed to keep everyone happy. Now, it appeared that the terms had changed. That fee had become 'per day' AND 'per person'. We had not discussed anyone else getting involved, but the decision had apparently been made for us. In hindsight we could all laugh about it, but at the time the looks that Anders, Anastasia, James and I exchanged as Rasmus sipped his coffee were anything but relaxed. We didn't want a conflict this early on, and especially the bad names we would all carry around Qaanaaq should it become broadcast.

I was thoroughly aware we had reached a crunch-point in our negotiations. We had stated what we had agreed, and Rasmus had said, politely as ever as a man of carefully reserved emotion, what he now wanted. Bend and break now, and we'd never do a fair deal again in all our time there. We would pay over the odds for everything and endure the lack of respect that accompanies a tourist or similar 'non-contributor'. If we were too tough, we risked Rasmus walking out, not completing the sleds and we could accidentally make an enemy of a man we liked. Honour matters a great deal in male Polar Eskimo psyche, and if he felt his was questioned, he could close up with stubbornness. Being swindled is a great insult and with awareness that many outsiders use the North to their business advantage, Rasmus was far from naive.

This position, though, a deal agreed upon verbally and then tweaked and changed to the advantage of the local, using intentional vagueness as a calculated tool to cloud details, we would come to call a 'Greenlandic invoice'. It was a formidable technique often with a guilt-trip neatly woven in and we came in time to expect them, not take offence, and learned to gently counter them to mutual satisfaction. Those with memories spanning pre and post modernisation in Avanerriaq have mused this may be a form of 'revenge via extortion' for ills committed half a century ago. Money, originally absent for Inuit with the exception of gifts, now meant all.

aki qagvaggamahoq – the price has increased.

An attitudinal change that struck me between our experiences and the writings of those around a century previously was that of business. Now gone are the days of long, protracted and slightly absurd negotiations for bartering and purchases. Then, faux-modesty and elaborate double bluffs preceded even the most basic of transactions and page after page of explorers' diaries recorded these in detail - charades, and mock shame about the poor quality of goods. The legacy of an anti-capitalist, pre-Contact culture ebbed away as the benefits of currency and trade gathered apace. Today, many Polar Eskimos are steely, but charming businesspeople with a light touch that never leaves a bitter taste. It pays to behave likewise.

As we were leaving the workshop the previous day, a visitor had passed by to see if anything interesting was going on. Wrapped up in a large jacket with her head hidden amongst a fur-lined hood, I was taken aback to hear an accented voice speak in near-perfect English. Navarana, her name we'd later learn, was a tiny lady in her mid-sixties and fiercely proud of her Polar Eskimo identity. Her spoken English was by far and away the best in Qaanaaq and, I suspect, the whole region.

Sat in our home in a sort of stalemate, James volunteered to head over with Anders and see if she was at home. Improved communication could, we hoped, bring our little conundrum to an end.

Twenty minutes later, we had drawn up another seat and reapplied negotiation-soothing coffee to mugs-various, and Navarana had a brief catch up with her old friends before turning her attention to us. Only just over five feet tall and with a slight frame, she had an easy smile and neat features. Clearly with a great deal of pride in her appearance, with her parka removed we could make out a mixture of traditional Greenlandic patterned fabrics and some imported European clothes. Her dark hair was specked with a little dark grey, and she wore her hair short. We learned that she had just completed treatment for cancer in the south and was on the mend.

I thanked her for coming and apologised that this time it was as much for her linguistic skills as her company. As I tried to summarise our sled-building quandary, she nodded at each point and smiled occasionally – both at Rasmus and me. With a sigh, a couple of minutes of Inuktun bounced around between Rasmus, Tobias and Navarana. The other four of us could only sit, exchange grins and wait. More or less what we had predicted had indeed transpired. The important point agreed about a set amount of kroner for Rasmus' time had to him been de facto voided by our trip to Qeqertat. We didn't really discover the logic behind this or why Tobias had been added into the deal on the same 'wage', but it turned out they wanted four times the sum we settled on at Hans'.

There were lots of intakes of breath, slightly awkward avoided eye contact and muttering in a variety of languages. I said to James, sat next to me and knowing full well that Navarana could hear everything I said, that we couldn't agree to it. It was a vast hike, we had been very clear about money before, and it was undoubtedly a bit of a mischievous game to extract some extra cash from the 'rich Europeans'. This being far from the case, our coffers looking pretty bare, and the whole issue of setting a precedent in mind, I played the game back. With a couple of reminders about past conversations and the fact we hadn't agreed a sled-build start date, Rasmus nodded in resignation as Navarana translated. I said that we wanted to be fair and honest, and also show the community we meant well. The four of us had already agreed how high we were willing to go, so I suggested a number, roughly double what we had settled originally and half what Rasmus was playing for. Sipping the last of his coffee and looking into it as if to find the solution at the bottom of the mug, he looked up at me with a reserved smile. "ii," he said, eyebrows raised – a good indicator. The deal was done, again.

We would begin work again immediately, with all hands to the pump. With Tobias and Rasmus, the four of us, and a constant stream of curious locals drifting in and out to lend a hand, we could be done in a few days. Navarana, already having been more help than she would recognise, also wanted to drop in and practise her English under the guise of offering more translation assistance.

Meeting after lunch in the workshop, we brought up a large box of lashing, special plastic for the sled runner 'shoes' and communal food. Around an hour after the approximate start time, Rasmus arrived with his toolbox and Tobias a while after. We used the waiting time to inspect the flat section of the first sled, already mostly put together. It was slightly advanced on the state we saw it in the previous day, so perhaps they had gone straight there after leaving our home. This sort of guesswork regarding peoples' plans and extraordinarily relaxed attitude to time was something we'd become accustomed to. For sure, it made a change to our more scheduled lives back home where lateness or flakiness is scorned. However, the rulebook was theirs and we needed to adapt or risk having a frustrating or isolated few months.

Politics aside, the sleds were simply remarkable. Very much unlike those you'd find in Scandinavia, modern racing sleds in North America or even the east of Greenland, their design was perfectly tuned to the unique landscape.

The basis for a Polar Eskimo sled shares some features with those of Inuit Eastern Canada, from where they 'evolved'. Those in the southwest and east of Greenland tend to have a lighter-weight structure more suited to ascending hills and with the sort of divergence you'd expect from centuries of optimising and tinkering. Assuming good access to timber, clearly a modern commodity that has only been enjoyed increasingly since the nineteenth century, a sled can be summarised by picturing it in three sections. Firstly you have two long, thick planks laid on their sides, with runners underneath and raised noses. Depending on the size and length of the sled you want, from a five-foot local run-around for town to a fifteen-foot load-carrier like ours, lighter horizontal cross-planks join those runners together into a flatbed. Finally, you'd add two upright *napariaq* stanchions and a crossbeam, a *napoq*, to the rear of the sled to use to steer and lash items to. Sleds of today are wider, shorter and with taller stanchions than in past decades and are endlessly being re-worked and optimised.

Your *qamutit* – sled – or *qimuggeq* if used explicitly for dogs, is complete.

This is I suspect how most people picture a traditional dog sled. The real magic comes though in how it is all held together. I'm confident that as a four we could have cut, shaped and formed a pretty reasonable sled from our background knowledge, hands on experience and using common sense. But, given a hard day out on the ice, ours would likely be shaken to pieces and snap in awkward places, lasting only hours and not the years of service a hunter would aim for. What is the difference? Lashing.

Polar Eskimo sleds, unlike (to varying degrees) others from around the Arctic I've inspected, use almost no rigid physical joins like screws, glues or nails in their main construction. This is the secret to their durability and long working lives, to the point where they resemble museum relics despite still completing sixty-mile journeys in a single day. Every section, from the crossbeams spanning the runners to the uprights held strongly in place, uses an intricate combination of ten or twenty-strand thick lashings and clever self-locking knots. Historically, this would have been a necessity – ropes, lines and lashings could be made from dried and treated bearded sealskins or entrails and there was no access to formed metal for nails, or adhesives. It works a charm though; on super-hard and bumpy sea ice surfaces, the shock the laden sled has to withstand at sometimes-great speed is immense. Rather like a road cyclist with a stiff, brittle carbon-composite bicycle will learn to their cost, too much rigidity combined with bumps and shocks means cracks and breaks. The Polar Eskimo sled avoids this masterfully.

Any modern tweaks to the ancient design are never fundamental, just convenient. For example, runner undersides (the parts in contact with the ice) are now nailed into place and every other crossbeam is not lashed to the runners but nailed once to the central brace (one nail allows rotations, not holding too rigidly).

Part of local culture that I had picked up years before but now needed to be adhered to carefully, was to watch and not ask. When learning a new skill, and whether you're a young boy learning to hunt or an outsider like us hoping to be educated, your eyes and not your mouth are the key. It follows with the generally quiet and reserved nature of communication that endlessly asking questions becomes tiresome. Instead, closely inspecting is the way. Counter to this, though, if you don't request assistance, none will be offered. Concurrently, every move a visitor makes is watched and judged, like an examination of your character. It may come across as unfriendly, but nothing could be further from the truth. A room full of Inuit, whether from Qaanaaq or elsewhere, is in general terms, alcohol removed, simply more reserved than one from most other places around the world, but then liable to erupt into laughter at the smallest thing.

Much to my relief, there appeared to be absolutely no bad blood given the last couple of days. Long quarrels and acid atmospheres are loathed in Polar Eskimo society – clean slates are pursued at any cost. On the contrary, Rasmus appeared to be in great spirits and his unique brand of humour, often at our and poor Tobias' expense, started to slowly unveil. The harder we watched, learned and contributed, the more relaxed everyone grew and the faster the jokes came. That barrier, perhaps higher with Rasmus than with others, exacerbated by his limited Danish and almost non-existent English, was slowly lowering. His stock joke would be to pretend to steal our things or take a greater share of something than expected. As he needed to return to his home quickly to fetch a tool, he picked up our large spool of lashing and, making sure we could all see, slowly pretended to put it in his bag and make his escape with it. A wide grin spread across his face and a happy 'ii', yes, followed a short chuckle. 'ii' can take on different meanings given context and pitch of speech. A breathy and deep 'ii' with a shrug is a sign of sad resignation to a fact, or even a way of saying no.

On another occasion, later in the day, we had bought a large, freshly made pastry from the store. This Danish national obsession has been enthusiastically adopted in Greenland, partly because ingredients can be shipped up long in advance and then the pastries made fresh, much like bread. They are rare in that they don't come frozen or tinned. Dividing the pastry up amongst us all, we had barely the time to carve the first slice out before Rasmus had offered us the one narrow slice to share between ourselves and picked up the tray with the remainder. Smiling and pointing to the pastry and then to himself, we laughed and made sure he ended up with the largest piece.

At the core of the distinctive Polar Eskimo humour is a kind of surprise slapstick and love for pranks. A seemingly sombre and reverent moment can quickly erupt into a joke with the grab of an ankle (simulating a dog bite) and enjoying the instant, short-lived panic on the face of the 'victim'. Another famous joke, perpetuating the Polar Eskimo fixation of strength versus the pathetic, was to secretly overfeed a companion's dogs the night before a long journey. This would slow their getaway with distended stomachs and make the comedian's spritely performance appear all the more marked.

To look at, Rasmus and Tobias represented two quite differing Polar Eskimos. Both with the facial structure and complexion that reflected their Eastern Asian ancestry; much had changed over the centuries since. Rasmus was short in stature with a wide frame, very common for Inuit men. His skills as a hunter were reflected in his round stomach and he maintained a smart moustache along with remnants of thinning hair atop his head. Another hunter we met later further clarified his choice of clothing, but indoors Rasmus wore a thick, button-up cotton collared shirt – rather like one you'd see on a stereotype lumberjack. Rasmus exhibited a curious mix of both supreme confidence and ease, with shyness. His prominent round eyes often avoided contact with those he spoke to in hushed tones but then a wide, long-lasting smile would appear as if from nowhere. His dynamic with us was hard to define initially. Obviously somewhat familiar with me from my previous visits to Qaanaaq, he took time to relax around our group, especially as we spoke in English amongst ourselves. One moment he was authoritative and we the humble students; the next he seemed meek and concerned about our approval.

In the 1950s, Frenchman Jean Malaurie, who spent many years in the region, experienced extreme mistrust and exclusion at first, and children 'ran off whimpering' at the sight of him. This, he soothed over time, as in his own words, 'I handed out presents right and left, I smiled, I talked'. (As an aside, those interested in the experiences of the early, empathetic visitors to Avanerriaq should read the works of those marked * in the Further Reading list. They shed light on 1910s to 1960s life there in an exquisite, charming and comprehensive detail that I won't attempt to paraphrase). Today, small children are cheeky and confident before teenage shyness sets in, to the sadness of older generations who remember the times of respectful children, and adults are in my experience almost never hostile. This curious distance though does occasionally manifest – children do still stand in nervous 'flocks' in doorways. There is more to the Polar Eskimo manner though as almost every outsider who has spent time in Avanerriaq has observed; the reservation and indirect style of communication can often be a façade with self-assurance, humour or even a strategy not far beneath the surface.

Tobias was as skinny as a rake and taller than Rasmus. Also moustached and with a thick crop of black hair, we gathered that his family was initially from West Greenland and were some of the first to move north after air travel connected the two isolated cultures. Extremely quiet, even amongst his fellow countrymen, he interacted with us from behind thick spectacles and showed his approval with a fleeting smile and positive sounding hum. He wore a black t-shirt and boiler suit trousers with a pair of ancient trainers.

We were done for the day and returned to our home to see to the dogs and cook supper. That evening there were things to discuss. Anastasia had recovered from her illness but there was an elephant in the room – an unfortunate side effect of our change of plans. We had forecast to be out of Greenlandic territory within just a few weeks of starting the Dark Ice journey, having crossed Inglefield Land and settled into sea ice travel. Unusually, Greenland only claims three miles of offshore sea territory, instead of the universal norm of twelve miles. We would be outside of their jurisdiction fairly quickly – thereafter even more responsible for our own behaviour and fate. Also, with the knowledge any call for assistance would be an international scandal and expensive enough to make our insurer's eyes water.

This worked out well regarding the legal status of our various nationalities. Anders, as a Dane, could stay indefinitely in Greenland and even work if he wanted to. James and I as UK citizens had a ninety-day visa-free period, even though Greenland itself isn't in the EU (in order to avoid fishing restrictions) and that the UK is not in the Schengen Area (a separate treaty to that of the EU and one that the UK decided to avoid). I did know, however, that Greenland's government has a fairly relaxed attitude towards extended stays as long as they made no attempts to work or otherwise disrupt the local economy. Anastasia as a Russian national and UK resident was more complex. She could not under any circumstances afford to overstay an accumulation of more than ninety-days on her issued visa to enter Greenland. Whilst it's entirely possible an overstay would not be noticed with Greenland's none-too-overzealous border control, any transgression could be catastrophic. In fact, once in Denmark, flights to Greenland are considered domestic and don't leave from international gates with further passport control. Her issue was that she had an ambition to gain British citizenship after the requisite number of years. Any black marks or questionable visa behaviour would be instant roadblocks in this process between two countries with strained relations.

The four of us had no plans to leave Greenland in under three months, so the conundrum was obvious. It had coincidentally been a tense week between Anastasia and myself. A couple of separate events, the common theme being about withheld information that led to extra work being placed on my shoulders, had left me quite exasperated. I was under the impression that her visa was of the extended variety, which made a stay of over ninety days acceptable. So, the new challenge was a surprise. Bizarrely, it had taken nearly a week to even mention, such was her desire to not confront the issue. 'Head in the sand' approaches to me only complicate matters and provide less time to work out a way forward. After a fairly awkward supper of Danish sausages and rice sides from our freeze-dry stores, we knew the only option would be for Anastasia to return to the UK and then use up the bulk of her time allowance later in the season when longer journeys were feasible with trained dog teams.

We were sad. Since the first time I met Anastasia in London and as we trained in Iceland on the Mýrdalsjökull icecap, atop the active Katla volcano, I found her a valuable addition to the team. Her skills were excellent, having been trained by some of the best guides in the business, and she was a hard worker. Nonetheless, by her own admission, Anastasia had long been happiest in her own company and joining a team, especially otherwise comprised of men (as far from unreformed though we hoped we were), was a tough decision. Perhaps it wasn't the right one in hindsight and she did often seek time alone to read or just enjoy the quiet. Some people are simply best cut out as soloists, whereas others are in their element amidst a team. Regardless, we liked her and she was part of the team. The surprisingly widespread scepticism from others, I will leave them anonymous to save their embarrassment, back home about me having a woman on the team was unfounded. This was a gender-irrelevant issue. As long as every member could do what was demanded of him or her by the journey, it doesn't matter.

Anastasia would stay for a few more days, at least to see the sleds ready to get on the move, and then we'd try and get her a place on the infrequent and unreliable flight south.

James said he was comfortable to run his sled solo, a brave call regardless of assurances from Anders and me that we'd do all we could to help. The world of dog driving was still an unknown quantity.

Meanwhile, sled building continued in earnest. Our instructors' delayed arrival had, though, given us a chance to really inspect the workmanship in private. Small details that a novice would have neglected made all the difference. For example, the main runner planks were angled inward ever so slightly, instead of being dead upright. This, we found, eases the change in direction of the sled; allowing it to skid to the left and right more easily instead of surging onwards like a runaway train.

After trading with Europeans in the nineteenth century, the whalebone and general odds-and-ends-constructed sleds noted by the explorer John Ross and crew were replaced with those made from timber. Goodness knows how difficult it must have been to gain a good glide on the ice and snow surface beforehand; the poor dogs must have had quite the job. The interface between sled and ice is critical and the Polar Eskimos, like other Inuit peoples, used the best technologies they had access to as their history progressed. Historically, the skilful art of icing the runners meant gradually freezing layers of freshwater onto the undersides, smoothing and then polishing them. One account even exists of shoeing the runners with carefully formed frozen fish and mud. Bars of metal became available decades later, bartered with explorers and whalers in return for furs and guiding services. These metal runners could be nailed into place and let the sled run far better than without. It also needed far less maintenance than icing, although could be improved with a glaze of frozen water or urine.

Curious as we were, the team and I had inspected other sleds around Qaanaaq as we wandered around. Left unattended outdoors with no fear of theft, each sled being unique to its builder and easy to trace back, they were fascinating. With a vast range of lengths, widths, ages and design tweaks, they did all follow the general Thule style – heavier set and tougher than others in the South and in particular the East, where lightness and climbing ability lends to an almost sleigh-like appearance. On one of these forays, down near the beach next to one of the smallest old homes, basic one-room affairs, we'd found at least a couple still with metal runners. Perhaps this semi-traditional technique suited some of the older hunters.

In the late twentieth century, plastics started being imported to the North and the hunters and travellers naturally took advantage of their benefits. Special high-density plastic runner shoes, our choice, are now industry standard, out of place though they may seem on a traditional sled adorned with furs.

Having shaped and joined two large, thick wooden planks for each main runner, our second sled was ready to have cross beams fitted. We watched Rasmus and Tobias work and occasionally called for their help if unsure or if our handiwork fell short of the standard needed. Using the first sled as a reference and template made that easier.

Large cuts and shapes would take hours with a handsaw and Rasmus unleashed his secret weapon, a handheld circular saw. A small audience of local men, and later Navarana, had gathered. Our sled-building antics had become quite the social event and it was an opportunity for people to congregate in the warm, not sit around at home, and to see what the strange young Europeans were up to. With a few loud bursts of energy with the saw, our runners were in shape and Rasmus beamed with satisfaction. On the final cut and with a couple of feet to go, the whizzing and whirring suddenly stopped. Rasmus, surprised, pressed the power button a few times and then inspected the saw. Anders quickly unplugged it at the wall to avoid a disaster but none of us could find an obvious reason as to why it wasn't working. Assuming a blown fuse or overheating due to intense cutting through dense wood, we mused the options with Rasmus and Navarana weighed in too. It was quite the mystery.

About half an hour later and after the last cut had been completed neatly by hand by Anders, a roof carpenter in a previous life, Rasmus came over with a grave look on his face. He pointed to his saw and made an exaggerated sad face. We mimicked the same, to show shared disappointment. Perhaps cooling or a new fuse could solve it.

"Rasmus is very sad about his saw. He thinks you should buy him another one," Navarana informed us, a little meekly given the negotiations only two days before.

A little wide-eyed and actually with a smile at first as I thought it was a joke, beside the obvious point that there was nowhere to buy a power tool from, I could only offer that we should try and fix it. The idea of us replacing it was again reiterated, a little more strongly, and I had to say no. We had not touched the saw and besides, thought it was likely to be a minor issue.

Logic seemed to follow that because the saw was being used on our sleds, we were responsible for anything that went wrong with it. With a sinking feeling in our stomachs and desperate to avoid another awkward episode, we managed to downplay the issue and hope that Rasmus would rethink things. Fixing the saw would of course solve all.

I spent the majority of the day, after James and Anastasia had carved notches into the ends of cross beams, lashing the beams to the runners. It became almost metronomic – even cathartic – once I'd mastered the process of running loops through sets of drilled holes and tightening them with the aid of a small piece of wood and a lot of heaving. Anders filmed and photographed these lashings, with their local unique quirks, as some way of recording them. In twenty years they could be consigned to history. Perhaps the local self-determined bans on snowmobiles and preference for dog sleds would end.

Two days of frenetic activity came and went. Rasmus and Tobias kept an eye on our work, occasionally tapping us on the shoulder and giving a pointer. They took on the critical finishing touches such as joining two plastic runner sections seamlessly to keep the glide smooth and hand-weaving the two-inch thick hauling loop which would in time join the dogs to the sled. In later months, the other three would turn their hand to rope weaving, not dissimilar to knitting. I did too, but the results whilst functional never looked quite right. Splice a strand into the wrong loop or gap and it never recovers.

Christmas was looming and Rasmus badly wanted to get out on the thickening sea ice and hunt before festivities began. A final day should see the sleds ready to launch out of the large doors to the shed; the latter designed to be large enough for a boat to be brought in and out for maintenance in the warm.

As we all heaved the sleds side by side to match the stanchion tensions and then add finishing touches, the main door swung open. A wall of deep frozen air wafted slowly towards us, wearing just jeans, shirts and a fleece. In came a young Polar Eskimo and another who appeared to have been just a passer-by and offering to help push the first man's sled up the ramp and in. The doors slammed closed and a heavy off cut of timber wedged it shut again. Slim but with a confident gait and clearly a local, but perhaps with a little southern heritage, he glanced at us but made no move to come over and introduce himself.

Rasmus signalled completion by knocking a couple of metal bracing pins deep into the wood runners at the front, presumably to protect them from splitting as they hit ice blocks at speed. Then, we stood beside them like two Rolls Royces freshly rolled off the production line. We stood to straighten our backs from the hours of stooping down, and tucked into some celebratory cake from the store.

The unknown man's sled blocked our exit so the grand launch, minus Champagne broken on the sides, would have to wait for later. We shook hands with Rasmus and Tobias; all of us very much pals again. As if by magic, Rasmus has got his circular saw running healthily again, presumably with a fresh fuse. I have no idea whether the whole thing was a cheeky ploy or an honest quandary, but no harm was done. With that, he donned his parka, lifted his toolbox and set out into the cold to get ready for a few days of seal hunting.

The hunter began to tip his sled over so that he could, presumably, do some work to the underside. His sled, whilst a 'single seater' (large enough for a driver, a storage box and some supplies), still weighed a good deal and if it fell awkwardly on a cross brace, could be damaged. We quickly scurried over to help. With five pairs of hands it was overkill for sure, but it broke the ice. Mikael introduced himself with a cautious smile and we shook hands. He spoke reasonable, slow English but once realising that Anders was Danish, quickly swapped over. Picking out the gist of the conversation and latching onto words I knew, I found out that he was unhappy with the runners on his sled after using it over rough rocky ground at the end of the last spring. To ready himself for a new season on the frozen sea, he wanted his steed shod with a fresh pair of shoes.

Sure enough, on inspecting the bottom, the black plastic, which we'd not seen before and later learned was very second-rate compared to the pricey white ones we had, was carved and pitted to within an inch of its life. Mikael planned to replace these with a mid-market green set, the white alternatives being in short supply, and also replace a few cracked crossbeams.

Mikael was the youngest person we'd spoken to thus far, perhaps in his late twenties. Just as I'd read from the handful of other explorers, authors and anthropologists with experience of Avanerriaq, many younger Polar Eskimos lack the relaxed self-assurance of those with a decade or two more experience. Indeed, they hold no position in society, excluded from serious discussions until of 'marrying age' or with their own dog team.

Instead of a quiet confidence and that distinctive humour behind a slight barrier of aloofness, Mikael seemed a little suspicious of us. In just half an hour he'd repeatedly laid out his hunting credentials; posturing, some of it with a glaze of machismo. Transport yourself into a more familiar setting like an office meeting room or a bar, and imagine a gradual escalation of showing off – one ego bruised by a perceived threat, no matter how restrained in its expression, and so retorting in kind. As outsiders we consciously did the opposite. We nodded, smiled and asked more questions. Disarmed and a modicum surprised, Mikael's frostiness thawed in front of our eyes and there began one of our warmest friendships. I think he was even embarrassed by ignoring us when he arrived in the shed and, as we sat for a rest between helping with his sled's servicing, he opened up.

"I have a met a few people from England and America who have come to Qaanaaq. They come, they take, they treat us like zoo animals. They leave." he explained. "I had heard that you had come to live here for the winter. Everyone has talked about it. I thought you are here like the rest."

Little did we know, Mikael had been watching out the corner of his eye how we watched and worked with Rasmus and Tobias. Perhaps combined with our offer to assist him too, Mikael had decided we weren't so bad. Before long, he had invited us out to his fishing spot, once we'd learned to drive our dogs, and he had an invitation to visit us for coffee. Anders and Mikael got on particularly well, aided by shared language, and it turned out Mikael had once or twice visited Denmark. This European experience meant that it was almost inevitable for his English to develop as well.

Having generously doused and towelled in a few gallons of Danish oil to our sleds and then, with some left over, to Mikael's too, they were ready to be launched. Moving dry and untreated wood from super-cold to warm and back and forth can be a recipe for cracking. Kim's 'timber yard' was up the hill next to his large shed, the highest building in the village. The wood resided outdoors, secure against concerns of theft (you would most likely notice someone wandering through town with an ill-gotten twelve-foot plank of wood) and so retained some natural moisture frozen in state. The drying effect of a heated shed would warp, crack and even split this valuable timber and so oiling liberally helps stop that happening.

With a parental concern for our new sleds and keen for them to find a snowy surface without scratched runners we, as a five, lifted and pushed them down the slope from the doors. I held onto a rope at the rear to stop them picking up runaway speed and hurtling down the beach into someone's drying rack, boat or dogs.

piagtoq – it slides well.

Often, dog sleds have brakes. I'd seen these fixed to the rear of modern racing sleds and traditional ones in Inuit Canada and Eastern Greenland. Usually a rubber pad or a piece of thick steel with teeth cut in, they are sprung and fixed to either the rear centre or corner of the sled for a driver to stamp on to slow the sled – the brake gripping the snow and ice. We actually had two of these pre-made, in Thule Air Base by a contact of Anders' and then helicoptered in, by my insistence that they'd be useful with untrained dogs, untrained drivers and some steep icy sections of terrain. Although fitting standing planks at the back of the sled so one of a pair could stand and steer with their bodyweight, we were assured there were 'other ways' and we never attached the brakes.

CHAPTER 6: Festivity in the Freezer

IT WAS THE DAY before Christmas Eve. Glancing out over the sea ice into the far distance, the moonlight shimmered off the surface and amongst the icebergs locked into it for the winter. We caught a rare sight of distant mountains, backlit by the lunar glow and breaking up the horizon. James and I stood atop the little rise that our home occupied, having endured another chaotic dog-feeding session – we were getting better each time – controlling the dominant dogs and making sure everyone got their fair share, all whilst keeping the guts and gore on our rubber gloves and off our clothes.

Once or twice we spotted a twinkle of light miles out from the shoreline. Blink and it would be gone – almost like watching shooting stars. These were hunters and fishermen in the pre-Christmas rush to bring in extra kroner and food for the table at their family homes. Extended families everywhere in Greenland are vast, especially in the context of such small populations. The onus to provide is traditionally still on the male head of the family. These hunters use their almost inhuman skill and sixth sense to feel their way across the ice with their dogs in the dark. Occasionally though, they would need to use a flashlight to check for something in their storage box or reflect off an ice block to see if it's navigable.

This rush has not always existed. Obviously, Christmas has only been part of Inuit and Polar Eskimo culture for a fraction of their history, but that this arbitrary pre-New Year celebration has latterly become an unfortunate yardstick in relation to when sea ice forms and thickens. I pointedly wish to avoid a misplaced debate about climate change and environmental policy here, but the formation and breakup of ice is, in measurable and objective terms, rapidly skewing.

Sea ice forms after the summer and then breaks and melts in late spring in most Arctic seas, fjords and waterways, with the exception of part of the Arctic Ocean, north of any land, which retains thinning but year-round ice. Each region has its own microclimate, currents and unique features, such as the low snowfall of Avanerriaq and its slightly elevated winter temperatures. Around Qaanaaq and other Polar Eskimo settlements from the southern Kane Basin in the north to Kap York and further south, ice used to form in October, after the September storms. At times, the ice was still sled-able into June or beyond, albeit with slushy snow atop the ice. Thicker ice, and ice for longer periods of time obviously translates to more mobility (dog sleds are faster and with infinitely greater range than a pre-twentieth century *qajaq* or larger boat). More mobility means better hunting and an opportunity to search out new spots to live and hunt.

The state of affairs today is stark, and inevitable grievances in the community ran deep. Ice now forms in December if the locals are lucky and no longer reaches the extent it did a century ago – a time when hunting territory increased seven-fold with the ice from summer to winter. Obviously, the earliest and thinnest ice is no good and it needs to consolidate free from storms and tidal surges for a few weeks. In some years, apparently there has been no safe sledding until Christmas, hence its recent significance, and early forays have led to unplanned swims for both dogs and men. Once or twice, these accidents have been fatal. The fate of the ice and dogs, and so too the Polar Eskimos, are intertwined.

Ice breaks very rapidly once the melt has begun, driven by warmer currents, daylong sunlight and periods of wind. Since the millennium there's been very little guarantee of sledding into May, except in the most sheltered and narrow fjords free from currents. This translates to a reduction of the ice-borne hunting season from eight or nine months to barely four or five. The awkward transitional periods are now longer.

We had been invited to spend Christmas at the home of Karen, a friend of Troels' – a remarkable schoolteacher who we'd met back in December. A mixture of Polar Eskimo and southern Greenlandic heritage but growing up in Aasiaat in the west, not Avanerriaq, she has called Qaanaaq home for much of her life. With a passion for education, she filled a number of concurrent roles in the community as teacher, priest at the tiny church built soon after the forced relocation, and if that were not enough, serial foster-mother.

Greenlandic society, in common with those sharing a tense settler-native dynamic, has had its share of troubles for quite some time, chiefly through a concoction of alcohol, lack of employment and inadequate education. Broken families result, some tragically by suicide (the rate of which in all Arctic nations is alarming) and others by separated couples and drunken abuse. Karen, apparently when she herself was still fairly young, began to take the 'waifs and strays' of Qaanaaq and even other villages under her wing. Not only did she feed and clothe them, but also provided an education in both written Danish and arithmetic far beyond the typical standard. Her most recent foster, a teenage orphan named Mikael (another Mikael), had been to study in Denmark and had ambitions to join the military academy in Copenhagen. Still shy and slightly built, he was nonetheless a testament to Karen. My only sadness was that he didn't see Qaanaaq as a life-long home. Qaanaaq needs talented and driven people to return and stay put if it is to survive, let alone flourish. Orphans in the nineteenth century were often underfed and left to fend for themselves, but on occasions grew to become the very toughest hunters and even revered leaders. Apart from him we often noticed one or two other children, perhaps between ten and fifteen years old, who came to Karen's house apparently for refuge and in particular if they weren't being fed enough at home. With parents or a single mother who battled with sobriety and tempers, the only other alternative is a sad inevitability to wander aimlessly around town in the cold.

Almost all Inuit communities have infant and juvenile populations out of proportion to adults. This trend is set to continue as families benefit from the reduced child mortality and better access to food and housing for which the revolution from pre-Contact, semi-nomadic population to modern-day community allows. The days of having to kill two thirds of newborn girls prior to naming them are over and thankfully, so are practices of strangling or smothering twins, deformed or sickly infants – a reflection of Polar Eskimo scorn for weakness, which still occurred in the 1940s. Active population control for pure survival is a fact of Polar Eskimo history, accented by a troubling mid-twentieth century period when birth control was actively doled out, perhaps to minimise fiscal subsidy from Denmark. The sub-one per cent birth rate has since recovered dramatically.

The family is a curious construct for modern Polar Eskimos, as almost all have now adopted the structure familiar to many in the south – exclusive marriage and raising children in a nuclear family unit. Pressure from Danes, both missionaries and secular, saw to this. It was not always thus. The pre-Contact Inuit culture of group ownership and unselfish sharing extended to human beings too. Unpalatable though it is by modern standards, women were historically seen as the possessions of a male-led society. That is not to say they were enslaved – they held enormous power in the home and the politics of kinship and families, for example. But, they ate last following hunts, after the dogs, the children and the men. Women were subject to curfews depending on natural bodily cycles and after birth, and could be shunned or even killed after miscarriages – indignities and atrocities men never had to endure. Arranged marriages well into the mid-twentieth century further shackled female liberty, and many were married in their early or mid teens to a proven hunter a decade her senior.

In modern-day Polar Eskimo culture, the exclusion of women from major life decisions is all but extinct. Nevertheless, the power of women in Inuit cultures is subtle. Aside from the traditional, discreet role they played, and typically less verbose nature, knowing looks, glances and a wrinkle of the nose could communicate vastly more than immediately apparent. A small, neat female nose has always been much desired by Polar Eskimo men and although falling out of favour, the touching or brief rubbing together of noses, much exaggerated in early accounts, did occur.

The exchange of wives on male terms was commonplace, although with durational caveats placed on such arrangements. This strengthened bonds within an extended group, aided procreation, and inadvertently reduced the effects of inbreeding on a small population, which incidentally were staggeringly low, puzzling early researchers. It transpired though that since the earliest days, rules governing the marriage of cousins were strictly adhered to. With no explicit knowledge of genetics, the Polar Eskimos had in their inimitable way ensured their survival.

The iron-strong marriage partnership and devotion of their 'inner selves' was separated fundamentally from sexual relationships and possessiveness was scorned in a kind of fundamentalist brand of what Malaurie charmingly termed anarcho-communalism. These arrangements even strengthened relationships between hunters and there was a widespread belief that brief exchanges would not result in pregnancy. Children were also frequently 'reassigned' to adoptive aunts, uncles or even unrelated families to bring up. The group was all – even when expressing a personal view, the phrase 'we Inughuit think...' rather than 'I think...' pervades.

It is of no surprise that these customs, albeit pragmatic, declined with the influence of conservative outsiders and the church. Vestiges do remain though. Even against the backdrop of our own modern, liberal European societies we were all used to, it took time to absorb Avanerriaq's current prevalence of adoption and lack of taboo attached to youthful promiscuity and its open discussion. Indeed, there is some local amusement, unlikely to be tempered by Scandinavian influence, toward social conservatism abroad. Only the continued rise of the church in Greenland is likely to object.

The dispassionate balancing of finite resources against a population to feed, shelter and transport extended to treatment of the elderly. Although now many Inuit communities have adopted the English term 'elders', their historic lack of reverence for the old is unlike other indigenous groups for whom they represented fonts of knowledge. Unproductive old members of a group would live apart from the rest and could be abandoned. Harrowing historic accounts exist of 'encouraged' suicide of the elderly by rolling off of a sled into the snow whilst a family was in transit, or even being complicit in their own hanging or stabbing by a relative following a party. Sobering, but thankfully now in the past.

Karen had finished her duties at the church, run an event for children at the school and somehow had found time to produce a phenomenal Christmas Day feast for us all. The generosity and unconditional warmth is even starker when you consider we had only met Karen once the week before.

Clutching a gift each, we kicked off our heavy down jackets and polar boots in the porch 'cold room'. The shame of bringing a miserly or thoughtless gift is perhaps worse than offering nothing at all – *in extremis* being wielded as a social weapon via gossip. The mix of wonderful smells of cooking, abundant warmth (she heated her house even more enthusiastically than most) and a glass thrust into our hands from a beaming Karen set the tone for a unique Christmas. Mikael, shy at first, did become increasingly loquacious after a can of lemonade had been gulped down and we sat down to the first of many courses. It was a curious mix culturally, representing the very best raw ingredients – it was easy to forget where we were. Given that the festival of Christmas itself was a Danish import, it's not unsurprising that the Christmas dinner itself borrows heavily from Danish culture, but local dishes did make appearances.

I later reflected on this strange fusion of culture, especially since it essentially pitted settlers alongside industrially deprived aboriginal peoples. This has often proved to be quite the tinderbox.

Around the world we hear tales of invasion, warfare, injustice and bitter exploitation of local populations by oppressive occupiers. The English in India. The Dutch and Belgians in Africa. The French in the Pacific. The Spanish in Central and South America. The Far East also supplies numerous examples and the result is predictable; a beneficial imbalance for the newcomers, who are often more technologically advanced, and the subjugation of natives. Other Inuit had suffered a great deal, most notably in Northern Canada, although some other small tribes (often now termed nations) in Russia and South America managed to stay off the grid until comparatively recently.

I was shocked when I first visited the territory inhabited by who a Polar Eskimo would term *allarraaq* – their cousins from Canada's Nunavut. A clue might have been in how the territory has only officially existed, distinct from the Northwest Territories, since 1999 following a long campaign between indigenous leaders and the English and French-derived Canadian government for land rights and limited devolution. The wounds are viscerally raw still and rampant racism appears to still flow liberally in both directions. Violent crime and substance abuse are common, and the reasons for this stem back directly to an eighteenth and nineteenth century foreign invasion of Nunavut, as with the rest of North America. Policing today is firm and serious work, unlike the 'caretaker' role some other Arctic police forces can enjoy. This, all in a country lauded globally as so amiable. It does not require a report of the substance of the recent Truth and Reconciliation Commission, which with its inherent subjectivity still makes for utterly heart-breaking reading, to explain what had gone on. With an early policy of conquest and thereafter, forced assimilation, the cultures of Inuit and First Nations of Canada were nigh on obliterated, even if not all of their people were.

Where next for Canada's nations? Then was then and now is now. Judging those born by pure chance into a certain nation for the actions of ancestors is reductionist and flawed. That doesn't erase past ills, but for reconciliation to not descend into a stalemate of bitter retribution, a new attitude is badly needed, on both sides, in order for anyone to move on.

I'm not going to suggest for one second that the Danish-Greenlandic relationship is perfect. After all, there is now Self Rule after Denmark ceded powers to a local parliament, and evicting the Danes with full independence is a real ambition (a poor one in my view in the short or medium term, but I tackle this in the Epilogue). Even the most respectful early settlers reported back sweeping judgements that Polar Eskimos could not summon abstract thoughts, were unable to express deep feelings, and were illogical with a tendency toward subservience. Indeed, many Greenlanders were enlisted as unwilling domestic servants.

In reports telling of the early Polar Eskimos, there is not a complete absence of violence, theft and other crime, but tales of murder are remarkably rare. When they did occur, most were related to restoring honour or settling a vendetta.

However, the integration of modern Danes into the communities does occur in a way I've not seen elsewhere. Many intermarry and work as colleagues. The preference for Danes in jobs that require technical expertise needs to become less of a default choice, but I've found the general atmosphere encouraging.

As an example and aside from the fact Greenlanders often display Danish flags alongside their own, have an affection for the Danish royal family, and have taken ownership of many Danish traditions, look at policing. The lone Danish policeman in Qaanaaq, usually alone across the entire region, is more overseer and guardian than steely enforcer. Though armed, as all Danish police are, and transient on rotation, they are seen as a positive contribution and attract little resentment. Today in general, only drunkenness, the odd theft by the village thief (a fairly harmless chap who liberates peoples' belongings only to have them retrieved the next morning) and sadly, abuse of children, are on the police's radar.

Knud Rasmussen, or Kunoorruaq/Kunuk, was the first to install a different legal system – dubbed Thule Law – attempting with some success to replace justice by revenge with compensation plans, but this was soon superseded by Danish law. After Avanerriaq was absorbed into Danish Greenland, as late as 1937, imprisonment was found to have little effect on the Polar Eskimo spirit and was a useless tool – the shame of compensation was far more cutting.

Compare this sole Danish policeman to the daily duties of the Royal Canadian Mounted Police, rural Canada's law enforcement, and barely a single similarity can be found. Serious call-outs are daily occurrences even in small settlements. Violence and poverty are not buried deep. I found every RCMP member I met to be thoroughly decent, but they carry the lineage of the organisation that was the face of colonial policy in times past. That symbolic wound will be hard to heal, no matter how many recruitment posters are displayed calling for new Inuit members. In the nineteenth century, there were Canadian villages, populated compulsorily, where social meltdown had resulted in more than fifty per cent of men being murderers. The RCMP modus operandi was inadequate, as Rasmussen found when he journeyed there (they later employed him to help), and colonial traders often negotiated with revolvers, not words. You can hardly blame the local resentment.

Why has this comparatively trouble-free truce developed in Greenland when it's failed so spectacular and tragically elsewhere? I think the reason is the attitude of the very first Danish settlers. Again, behaviour was unlikely to be consistently admirable but they, most notably Rasmussen and also Peter Freuchen, the last to live with the Polar Eskimos in their 'virgin state', traded instead of confiscated. This was a time of explorers naming whatever they found, whether mountain, fjord or trading station, often regardless of whether it already had a local name.

These pioneers were visionary, ahead of their time in respecting native people, and duly garnered local respect. They are still spoken about in the warmest terms in Avanerriaq. At times other settlers and missionaries followed suit although some North Pole-seekers, mostly Americans, and whalers, ran the wrong side of the exploitation line. Unusually when viewed in a global context, enough colonials and settlers in Greenland acted with a base of moral integrity – enough to tip the balance of hearts and minds. Wider resentment rarely surfaced, except during a post-war period when Danes fell out of favour due to an unwelcome protectionism of the increasingly world-aware Greenlandic people. Relationships and working arrangements built and these did so around mutual benefit to one extent or another. It was also easy to see in the twentieth century how medicines (often to counter the new diseases that the Europeans imported – in fact just bringing the mail north would lead to 'Etah having the flu'), shaped metal, coffee, weapons and building materials accelerated and revolutionised the Inuit way of life. Most of this was for the better and the pragmatic locals knew it, adapting to the quantum leap in technology with admirable swiftness.

As a caveat, I want to condemn one wretched import that this colonisation brought along with it – to Avanerriaq via Gustav Olsen in 1909, much later than in the South. I most likely would have few supporters in Greenland for this point of view and so it should be taken as such, but the conversion of the pagan and animist shaman/*angakkoq*-driven people of Greenland, for whom beliefs and taboos were part of the moral compass of society, to Lutheran Christianity is not positive. Whilst as denominations go it is not the most oppressive, it is conservative and noticeably joyless. It is also at odds with much of Polar Eskimo culture – damning their survival-driven attitudes for the weak being social parasites, and for retaliation – far from Christian virtues. As such, gentle evolution from one world-view to another was impossible. An immediate revolution was inevitable.

There soon became very little space for traditional Greenlandic beliefs, many of which tied the people to the land, the ice and its creatures in a respectful way. It was firmly believed that animals willingly volunteered their bodies to be eaten through a desire to help their hungry 'brothers of the land and ice'. Though it was spirituality driven by an almost total lack of scientific knowledge, they had a reverence for the animals they harvested and exchanged souls with after death (deemed 'breaths'). Days of mourning were held following the successful hunt for a polar bear, the animal they felt closest to.

Concepts fundamental to life had different interpretations to those we in Western nations take entirely for granted. Possibility and impossibility, life and death, dreams and reality, beginnings and ends were all understood on a lateral plane to ours.

Their beliefs and superstitions were custom-made for the Arctic and to an extent they worked. Christianity was alien, unsuited and possibly even **less** based on reality. Yet the Polar Eskimos, who usually know their own minds so resolutely, adopted it in a remarkably docile manner – the last Greenlandic Inuit to be converted. It was a lazier and more servile belief system than theirs – it introduced 'sin' in addition to right and wrong. A number have mused that this compliance may be superficial – good acting to garner favour. Today, though, the widespread religiosity has some constructive effects, such as a community hub and a campaign to limit drinking (by prohibition lobbying amongst the Blue Cross group). On the other hand, a worryingly evangelical 'Free Church' is gaining cult-like momentum.

Of course, any benefits can result just as well from other social projects. The replacement of pagan beliefs with European religion has caused a rupture amongst the connections between Inuit (here I mean across all groups, including Polar Eskimo) and their natural world. It is interesting though that when calamity strikes, the people often fall back on traditional beliefs, taboos, ghost-stories and rituals, not what the missionaries imposed. A tale is told of a beautiful woman from Neqi singing ancient *ajajas* (a phonetic southern term for pagan *ingmerutit* songs) as she lay dying, despite having been baptised.

Odin

CHAPTER 7: Friends

IT WAS JUST a few days before yet another landmark, New Year, which tends to be more of a community celebration than one for family and close friends. Again, it's a fairly spurious Danish import since the Polar Eskimos would have had no concept of the Western calendar before being 'informed' of it. Indeed it has little practical relevance. The major annual moments that punctuate their lives are the disappearance of the sun for the winter and then its return in late February. Both are, too, commiserated and celebrated respectively.

Time was traditionally measured in sleeps, *hiniks* (again, the sound 's' is denoted by the letter 'h'), as day lengths are so variable and extreme, and also lunar months. Of course, concepts of seasons were, and are, at odds with those from the south and were adopted latterly, along with days of the week. This moment of inheritance is hard to define but occurred comparatively recently – perhaps 1818, contact, or 1910, Rasmussen's arrival.

Shared celebration and extravagance when hosting others have long been part of the fabric of Polar Eskimo communities. A party for a child might have been so generous with gifts, and also an unlimited guest list to feed, that the host might be ruined for a month, yet remained blissfully happy. This mindset caused friction when some decades ago the Danish encouraged saving currency (of course itself an imported notion) for 'rainy days' or to save up for new imported goods. A sharing culture and distaste for misers or capitalism waned with the pressure of modern Arctic life.

For the four of us, there was extra excitement to be had before the festivities. Our dogs were to be roped to our sleds for the first time. The result remained to be seen, but we were delighted that our early forays could be performed under cover of darkness and away from the assured laughter of veteran dog drivers.

We had also begun to get used to social life in Qaanaaq. Before we'd even had a chance to head down to our dog hill, we had been visited by Peter again and his girlfriend Else, plus her children.

These sorts of unannounced home visits have been part of the fabric of Polar Eskimo and wider Inuit society through history. It is an honour for the host to be visited, so with an 'open door policy' and a cheery call of 'alluu!', it's not something you need solicit. Well-stocked homes nowadays have led to the gradual loss of quaint but practical traditions – fifty years ago Else and Peter would have brought their own spoon and bowl in anticipation of a shared meal.

It was that morning we sat, fascinated, as Peter regaled with no lack of pride that his great-grandfather was Oodaaq. Along with Iggiannguaq, Hivso, Ukkujaaq and the Americans Robert Peary and Matthew Henson, they claimed precedence to the North Pole in 1909. Subsequently shown to be just another false claim with conveniently omitted proofs, nonetheless, the fundamental role the Polar Eskimos played as guides and dog drivers were the key to the hundreds of miles they did travel. Often, Polar Eskimos guided out of the sheer curiosity of being part of the 'living saga' of hapless southerners. Apparently the visits and expeditions with Cook (another false claimant of the North Pole) and Peary were discussed at length in Polar Eskimo settlements for decades after. It is the local opinion even today that Peary or Cook succeeded in their goals, which one depending on the camp they were from, not least because a failure would reflect badly on the honour of the guides. In hard reality, the total lack of landmarks on the Arctic Ocean makes locating one's position absolutely impossible without technical instruments.

You will notice that through history Polar Eskimo names have changed somewhat in their style. Firstly, names are often now more Nordic or Christian in origin. Apart from names we've come across so far, like Hans and Peter that are widespread, Sofie, Rosa and Enok appear again and again. More dramatically though is the change from the traditional Inuit nomenclature of solitary, highly descriptive names to the binomial given name plus a family name many of us find familiar. This was an administrative decision by the Danes in the 1960s. As a sign of the split loyalties between the charms of the past and the practicalities of the present though, Polar Eskimos often have a local name and then a westernised name too. They can also choose an additional name at pivotal life events later in their adulthood. As a bittersweet nod to the indiscretions of those early explorers, the family names Peary and Henson often appear today. A villager known as Tikkili is vocally proud of his black heritage as a descendant of the latter, perhaps with good reason as Henson distinguished himself with a humble and collaborative attitude toward local Inuit in the 1900s.

A name took on phenomenal spiritual importance to Polar Eskimos, and linked to the souls of deceased relatives. Until older, it is both this belief and the recycling of a small batch of names that is the reason behind parents not scolding naughty children. To reprimand might offend the ancestor's spirit, cause it to depart, and leave the child dead. Meanings of Polar Eskimo names might seem comic nowadays, but in my view their deference to our European convention is a huge cultural loss. Eqorsuaq meant 'big shit' (believe it or not a name won through respect with its literal meaning lost), Angmalortoq 'he who is round', and Aninnguaq 'the unsympathetic one'.

Finally free to go on our first canine adventure, we played it safe. A full team of ten would surely result in a stampede of dogs heading in ten different directions, run-over drivers and the sled ending up upside down in a ditch. We needed to gain the control, respect and trust of our dogs – most importantly, the stronger personalities.

Fixing Dave, Thor and Odin to our first sled took forever. We got wound up in ropes, clumsily clipped and unclipped hooks and the dogs were as confused as we were. Thor bit Dave, which Dave responded to by screaming blue murder and hiding behind an oil drum.

Anders had been practising his whip skills and so headed out ahead. Thor was keen to run, having been relatively immobile for months of summer, and followed along with the more circumspect duo behind. Whipping from side to side, Anders halted the dogs' enthusiasm before they could overtake us. This would be the lynchpin of basic dog control and needed to be mastered before even considering a free run. With a piercing yelp that the rest of us couldn't help but laugh at, Anders leapt as a mis-aimed flick of the whip caught the back of his leg. It wouldn't be the last time for any of us.

All in all, though, it went well – perhaps better than we expected. The only commands we tried were the simple 'hak, hak' (some early visitors wrote this phonetically as 'aak') to get them moving and 'aeeee' to attempt a stop. At first we barked the orders almost like a drill sergeant but soon realised that the dogs could hear us easily enough at speaking volume – more than capable of separating commands meant for them from general chatter amongst ourselves. All we had managed was to head along the frozen beach, onto a section of the offshore ice, loop around and then come back. It was a mental hurdle out of the way though. Working with our dogs was no longer a hypothetical idea for the future – we had begun our journey and could imagine building up to our dream of nonchalantly harnessing two full teams up in twenty minutes and then driving thirty miles under total control. Every moment spent watching the dogs and how they behaved and interacted with each other and us was a lesson.

Impatient to get a full team hitched up and able to start making educated decisions about whether some dogs needed to swap teams to balance pace or avoid fights, we planned to try eight different dogs the next day from the other prospective team. Instead of taking the easy option of heading east along the beach into the main dog staking area and using well-worn tracks, we wanted to start our own route out onto flatter sea ice; straight across the turbulent rubble ice of the tide crack from where our base was. Our idea to slow the whole process down and give us time to think and gain control was to weigh down the sled. An empty sled with a whip man out front and another laid on the flatbed or standing on the back would weigh less than four hundred pounds. For a team of eager and frustrated dogs capable of hauling more than three times that, the effect could be the same as standing one leg in and one leg out of the cockpit of a Ferrari and hitting the throttle. We 'borrowed' a pile of freighting pallets, very common across all Arctic communities in random piles on edges of settlements, and lashed them into a four-foot-high pile at the rear of the flatbed. Job done, we hoped.

With James and Anastasia's team the next guinea pigs, we had needed to swap around harnesses so that we had a full set. All dog harnesses are custom hand-stitched by their drivers for each individual animal and a handful of our dogs were delivered without or with ones a handful of strands short of snapping in half. Harness stitching and, sigh, repairs for the more chewing-fanatical of the dogs, became a speciality reserved for

James' and Anastasia's evenings after dinner as their artistic flair seemed to overshadow Anders' and my own.

We had two dogs, Houdini and Lyka, both incidentally the escapology and rope/harness/anything chewing enthusiasts, who were still growing and so we knew they'd need repeated re-measuring and new webbing cut and stitched. The number of times we would open our door to be greeted by an irrepressibly happy young dog, one or the other of them or even both, having joyfully chewed straight through our handiwork, couldn't be counted. Some dogs could be trusted with their harnesses left on and on nylon ropes, but others needed chains and a snug-fitting collar to get through an evening unsupervised and chew-free. We even had to divide the inseparable pair as Lyka had chewed Houdini's collar itself, allowing him to run free down to the other dogs and parade his liberty. Retribution for this cockiness we'd soon learn was building in the memories of the other dogs – Houdini certainly thought, with his youthful exuberance, good looks and strong stature, that he was top dog. Not for long.

It was approaching midday by the time we were loaded up and ready, with Comedy Dad on the longer trace or *ipiutaq* (a thin rope connecting dog to front of sled), and a deep red glow appeared on the southern horizon for a short period as if to taunt us before fading away. To our eyes it was mostly pitch black, but if we switched our headtorches off for a few moments and let them adjust to the dim starlight, a shadowy deep blue hue bathed the broken ice ahead and offshore.

With James this time the man with the whip, the team being his, he walked out ahead with Anders and Anastasia beside the sled, ready to jump in should anything go wrong. I had volunteered to ride the sled ahead of the pallet pile and try my best to film our launch across the fifty yards or so of pressure ice. We'd previously walked out to make sure there was a rough way through and no dead ends, but a number of jagged pieces of ice and large troughs would make it far from simple. We hoped that by the time we'd used it a few times, the carved tracks would smooth out obstacles and get progressively easier.

Off we went. The dogs, unfamiliar with each other, ran and then stopped, jumped over each other, and then ran again, only sometimes in the right direction. James was doing a great job at the front and held his nerve. The temptation as the dogs pick up speed and the intimidating sled gains momentum is to get out of the way, a disastrous move, instead of stamping down authority with the whip – a Gandalf-like 'you shall not pass!' I was bouncing around from side to side, one hand clutching my camera which filmed from a point-of-view angle and the other holding the wooden slat underneath me for dear life. The light was low but it was picking up the view well as I studied the screen and tried to keep it smooth. Then, we hit the rough stuff. James had ended up some way ahead, scouting the way forward and encouraging the dogs with 'hak, hak'. A gap had grown which the dogs then accelerated into, bouncing the sled off a large ice slab to the left that catapulted me around. Two dogs let their ropes, slack for a split second, snag on a spike of ice near a crack in the surface and were stuck. The sled careered towards them and they struggled free just in time before the two-hundred pounds of wood came clattering over. Finally, two large ridges combined with a burst of speed from the dogs and the sled shot off, becoming nearly airborne. The impact as we hit the solid ice was spine jarring; no shock absorbers on these chariots of the north.

"Aeee, aeeee!" James yelled and remarkably, most of the dogs slowed to a stop. Immediately, a scuffle broke out and all four of us jumped in to remonstrate. Not ready to saddle up and drive toward the sunset, or where we imagined the sunset might be, our first outing was essentially a glorified dog walk. We took turns getting the dogs to follow us with some discipline and generally getting a feel for it – at times with the dogs making off in four different directions. About a mile out at sea, we curved round and stopped for a chat. The dogs, standing to attention and anticipating more action, seemed to be willing us to issue the desired command. In front of us I could make out a few icebergs silhouetted against the starlight. Beyond that, nothing. Facing back the way we came though was spectacular. Granted, Qaanaaq is barely a village by usual standards, but the dim, warm, yellow lighting from homes sparkled against the pitch-black background like a Christmas tree. It was so inviting; comfort, safety and familiarity in the middle of unimaginable wilderness.

I walked the dogs back towards the light, finally giving them something to aim for. My whip flicked back and forth ahead of the dogs' noses inexpertly but effectively. A cone of light from Anastasia's head torch illuminated the dogs and my body threw a shadow across them. Asking if everyone was aboard and glancing behind to check, Anastasia and James were knelt on the flatbed and Anders stood on the rear planks, a mitt on each upright 'handle'.

"Shall we give this a crack?" I asked.

With nods in response I stood aside with an eye on the spot on the sled I'd make a leap for. Whipping ceased, I half-whispered 'hak'. The dogs erupted into an exuberant sprint, straight towards the lights. At least they were going the right way. Having settled into a trotting pace, I took my eyes off the dogs to exchange satisfied grins with the team. There was no point in getting ahead of ourselves and trying directions, but the ice shot past and soon we'd be in town. I needed to stop them again, with the mental image I had of the four of us haplessly zooming into the centre of Qaanaaq, all yelling "aeee!" and the dogs not paying the slightest bit of notice.

With time still to spare, I hopped off and ran alongside the sled. "Aeee!" I called. The sled slowed, a couple of the dogs glancing back at me, unsure of how much respect to afford this interloper fancying himself their boss. Comedy's ears were facing back towards me and another couple of assertive commands brought him down to a walk. Then came a halt, followed by the rabble of the rest of the team.

Somewhat smug, I handed the whip to James and Anastasia to walk them into our parking spot at the foot of the dog hill. The whip, one of two we were generously given for a nominal price, was crafted with a wooden handle, perhaps a foot and a half in length. Lashed tightly to the end with a strong thin cord, ahead of a nodule on the end, was the start of the sealskin whip itself. Starting half an inch wide and linking to a thinner section a couple of feet down the line, it then narrowed to a thin tip a dozen or more feet long. It was this thin tail section that in practised hands can create the sharp crack sound that so focusses the attention of dogs and humans alike.

Having bumped and whacked our way through the ice crack along the original tracks, and with dogs individually walked up the hill to their spots, we committed ourselves to a daily routine of practice and training. We wanted to be proficient enough to cover serious distances before twilight was appearing along the horizon at midday – February perhaps.

We had given in to tunnel-vision in our hurries to get out with the dogs, with our insistent and regular coffee meetings with Peter, Else and others, and the busy evenings of practical work that was necessary. If it wasn't making or repairing dog harnesses, it was linking hundred yard lengths of chain we'd sourced from the store and finding the right cords to connect 'spinner' loops at intervals to. They'd make us a portable dog-staking system we could use when out of settlements. Dogs could chew all but the thickest, most resilient and tightly knotted cords and ropes, as they took great pride in demonstrating, so it was a daily ritual at first to recapture loose dogs and rethink our staking point construction.

The most amusing episode came barely a week after we'd adopted our crew of dogs. Garfunkel was the beneficiary of Houdini's chewing prowess, who was loose, but easy to recapture through his tendency to stay around our home or the other dogs. Missing, Garfunkel was a concern as one of the meeker southern dogs and fairly hand-shy. On feeding duty, I called the others down and we swept east across the beach and lower dog hill. We scanned for a loose dog amongst three or four-dozen others, initially sleeping or resting but instantly up and barking at the slightest hope of food or excitement. Peter, Rasmus' brother's team were dogs we recognised, located in one spot in the centre. Perhaps Garfunkel had gone back to be with his friends.

Our hunch was correct. Moving with the wiliness of a fox and the suspicion of an animal more than once freed and recollected, he looped around always with an eye on us. The next twenty minutes had us in stitches of laughter. Each of us had grabbed something to entice Garfunkel with, from dog kibble to flapjack to cheese. Having roundly failed to get within even ten feet of him using the promise of treats, our tactics resorted to simple pursuit. We were down to James' pocketful of Danish cheese and the wits of the four of us dashing around in polar boots – not the most nimble of footwear. A hunter we'd not come across yet was feeding his dogs at the top of the slope and having seen our dilemma, came down to help. With a quick grin, he joked and gestured with his hands that we should shoot Garfunkel and it would solve the problem of catching him. "A problem we all have," he said, before giving chase too. The poor animal must have been half frightened and half entertained by our attempts. On one occasion, his jacket flapping open to dissipate the heat caught in the insulation, James got close and made a wonderfully committed full leap towards him, landing only a foot or two short. He laughed, lying in the snow amongst scattered rocks, banged the ground with his fist and got up to try again.

Finally, with a nifty move from three of us, including our new friend, blocking a likely escape route and the others tricking him into a false move, we got hands on our runaway. Triumphant with a hint of shame, we shook hands and laughed with Enok, and took Garfunkel back for some food, an attempt to show him we were friends not foes, and a chain to replace his rope. We didn't want to go through it all again.

Finally attention could turn to our neighbours, one of whom we promised to visit before heading out to celebrate the arrival of 2014. Between the sea and us sat a fairly newly fabricated red house. The inhabitant was a middle-aged man and he seemed to have little interest in getting to know us. It is usual, if at a distance or heading in different directions, to nonetheless raise an arm in greeting, whether friend or stranger. After four or five attempts with him, we gave up, confused. Months later we would learn from another villager that he worked as a mechanic, assisting in maintaining the town's facilities. Also, the reason as to his seemingly antisocial nature. He had lost two children and his wife, one after the other, to suicide. Shocked and saddened, we would find that before our brief time in Qaanaaq was over, three more would take their own lives, from a population below five hundred. Often it was the youngest that fell victim. The combination of darkness, alcohol, lack of employment, inability to escape unrequited love, poor education, and a view to a wider world with opportunities they'll never have, can be toxic. Prior to Contact, suicide was rarer and limited to when resources were scarce and it was considered for the good of the group, or after being cast out of a village. Suicide – *imminortoq* – literally means 'goes away from home'. Being outcast is like a death sentence for the Polar Eskimo psyche.

Next-door was a friendly, slightly-built hunter and his wife. We assumed his dogs were elsewhere, but one did live outside his front door. A dirty white and with an unkempt and dishevelled mop of long fur, he was probably the ugliest sled dog I'd ever seen. Young, friendly and with the most incredibly sweet temperament, we fell for him immediately, sneaking him treats and a few minutes of belly rubs and ear scratches each day. We nicknamed him 'Yeti'.

Opposite were two homes, larger than many. On the left was a family of four. The mother, we were told by more than one person, was a troublemaker and a 'complainer'. Unceremoniously called the 'village bitch' by others, we steered well clear but tried to raise the arm of diplomacy and wave whenever we saw them outdoors. They had a fresh brood of pups outside with their mother. In the other home, painted yellow and clearly well cared for, lived an elderly lady named Regina.

I imagine Navarana knew Regina since they were children. They were approximately the same age and neither lived with family. Navarana had quite the adventurous life and was previously married to a Canadian Arctic academic. Still on good terms, she regularly visited her children and grandchildren living in Canada and Denmark. Navarana, by virtue of the fact of being Polar Eskimo by birth and upbringing, had a strong affinity with Eastern Canadian Inuit and had even visited ancestrally related family on Baffin Island a few years before. She did tell us though that Regina was lonely, had enjoyed our brief 'welcome' conversation in the street, and would love us to visit for tea and cake. Widowed and with her children living outside of Qaanaaq, Regina found that even getting involved in the odd community event and particularly, cake-making contests, didn't stop living alone difficult. Navarana seemed concerned that we wouldn't want to go; that it would bore us and that we were more interested in our own work that had picked up a pace. We reassured her as she tried to cajole us that we would be delighted and didn't need persuasion. She also invited herself in case language barriers were to crop up.

It was still afternoon and the more elaborate festivities wouldn't begin until later. We had been told, very much still 'curiosities' in town that we were, we'd be expected at at least three New Year gatherings. The four of us spent a good few hours with Regina and Navarana, unrushed and transfixed. Her home's entrance way set the theme for the interior. Painted and papered with cosy, warm colours and with every inch of wall space covered with some sort of photo, souvenir and memento, some unfamiliar with Inuit homes might call it cluttered. To us though it was just fascinating. An entire life in the Arctic was proudly displayed, from cooking utensils including the local *ulu* – woman's knife (a curved half-moon blade set into a bone or ivory handle and unique in shape to the community it's from) to small fur boots, *kamiit*, sized for a child – her daughter perhaps. I have hereafter anglicised the singular word *kamik* – one boot – to *kamiks* for a pair.

Regina smiled from ear to ear – greeting each in turn and piloted us onto a pristine sofa that must have been shipped up just a year or two before. She was very mobile and energetic, although slightly uneven as she rolled from foot to foot across the floor. On a tray which she'd pre-laid for us, evidently with quite some forethought, was a huge iced caked adorned with fruits – strawberries, cherries and apricot slices – undoubtedly sourced from an imported tin but still an expensive rarity. A large teapot sat beside six dainty and exquisitely designed and decorated cups.

A couple of hours of passed exchanging stories, during which we demolished the vast bulk of the cake, almost embarrassingly fast. Sometimes it was apparent that Regina didn't fully understand what we were saying, so Navarana jumped in with a minute or so of Inuktun. Articulating with ease and a graceful, unhurried flow as she spoke really accented how inadequate I felt for not even having a remote grasp of the language yet. Soon we were poring over a fragile old photo album that documented her incredible life in the North. She had been quite the traveller in her youth and although not in the 'driving seat', as was never traditionally accepted for women, we marvelled at black and white images of her riding the family dog sled on one quest or another. Happy family photos, at weddings there in Qaanaaq, came next and then more modern ones as she worked cleaning at the municipal building. She sighed as she closed it, thumping it down on her knee in a nostalgic resignation. "My family are gone from the North and do not come here now. I miss my dogs and adventures." Before we left to feed our own dogs in time to join the party in the village, she made us promise to come back and take whatever we needed from the storage shed. Dog harnesses, ropes and all sorts were ours if we so wanted. Touched, and in equal parts saddened that she clearly sought company in a community not well prepared to support its elderly, but fascinated by her past, we bade her farewell.

This moment is right to broach one of the defining cultural norms that I, and before me so many commentators, noticed as being nigh on definitive of a Polar Eskimo, and one I don't believe I've seen contradicted. That is, the flexibility and nuance of their tone and how confidence and modesty are balanced. Instructions and advice can be imparted with brevity and vice-like earnestness. Any questioning of knowledge would be a slur of the highest order. Counter to this entirely, when speaking of possessions or if in need of any assistance, a deference and almost servile polite hesitance takes over. To offend someone deeply is avoided at all costs and your undivided attention is broadcast with soft, repeated 'ii's. Yet, feelings are often masked, especially when impressed. These unpredictable exchanges, especially alongside the bewitching sound of fluent Inuktun, are abiding memories.

Understanding Polar Eskimo life is not straightforward. Without you becoming part of one yourself, the secrets and subtle details of family life are well guarded. You can experience snapshots in the homes of those you befriend, and when travelling on the ice. In public, you see a different side to the community, like in the festive period, and it can be quite a contrast. Of course, it's necessary to generalise as outliers – super-extroverts and recluses – reside in every community, whether in the frozen North, another indigenous group, or a European city. Cultural norms do exist, reported through the writings of the explorers throughout the Age of Contact, or today.

Even with their misunderstandings and prejudices, Rasmussen later, and then Malaurie who witnessed the formation of the American base at Thule and one of the last to see Qaanaaq as it was before relocation, still offer a window. They could not hope to record a virgin state given what aboriginal culture had already been lost forever by the time they arrived. And now, in the twenty-first century, the same is true. We all add a little to a picture.

It is inevitable these cultural norms may provoke some, but I implore them to think again. Of course, not every member of a particular society subscribes to or complies with these norms. Saying 'Polar Eskimos do this or that' is crass. But nonetheless, norms emerge from a mixture of stereotypes and observations. Polar Eskimos en masse may appear pensive, but perhaps this is simply a resigned courage inherited from centuries of living in the barren North. My fellow Britons and I are world-renowned for our fanatical commitment to forming queues, and for apologising when we're not sorry, just to diffuse an awkward moment. This hasn't cropped up from nowhere – it happens with regularity. So, the same applies to any coherent social group. We all have our en masse characteristics, even if we are all individuals. These collective traits make the world interesting, but to perpetually speak about any humans as if homogeneous organisms is to do them a disservice. Doing so fed misguided early racist stories of savages.

After meeting Troels, via an impromptu bump into Peter (very nearly literally as he was a tiny bit unstable on his feet – his festivities had already begun), we visited Karen, some other Danes including the community's nurse, Merete, and other locals. Some people had been preparing, baking and cooking for seemingly days and the atmosphere around Qaanaaq had tangibly loosened up. It was a long way from a carnival atmosphere, but there was a sense of a temporal landmark amidst the dark, long winter and something to celebrate.

After a handful more social stops, instructions were clear. We must go to the village's communal sports building. One of the suspiciously smart and modern additions juxtaposed against the modest architecture of Qaanaaq and the wider Avanerriaq, the hall was impressive for somewhere so remote. Straight answers proved elusive, but the sporadic and rapid assembly of new facilities raise questions about their source. Greenlandic investment in the North? Unlikely and something I want to tackle in depth later. Danish funded? A quiet gift from the US government as unofficial reparation for the forced relocation of settlements to make way for Thule Air Base, and almost-certain 'loss' of a nuclear weapon and contamination following a B-52 crash-landing in 1968? The end result is the same in any case – the people benefit from a blatant subsidy.

The creation of the Thule Air Base is still controversial. It went over the heads of all local inhabitants – reminiscent of the US purchase of Alaska from Russia for a mere few million dollars, **including** and irrespective of those living there. Indeed, there was a risk of Greenland being sold in the eighteenth century, its people hapless and unaware pawns in an 'Age of Land Sales' – and of human beings. Whilst the Uummannaq camp had been a central location for infrequent ship landings, trading and a few Danish administrators, it was still small when thousands of American servicemen, landing ships, aircraft and bulldozers arrived to rapidly build a vast Cold War military installation in the short summers of 1951/2. Most of the US personnel were not even told where in the world they were being sent to in order to work on the construction site.

Unaware, the reaction by Jean Malaurie as he sledded to the area with Polar Eskimo friends after a year living in Avanerriaq was that of bewilderment. Rumours of melting the whole ice field, of atomic bombs and stealing their women were rife. Some sensed opportunity and that they were about to become rich – conflicted in their views about leaving their past, at times brutal, lifestyles behind. Remember, these peoples' hardiness was necessary due to where they were born, not something they opted into. For the first time, they were aware of what other people had, and they hadn't. Even the young Danish administrator seemed confused about the pace of goings on and was powerless to negotiate terms on behalf of the hunters – the idea of demanding the Americans pay a modest 'ground rent' was rejected. This miserliness, when the US financial investment made just that year was more than double what Denmark had spent in total in Greenland since the mid-eighteenth century.

Knud Rasmussen's little white house, by then having stood for decades, and small Polar Eskimo dwellings were dwarfed by a cutting-edge, near billion-dollar airbase. This house was ingeniously divided in two, sailed to today's Qaanaaq, and now stands proudly as a repository for Polar Eskimo artefacts. In the shadows too by then was Oodaaq's home, Peter's explorer guide forebear, being a gift to him from the Danes, and also Peter Freuchen's.

Ultimately, given the American paranoia about security and communism, they had to go. Fear amongst the Polar Eskimos grew – they felt a sense of abandonment by the Danish, even the king for whom they had affection and allegiance. They dreamt up a story that this was Peary's plan all along, those decades before. Diesel was contaminating the water and making hunting impossible. The seals and whales wouldn't return, they lamented.

In just a couple of years, initial friendliness, souvenir photos and informal trading with wet-behind-the-ears servicemen barely out of their teens turned to eviction. There was soon a contact ban between those living on the base and natives in the tiny settlement. Hans Jensen, then a young boy, was one of them. Navarana too. In 1953, they were ordered with a few days' notice to leave their home of hundreds of years and set up camp again at Qaanaaq, over a hundred miles north. Decades passed with increasing trade in alcohol, tobacco, sugary food, the arrival of a different breed of more bureaucratic Danes, and their new spectre - regulations.

The countdown to the New Year continued. Over a hundred people had congregated in the hall itself, seated either on the floor and watching the activities in full swing in the centre, or eating in groups around a set of rickety-looking tables. Some of the younger children were playing games in the back corner; by far the noisiest group and without the shyness we'd notice they tend to acquire when on their own around adults, and especially strangers. We smiled and waved at some familiar faces and joined the line to see what the fuss was about. With two raised platforms, one with a young man sat behind a modern music system and with a loudhailer, the other had a large pile of boxes and two or three more men sat as if awaiting something. The action was in the middle of the crowd. Two pairs of men were squirming around on the ground, locked in a tense and curious sort of wrestling match.

Tests of strength have forever been integral to Inuit culture, mostly amongst men. They attract a jovial atmosphere but a serious undercurrent remains in how respect and hierarchal positions are doled out to the winners and losers. Not only the young, unproven and ambitious hunters get involved – many of the older generation of hardened Polar Eskimos can be formidable.

Boxing, sparring and outright fighting which has a habit of causing both injury and discord in a small, tightknit community was substituted by surrogate contests. Often these rely on hand, wrist and shoulder strength. With scant resources, ancient grip and finger-strength games were easy to organise but the particular competition playing out for this New Year festivity used a couple of pieces of wood connected by a strong cord. The aim seemed to be, sat behind it on the ground and with legs to the side, to wrench it towards yourself and make your opponent lose their grip. We watched a couple of matches, apparently part of an organised but slightly chaotic knockout tournament. Games like this were, and are, commonplace as entertainment and time-killers on the edge of ice floes or after a long day on the trail. However, this seemed like an annual culmination. One, between a mismatched pair, ended with a single concerted heave. The other was more close-fought, with victory coming only after one man lost his purchase on the ground and slid forward.

We weren't Greenlanders, let alone Polar Eskimo, and so assumed we'd just observe from the wings. The man with the music, with fashionably styled hair and a soul-patch, beckoned us up. Hairstyles are now fairly conventional, having evolved from long, uncut hair liable to hide their faces or held with a leather band, via bowl cuts of the mid-twentieth century. He introduced himself in a combination of English and Danish as Peter Peary. A descendent of Robert Peary and his relationship with the young Polar Eskimo girl Aleqasina, he took the European name Peter for ease, but his real name was Aleqatsiaq. We were quickly added to the strength contest roster and he said to us with a smile, "you live with us now so you are part of this too!"

Anders was pitted against a young hunter probably in his late teens. Stout and broad-shouldered, it could go either way. Anders though stood around six foot and along with the training he did for our journey, was gym-focussed. Rather disappointingly, James and I were lined up as contesting each other, but perhaps one of us would experience a wrestle with the locals in a later round. No-one really knew what was going on – everything seemed based on the sheet of paper Peter Peary held in his hand and scribbled on with a biro. One minute the four of us were sitting and chatting, Anders attempting to politely escape the highly amorous advances of a middle-aged Polar Eskimo lady, and the next he was summoned into the 'ring' – the large gap in the middle of the now substantial crowd.

No alcohol was openly visible around the hall, with children still playing and sat with their families (many Inuit children are rarely given enforced bedtimes anyhow), but a good quantity had evidently already been consumed earlier in the evening. The Danish-imposed points-based rationing system is gone, but strong liquor is still not allowed, only beer and wine. The volume had risen and above the cheering was the enthusiastic hollering of Anders' admirer.

Without practice or knowledge, Anders nonetheless steamed through his first round, forcing his adversary to release their wooden handle in less than ten seconds. It was more through brute strength than technique though and as he sat back down with a proud grin, said he needed to watch the others carefully and learn the body positioning. Without this, a more evenly matched opponent in terms of strength would beat him on technique. It turned out Anders, whilst still slightly bemused, was keen to take the fight to the locals! There was a sideways leaning knack and elbow-locking that we noticed many employed, and we needed to try to emulate.

Half an hour later and after Anders' second round, which he duly won too, Peter Peary broadcast across the crowd, "Alex and James (pronounced 'yam-es' locally and one of many nicknames he would accrue), come up!"

Not taking it particularly seriously and having never tried it before, James and I were laughing as we sat down and gripped the wooden handles. An adjudicator came over to correct our handgrips and gave us a few gestured pointers, none of which really sank in. Then, with a drop of the hand, we pulled, squirmed and wrenched for all we were worth. Fairly evenly matched, we grimaced and then made eye contact. We made each other laugh again but kept the pressure up – we certainly weren't taking it easy on each other. Unlike many of the sub-ten second matches we'd seen, it seemed to go on forever. The noise had grown and the locals, young and old, male and female, could be heard yelling encouragement. Eventually, the sweat from our exertions caught me out and I felt my grip on the smooth handle begin to slide. Trying my hardest to the very end, the wood pinged from my grasp with a massive force and both of us were flung onto our backs. James, still holding the contraption, ended up with one handle catapulted straight onto his forehead with a bump. Aside from the sore palms of our hands, he would be left with a reminder of his great victory.

Anders kept on going, round after round, with harder and heavier opponents each time, and James proceeded one more round before dropping out after a hard-fought wrestle. Eventually, quite unbelievably and it had to be said, hilariously for us, Anders and most of the Polar Eskimos we were sat with, he was in the final. The other man was well built and had stood out in previous matches as having the technique of locking the handle into his body well practised.

The tension in the room was palpable and once or twice we winced as Anders lost the initiative and had to claw his composure back. Nearly a minute into the battle, a marathon compared to most, the Greenlander finally relented. Anders was the victor, just an hour or so after unwittingly stumbling into a game we'd never played before.

It did cross my mind that this could not be such a good thing, diplomatically at least. How would the community react to an interloper appearing from nowhere, beating local competitors (for whom machismo is part of the fabric of society) at their own game and collecting the spoils?

I did not need to worry; the reception was nothing but warm. Stranger and acquaintance alike congratulated Anders and we had to practically restrain his biggest fan from kidnapping him; further down the road of inebriation as she now was. Winners of each category: youth and adult and a reassuring show of the times, female, were invited up to receive the prizes. I'm sure that contests between women existed throughout Arctic peoples' history, but unlikely in ones with a traditionally male slant.

Prizes had come direct from the town's store and presumably had been 'sponsored' by the company that feeds it. For the teenage winner was a music system. Anders was the last to be invited up and he did so to a roar of approval and applause – the loudest noise I'd ever heard from a group of Inuit, with exception of one chaotic experience in a cramped, makeshift bar in the east of Greenland that I'll spare you.

As a fitting prize, and almost embarrassingly generous given the circumstances, the stout hunter who had stood guard on the other platform thrust a long cardboard box into Anders' hands. A rifle. These, whilst a mainstay of the community for whom hunting was integral, get increasingly expensive the more remote a community you try to buy them in. I bought ours further south, with the knowledge that if they lacked stock of the very high calibre we needed, we'd be stuffed. Up in the Far North, a rifle (more expensive than shotguns, the basic anti-bear weapon of choice prior to a bizarre ban on solid-shot ammunition) was a treasured possession, almost reflecting the value attached to them when first traded with the early explorers. Anders' new possession was chambered to take high-energy small calibre bullets, ideal for hunting prey with minimum damage to the skin and fur. He'd later trade it in town so that someone in greater need of a hunting weapon could use it, but it symbolised his local celebrity status. Children, teenagers and adults alike now knew of Anders and seemed happy he won at their game. Any fears of an upset or loss of face were unfounded. Perhaps the difficulty other researchers have reported 'getting on' with Inughuit stem from the lack of respect afforded to those without physical or outdoor aptitude.

By the time we got home, we had meandered via three or four houses belonging to people we'd met just that evening and finally got to sleep by 2am. The next day was a feeding day for the dogs but one we'd not use for running them. Instead, as our confidence was building quickly, hopefully not with unfounded self-assurance, I wanted to plan our coming months. We needed structure and landmarks to measure our progress by. A whole winter and spring seems like a long time, but it could so easily slip by.

An important job to be completed before anything more ambitious was to relocate our 'dog headquarters'. In a flurry of activity; laying out new chains, anchors and rope links, we moved our menagerie, and an old wooden crate as a food store, down onto the sea ice itself. This put us in line with the majority of dog teams run on a regular basis, and spared our neighbours a daily cacophony.

Dog feeding and our plan for their training near Qaanaaq, and on long journeys, was a sprawling debate. It needed to match their demands yet be affordable and efficient for us. They were our engine room and needed to be in fine fettle.

Our approach was still traditional, exclusively working with the seals from the hunting community lockup. Options otherwise for fresh game meat were limited. Quite rightly, the Inuit's special dispensation to harvest mammals and fish otherwise protected by law on a quota basis did not extend to us. The mixture of meats used by the Polar Eskimo people for their own food and that for their dogs; seal, walrus, caribou, muskox, polar bear, narwhal, beluga, minke whale, small fish and Greenland shark, mostly fall under the quota system. Licences are only issued to those who rely on hunting as their main occupation. This both allows for the people to live traditionally, as they wish, and to make sure that modern advances don't lead to over-harvesting. When you bring modern boats, skidoos, radios and modern weapons into the mix, as in other parts of Greenland and in Canada, the balance swings decidedly against the quarry. The people of Qaanaaq and the wider region were determined not to step onto that slippery slope.

This is an avenue where the Polar Eskimos' cousins across the water in Nunavut have tragically lost their way. With the destruction of thousands of Canadian Inuit dogs, a shift in mindset from traditional transportation and hunting to machines and southern practices was inevitable. There is still today controversy surrounding the huge loss of dogs in the 1950s to 1970s, perhaps as many as twenty thousand – some were lost to disease, but stories of systemic eradication on 'public health grounds' are widespread. Reports by Inuit, the RCMP and other commissions blatantly contradict and no clarity has resulted. Regardless, the dogs were integral and whether their demise was intentional or not, Canadian Inuit culture also began to implode. Today, many inhabitants of the Canadian North are now **afraid** of sled-type dogs – what a sorry indictment.

With traditional dog sled travel replaced by snowmobiles and all-terrain vehicles, then came boats with outboard motors to supersede kayaks and rowboats. Firearms had long-since replaced harpoons and lances. Hunting, with ever-growing human populations in permanent settlements, had become industrial in scale.

My own time in Nunavut has totalled just a few weeks in its eastern parts, but the contrast to Greenland became instantly clear. Wealthy trophy hunters, accompanied by an indigenous guide, can hunt polar bears from snowmobiles. There is also the infamous commercial seal hunt, and most depressing for me – the Canadian narwhal hunt. Narwhal, the small 'unicorn' whales of the North are harvested in low, sustainable numbers by kayak and harpoon in Avanerriaq – in fact, Qeqertat exists for that very reason since pods of narwhal collect there each summer. In Nunavut though, locals told of summertime killing frenzies offshore from flotillas of motorised freighter canoes and hunters blasting away into the water with hundreds of bullets. Some are so imprecise that even other boats are holed. Many dead narwhal sink and are lost. Those collected, with few exceptions, have their meat and skin thrown away and the valuable tusks, some rare double tusks in particular, are promptly sold to the South. It's a shameful waste and frankly, beneath them. Greed and recklessness have, for some, replaced skill and respect. Arctic caribou herds are suffering in a similar manner, with some sub-populations already extinct. Where do you point the finger though? At the perpetrators, or the system that changed a whole society so irreparably that points of traditional reference are now skewed to the point of oblivion?

Hauling two or three half seals we'd exchanged for a fistful of kroner across town in an old plastic sledge, we took turns at butchering. We no longer did so outside, a misjudged early tactic, and without a semi-cold room with a strong ceiling-hanging hook like most hunters, we made do. We set aside the area near the front door for long-term storage and the little boiler, and allowed a day or so for the deep-frozen carcasses to thaw.

What follows is gruesome – there is no getting away from that fact. Once thawed, the smell of the seal is horrific; a combination of raw meat and a fishy odour, made far worse by any time in the open air. Whether the seal is as it was caught, or already skinned, it's a sad sight. I'm a meat eater at home and am thoroughly aware of the need to face up to the realities of what happens before farmed meat is neatly shrink wrapped for a shop. As a biology graduate though with a lifelong passion for the natural world and animals in general, it's tough to reconcile.

We took turns, as the mostly strictly adhered-to rota duty, butchering every couple of days. Missing out on your turn would be looked upon gravely by the others, given our lack of relish for the task. We had different techniques, but I preferred to shut myself into the small washing and bathroom area of the home and close the door, attempting to keep the smell in. With a mostly thawed half seal in a large plastic tray, a combination of sharpened knives, brute force and an axe, I separated limbs, sections of meat, blubber and internal organs. The ravenous dogs would consume all this and we tried to make sure each got a mixture. If one dog ate just meat protein and the other only energy-rich blubber, they'd fare very differently out on the ice.

I tended to do the whole thing breathing through my mouth only, so as to limit the stench and I tried to keep bloody splatters off my precious clothing. On one occasion, I recoiled back onto my haunches as I made the macabre discovery of an unborn seal pup inside its mother. Its white fur contrasted against the dark colours of meat and organs. I can't say it didn't affect me, but I butchered both carcasses so as to make use of them – not lives lost in vain. Job done at last, the buckets full to the brim with butchered seal and bones ended up being satisfyingly plonked outside the door on a base of newspaper. It was over to the designated 'feeders' who'd sledge or carry them down to the dogs.

A final part of the butchering ordeal was the clean up. A pipe in the floor took the effluent out of the house and emptied onto the slope outside. Like most houses we'd seen around Qaanaaq, this ice flume (the contents froze soon after release into the open air), comprised a fusion of clear ice and blood red flows.

Garfunkel

CHAPTER 8: Four Become Three

TRAINING WAS going well. Lyka had been demoted from any sensible role actually hauling the sled and we either left her behind or allowed her to run free out front, usually counterproductive as the dogs would follow her and not our directions.

Whilst James and Anastasia were happy with the steady but encouraging performance of Comedy Dad as their lead dog, Anders and I were less optimistic about Crazy's potential. Although keen, fit and able to run ahead of the main team (some dogs abjectly refuse to break ranks), he lacked the concentration and intellect to keep a straight course without a track or sled to follow. If given a blank canvas of virgin snow on a flat sea ice surface with the odd iceberg dotted around, frozen in, he would struggle. An excellent lead dog is able to fix onto a distant landmark and run on that course unless modified by a call of "haruu!" or "atsuk!" (left and right).

It was with that disappointing end of term report that we demoted Crazy. Perhaps we could use him up front in situations where a lead dog was tired and we needed to cover lots of miles along an existing sled track, but he couldn't be the main choice. Thor was intelligent, confident and strong, but refused to run outside of the team. From day to day, training from dimly lit ice expanses to jumbled rubble fields, we cycled other potentials through. My real hope was that we'd find a potential lead without having to poach a dog from James and Anastasia's team or even buy another.

Each time, we exchanged the normal length ropes for the extra long 'lead' trace, occasionally leading to scuffles and horrible tangles, but persevered. Meanwhile, James was really getting the hang of gaining the trust and respect of their his and usually led us out onto the ice, giving our six to ten-mile daily forays some structure.

A few were not even worth trying; OJ and Dog With No Name, for example. OJ had also been causing headaches all on his own. Seemingly capable of winding up any dog within a close radius, he lunged at Thor one evening as we walked him past. Thor, who was on his staking rope, flew into a rage and caught hold of OJ's thick neck fur. He simply wouldn't let go and OJ eventually gave up his defence. Still, Thor persisted with renewed verve and my attempts to deescalate had to become more pointed. Eventually, I managed to separate them. OJ had wounds to his neck but would certainly recover – would he ever learn? Thor too was feeling sorry for himself after my intervention. Only the next day, as the sole dog still severely hand-shy, OJ slipped his collar. His wiliness kept him free for over a week. Curiously, he came running out onto the ice each time we took the dogs on training runs, but always kept just far enough from reach.

Resigned to the permanent loss of a dog, we purchased his replacement. Enormously handsome, sandy-coloured and of Dave-like proportions, we named him McMuffin, or Muffin for short. It would turn out that Muffin shared more in common with Dave than just his height and bulk of thick, healthy fur. His reluctance to partake in daily exercise was so marked that he even tried repeatedly to ride the sled instead of run ahead of it. After a couple of unceremonious heaves off the platform, he began to get the idea. His friendship with Dave was born, as was a very theatrical submission performances towards Thor.

Our quest for a lead dog led to Enrique. Loveable as he was, we were sceptical about how good a listener he'd be. Usually singing his heart out and running around like a fruit loop, perhaps he lacked the reliability we were after. We were wrong. Leaping at the end of the rope in pure exuberance to get going and with the independence needed to have the team give chase, we started Enrique off on an existing straight line of sled tracks heading east. So far, so good. He occasionally looked around at us for reassurance but his ears were often rotated back towards us to listen. Thankfully he halted without too much of a fuss as we called "aeee!"

The true reckoning would be without tracks or another sled to follow and so we walked him out to the south. On the horizon were some huge icebergs, some bumpy ice in the nearer ground, glacier-strewn land in the distance and Herbert Island to the half-right. Anders stood out front with the whip and 'released' the team from a walk instead of from a standing start. He missed his target of leaping onto the front of the flatbed, ahead of where I was slumped, and had to make a desperate jump for the standing spot at the rear. He was nearly left behind altogether. We went straight for a while, but it was a real test of Enrique's training as a pup and young sled dog. We didn't know if he was practised in using landmarks as reference points, receptive to 'left' and 'right' commands, or able to resist distractions. Soon, he deviated right a bit, but a call 'haruu!' brought him straight for a while. It was a bit hit and miss; he was no natural lead dog for sure. Anders and I discussed that evening that Enrique would be our default lead dog, and we'd bring out Crazy if Enrique was playing up, needed a rest or if there were easy tracks to follow.

Anastasia's forced homeward journey loomed nearer. There had been a hiatus of flights over Christmas, down from the already infrequent weekly services, operated with subsidy, by Air Greenland. We'd managed to squeeze her on after a cancellation, and sorted out the logistics back home via the Greenlandic hubs and Denmark.

Finn and Hans accompanied us to the airport to see her off, as a couple of Danes on the incoming aircraft were staying with Hans for a week. The Danes were on a government contract, and Hans relied on their patronage and those like them at the guesthouse in the darker months of the year.

Losing a quarter of our team, and an important one at that, was tough. She brought unique skills to the mix and would be tough to replace. There had been tense moments, often generated by an introverted nature that otherwise gave Anastasia her strong character, which undeniably impacted communication. She loved the dogs in particular, and so our final words before she headed out the airstrip-building door and across the snow to the aircraft steps were to reassure they'd be fine and raring to go on her return. With that, we were a trio, and would be so for quite some time. In fact, the sun would be high in the sky before we scheduled her return to optimise those remaining days from the original visa-allotted ninety.

We felt ready for longer dog sled trips, beyond the 'safe' ten-mile radius from Qaanaaq we'd relied as we trained ourselves from newcomers to half-competent drivers. Each day we solved problems, rid ourselves of bad practices and found new and better ones. Some we picked up naturally and others by watching locals. From finding safe but accessible spots for our rifles to working out the detangle technique for the mucky, tightly braided dog traces, we were improving.

We had scavenged a couple of pads of foam from an old truck on the rubbish tip and having cleaned and snow-proofed it with tarpaulin, strapped them to the fore-section, the spot chosen by the Polar Eskimos for their seat. Some dog drivers sit at the back, some stand on the rear; mostly dictated by the area of the Arctic they inhabit. In Avanerriaq, passengers and family could sit, legs forward, further back, but the driver slumped casually at the front, whip dragging to the side, ready to flip forward. We had a habit of standing to get a better view and to help our fledging whip technique avoid snags. Some hunters had noticed and chuckled about it. We had spotted how advice was broadcast with total conviction, yet often contradicted directly with other guidance we'd heard just the previous day. Soon it became obvious we'd have to use our own judgement, perhaps learning once or twice the hard way from near-misses from fast moving sleds only just under control, and bruises from whips and pieces of wood and ice.

We set our sights on Siorapaluk, the northernmost native settlement on Earth. It made sense since we'd already visited Qeqertat on foot, and the settlement was the only inhabited one left without prolonged overland traverses to the south of Avanerriaq. It could just about be managed in a single push of around forty miles.

Mikael, like the other hunters, had been busy. Most had decided at Christmas whether they would concentrate on hunting, mostly just for seals in the midwinter, or fishing, and were underway the moment ice conditions allowed.

Stopping by our home one evening, he said we should come out and meet him the next day at his fishing hole. Intrigued and unwilling to turn down invitations to further our education, we shifted our Siorapaluk plans to the day after. He had sweetened the offer by not coming by empty handed; instead with a large frozen Greenland halibut in each hand. Generously, he told us these must be our dinner. They were in perfect condition; certainly not his rejects. It was odd to me as I considered that with the summonses we received almost daily, they seemed to often offer incentives, as if we had to be persuaded against our will. It was a surprising dynamic of the balance of power – nothing like the cold suspicion we could have faced. If only they knew that socialising – really integrating – was not a chore.

We took both teams of dogs with Anders and my team in the lead so that James, riding solo, could have an easier time setting out into the darkness. There was a gentle breeze from the east, which made me pull my neck gaiter up over my face. The wind chill was probably around minus forty.

We criss-crossed track after track, some parallel to our direction and others perpendicular. Enrique was getting confused easily and I needed to hop off the sled and correct him a few times. Twice, a couple of the dogs in the main team caught a scent towards the beach and Qaanaaq, presumably of fish, meat or other dogs and made a dart for it. The tangled lines and dogs caught around and under each other tested our patience but we persevered. As the spider's web of tracks in the snow dissipated, we ended up following a single set of routes that we hoped headed for the fishing spots. A couple of twinkles of light started to appear, just a mile or so away. Anders and I were able to think about best routes and even chat a little as the dogs ran without fidgeting or randomly veering off to the left or right, or even stopping of their own accord. So, this was what driving dogs should be like.

Obviously, Mikael would have his own dog team set out around his fishing location in a series of staking points. Perhaps he would only take seven or eight animals since it was only he and a ten-foot sled. We were about two miles offshore and no longer in front of Qaanaaq. The ambient light from town had faded and the stars were on full display, bathing the ice in a faint blue hue, instead of the orange of electric lights. To avoid running straight into his dogs or someone else's, hidden in the dark, I halted our progress a hundred yards short and walked the dogs in on the whip.

I recognised his sled on the left of three fishing huts and made for it. We only planned to stay for a few hours and so wouldn't set up a full stake-out system. Instead, we'd use an ice screw to secure the sled and avoid a runaway, and leave the dogs as they were to rest. If there was a fight, we would hear and be able to return and remonstrate.

The Polar Eskimos had devised a remarkable system for fishing in the years since they had access to basic wood and timber products. Instead of using a domed snowhouse, *illuliaq / igluigaq* in Inuktun, (what a westerner might term igloo), or a *tupeq* tarpaulin over a sled or other makeshift shelter, these multi-day fishing excursions demanded better accommodation. After all, they did not thrive off needless suffering; comfort and the ability to make oneself so is a sign of competence and good sense. Sat atop a large sled base and able to be drawn by dogs or behind a sled in tandem, each fishing spot had a small wooden hut. Perhaps only eight feet by six, they were a mobile home from home. In front were holes in the ice and fish laid out in neat rows.

Mikael was nowhere to be seen, but we could see a warm glow around the shape of a door to his hut. Sensing our arrival and as we had finished securing the teams, he opened the door. A jet of condensation poured out, as you'd expect from a deep-freezer opened in a warm room. He quickly closed it and walked over, a wide smile across his face. We greeted his dogs as we passed them in ones and twos, a group we'd not met before. Some couldn't care less and lay there aloofly whilst others, the younger ones we guessed, came up and greeted.

In the manner we'd grown used to, we made our first greeting in a mix-mash of English, local words and Danish. Mikael often practised his English, usually slipping into Inuktun or Danish for harder phrases, the gist of which we usually grasped, and then spent periods speaking in fast, fluent Danish with Anders.

From a self-built wooden reel set four feet high on a creaking frame, a line ran under tension straight into a hole in the ice. I shone my headtorch to see a square-shaped hole, *agluaq*, around six feet square, and a pile of snow and ice to the side that had been excavated. A wooden pole with a sharp metal spike on the end lay beside it. In just minutes, the surface of the dark, foreboding water would start to freeze over if not re-broken and churned up by the spike or a shovel.

It was possible to see the true depth of the ice, around two or three feet thick, and the thin snow-pack on top. This, remarkably, is easily strong enough to land a small aircraft on.

Since the line was down and he was waiting for two or three hours for the magic to happen under the ice, Mikael ushered us inside. I remained outside for a minute or two to capture the surreal scene on my camera with a long exposure, so as not to ruin the ambiance with flash. The image of the little wooden hut on runners against the icy wilderness and star-studded sky was almost cartoon-like.

Joining the others inside, I yanked the door open, which was stiff with accumulated ice around the edge. I quickly jumped in and closed it, so as to minimise the heat lost.

They were sat in a line on a low platform, an *igleq*, not unlike those used in the *iglu* homes of pre-modern day Inuit, whether a stone and peat winter house or a hide-skinned shelter in summer camps. This kept the cold air separate and near the floor, in the *qaaneq* area (the namesake of Qaanaaq itself), away from people and possessions. A space was kept free for me and I sat, having removed down jacket, hat and gloves. James gestured to be careful and pointed behind me. I almost jumped; a few inches behind me there laid a man, sleeping. He was gently snoring and was apparently undisturbed by our arrival. He was covered by a grubby blanket but otherwise fully clothed. Mikael was sharing the hut with him and they were alternating fishing duties.

Mikael explained how the lines needed to be down for hours to get enough fish, and the baiting and sorting of fish took time, so they worked through both day and night, since there was no objective difference between the two. This meant sleeping when the opportunity arose. If the going was good though, a three or four-day slog of constant shift work could bring in literally hundreds of fish – more than two sled loads. This, minus the haul he would keep for his family, could then be given to the Royal Greenland fishery building in Qaanaaq to be basically processed and stored for export or local sale.

Rather alarmingly though and raising the question of how broader issues impact the psyche of a Greenlander concerned mainly with day-to-day practicalities and traditional beliefs, he told us how he thought fish populations react. "The more we fish, the more will come," he said confidently. Certainly, on a micro-scale, if you remove some fish and their food therefore flourishes, more will indeed fill that void in the short term. As any environmental biologist will tell you though, that logic if scaled up can cause catastrophic population collapse.

The ice, from Qaanaaq to Qeqertat and to the far reaches of the vast fjord, is the region's most reliable in winter and spring due to the enclosed nature of the geography and lack of warm upwelling of water that can cause polynyas (ice free areas of sea year-round). Chatting to Mikael about fishing was fascinating. He was so keen to explain, to tell, to boast the skill that both he and the older hunters had. He retained that youthful need to show off that others have observed in Inuit people, but that never came across as obnoxious or confrontational.

Mikael tended to wear a combination of modern, USA-inspired clothing and traditional garb. It hadn't escaped my notice that the younger the Greenlander, the more fashionable and imported their clothing tended to be. Was this because they hadn't yet chalked up enough significant hunting successes to outfit them in skins and furs, a fashion decision, or a sign of the times steering away from tradition? It wasn't clear.

The hut, it turned out belonging instead to our sleeping host, was well stocked. In the corner were a couple of large, twenty-pound petroleum burners. Confusingly, petroleum is the term used not for what the British would put in their unleaded cars, but for the simpler fuel we call naphtha or white gas (which is liquid, not gas). One was on heating duty and on full blast – the metal cone and element on the top glowing a cherry red. The other had an old-fashioned accessorised tungsten filament cap atop the burner. Once up to temperature, they produce the most dazzling and constant white light, at least enough to compete with a one hundred watt household bulb. Sorcery!

As we arrived, he was busy preparing a flask of coffee, a staple for the people of Avanerriaq since the very first trading began in the eighteenth century. He also had a shop-bought cake that he was eager to share. The heat was almost oppressive, with the door sealed shut and only a small vent in the roof to allow condensation out. Any incomplete combustion of stove fuel and a layer of dangerous gases would collect near the floor, unable to escape.

We had our long-sleeved merino wool t-shirts – standard nowadays in the outdoor industry due to their breathable comfort, and ability to resist taking on odour. Mikael, partly covering an arm of tattoos he'd inked himself, had on a checked, cotton, collared button-up shirt. It wasn't quite thick enough to be true 'lumberjack', but the pattern was similar. Rasmus also wore them regularly, and others too. It puzzled me. Cotton, whilst breathable, holds moisture and dries slowly. It can also chafe skin badly under even light exercise. It was not traditional wear for sure, presumably not being imported until decades into trading agreements. Surely if, as a Greenlander, you're going to forgo truly traditional garments for ones developed elsewhere, you'd choose modern wool weaves, down insulated jackets (we'd seen none so far) and even breathable synthetics. Yet, cotton it was. I asked why.

"It is warm! It is better than other clothes like yours!" he joked mischievously. But why the awkward collared button-up? Wouldn't this catch on other clothes and not sit as neatly as a t-shirt? I never quite worked it out; regardless of how many times I enquired over the months. The moisture and sweat issue might perhaps be of a lesser concern for

Inuit as they, with centuries of using clothes that can't release sweat and ice, routinely never ran or overexerted for that very reason. Trapped sweat turns to ice. Ice kills.

It was time to tend to the fishing. Our spell in the comfortable but by now sweltering hut was over, surreally so considering our precarious position sat a mile offshore in the Arctic winter.

Outside and only using the minimum of artificial light so as to let our eyes become accustomed to the faintest natural glow, we set to helping out under close supervision. If we made a mistake, at best hours of work could be wasted, or at worst precious equipment, lines, and hooks lost. James broke the ice on top of the surface, which was half an inch thick. Then, we took turns at turning the reel. Entirely self-made and based around an old cable spindle, a bent metal handle controlled the turning of the reel set four feet off the ground on a rickety wooden frame. Nothing was particularly circular, so it turned with an asymmetric and scratchy unease.

There was a single line, which was under enormous tension, and its length became evident before long. Depending on the number of hooks, an Inuit fishing line of this style could be between three hundred and a thousand yards long. Tangles or knots could be a disaster, so the spooling had to be expert. I had been on my shift for ten minutes and nothing had yet appeared from the slushy black water, not even a hook. They did not want to fish directly underneath ice that has sled, dogs and activity on. Vibrations can scare away the fish. Instead, they took account of the current and dug the holes far away from the target waters.

Finally, a hook appeared with bait still attached. Then another. Then another. The next was empty altogether. Each time, Mikael grabbed the hook with a gloved hand, and sat the hook into one of hundreds of cuts made into the top of a cardboard box – the key to keeping all in order.

Finally, from the gloom of the pitch-black water and with glinting reflections from our LED headtorches, a small flatfish appeared on a hook. A Greenland halibut. We all cheered, but Mikael nonchalantly tossed it over the snow pile and onto a raggedy mixture of small fish and rays – the bycatch pile. This would be for the dogs, nothing wasted. It flipped and flopped around for a second or two, then accepted its fate as the rest did before it.

We kept spooling and fish emerged on perhaps a fifth of the hooks. The catch was good – over thirty fish. About twenty were big enough to be gutted by Mikael's filleting knife whilst still 'warm', and then laid out in neat rows of ten, well away from dogs. Finally, once all the notches on the cardboard box, marked with 'tinned vegetables' on the side and clearly borrowed from the store, had a hook neatly placed in them, the final act had to come. Anders' spinning of the handle slowed as resistance increased and it then jammed. Mikael beckoned to James for help and they knelt down to grab what was stuck in the entrance to the fishing hole – a large aluminium plate, where the mammoth fishing line finally terminated. Without it, the line would never draw out straight underwater and could tangle on itself and possibly other lines; uncontrollable and hopeless.

harvartooq – there is a current.

The plate relied on the flow of water. It was difficult to visualise whilst standing atop the ice. It was so still, so calm and so cold. However, just a yard or two below our feet was a strong current, driven by the complex Arctic waters and the upwelling facilitated by unusually extreme local depths. The plate's surface area would catch the current and be quickly dragged under the ice to where the expert Polar Eskimo in charge wanted it to end up; hopefully in the deep teeming with large, mature fish. The power of the water was frightening. To fall in through inexperience or a momentary lapse of concentration would guarantee a lonely and unpleasant death. It is, along with polar bears, storms and crevasses, the greatest fear of the polar traveller, whether native or visitor.

The same spring as I first drafted this book, a Dutch friend of mine was lost under thin ice, along with his sledging partner. They were Marc Cornelissen (46) and Philip de Roo (30), the latter with whom I had started planning a polar project. In the Arctic Archipelago of Canada's Nunavut territory, they were investigating thin ice just a few hundred miles from where I'd been with my own team. No-one will ever know the full truth and only Marc's body was recovered, along with their alarm-dog who survived, but one appeared to have fallen through, the other activating the emergency beacon before himself falling in. Once in the water, unless very lucky, the currents take over and the chance of survival is minimal. It was a sobering reminder of the indifferent finality the Arctic can show to even the most experienced.

Meanwhile, the fishing process was once again repeated; a bucket of pieces of bait fish was fetched from the warmth of the hut and with the metal plate once again released to the fate of the current, each baited hook was dropped into the water. Really, it was a one-person job, and Mikael sped up the process by taking over. He seemed to appreciate the company though as we chatted in our cold, surreal locale.

Hours later, we returned via our outward route to Qaanaaq. Mikael planned to stay for another day or so, and we might pass him and the other fishermen as we set off to Siorapaluk.

Some of the evening had been spent studying Mikael's sled layout and adjusting our own. You might be forgiven for being confused as to why storage might be an issue on a dog sled that measures a full five yards from front to back and over a yard wide. Besides, surely they also have no limit to how high you can pile goods.

In a typical Kevlar sledge I might myself pull behind me, all my worldly goods from technology to fuel and food is minimised in both weight and volume. All must squeeze into a cylinder of less than two yards long by perhaps two feet wide. A dog sled is like a large transit van in comparison, surely?

The dogs are the ultimate limiting factor. As long as you're not going to aspire to excessive distances like sixty miles per day or high speeds, above ten miles per hour, the rule of thumb is to allow roughly a hundred pounds of freight per dog. This must, of course, include the weight of drivers, should they choose to ride and not ski, run or push. It's testament to the phenomenal stamina, focus and toughness of the dogs that they can haul their own body weight or more for hours on end. Many humans would balk at carrying fifty per cent of their weight on their backs, with the most demanding military courses expecting up to a hundred per cent, but at a slow yomp, not a run. Hauling a sled, more comparable, I have hauled from seventy to nearly seven-hundred pounds (thirty-five per cent to three hundred and fifty per cent of my bodyweight) but at the upper end would only achieve a quarter or less of the distance a dog might.

We had also watched how other local Polar Eskimos laid out their own sleds. A single hunter on a small sled would tend to, remembering that Inuit of this region don't tend to stand on the back, layer his flat belongings and if lucky, his catch, under a tarp and then sit on top with a caribou skin for comfort. A small wooden crate would sit in front of the stanchions, containing a lamp and fuel canister. Occasionally, he would store a flask of coffee there too. This meant though, importantly, a bow-end laying position for the drivers. He would lay either way around, or even sit upright with legs hanging off the side, if his stature was small enough to avoid dragging boots in the snow.

Transporting a large load or his family wouldn't alter this greatly. The box remained at the rear, with his wife, children or parents sat on insulating skins just ahead, and the driver taking control at the front and his whip casually dragging to the side, free from snags.

We had begun to get out of the habit of standing as our confidence improved; whip technique became passable half of the time, and we took on bumpier surfaces. The latter, if we were standing, could easily throw us off balance. This didn't stop us channelling our inner-Machiavelli though by catching each other off-guard – using a shove to send one of us 'overboard' and tumbling in a ball into the snow.

I remember one particularly pitch-black training session, some miles offshore from Qaanaaq and with its twinkling lights barely visible. I stood up to look back towards Herbert Island to re-orientate myself. James was on the back of the sled, sometimes hopping off to run, push and warm up. Anders was next to me. Before I knew it, I felt a tap on my side; enough to send me over the edge and onto my shoulder. The force of hitting the snowy ice from a sled moving at six miles per hour led to a spectacular tumble of two or three full somersaults before coming to a stop, unharmed. Both laughing their heads off and encouraging the dogs to pick up speed with calls of 'hak!', the sled rapidly disappeared. Neither had their headtorches on, practising travel using ambient light, and so I squinted as I began to run, giving chase. There's no need to overstate the risk, but being left behind even temporarily without any equipment or rifle did motivate my pursuit. Deciding the joke was over, James and Anders called a halt and filmed my panting, half-scowling and half-laughing arrival. They knew however that what goes around, comes around. No-one was truly safe from practical jokes, from each other or Inuit.

To complete our sled outfitting, we fixed a canvas sled bag to the front end, with sleeping bags and skis strapped on top, and we ourselves occupied the second quarter. Behind us, we designated the next quarter to robust cardboard boxes (to keep items upright and safe), a plastic barrel with other supplies and dog food at the bottom, safe from canine raiders.

All of this could be secured against wind, snow and accidental losses by a tarpaulin, and then tightly lashed down with rope. Of course our 'training weights'; the shipping pallets, were shed. The final sections of both sleds were left for our home-built boxes. Given that we needed more space for fragile and easily lost equipment, like mitts and our rifles, to be stowed safely, we'd built larger boxes than the locals and added lids too.

These additions, along with the huge chain lengths neatly spooled so we could stake the dogs anywhere, completed our steeds. It amused me that just weeks before, I was considering the relative weights of types of edible oils and agonising over the use of titanium over aluminium. Now, we had a large hand axe, nails and brackets for impromptu repairs and even a spare wooden plank aboard. A different game.

Pinky and The Brain

CHAPTER 9: Enigma of Siorapaluk

OUR FISHING ESCAPADE was complete and we refocussed on the apparent indecision amongst the hunters about Siorapaluk. The second settlement to Qaanaaq in terms of population (albeit changeable and decreasing), it sat on the shores of a fjord two headlands along to the west and is the northernmost survivor after the retreat of the Polar Eskimos over past centuries.

Although before Christmas there was a route from village to village, as proven by the arrival of our Siorapaluk dogs, conditions had been changing daily. Historically, the majority of the fjord right out to Herbert Island and islands beyond, and to the west almost to the Smith Sound, was well iced-up over winter and spring. Dramatically, this has reduced to such an extent that recently even Siorapaluk in midwinter has become touch and go. Headlands often present thin ice, *hikuaq*, just offshore. Lots of fjords mean lots of headlands.

The small population of Qaanaaq and its municipality, especially considering the even smaller band of below two hundred Polar Eskimos it grew from at the time of outside contact, does imply a high level of inter-relatedness. Having villages stranded by poor ice, or rough seas in midsummer, can split families apart and cause a plethora of other supply problems. Besides this, hunting territories are decimated in size.

The only sure solution for finding what lies ahead in the darkness is carefully scouting ahead with a small dog team and tiptoeing along frozen beach and ice foot sections where necessary, but there is a modern contribution. (An ice foot, known locally as *qainngoq*, is distinct from a beach in that it is the narrow remnant of sea ice that clings to a shoreline when the rest has broken up and dispersed.) The Danish Meteorological Institute ran a feed of infrared images available from the various satellites orbiting the Earth. Those in Qaanaaq with internet access could see these directly, but for the majority, a printout was pinned to the outside of the village store. Able to 'see in the dark' using invisible wavelengths, somewhat blurry grey images could highlight, to a trained eye, where the ice was thick, thin or absent altogether.

The previous week was hopeless and dejected rumours around town told of their imprisonment in an ever-reducing zone of ice. Sea ice was their world and that of the dogs. All around them otherwise were mountains, cliffs, crevassed glaciers and only small expanses of navigable hills. Broken or, even more tantalising, thin or reforming ice was like all roads being suddenly closed in a bustling modernised country. Things grind to a halt. Waiting and resting can become torture. Ultimately, it could spell the end of a way of life.

We saw Peter the next day. We'd picked up on the custom that home visits could be random, self-invited and at more or less any time of day – we had received guests at seven in the morning and near midnight – so we opened the door and shouted "allo!"

Else, Peter's girlfriend, and her two children lived in the house; one of the more modern prefabs in Qaanaaq. Else had come up north from the West Coast years back and had one of the handful of municipality roles at the town building. Her English was better than she let on, but she could be bashful.

Peter, we guessed, had moved in and left a more basic home nearby, apart from a tiny one he still kept in Qeqertat.

Already back from school, normally only in session through the mornings (and from many accounts, paid lip service to in duration and diligence), both young son and daughter were home, tucking into a thin stew. I'd seen similar before – a stock-based mixture of diced vegetables from the annual sea freight import, some noodles and meaty chunks of fish and seal. Tasty, economical and nutritious, it was a common staple amongst other indulgent Danish-inspired dishes. The children concluded their meal with sweets.

The over-consumption of imported confectionary and unhealthy food in general is now endemic across the Arctic. Limited healthcare, especially dental, hands-off parenting and the ease of importing sugary goods that don't expire, have conspired to create a real problem. This is new. Traditional diets saw to mouths full of healthy teeth in the 1940s. Within a decade of then, many Polar Eskimos were toothless. In addition, for right or for wrong, the southern obsession with a skinny body image had not permeated in Qaanaaq – perhaps not obesity, but carriage of extra weight held no shame. Rather, the historic association between a round stomach and success as a hunter and provider for family, proudly termed *assak*, still lives on to some extent. Of course, the ingrained cultural habit of a eating excessively well whilst the going was good is now out-dated. In real terms, the safety buffer of air travel and centralised government now mitigates genuine risk of starvation. Peoples' belongings now far exceed the capacity of their dog sled, unlike just two generations ago. The mindset though and all the societal connotations are hard to shake off.

We were treated to a large pot of tea, a huge bowl of sugar and some freshly baked buns. A staccato hour or so of chatting amongst ourselves passed. It seemed the norm; again the Western need for endless entertainment without a single silent minute was absent yet comfortable, and I noticed the enticing glow out of the window from the daily gains in twilight overpowered by the harsh lighting inside the home.

A half hour or so after we'd arrived, two young Polar Eskimo women let themselves in and quietly set themselves on a corner sofa to chat. Occasionally, one of them giggled and glanced over. I did not recognise one, but the other was Arnannguaq, a mother in her early twenties. Else, and thereafter everyone else, had teased me that she had a soft spot for me. We'd never spoken and her English was non-existent, not to mention a shyness, avoiding eye contact at all cost, that precluded anything approaching a conversation. My attempts to laugh it off were only met with partial success.

With a loud bang of the door, frosty air shot through the room. Peter was home. He came in displaying one of his mischievous smiles.

"ii," he said in cheerful, typically open mouth, half-laughed Inuktun. "Kammak!" Peter patted me on the shoulder and I returned the greeting. Peter and I were developing a running joke, quite why I'm not sure, for using this word, meaning 'friend', each time we met.

"Good day out?" James asked him.

"Mmm," Peter grinned. "Dogs. Food. Qimmeq." His English was limited mostly to individual words, without the sophistication of Navarana, Mikael or Else's. He tried hard though to add in local words too, and we began to learn via that rather inexact method.

He was dressed in the most traditional outdoor outfit I'd seen yet. So far, many hunters had a hotchpotch of perhaps seal boots or a fur jacket and then shop-bought overalls and woven gloves. For around town or an hour or so on the hill or ice, this was usually sufficient. For any more serious travel, out would come the full wardrobe of prized and handmade

133

garments. Peter had been out all day, moving his sea ice headquarters around, including large wooden crates of supplies, and tending to a pregnant female dog of his.

Peter was not a tall man and despite deceptively remarkable strength, something he took pleasure in proving with arm-wrestles, had a slight frame. His boots were *kamiks*, soft sealskin hand stitched with soft undersides, grass padding (originally collected in summer from the fertile spots beneath bird cliffs) and polar bear fur lining at the top to stop draughts. Polar Eskimos are known for their pride, and this is never more apparent than with their ease on the ice, their unique environment. Falling over is so, so rare that any gaffe by a friend, or especially a foreigner, is met with raucous laughter. Much of this is down to those skin soles. Superior to modern plastics or rubbers, they were the secret to sure-footedness. As a trade-off, they did wear out, needing a replacement to be stitched in usually by their wife.

Mercifully now redundant, a daily chore for Polar Eskimo women was to prepare skins for use as clothing. This involved hours of chewing to fully remove the flesh and fat, softening the hide and conditioning it for use in the toughest of outdoor conditions. Chewing could also restore frozen *kamiks* to their former glory. Many women by their mid-thirties would have teeth worn down to the gums. The magnetic charm of the younger Polar Eskimo women, that early settlers waxed lyrical about, would originally have by this age given way to a weariness and premature aging that their tough life forced upon them.

Peter's faded, blue, hand-stitched canvas *annoraaq* (from this word we derive anorak) with a fur ruff hood had kept the bitter cold at bay. It had a *kineq*, a large central pocket on the front for carrying valuables – amusingly including his Samsung smartphone, which he set down on the table, warming it first to lessen condensation. Looking closer, I saw the inexact stitching which held it together; strong, thick cord and large loops, totally unlike the regular machine-patterns we're so used to.

The main event though was without doubt Peter's polar bear trousers. The hallmark of a successful Polar Eskimo hunter, these *nannut* were his pride and joy; historically, poor hunters would instead wear lesser dog skin trousers – also taking meat from the racks of grudging neighbours. They were thick, off-white and met the top of his sealskin *kamiks* perfectly. If they weren't a deadly serious and vital part of Inuit culture, they could raise a chuckle. I was impressed by the quality of their fit and how much time and effort it must have taken to remove, treat and prepare the fur and skin; only a single pair could be made from a whole bear pelt. Totally windproof and with hairs unable to absorb moisture and thereby ice up, they had stood the test of time. Only in the bitterest winters would they be supplemented with a fox skin draught excluder – nowadays replaced with fleece or wool.

By the time Peter had settled down for a coffee, he'd taken his glasses off. He squinted and blinked at them, wiping off the copious moisture that had clung to them as he'd come in from the cold to the warm; perhaps a fifty degree rise. He was also changed into casual trousers and a Reebok sweater.

It turned out that Peter had friends in Siorapaluk and wanted to go too. The bad ice was a community-wide issue and Peter could only offer shrugs. He did say he'd try the journey and would report back. When, we had no idea.

I asked for views as we walked back along the snow and rock-strewn rises and dips in between buildings and past the fuel silo that dominated the centre of Qaanaaq. We needed to stretch our legs, figuratively speaking, and become more ambitious. Before we'd know it, it would be February, and then spring, then the thaw, and then it would all be over.

The confidence of progress was brimming in our fledgling team. Anders, always one to take trials in his stride and nonchalantly pass over setbacks with a joke, seemed at ease both with the people we met and on the ice. James was a phenomenally fast learner, and found his enforced solo efforts with a whole team of unruly dogs to be rewarded – he was ahead of Anders and me in the training stakes and it couldn't be put down to 'having better dogs'. More than that though, we were having fun. Every day we learned, whether by experiences and mistakes with the dogs, or spending time with neighbours and new friends. Slowly but surely, bridges were being built. Suspicion and long-jaded views were absent and I hoped, realisation grew that not all of 'us' were the same.

It is futile to suggest that we were doing Qaanaaq and its people a great favour. We weren't. The truth is that we arrived there with the intention of launching north after a few days. Situations had changed though, and so had we. A single-minded focus on an arbitrary goal, although important in the wider scope of my career, was worthless here and I was uncovering value elsewhere. We exacted no drain. We were funnelling our meagre funds directly into the local community and had a platform, thereafter through our lives back in Europe, to share our experiences. If instilled with knowledge and a purpose, a subset could surely exact influence for the betterment of the Polar Eskimo future and self-determination.

It was decided – we'd set out for Siorapaluk alone. If we came across an impasse, we'd turn around or find a new way – simple as that.

To the west, the beach followed all the way along to the local rubbish dump and further yet to the airstrip. Beyond, tracks led, snaking as they followed the shoreline, to the dilapidated shelter we'd hauled to on the test day back in early December. They went further though, so we had a choice. Perhaps they'd peter out as they reached storage crates or seal hunting cracks in the sea ice offshore, perpendicular to the beach. Or, they could end up running all the way to the first, sharp headland. Finn had regaled us with horror stories of that particular landmark. He told of a tiny ice foot, the slither of ice joined directly to land, vertical and unstable cliffs, and thin or absent ice just a few feet from the apex. These ice feet are no haven, and have spontaneously collapsed under the feet of dog teams. He said that he'd had to shuffle around the corner, arms up on the rock to steady him and not fall backwards off the edge. In the dark and with sledges, it sounded dangerous. With four-foot-wide dog sleds and a team of dogs who aren't known for their sense of self-preservation and restraint, it appeared suicidal.

The other option was to head out to sea and, rather like our straight-line ski to Qeqertat, aim to sled amongst the icebergs and offshore sea ice, 'missing' the headland to our right. There were some tracks that way too, but they could end up anywhere. We needed to take responsibility for route finding and not be lazy. It would be a very different prospect to Qeqertat though. Heading away from the fast ice of the fjord and out towards the ice edge, we'd encounter pressure ice, headlands, thin ice, shingle fields on shorelines and even open water. It could take five hours, being six or so miles nearer as the crow flies than Qeqertat, or three days if we had to tackle obstacles or divert. We could choose to camp, or save time if we happened across a hunting shelter. Of course, the darkness would cloak what was approaching and make everything ten times more treacherous.

After an early breakfast we loaded up the sleds, now becoming slicker – after all, the faster we strapped it all down, safe from tumbling off and hitched the dogs on, the less chance they'd have to fight, tangle up, and pee on our things.

The stars were out in force and the three-quarter moon emerged from the hills to the north. I checked the rifle, making sure that the magazine was seated correctly, there was no snow in the action or muzzle, and stowed it easily to hand in our rear box. "Not today please, *nanoq* (polar bear)."

A hunter and his son passed by in the distance – in the dark of course, without lamps. They'd been shooting along towards the twinkling lights of Qaanaaq for the past couple of hours. Where they'd been we didn't know, but we raised arms in greeting. A gentle breeze had appeared from the direction we were headed. At around -25°C in Qaanaaq, where fractionally warmer air will tend to pool, and -30°C out on the ice, the mellowest wind makes all the difference. In still air, it takes a temperature of below -30°C or -35°C to compel a person to cover their face. Mitts, or excellent gloves if using hands for dextrous tasks, and insulated socks and boots, are de rigour from only modest sub-zero temperatures. However, even at minus twenty or fifteen below, a breeze can chill to the bone and put noses, cheeks and ears at risk of frost damage. A balaclava or extendable neck gaiter, allowing breath to escape and not trap inside clothing, becomes an awkward necessity. At -40°C or below, all bets are off – the air feels as though it burns your lungs even in motionless air. With wind, it can become a living nightmare.

"Hak!" I called as we set off ahead of James. Enrique leapt into action and as Anders draped himself across the padded front of the sled, I jogged alongside before hopping onto the rear standing planks. A slit, cut into the first six inches of the whip leather, allowed me to hook it over the 'handle' to one side and let the full length run freely to the rear as we creaked into motion.

On a map the Piulerruup Nunaa peninsula, on which Qaanaaq sits on the central south coast, appears as a wide rhomboid in shape. In the centre, a small icecap atop the rocky hills dominates, from which glaciers flow. To the east of the village are high cliffs (Peary's 'Red Cliffs'), a narrow fjord to the north towards the inland ice (Prudhoe Land is nominally given to that icecap region, even though just an offshoot of the mammoth Greenland ice sheet), and then east into the vast fjord which finds Qeqertat near the far end, before widening into a glacier outlet system. To the west of Piulerruup Nunaa are two narrow fjords pointing to the north, past the notorious headland. The first is the MacCormick Fjord and the second, the Robertson.

Siorapaluk is sat on the far shore, halfway along the Robertson Fjord. With the mental image of our route in mind, in case we needed to make rapid decisions, unable to refer to map or GPS at leisure, I tried to reply on my imagination to complete the layout. After a couple of hours, the lights of Qaanaaq to the rear had faded and we were once again immersed in this deep, dark world of ice. Icebergs passed to left and right, but the surface was ok. The snow was thin and compacted, but enough for the dogs to eat as they ran. In between frantic jogging sessions to warm up, Anders and I had time to chat. In the gloom, the stars allowed us to make out the outlines of the hills and high glaciers to the north. The Qaanaaq Glacier itself came and went, tiny in comparison to most.

The ice, flat here and mashed up in isolated but significant pockets there, was bathed in an ethereal blueness. There was no need for artificial light as our eyes had become accustomed to the dimness of winter. It felt special. Off we went at last. We were doing it ourselves – with the advice of the Polar Eskimo people forefront in our minds – but without handholding. It was clumsy, slow and far from neat, but with each excursion, improved.

I became uneasy as time progressed. Nothing seemed to have changed with the surface. The breeze grew steadily, and I found myself periodically rewarming my nose with finger and thumb in its mitt. A rumour of an overland path through the lower hills, cutting off the whole headland section altogether and appearing mid-way down the MacCormick, existed but it looked steep and forbidding. Rocks routinely poked out of the snowpack and would cause havoc with a dog sled, especially a large, heavy one.

When would the ice thin? When would the pressure ice appear? Would we get warning? Would the dogs drop into deep, freezing water? Were the tracks we kept finding and losing created weeks back, and leading us straight towards a non-existent route?

As leader, and having route-found dozens of times before on all manner of ice routes, I knew it was an inexact science and ultimately my responsibility. Dogs on coastal headlands in the dark though, were new to me. I didn't want hindsight to show that we needed to redirect up onto the ice foot, now, well in advance, to find a way around the rock and back onto reliable sea ice.

Another hour passed, and we stopped for a break and dog detangle, just as the shadow of the cliff came to an abrupt end. The headland. The tracks were faint, and weaved around as we picked them out ahead. The ice appeared thick and safe.

James was all iced up, from neck to forehead. Wearing his 'gorilla' balaclava, the extreme cold had frozen the moist air that he exhaled and encrusted a white covering to everything apart from his hood, and the gaps for his mouth and eyes. I had just been using my neck gaiter sporadically, so found it easier to speak, and Anders removed his own facemask to reveal strands of long blonde hair escaping his beanie hat and an amusingly unkempt mid-length beard . In seconds, it had frozen up too. Besides all this, we were comfortable. Superficial frosting doesn't affect body temperature and is part and parcel of polar travel. That was not to last.

The temperatures began to tumble, and settled at the coldest we'd experience in our time in the land of the Polar Eskimo – around -42°C and unusually low for midwinter. As spring breaks each year, lack of meaningful sun radiation and the end of winter triggers the characteristic air movement, so the mercury plummets to its minimum. Even at sea level, -35°C in a settlement during early spring is typical, and here on exposed expanses of open sea, it rarely warms above -40°C. Weeks later, the sun would return us to -20°C or -30°C like winter, before summer came. Oddly, we'd experienced a dip early.

issi – the cold.

We were all suffering to some extent with the chill that day. The lack of concern I often, when man-hauling, show to low temperatures is vindicated by the fact physical exertion generates heat; usually too much of it that needed venting. Entirely counter to that, dog sledding on flat sections where we did not need to help the dogs by leading them or pushing from behind, or using bodyweight to skip the sled left and right around ice blocks, was not energetic. My feet and hands were toughest to keep warm. Your core warmth, as long as you're dry, wind-proofed and well fed, is straightforward to maintain. Your face has phenomenal natural blood flow, and needs just a thin wind-proof barrier like a buff or balaclava to create a microclimate of warm air, and thereby comfortable skin. Feet and hands are a different matter. They are far from the heart and lack the bulk of body mass around them that reserves and retains heat. Blood flow is vital if you're going to keep sensation to the tips of your fingers and toes, and once it's lost, it's hard to regain it in extreme conditions. Cold injury, frostbite and even necrosis and septicaemia can follow with alarming rapidity.

We all wind-milled our arms around to use centripetal force, coercing blood into fingers. We stood up occasionally, notwithstanding it being a bad habit, to let gravity do the same for our feet. Banging them together gently, as we'd seen Polar Eskimos do, or going for a quick jog could also help. Unlike faces, even with thick layers of carefully vapour-barriered insulating gloves and boots, it was a tough fight. The pain of sensation returning to a rewarmed extremity is excruciating.

Spirits were nonetheless high and we were praising our dogs, like proud parents of children who'd remembered their lines at the school nativity play. We agreed to push on and not commit to the ice foot. It seemed ok, there'd been no recent bad weather, and so perhaps the ice had recovered. We had to keep our eyes peeled though, and use torchlight regularly to scout ahead. Closing one eye whilst torches were on helped avoid total loss of accrued night vision.

Eventually, we bumped, swooshed and creaked our way past where the headland was. There was a distinct line of demarcation as we progressed from older, thicker ice onto a newer, coarser surface. This was where the breakup over past weeks had been. New ice forms fast and thickens impressively if the conditions are right – calm, super-cold and untroubled by currents or swells. Not believing our luck, we waved back to James, yelled a holler of success, or relief, and went back to scanning ahead for signs of danger. Pride comes before a fall – and a fall for us would be cold, wet and fatal.

As Anders took command of the team, coaxing them back on track when they strayed or got confused, I took a rest at the back. I hopped around to face backwards, still stood one boot on each standing plank and steadied myself by resting hands on stanchions and my lower back on the crossbar.

Behind me was James' team. About fifty yards behind, it was a rare chance to watch them work from the front. With ten gazes fixed

140

unflinchingly ahead at me, they ran with poise and confidence. They were getting stronger; the consequence of plenty of good food, training and adequate rest away from antagonistic dogs. It was a welcome difference from our normal view, a panorama of the rear ends of a whole team of pack animals, tails raised and with regular olfactory accompaniment. Sled dog flatulence is like no other.

The dogs have no such aversion or squeamishness to such bodily functions. In fact, they saw it frequently as an opportunity. We regularly caught OJ or Scar happily gnawing away on a frozen log of excrement. Invoking our disgust and amusement in equal measure, whilst running one day, Enrique whilst out front decided to void himself on the move. The loose stream that decorated the pristine snow was instantly shovelled up by Thor as he ran behind. Extraordinary.

Each animal had such an overwhelmingly strong personality, even those markedly submissive compared to others, that we could tell them by body language in the shadows of the darkness, or by their barks, howls and wails. Houdini had been the biggest transformation. Still so young and clearly not well socialised before we bought him, he'd only run with a team three times. He showed potential for growing into a truly enormous, powerful dog, but was apart from being one half of the escape duo with Lyka, very arrogant. With delusions of dominance and superiority even with the much older and experienced dogs, he'd aggressively food guard and *qalinguuqtuq* (show teeth), even at Thor. Within just two or three days though with us, a couple of pretty conclusive 'educational exchanges' between Houdini, Thor and others and another pretty brutal scrap, he was in his place.

Houdini was never destined to be a submissive omega, like Garfunkel, or a pacifist like Dave, but his time for competing for king dog status was far off. Bringing him back down to Earth served to settle his team. We'd given up trying to stop him, Lyka and occasionally others from chewing lines or harnesses, so they were added to the handful who'd be secured with chain and collar overnight and then re-harnessed each and every time we ran them. Others, like the venerable hitmen, Jason and Leon, could be left in carefully sized, stitched and repaired harnesses and with just a rope to their stake point, with no drama or risk of escape.

A kind elderly hunter, one of the audience we had accrued in the sled-building days, had pulled us aside in hushed tones in the communal

141

workhouse as Rasmus and Tobias were discussing how to proceed with the sled runners. He thrust a small, black pouch into my hand with a smile.

I pulled on the thin black ribbon that bound the fabric pouch together and opened it. Inside was the definitive do-it-yourself arctic sewing kit. A large and simply designed yet robust thimble sat neatly aside various cords and needles - none of them as you'd expect to find in a haberdashery store. The cords were of wide gauge and some of traditional flattened narwhal sinew. A couple of needles were like sailmaker's, with huge eyelets and extended in length. Others were more fragile and must have been either bone or tusk of some sort. All were razor sharp and it became clear the collection was this man's treasured possession. It was one of the tools of the trade of a true dog driver and hunter that made a Polar Eskimo what he is.

"Take it. Use it for your dogs. Just hand it to me again sometime," he generously offered. Then, taking a length of cord from a pocket and picking up a section of spare blue webbing offcut we were practising on, he showed us some locking-stitches we might find useful. Gleefully showing us his expertise, the needle passed through two pieces of thick nylon as if it were thin cotton. We knew from experience that it needed quite some elbow grease. Watching him work, I wondered how many thousands of times he'd hand-stitched webbing into harnesses. As a child, he would have learned on other materials like tanned hide and canvas – a lifesaving skill in the North.

"Not a job for woman!" he suddenly laughed. "Man's job."

We all, Anastasia still of course with us then, nervously chuckled. The man meant nothing offensive by it. The elderly couples I'd met had a real sense of team about them; happy in their division of labour and proud of their own skills and those of their spouse – complementary, as they have grown over decades. He was from another generation and another culture where gender roles were decades from being evened out – and perhaps they never will be. I never managed to properly pronounce his name, he having not adopted a more contemporary one, let alone managed to spell it. But, his donation of the pouch was generous, and we reminded one other that it must always be cared for until the moment we returned it.

Midday's brief glow was fading. The glimpses of mountain shadows were disappearing back into the blackness and the tantalising openness of the fjord to our right had to be consigned back to imagination.

Enrique was starting to struggle, and so the reliable, if dawdling Comedy Dad took the lead, with his cohort just behind. Around six-hundred pounds of sled and supplies slid slowly behind. Four or five miles an hour, a slow jog, was our cruising speed, and we knew it was poor. We would never achieve the pace of a light racing 'single-seater' sled or that which a team of walrus meat-raised Thule monster dogs at the top of their game could. But, we dreamed of tangle-free, well, relatively anyhow, six or seven mile per hour journeys. It would make tentative ideas of a genuinely long dog sled trip feasible. We had a long way to go.

I expected a repeat of the worries and hazards of the first headland as we approached the second. Looking at maps, basic though they were, it looked more gentle and rounded. Instead of tight, aggressive contours indicating cliffs, I saw a gentle rise before more daunting hills. Before bringing out the little GPS unit and warming it in my pocket to double-check our position, I tried to estimate our distance back to the first headland, thereby guessing how soon the second would be upon us.

This though, wasn't necessary.

As soon as I'd called over to James and Anders that we should be upon it soon, a raised arm from both of them to confirm receipt of the message, a bump. Then another. Small blocks of broken ice atop the otherwise smooth frozen sea. A couple of rocks were lying around too, as if casually rolled down a slope from land.

An ominous, intimidating presence slowly grew to my right, and I could just make out the slightest contrast between the dark sky and something one shade darker underneath. It was land; a hill.

Nothing we could see ahead, using blasts of torchlight now to be sure, was of concern. Tracks from past sleds were faint, absent or obscured, but the ice was a bright white, an indication of thickness (in simple terms, greyness means danger).

Again, no thin ice, fractured zones or tortured pressure ice were to be seen. The route seemed good. I was looking forward to seeing if someone in Siorapaluk could, on our arrival, send news back that passage between the settlements was once again possible. However, an unexpected struggle was to rear its head; one more insidious than dramatic.

Snow cover is dependent, of course, on how much snowfall has occurred, but there's more to it than that. Snow doesn't stay put. On icecaps, it's formed by persistent and powerful unidirectional winds into bizarre, beautiful and sometimes demoralising sculptures and ridges called *sastrugi*. This can of course happen on sea ice too, but less frequently – wind is more multi-directional due to lack of gravity-driven wind systems and is less regular. In Avanerriaq, where as we've found snowfall is famously light, the wind that does materialise moves the snow around. It can be scooped off a flat area, leaving behind an icy, scoured surface of briny sea ice. This can be fast under sled runners, but tough on the pads of dog paws. The snow can 'catch' around landmarks like icebergs or large rocks. The eddies of wind cause spindrift and create quite a pile or dune behind – perfect for collecting fresh snow for melting over a stove. Finally, the larger-scale effect of winds and varying snowfall around hills, fjords and mountains means that air funnelled in one direction or another can leave snow in one fjord, and none in the next. We were about to feel this pain.

Slowing seemingly minute by minute, I could hear the soft swishing sound of the plastic meeting the ice and snow increase in volume. The swish became a laboured creak as the wood flexed and worked its way forward. The dogs changed their gait, even peeking back over their shoulders to see what was happening. Had we added another couple of hundred pounds to the sled, they must have thought?

We had entered a zone of deep snow. It was a little above minus forty, where friction is insufficient to allow glide. So, our one saving grace was that the snow was as resistance-free as possible. Timing was unfortunate, as the dogs had nothing concrete to fix their gaze on and 'run to'. This affected motivation and they had already come around twenty-five miles – not insignificant. Increasingly, our lead dogs were getting demoralised and stopping. Comedy in particular was making hundred-yard pushes, then halting without command and just staring at us. Having immediately started to help them ourselves, either with someone pushing from behind and a driver painting a spot of torch light ahead of the dogs as a target, we were at a crawl. I was getting bored of calling out 'hak' to the dogs. The word was losing its effect. It was going to be a real slog into Siorapaluk. It had better be worth it!

The land to the right seemed to go on forever. In a slight déjà vu from our long walk back to Qaanaaq in December, I was willing the headland to pass and the beckoning lights of civilisation to magically appear ahead.

Eventually, we were rewarded. Warmed up by the exercise of walking alongside or pushing the sled, suddenly in the space of a couple of seconds, presumably as an unknown rock in the shadows got out of the way, lights. Not many, just a handful, but it was all we needed.

The danger of the sea ice, and our uncertainty of what was ahead almost became side-lined in our minds. We were focussed purely on getting there. Of course, going by the stories from hunters and the latest charts we'd consulted, we knew the poor ice and edge of the annually expanding polynya was near. But, it was pathetic really. This was a simple village-to-village transit trip. It wasn't a world-first new route. Also, the goal wasn't even really that mandatory. We could camp if progress slowed to a stop. It just seemed like something we wanted to do. Stopping short in sight of the settlement because of a little snow seemed daft. Deep down though I felt inadequate. I knew I could do ski and hauling routes, no matter how bad the ice, and had done so for thousands of miles. This was different though – a totally different skill – and we were beginners learning the ropes. A fifteen-year-old hunter 'in training' could do this journey solo with ease.

kaussuaraa – pushes sled…

Nearly three hours later, ridiculous considering the mere final eight-mile stretch across the Robertson Fjord, I could start picking out details amongst the lights. One, the brightest, sat atop a metal pole and seemed to illuminate the beach and a sort of jetty. Then, the handful of little buildings, basic and more akin to those in Qeqertat than the 'metropolis' of Qaanaaq, started gaining detail. I could see a door, then windows. The light was dim, but orange and warm – totally at odds to the blueness of the natural darkness.

I can't recall what time it had become before the surface offered up a spider's web of sled tracks, pieces of wood, ropes and other detritus that signified human habitation. We'd reached Siorapaluk.

We assumed the sleepy village, only two or three times more populous than Qeqertat but with electricity and a few more facilities, would be closed down for the night and we'd camp on a spare patch of snowy ground or on the ice itself. James held the dogs, none of whom needed much encouragement to lay down. Before Anders and I had a second to cross the bumpy ice crack and hop up onto the raised snowy and gravelly beach, figures began emerging one by one. Tired and still trying to figure out what was what, I double-took as I heard the familiar call, "Kammak!"

Peter Duneq walked straight towards us at the head of a group of about five. Our welcoming party were all puffing away casually on cigarettes and were curious to find out what the unexpected excitement was all about. We'd not messaged ahead and were strangers to all, bar Peter.

With a slightly surprised yet half-impressed look on his face, presumably that we'd have the gumption to try the journey solo and to have made it, he gave us all a back-slap. I asked him about where it would be best to put the dogs. Expecting to receive a trademark shrug and vague response or even be kept well out of the way, somewhere awkward, instead we were enthusiastically pointed over to the beach. It was a prime spot, the perfect length to fix the chain, and there were anchors frozen into the ground to which we would affix the stakes. There would be no need for ice screws.

I don't think I've ever seen such looks of disapproval in my life, but our every move was watched with interest as we set the chain and started to offload the dogs from sled to their spots. It wasn't perhaps the process they used, and I was beginning to learn that there was often their way, and the wrong way. The Polar Eskimos have total conviction in their opinions – 'The [Polar] Eskimos can work such a spell that, they make you feel that they are always right…brilliant eyes staring into mine to convince me' as Malaurie noted. Amusingly though, this could vary wildly from hunter to hunter. It reminded me of the incredulous feeling I had when, in training years before, two military instructors showed me how to do something, both totally differently. Minutes apart, I was then balled out by each man as I haplessly followed the advice of the other. It helped hasten my decision to jump ship.

"Give them lots! They have run far," an unintroduced Polar Eskimo man told us, as I dragged forty-pounds of meat and fish from the sled. Happy to oblige, I made sure each animal had its fill, and the others, including our new acquaintances, kept the dominant dogs from stealing the food of the more timid ones. I was relieved to learn later that this endless game of keeping one dog back whilst feeding another even had a name, *mianerigai*. I was getting quite good at estimating what two pounds of food looked like. Rather like a skilled sommelier who can ensure that each glass has the correct amount of wine whilst emptying a bottle in a single pass, I beamed as our supply exhausted perfectly after feeding the final dog.

One of the older hunters surveyed the sleds down to the smallest detail and then walked along a few of the dogs. He gave a shy smile and nodded. Approval, perhaps.

He then shrugged at the ice screws hung on the rear of our sled. We knew they weren't traditional, or even the more efficient system. Having seen dogs staked on ice over many years, I knew very well that Greenlanders carved horseshoe-shaped loops under the hard ice with a sharp knife. Through this a thick rope or chain can be passed to form a super-strong anchor. Our skills did not extend to this, that early on at least, and our collection of ice screws made them simple and quick if placed properly. Still, as is often the case with modern developments that the Greenlanders saw little or no need for, they provided ammunition for teasing the curious newcomers.

There was never going to be any possibility of camping. I got the feeling that, perhaps not unlike how visitors are greeted in many frontiers around the world, it would be seen as a dishonour to allow a guest to sleep outside. Before we had a chance to get our bearings, having noted there were a few storage sheds along the beach and then homes dotted up the increasingly steep hill to quite a height, we were led across to a small, green disused home. Peter helped me load up some supplies for our evening – sleeping bags, food and more – onto a little old sled that was sitting around, and we pushed it up the hill to our doorstep.

Inside it was pitch black, and our torches lit the way through the freezing air almost like a sort of found-footage horror movie. Then, after some tinkering by a young teenage boy who'd joined us to see what the commotion was about, there was light. A couple of dangerous-looking bulbs hung from the ceiling connected to exposed wires, but they made it homely. Central heating was a non-starter, so after our new friends had left us to eat and sort our gear out, we closed a couple of doors to limit the airspace to a minimum – the kitchen area and a small main room – and set our three stoves up to pump out some heat. Fuel rationing was a non-issue, unnatural though it felt. We had tons of it back in Qaanaaq, sea freighted up the previous year, and could even buy more locally.

It was evening, and after a rapidly devoured freeze-dry meal along with some local treats we'd brought along, a second wind buoyed us. We would go and explore Siorapaluk a little before 'bed'.

In Siorapaluk we'd found almost an intermediate between Qaanaaq and Qeqertat. The homes were newer and larger than in Qeqertat, and shared the robust foundations of those Qaanaaq. It was tiny, and lacked any of the infrastructure those in power in Nuuk had afforded Qaanaaq, the municipal hub. Power was the main distinction though. Light makes the world of difference.

We rounded a corner of what we assumed was the communal building, housing the store, place for post and supplies to be sorted, and possibly a room for schooling the dozen or so children. It must be so difficult to plan and effectively educate children (as across Greenland, the young make up a large proportion of the demographic) who are all different ages and stages. You can't have a separate class and teacher for the five year old, the ten year old, and the fifteen year old. However, small local schools are vastly superior to centralised residential boarding schools, or even shipment to Copenhagen, piloted decades ago on European lines to promote colonial languages and values. Long since discontinued in Greenland (Qaanaaq's took in Siorapaluk's children), their legacy in Inuit and First Nations Canada is one of abuse – dismantling an entire culture.

A long, dark red cabin ran along the bottom of a rocky ridge, poking through the snow, and the lights were on inside. A man, one we had met with Peter on the beach and I believe whose name was Kunuk, stood with his two children in the doorway. We rarely saw names written down and they are often mumbled in introductions. Indeed, to use names at all in greeting is a modern habit, such was their historic spiritual value. Acknowledgement after some time apart used to follow the indirect "are you human?", to which the reply comes "yes, I am a son of a hunter."

Of course, Kunuk and family said that we should come inside, and the two young children ran away shyly as we stamped our way up the narrow wooden steps with our oversize polar boots on. Flexing our sore toes in bare socks, the warmth of the heated porch space slowly penetrated, where we thankfully piled our boots.

A large water tank sat to the right along the entry corridor and led into a single main room. It had the feel of a railway carriage. Windows ran along the whole southern aspect and must have had extraordinary views of the sea, and the infuriating headland, in the bright light of summer. I noticed a leaky-looking can of heating oil on the water tank and wondered how sensible that might be. I supposed we would find out, as we were hurriedly offered the only seats at the tripod table and a large pot of tea. We insisted that we couldn't take their seats, but the family, now totalling three children and also Kunuk's wife wouldn't take no for an answer. Two foam mattresses lay in the corner, presumably the 'overflow' bedroom as their brood had grown.

All around the room was evidence of hunting and a far more traditional taste in decoration and goods than the strange hybrid-feel of Qaanaaq's homes. Whale baleen hung on the wall. Fish had been prepared on the worktop and were being readied for drying. A small sealskin drum, called a *qilaut*, was perched on a small shelf – the latter very much a do-it-yourself effort of plywood and two rusty brackets with screws only halfway into the wall. Next to that, was what must have been a fifty-inch flat screen television. Keen to be polite, the children's mother had muted the cartoon the children had been enjoying, much to their consternation. Anders mischievously pointed out the obvious juxtaposition, but we'd heard complaints already from the elderly of Avanerriaq that they felt television had corrupted the youth into laziness and sealed the fate of traditional oral storytelling.

This time, even Anders' Danish fluency wasn't a trump card, and the language barrier ran deeper. Although exposed to Danes since the early twentieth century, there is no official requirement for people, especially those in the smaller outposts, to achieve Danish proficiency, especially if the need locally is limited.

Kunuk had a masterful plan to smooth the flow of communication: music. Taking the fragile-looking drum off the shelf, he picked up a short section of what appeared to be polished tusk ivory. In a basic sort of rhythm, he held the drum up and tapped the skin, which was perhaps ten inches across, with both ends of the ivory. It made a non-melodic tapping sound with only a hint of resonance. Then, startling me as I sipped from my cup of tea, the real performance began – a drum dance – *ingmertoq* (or *mumertoq* if performed by a shaman). Smiling and giggling, the whole family watched as Kunuk began to sing all of a sudden. It was loud, enthusiastic and to my uneducated ears, discordant. A round of applause rewarded his minute-long song, which had started to repeat cyclically. Now, it was our turn, whether we liked it or not. James chuckling coyly as the drum was thrust into his hands, and then Anders. Finally, I tried my own humble rendition, trying my best not to split or rip the paper-thin dried skin.

I placed the drum back, relieved more than anything else it remained in one piece, and as I did so noticed hung on the wall a parka with an *amaut* section. Not an extended hood as many believe, this woman's garment would have been used to carry her children as infants. It was designed so the baby or toddler's front was held securely against its mother's back and could be swung around for nursing. This one was traditional as a series of stitched skins, but many now opt for washable thick-weave woollen *amauts*. Still excellent at isolating an infant from the elements whilst on the move, thankfully today precautions are taken to avoid its 'natural functions' progressing unimpeded down its mother's back.

That night we slept well. We'd managed to get the internal temperature of the little old home to around minus ten, which is comfortable to sit around in, and laid out our sleeping pads in the spacious main area. We didn't want to overdo it and pump too many gallons of fuel through the stoves. Once you defeat freezing point and send temperatures into positive figures, condensation becomes an issue – on walls, fabrics and anything that was previously deep-frozen.

There wasn't a great deal of point in hanging around Siorapaluk for more than it took to meet people and get a feel for what life was like; how it differed from other places. Views down the fjord and up across the cliffs were made impossible by the obstinate winter. We could have been anywhere – a tiny cluster of houses in the middle of a vast, freezing black nowhere. It was extraordinary to think that people have chosen to call it home for centuries.

Peter came by the next day with his cousin, who he was staying with, and we shared plans. He'd only travelled to Siorapaluk on a spur of the moment decision. It served to satisfy his, and others', curiosity about the condition of the sea ice, and an excuse to visit family and friends. The majority of inter-village journeys for local people occur in the mid winter to late spring, by dog sled. Before the ice forms properly and thickens beyond an inch or two, and during the *imarortoq* breakup in May and June (or even earlier in recent years), it's a no go. The water isn't clear enough to boat safely, and not thick enough to sled on. In the short summer, boats such as a *qajaq* can be used. The only way to circumvent the traditional

150

methods are to use one of the infrequent Air Greenland service shuttles by helicopter – the expense of which is beyond justification for many. The sea is therefore the key to travel for the Polar Eskimos, and it has always been that way.

Peter wanted to go back to Qaanaaq. Offering to wait a while for us to sort our dogs out and reload the sleds, ready to go, he wanted us to come too. Peter's setup was a great deal simpler; a small eight-foot sled, well worn in by the looks of it, and half a dozen of his dogs. They all seemed particularly friendly, but without the frantic exuberance of some of ours. The reason, I learned as Peter joined me whilst I was giving them a head scratch, was that they were young – last year's pups. Another reason for embarking on his seventy-mile round trip was to train them. I had no doubt that, going by his older dogs we had bought and others we'd seen, he was a master at this.

Anders pointed out, quite rightly, that Peter would outpace us perhaps two to one. All three of us really wanted to travel in convoy though; a guaranteed opportunity to boost our education and experience. We wanted to be independent, for sure, but we also wanted to share our time with the people we were growing to so admire. I warned Peter we'd be slow.

"Fine! I wait," he replied, laughing. He probably knew how many times he'd end up stopping and waiting for us. Perhaps having him as a scent and sight to chase would shimmy our dogs along.

As soon as we'd pointed the sleds in the right direction and harnessed the dogs, plus carefully spooled up the long, clinking chain so as not to allow knots and kinks to form, it was late morning. I doubted we'd reach Qaanaaq any time before ten in the evening – perhaps later.

Bored by our tardiness and taking our final strapping down of tarpaulin as an indication we were ready, Peter stood about a hundred yards down the beach, in front of his sled and team of dogs. They were barking and lunging on their traces. In an instant, they were off. I didn't even hear a verbal command, and Peter nonchalantly sat down on the sled as it nearly shot past him.

Clattering aggressively but fluidly over the bumpy tide crack and broken ice, he reached the flat surface in seconds and was fast out of sight. The range of the handful of dim, low set lights that lit the foreshore in an eerie glow was short. Peter had vanished. We needed to get a move on!

"Hak, hak!" James called as I did an 'idiot check' to make sure nothing was laying around in the snow. With that, it was goodbye Siorapaluk.

Peter obviously wasn't using any artificial light, so we'd need to pick up his tracks. Sled marks that had been left in the snow for days or weeks, and not been subject to wind, take on a softened look, with sharp edges lost. Given this, we soon spotted the fresh pair of parallel lines heading into the blank distance and sets of neat dog paw prints all around.

Having eaten well and rested, now with a serious target to chase – the irresistible scent of unknown dogs, they ran and ran. To maximise our chance of not being humiliatingly left in the 'dust', only one of us rode a sled at once – otherwise jogging behind to lighten the load.

"I see him!" Anders called. Soon, the soft glow of midday would silhouette Herbert Island against the backdrop of lighter blues and even a little redness.

Anders had been right. Squinting into the distance, I could make out an unnatural shape, and ten minutes or so later, we'd pulled up behind. Peter was smiling and casually chewing on some dried fish he'd stashed in his little box at the rear of his sled's flatbed.

Naturally, he was adorned in his furs. Incredibly though, not all of them. It was twenty-five or thirty below, but he hadn't donned his outer parka with the fur-lined hood. He was that comfortable. Dog sledding is most likely the coldest way to 'be' in the Arctic, unless negotiating highly turbulent ice and working hard with the dogs. You aren't actively hauling, you're travelling at speed that creates a 'wind', plus you might be forced to face the breeze. If lying sideways, the blood flow that standing up might force into your feet and toes is now perpendicular. Yet, it was just like a slightly chilly autumnal evening for Peter. It had always struck me as remarkable, and I was envious. In 2012, I'd stood on an ice edge with an Eastern Greenlandic Inuk, Georg, who'd been a regular helper with many of my early journeys. With no direct sun and temperatures below minus thirty, he wore no hat, and drank a can of coke with bare hands. Another world.

As the ancestry, complex migrations and ultimately, the geographical source of the Polar Eskimos becomes better understood, their adaptations begin to make sense. Although sharing common traits with Eastern Asians and some indigenous American groups, such as the 'Mongolian Blue Spot' birthmark, thousands of years in the cold with brutal ecological selection pressures have aided them. Wally Herbert postulated they have enhanced facial blood flow and fat to insulate, and small earlobes to see off frostbite, but I'm not aware of any robust evidence to support this. What they did have for certain were tricks of the trade – stories tell of how holding a few pieces of grass between your teeth disrupts the wind flow and keeps lips warm.

With my face safely protected from the lightest of breezes, we all circled around. Peter took the mick out of our pace and showed us a quicker way of detangling our dogs' ropes. His polar bear trousers and *kamiks* were as we'd seen in Else's home, but his 'mid layer' was the most wonderfully aesthetic *qulittaq*, a jacket stitched from caribou hide. The scene, if we were excluded, could have been taken two hundred years ago, down to the smallest detail. Then, suggesting we do two more stops en route to Qaanaaq, roughly around the two headlands that our route would 'clip' as it curved gently east, Peter gesticulated for Anders to go to his sled.

It is a great source of pride to show off the ability of a dog team, and to either appear unwilling or unable take passengers can be seen as admittance of having a substandard team.

"ii, ii," he confirmed. "Faster." Anders would ride with him. Quite where he would fit, we had no idea. With the wooden box, a bulge of supplies ahead of it covered with green tarp, and the small patch covered with an *ameq* reindeer hide for Peter to perch on, it seemed full up. Onwards we would go though one way or another and I imagined Peter's small band of dogs peering around and wondering what they'd done wrong to deserve a payload increase the size of our Danish friend.

James and I worked both the dogs and ourselves hard the next session, determined to not allow such a gap to build. We kept Peter in sight throughout, and the first headland passed to our left, slightly more visible this time around. We were in the wide opening to MacCormick Fjord and driving towards the leading corner of the stretch of coast that was host to Qaanaaq. It was the best of the brief midday glimpses of the world around us we'd seen. Icebergs large and small peppered the flat sea ice, and the hazy rocky outcrops at the head of the MacCormick were tantalising. Each day at such extreme latitudes, light levels develop rapidly. We gained twenty minutes of additional twilight each day.

James headed out ahead with Peter next, and spent a good portion of it hanging over the crossbar at the back, trying to get some smooth footage of us approaching with his camera. Cameras were about the only thing, with a couple of essentials, in Anders' and my jackets. They needed to be kept warm and dry. I preferred to run light and keep from weighing down our light, puffy down jackets. At odds with this, James had accumulated a comic reputation for having everything apart from the kitchen sink in his jacket pockets. At times this was useful, but I did feel for the embattled seam stitching of his jacket. The clink, clink of his jacket on the occasions when he jogged or ran must have been heard across the water in Canada.

Two sleds were approaching. Dog sledding is actually remarkably stealthy. Unlike the cloud of dust that might be kicked up behind a cart or a vehicle on a sandy desert track, sleds move along without a fuss. A good driver speaks to their team calmly and quietly. There's something unique and thoroughly deserving of respect when you observe a veteran sledder – the control, the ease, and the teamwork – it's almost mystical.

"Aeee..." we heard Peter call ahead. We did the same. An oncoming team was a new experience. Without lanes, markers or any sort of rules of the road (apart from, we'd later hear, that powered vehicles yield to sleds), it was worth being cautious. How embarrassing it would be if our rowdy team of misfits careered past Peter's well-behaved team and barrelled straight into a stranger's team of dogs. Dogs often interpret a straight-on approach as aggressive, and few Greenland dogs need more than a little encouragement to scrap.

To my relief, we seemed to settle our dogs down – they needed a good rest anyway – and I anchored the sled at the front with an ice screw, which was promptly peed upon by Batman. An empty sled can be easily kept in place by pushing it onto its side – a sort of handbrake – but any sort of payload precludes that.

Our two new acquaintances were quite shy, and similarly dressed to Peter. They turned out to be Peter's cousin, another one, and his son. The older of the pair raised his arm to greet us and pulled out a flask. Offering us a piping hot mug of tea, this small family reunion had their impromptu lunch break. As I'd noticed was normal amongst men of most ages, and many women too, they smoked. It seemed a shame – aside from the fact cigarettes are expensive and a drain on meagre incomes, or the health impact, or just my personal aversion to smoking – because the acrid smoke spoiled such a pristine scene. I felt sad that along with bringing with them rifles, tinned food, medicine and timber, European pioneers also brought tobacco. As with coffee, alcohol, religion and confectionery, it today is at the heart of many modern Inuit cultures.

We communed in a circle – three traditionally garbed Polar Eskimo men in furs and three young Europeans in bright goose-down jackets and fleecy hats. No one spoke much. Having thanked them for the tea and offered them some biltong, they held their flask mugs protectively against their bellies, hands wrapped around them to keep warm. Everything and everyone was bathed in the pervasive dark blue hue of winter twilight. Every few seconds, my attention was caught by the little spot of bright red light that appeared as each man inhaled through their cigarette. It was peaceful with a sort of quiet companionship, punctuated by soft hums and sniffs. It may surprise you to hear that, given this silence, by and large Polar Eskimos find solitary time intolerable – they crave human bonds - and seek to convene at meeting points when on the ice. In settlements, this manifests in the daily need for home visits.

Beside us was a large, beautifully-shaped iceberg locked hard into the sea ice. It would be many months before it would be released from its winter prison to continue its journey west, away from the glaciers and then south into Baffin Bay.

As suddenly as they arrived, it was decided it was time to move on. Mutual inspection of sleds was a ritual, especially when it came to ours. Huge transit sleds are unusual and word must have spread around town. What struck me most was the state of aesthetic disrepair a sled can take on whilst still being perfectly functional. The wood on so many sleds we'd seen was darkened through years of use; weathered, almost like driftwood. The lashings were worn and dirty – the soot of dirty stoves and rich oils of walrus and seal blubber soaking their way into the fibres over hundreds of journeys. Yet, they still flexed and moved over the ice like a living, breathing entity. Occasionally we spotted a running repair like an extra iron bracket to brace a crack, but it was rare.

With an approving smile and backslap, having tugged at our lashings and sled bags affixed to the sled's front section, father and son dropped their empty flask into their sled box with a thump, and uttering a command we'd not heard yet, expertly pulled off in a loop around the sleds and dogs littering the area. I watched as they near-silently continued on to Siorapaluk.

I said to Peter that since he had Else waiting for him back home, ideally to return before it was too late at night, perhaps I should forgo my turn to travel with him. Our slowness was our problem and it shouldn't impact him. He wouldn't hear anything of it. Peter seemed to genuinely value our company. The context mattered a great deal – Qaanaaq, or any small Arctic hamlet, is quiet and could be seen as repetitive in the winter – so we did provide an element of entertainment and novelty, just by being there. Peter liked to practise his English too, but didn't have any sense about him that he saw us as a source of cash. He had never asked for a single krone from us. It was encouraging – perhaps we were progressively lowering that wall and making good names for ourselves. We were cautious though about becoming reliant on those who in objective terms had far less than we.

Expecting to have perhaps a final stop to detangle lines before reaching the bright lights of relative civilisation again, Peter and I took off. Light was fading fast to pitch-blackness, and I watched as the stars grew in brightness and number every passing minute.

Peter was relaxed as he sat on the front end of the caribou hide. His behind was in the middle of the sled, and by virtue of his short stature, could sit with his legs down, boots parallel as they skimmed a few inches off the snow surface. I was less lucky. I had to regularly shuffle around to keep enough blood flowing to feet, arms and elsewhere. My legs would drag dangerously on the snow if I mimicked Peter.

We began to talk – he was more relaxed than when in a group. There was less, for want of a better phrase, showing off. Also, he was more ambitious with his English, and equally generous in helping me link English words with their Inuktun counterpart. His sentence structure wasn't fluid and tended to rely on a limited set of vocabulary and the present tense – much like my hopeless attempts at schoolboy French and Spanish would sound now. With no formal tuition, his efforts were nonetheless impressive.

We talked across a whole spectrum, Peter regularly telling me about how much he liked his girlfriend Else, and vice versa. Once or twice, with a mischievous twinkle in his eye, he made a racy allusion or joke. Risqué or crude sexual references are never far buried, driven by humour and pragmatism about bodily functions. To illustrate, an *ajagaq* is a group game made from walrus ivory and involves aiming an awl at various mimicked bodily orifices.

More business-like all of a sudden, Peter told me about how he wanted to find people from abroad to visit in the summer and fish for Arctic char with him, paid as a guide. I asked him about his life in the North, and about whether he'd ever go south to Ilulissat or even further. Immediately and with passion and insistence I'd not seen in such a normally quietly jovial person, he said no. Alas, two years later, he had done just that, albeit to return later. Going on, it became so obvious how important the cultural distinctions between the Polar Eskimo and the rest of Greenland are to them – the traditions, the formidable ancestry, the retention of skills and survival knowledge. They even have words for 'other' Greenlanders, *quvanngarnihaq* – a *kalaaleq* in the west and *tunumioq* in the east.

Rounding the final headland (a *nuuk* – a cape/point and the namesake of the capital) that caused so much concern on the way out, we had another couple of hours skimming the straight coastline to Qaanaaq. That headland was the same one built up in our minds, fed somewhat by Finn's stories, as being perilous for man-hauling sleds around – dark and foreboding and with a drop into thin ice on one side; a vertical, unstable cliff to the other. Glancing to the side towards where it would be, and picturing its shape in the shadows, it didn't seem quite so bad.

The dogs had been trotting along with ease for miles. Our total weight was perhaps only half of my own sled, and with only marginally fewer dogs – all with excellent lineage and physique – it showed. Peter's dogs barely fidgeted, totally unlike ours. A rhythm and discipline pervaded. As we rode each bump though, over cracks in the surface and between icebergs, small obstacles were beginning to have an effect. Even on good quality, freshly formed sea ice that hasn't suffered the pressures of pack ice dynamics, it's never a billiard board. With each extra exertion, the dogs slowed. I noticed one or two look round for reassurance momentarily – their expressions could have said "Come on! When are we home? The extra person is heavy!"

I knew that the Thule dogs could achieve double the distance we planned for our day, but they were still growing and in training. Peter began speaking in Inuktun. Turning to him, I thought he was speaking to me. Finally, he'd felt the chill of the bitter cold and added his parka, then pulled a fur hood around his face.

The low, calm words Peter uttered weren't for my benefit. Peter was speaking to his dogs, and they were responding to the tone of his voice. The pace picked up, and they steadied. There was no need for the theatrical overtones you might hear from 'dog mushers' who race for sport in the south or the yelling of the exasperated novice. He was encouraging the team, making them feel part of the group, and reassuring them. Their trust in him was absolute, knowing him as their master and carer since their first memories as new-born pups. On we ran.

The lack of space and bumpy nature of the items stored on the sled, under the caribou hide and tarp meant that it was far from comfortable. I shuffled around regularly as I needed to encourage new blood flow into my extremities. Sometimes I sat facing directly forward, with tips of my boots lightly brushing the snow and lifting them as I saw an ice block approaching. For a while though, at times when Peter and I weren't speaking, I looked back. I could see James and Anders behind, increasingly losing the race. Mostly they were laid out on their spot on the sled, but I could just about make out one or other occasionally hop off to run, stand on the back, or flick their head torch on for a moment.

Peter's posture had changed a little, but his seating position had not. He hunched forward more and was tapping his *kamiks* together intently – *kuhuliktuq* – the universal signal all cold climate inhabitants share.

"Cold?" I asked.

"ii, it's cold – *issittoq*," he replied with a sheepish grin. He wasn't immune after all. The lack of sun compounds any feeling of chilliness from the actual air temperature. I remembered feeling a great deal warmer on the Greenland ice sheet at nigh on -40°C with the sun in the sky than I did on this shadow-enveloped sled at somewhere around -30°C.

Handing me his whip, similar to ours but with a smaller wooden handle, he hopped off. Just as we had begun to do at regular intervals, he started to jog along. I knew his clothing would not allow enough sweat to escape, despite their loose fit, to vent moisture. He wouldn't be able to maintain it for long. The dogs had picked up the pace in response to the hundred and thirty pounds of lost bulk.

"No go without me!" Peter joked to me over his shoulder. I flicked the whip forward, over the heads of the dogs. I was rewarded with a good swish sound, but no sharp crack as I'd hoped. Many hours more practice would be needed for that. It had the desired effect though. The lead dog and a couple of others flicked their ears back towards us. One momentarily turned its head back for a glance. Peter gave a command that

I couldn't pick up properly and the dogs held back a little – enough for Peter's lolloping to keep up with anyhow.

In a fluid movement, so casual that he must have done it thousands of times without missing his aim, Peter's behind connected with his seating spot. It sounds easy, but we'd found hitting our own moving targets to be quite hit and miss – especially when a gleeful teammate takes pleasure in giving you a shove back off again!

We'd seen a glimpse of the northern lights for the one and only time that winter, being rare in the region and locally known as *arrarneq* – the dancing spirits of stillborn babies.

I could hear a beeping sound. It was so out of place. The environment was so natural, with a headlamp seemingly the most incongruous assault in sight to the innocence of the Arctic, that the sound of a beeping phone seemed alien.

With bare hands, having extracted them from his sealskin and *aeqqatit* (polar bear fur lined mitts), a similar pair I'd soon acquire for myself, he fished around inside the little sewn pouch on the front of his smock. The beeping increased in volume as it appeared and Peter held the phone to his ear. In fast and half-mumbled Inuktun, he had a two or three-minute conversation, before returning the phone to the pouch. I smirked at the whole experience. The apposition of new and old was clearly unrecognisable to Peter; his perspective was so different to mine.

It was Else. She had wanted to know what time he was due home. Also, she had more serious news. Word had reached Qaanaaq that there'd been an accident in the South – in Ilulissat.

Air accidents are fairly few and far between in the Arctic, perhaps counter intuitively. You might think that the winter darkness, extreme landscapes and inclement weather might make flying disproportionately or even unjustifiably hazardous, but not so. In absolute terms, problems are rare. Perhaps if you scaled them up to match the number of flights, say to and from the UK each year, the statistics would look less favourable. Apart from sporadic helicopter and seaplane crashes in the 1960s and 1970s, the USAF nuclear bomber crash, and a handful of heavy landings, Greenland's flying history has not been dramatic.

I'd flown in and out of Ilulissat, central west Greenland's main airport (still only a single runway and small terminal building), a number of times and then north to Qaanaaq via Upernavik, so I was aware of the dangers. There is nowhere in Greenland's small halo of ice-free landmass where there's a totally safe place to land. There are always hills, mountains, ravines, scree slopes, melt-rivers and more to contend with. Upernavik's airstrip is especially short and atop a cliff. It needs a handbrake start in order to take off, even with a short-take-off Dash 8 turboprop aircraft. Qaanaaq's gravel airstrip is directly beside the sea. Ilulissat's more elaborate runway is nonetheless nestled amongst inlets and steep hills a couple of miles from the hilly town itself.

The news was worrying. Else had family on a flight from the South in Kangerlussuaq that was to land in Ilulissat. Apparently, the Dash 8 had crashed as it came in to land. There was no other information and the rumour mill was in full flow, compounded by the fact families were so widespread, and so personal association was likely in any accident.

It was time to get back to Qaanaaq. Having agreed amongst us that a final stop and meet up with Anders and James was only needed if we must detangle ropes, we decided to push on. Waiting for them would waste time, when we knew very well they were more than capable of guiding the dogs in on their own. Once on the outskirts and having released Peter to zoom along the frozen beach to his home, I could at least make myself useful by preparing food for dogs, the staking area, and even some supper for the guys. They would have had a long final leg, in the pitch-black and without my assistance, most likely over an hour to the rear.

Peter gave the dogs a pep talk with some more animated commands and they sped on, motivated. They seemed strong still, the steam-like condensation from their heavy breathing wafting back towards us in clouds. They were born for this – it's what they do and what they love. Tails high, we got the customary 'end results' of their raw food diet. It was something I was slowly getting used to. The relative cleanliness of human-powered sledge travel this was not.

We had spoken less after the phone call. Peter looked more tense and focussed. He did relax a little though as we picked up the first little dot of light – Qaanaaq – and we talked about whip design and skills.

Peter decided to take a different route in for the final half dozen or so kilometres than the offshore one the three of us had used. Ours was the conservative option. Peter aimed squarely for the direct approach. He didn't cut in aggressively and find the beach though as it would mean plenty of wiggling as we following the shoreline. Instead, he wanted to pick his way through straight to the rubbish dump and then along the smooth beach to his home.

The going got rough. Peter swung his legs forward to protect them from the blocks of chaotic ice which we found passing us at speed on both sides. I glanced round, mitts now holding onto the wooden beams tightly for grip, and realised James and Anders were well out of sight. I felt like I'd somewhat abandoned them, but knew that it was within the bounds of what we discussed, they were perfectly capable without me, and I couldn't hop off now and wait for them. I had no rifle and they could miss me easily on a different route.

With Peter's total trust in the judgement of his team to choose a safe route amongst the jungle of smashed sea ice and small icebergs, the lead dog darted left and then right. His team obediently followed. If the direction was not quite right, all it needed was a gentle 'haruu' or 'atsuk' from Peter and the correction was immediate. The performance was so casual – like guiding a car along a motorway. The sled bucked and flexed over the bumps. The runners swished on the ice and the lashings creaked as the tension built and released repeatedly.

Again though, I felt guilty that because of my weight, the dogs were slowing. Their attention was buoyed by the changes of direction and having to jump and avoid obstacles, but the energy required had skyrocketed.

Gentle vocal encouragement was no longer having the same effect as before and some of the dogs had started to fidget or even let their line go slack a few times. We couldn't stop – there would be no point – we needed to get to Qaanaaq. The momentum had to be maintained. The dogs would get their rest, a huge evening meal, and even some praise, but not yet.

The whip has many uses. Ninety per cent of the time, it's used over the heads of dogs to gain their attention, or to one side or the other to correct their direction. With an inbuilt fear of the whip, and we knew why, having cracked our own legs and even necks once or twice during practice sessions, they could be controlled by it. Whilst walking, we could also corral the team and hold them by whipping gently in front of the lead dog.

If a major fight broke out amongst a team, involving more than just a couple of them, it had to be quelled. Fatalities are rare, but sled dog fracases are not like a little scuffle between two lapdogs in the park. Hunters had told us stories about horrific flesh wounds and even the disembowelling of one unfortunate animal. Remarkably, and testament to their sheer will to survive, that unfortunate animal made a full recovery without veterinary care. These sorts of fights are easily halted by judicious use of the whip and whip handle, scattering the dogs and separating the worst culprits with well-aimed thumps. It's hard to watch and harder to undertake, but a vital aspect of Greenland dog ownership.

The final use of the sealskin dog whip is to physically motivate. It's the least palatable to those with European sensibilities and with little exposure to working dogs in the north. An almost cartoon-like image can pervade of dogs, reindeer, mules or other draught animals being whipped along with lots of yelling and hollering to get a team to run. It's inaccurate and unhelpful. Also, it would be ineffective. Dogs react badly to violence and would end up basket cases if habitually subjected to it. Sled dogs, by virtue of artificial selection, don't need fundamental encouragement to run – it's in their genetics and they love it. A frustrated dog driver with misbehaving dogs must remember this – also that ultimately their fates and those of the dogs are intertwined. You are a team.

However, there are exceptions. A tired dog which has no appreciation of the need to run a little further and with no way of learning when it will end, can need motivating. It was not something we as a team had employed for one single reason – our skills with the whip were still lacking. Our accuracy and judgement of distance, whilst avoiding the long tail of the whip getting snagged beneath a runner was months or years from perfection. If we tried to place a single crack of the tip of a whip on the behind of a particular dog, the chance of success would be zero. It might hit the wrong dog, catch around a rope, or hit the dog on his side, back or head. The result would be fear, confusion and the opposite effect to that desired – he'd stop and cower.

Peter though was phenomenal. He looked around to me and told me it was time to go faster.

"Hunde tired," he said in a mixture of Danish and English.

With accuracy like that of a championship archer, a small flick of the wrist sent the whiptail from sliding alongside the runner and over the dogs. The final couple of inches placed exactly on the backside of the lead dog. There was a little yelp and the dog pushed on, fast. A couple of other slacking dogs received the same treatment and that was it. There was no need for a repeat.

Qaanaaq and the rubbish dump had appeared fully into view, atop the jagged peaks of broken ice. We needed to find a way across the most violent pressure ice, around the tide crack, and onto land. Peter spied what he thought was a gap. The dogs changed direction at his command and surged towards the shore. The sled flew, clattering and bouncing from rock-solid ice blade and block to the next. We must have got air once or twice. A large rise appeared ahead, three or four feet high, and the dogs leapt up with ease. At an impossible angle, Peter, the sled and I followed. I felt it tipping to the right and I countered by flinging myself to the left, rather like a motorcycle sidecar rider. An inch or two from capsizing, we landed with a spine-jarring thump.

Peter turned to me as he set the sled's direction anew – along the smooth, icy beach. He laughed, enjoying the fun and drama, and I joined in as we exchanged jubilant back slaps.

We must have covered the final couple of miles in just a few minutes. The dogs sensed home and the surface offered no resistance. Soon, we were at the foot of the hill below our home – the western extent of Qaanaaq. I clambered off, pleased to get blood flowing once more, and bade farewell. We agreed to meet for coffee soon and with the necessary urgency from his call with Else, he called 'hak' and sped on to home.

I was envious of the control and focus he'd instilled in his team. In time, we aspired to the same. For sure, some techniques we'd not have time to fully master – to make a team lie flat to the ice, to divide into two sub-teams to avoid a runaway sled on a slope, to have them walk calmly 'off lead', and so on. Time would tell if we could achieve even half of these.

Later, we'd hear more news of the crash. Mercifully, there were no fatalities or serious injuries. According to a report the Dash 8 had come in to land, perhaps against local advice, in forty-knot crosswinds. The impact of the landing collapsed the main landing gear and it then proceeded to skid to the side of the narrow runway. Critically, it didn't then roll off the edge; instead, it slid nose first down a steep slope and came to a halt. If it had exited sideways, it could have rolled, destroying the wings. The consequences could have been catastrophic. It was a timely reminder that we were in a truly frontier region of the world, which offers few second chances after poor decisions.

I had time to walk up the hill to our little yellow home, unlock, and ready it for the boys' return. Kibble was bucketed up (we didn't have a seal butchered ready) and I prepped some food for a large helping of *biksemad*, a hearty Nordic dish. One of the couple of small windows overlooked the hill, so as I peered out to check, it was easy to see the white, fast-flicking light of headtorches arrive.

I met them at the foot of the hill as they had finished staking the dogs, and helped protect our boxes and supplies near the pallet storage area. We'd collect them the next day at leisure. Anders and James looked tired. The dogs' energy had waned much like Peter's towards the end and it was obvious they'd had to work for it. They had done a phenomenal job though and plenty of ribbing rocketed back and forth as we finished up the serious work. We were on the way to grasping one of the most ageless and irreplaceable Arctic skills.

That evening, back in the warm, the previously unknown chore inevitable when running dogs in traditional fan hitches – the famous detangle of ropes – was cause for self-pity. For a trip under an hour, the tangling effects are barely noticed and don't present an issue. Beyond that is different.

Dogs often have a preferred place in a team. The most confident might dominate the middle, like Thor often did, and the more lazy or conflict-averse could stay to the left or the right. Dave stayed left, and if caught on the right for any reason, spent every second trying to hop back over left to his comfort zone. As such, they fidgeted. I did often think that some lazier dogs, with guile, realised that hopping over and under ropes gave them 'time off' pulling. It needed to be discouraged, as the positive reinforcement that fidgeting is in their interest will only lead to more of it. The hopping over and under with up to a dozen dogs led to the most extraordinary knots in the traces. Pulled tight by the force of the team, the effect was a chaotic muddle that obviously reduced the 'fan' of the hitch. At first, the lines were all long and enabled the dogs, even those at the flanks, to run with their energies focussed in the forward direction. The tangle at its worst, our threshold was for a yard or so of it, meant the flanking dogs could have their ropes pointing out at near perpendicular angles, wasting their input. At least the traces were synthetic rope, as they were formerly made of sealskin – even harder to unknot and always at risk of being chewed.

We hoped it would improve in time as the team got used to each other and fidgeting reduced, but at first we needed to detangle this mess almost every half hour. It couldn't be done from the 'dog end', but instead at the sled end where the ropes fused into a single point onto a thick spliced rope, called a *pitaq*, connected to the wooden strut.

Nerve-wrackingly, bearing in mind these dogs do not respond to "dog, come!" if let loose, the only solution was to stop them, let them settle down and rest, then disconnect the team entirely. One person, or the only person if alone, would then stand with their full weight on the huge, long knot and the other could manually undo it by hand. It was like a game, but made unpleasant by the intense cold and dog excrement frozen onto the lines. It needed dexterity, so mitts had to come off in deference to bare hands, regularly rewarmed under armpits, or with contact gloves. Finally and satisfyingly neat, the main loop was slipped through the looped ends of traces and with some relief, we were ready to go again. If a foolish person was to call 'hak' during the detangle, the dogs would leap up and run free. I doubt we'd ever see most again, left stupidly alone with a sled in the middle of the wilderness.

To make life easier, the tool used to 'complete' the loop for the main spliced hauling rope was an oversized karabiner. Some locals also used this modern addition, but others relied on *urhiq* - traditional bone or ivory hooks, as had been the case for millennia.

OJ

CHAPTER 10: The Rising Glow

OUR TIME in the North continued apace. Each day saw a glimmer more twilight in the sky around midday, stretching a few minutes further into the morning. It was still distinctly winter and civil twilight (when artificial light isn't needed – think the half hour after a typical sunset) was far off, but collective spirits rose in anticipation.

One evening after a good day of training one of our teams out towards Herbert Island, but not as far as the thin ice surrounding it, I had fed the dogs and was wandering past the three still placed outside our house, one on each corner. Phoenix had been building both in stature and in confidence and greeted me much as a pet dog would. He had a wonderful temperament, quiet and very handsome in a different way to most Greenland dogs, with his fox-like face.

I said goodnight to Dave who was already curled up in a ball on an old cardboard box, which made ideal warm sleeping mats, and as I walked away, noticed something. Double taking, I stepped back and looked again. The others were inside and had got into comfortable clothes for an evening of chatting, planning, eating, and perhaps a rerun on Danish television we'd managed to connect to on the highly limited local broadcast. They were reluctant to shift as I called inside to come and see, but a few minutes later appeared onto the rickety wooden porch outside the raised front door. All buildings, due to the pre-fabricated nature of the homes, the permafrost and the hilly ground, were raised on wood or cement. Stray dogs often took up residence underneath and it was a job to close up the gaps.

I pointed to Dave and walked over to him. Sleepy and unbothered by my approach, which he'd usually interpret as time to eat or time to go running, he opened his eyes and rotated his rounded black and white ears towards me. I reached down towards his underside – a mass of fat and thick winter fur – as James and Anders craned over the side of the ledge to see. Frost had already begun to form in Anders' long blonde hair; not so in James' as he'd joined Anastasia and me to adopt low maintenance cropped hair.

I picked up and 'presented' what I had spotted.

A black and white female pup. She had sought warmth and refuge with Dave, a giant hot water bottle. She was incredibly lucky that she chose this particularly docile dog. If she'd chosen another, it might have ended differently. Amusingly, their similar coat colour had provided camouflage and it was pure chance she was noticed.

I carried her in, narrowly avoiding the initial 'shower' of excitement, and checked her over for any injuries. Tiny, probably just four or five weeks old, she was hard to not find irresistible and had bright, large eyes set against her dark fur, broken up with small white patches. We couldn't keep her, obviously. She belonged to someone's female dog in town and would have been of no use to us anyhow, especially if we decided on a long icecap journey in future months.

Having endured an evening of unsuccessfully corralling our deft little escapologist, now named 'Goliath', and clearing up the puzzling quantity of 'presents' she left us, we asked our friends if anyone had lost a pup.

The culture surrounding dogs is different to what we're conditioned to at home, especially in the exceptionally canine-affectionate England. There was a predictable indifference, as if an AWOL dog was of little consequence. We knew that she must be sought after somewhere though, since she was female. Dogs need time, money and resources in a place where all are in short supply, so dogs don't survive by accident. She was too well fed to be a stray. Most females, along with weak males, are quickly put down at birth and fed to the adults due to the overwhelming demand for male sled dogs. For a female to survive to the weaning stage, she must be intentionally bred as a rare team dog or breeding bitch.

The ever-reliable Navarana came to the rescue again a couple of days later. Goliath had lost none of her cuteness factor, but was a full-time job and having her in the house was fast becoming a health hazard.

"She's Regina's!" Navarana said, stood on our doorstep. Her words were obscured behind a thick fur-hooded parka. Not knowing she even had a dog anymore, surely enough leashed around the back of her house we found a rusty and white female dog. She was evidently anxious and, with a relieved Regina arriving, we reunited mother and pup. The problem was obvious, and we were fairly sure of why there was only a single pup left from the litter. Now that the pup was mobile and curious about the world around her, the mother couldn't fetch her back when she strayed. Vocal protest could only do so much and once out of view and earshot, any pup would have little chance away from warmth and food. We weren't even sure why Regina had a dog since she didn't travel by sled anymore and showed no evidence of wanting a housedog. Puzzled, we tried to suggest leashing the mother was the problem; perhaps a fenced area, which other locals had fashioned outside their homes, or letting the mother loose could work if she could be trusted. Unsure of whether it had sunk in, we took our leave.

Two weeks later, on returning from a long day training the dogs, we found Goliath's frozen body next to our wooden steps. Phoenix was standing beside her, cautiously nosing at the sad, lifeless pup. It seemed so unnecessary and brutal, but we had to suspend our own standards. The Arctic is tough, but isn't cruel. It's just indifferent. The people who've lived in and adapted to the place have had to match it at times.

We had spent many of our evenings in Qaanaaq, when not out exploring across the sea ice, with friends – Troels, Merete, Peter's extended family, Navarana and also another young Polar Eskimo family who came to visit at least once a week. We also had a wider network around our own age, an at times impenetrable social group, from Aleqatsiaq to a small group from Nuuk, who attracted much gentle teasing – *qavaghuqtuq* – meaning 'does or says like a South Greenlander'.

Our closest companionship though was undoubtedly being forged between Peter, Else and us. Peter's enthusiasm for his community, and the history and traditions of the Polar Eskimo people was infectious and he was keen to share.

We were still primarily using seal meat to feed the dogs. The job had become no more popular and Finn had been the first to show us how he had a special room, apart from his main building, in which carcasses could be partially thawed and thereafter butchered whilst hung from a ceiling hook. We didn't have such a facility; our little rented home presumably not built for a hunter, and still used the wet room. Peter had seen our system in action and, disapproving of this deviation from standard practice, wanted to teach us one of the cornerstone skills of any Arctic hunter. The fact we couldn't install our own hook butchering area was immaterial it appeared, and learn we must.

Else generously fed us with buns and tea, along with the children who'd already finished school. It was just as well we all had strong constitutions and were more or less immune to the macabre sights and smells of animal innards, otherwise eating afterwards might have been advisable.

Beckoned through to a little space that had been blocked off on previous visits, we found their water tank and a storage rack or two for *kamiks* and smocks. At the far end, next to a small door that led to a wooden walkway along the frontage of Else's home, was our educational tool.

I wasn't entirely convinced that the large steel hook affixed to the ceiling was going to last the day; screwed into a ceiling panel as it was and not into a beam or joist. Beneath it hung a thawed and so far untouched adult ringed seal, the most populous of Arctic seals and a common source of meat. I suppose using a European equivalent; these seals are the sheep or cattle of the Arctic – for skins, meat and even fuel.

The hundred and forty-pound bulk of the animal was lashed to the hook by cord that bound the back flippers together. It's such an indefensible emotional reaction for an omnivorous southerner, but I found it hard to be entirely dispassionate.

Peter was going to demonstrate how a proper butchering is done and then see how we fared. The aim, as it has ever been for the Polar Eskimo and other Inuit and northern groups, was zero waste – even bones could be used as tools or hooks. Eyes, marrow and blood were consumed too. Resources now have a 'buffer' after the lifeline with the rest of the world was established. Starvation and genuine threat of loss of life for want of the basics are more or less unthinkable but this has most certainly not always been the case. Hunting used to be even harder than now, so every part of every seal, bear and fish had to be carefully dealt with and not spoiled.

Beneath the seal was a large plastic bucket tray, the same sort we'd found at the store for thawing our own carcasses in.

Peter drew up a tiny homemade wooden stool and purposefully adjusted his glasses. In his hand was a razor sharp eight-inch knife. He proceeded to work with incredible speed and accuracy. This would have been honed whilst hunting and butchering larger mammals out on the ice itself. Animals such as walrus and polar bear are too large to sled back to a settlement whole, so are butchered at the spot of the kill before they cool

170

and freeze. Speed would be of the essence and this efficiency continued at home.

First off came the skin, excised neatly in large, continuous sheets from the body and only with a thin layer of supporting blubber behind. He folded these neatly like linens, as Rasmus had in the storage hut, and set them on a plastic bag on the floor. The seal was transformed from an attractive short-furred animal with grey and black patterning to a light pink with a 'wet', oily texture. The blubber sections could be cut off in large strips, being careful not to reach the meat itself yet. Dogs are not as keen on blubber, but this calorie dense layer that keeps the seals warm in perishingly cold temperatures would be fed first when they are at their most ravenous and would eat anything. The fat's energy, combined with the protein-rich meat itself, would cover their nutritional needs year-round.

It was all so neat and clinical. The fact the seal was suspended and could be rotated easily with one hand made it much easier than how we'd been making do back home. The bucket was thus far empty, but Peter then used the full length of the blade to open up the chest cavity, slicing effortlessly through muscle and connective tissue. In a single, sudden and cadaverous slopping motion, the innards of the seal flowed out into the bucket. This could be liberally fed to the dogs as it was. Remaining was the actual meat itself; dark, rich and mostly free from fat. This was the most skilful phase since it needed to be parted from the bones with minimal wastage. Steak-sized pieces were building up in a small pile beside Peter. He glanced over his shoulder with a gleeful grin accompanied by 'ii'. We all took over one by one and James was left to finish off the final sections. In less than half an hour, the seal had been expertly divided up ready for us. Plenty of thought had gone into how the dogs would be fed, the state in which the skins needed to be in order to be worked on, cleaned and prepared for tanning, and keeping choice cuts for human consumption.

If that lesson had not been enough, we were to experience another education in how things **should** be done the following day, which not coincidentally was, as February was well apace, sunrise day. The annual event of the sun rising for the first time after the long winter energised the whole community.

The day before had been an unusually overcast day – possibly only the second or third we'd experienced in over two months. Even in the dark, we'd been able to ascertain the weather by whether the stars were out or not. The moon – *aningaaq*, if risen, could also tell us a great deal, from being obscured, hazy or sharply in focus. Traditionally, the moon was believed to be chasing its sibling, the sun, around the sky. Every natural feature had its backstory – land being rocks that have rained down, and light and dark to benefit the hare and fox respectively. At the more extreme end of the spectrum, wind and rain are said to be the released contents of a caribou nappy worn by a giant baby in the sky - always a light tone.

Workable twilight had dominated the daytime hours for a week or two and soon we'd feel that wonderful direct warmth, albeit the feeble polar sun at minus twenty, on our cheeks. I hoped the day of its actual return (a day later than it's official reappearance due to the mountains being in the way at the point it was to rise) wouldn't be on a day of cloud cover. The people of Qaanaaq and the whole region would be horribly disappointed and the celebrations – *hiqinniaqtuq* - would be merely symbolic. I heard that people in past times had been so excited by the sun that some would spontaneously perform handstands.

The mood and atmosphere in town visibly lifts; activity booms. It beckoned, after the temperature dips of early spring, warmer air and the fruitful summer months. It's well known worldwide how the sunlight can benefit health, both mind and body.

Dozens of the townspeople, and surely in the other Avanerriaq settlements too, had climbed the hill behind the community to get the first glimpse. Mercifully, the dull, overcast clag of the previous day had lifted just in time and it was hard not to stare, mouth wide open in the -30°C air, at the pin prick of super-bright sunlight as it peeked above the distant mountains. Not even half an hour later, it was gone.

Some traditional songs had been quietly chanted by the church group atop the hill, another ad hoc singing band joining in too, accompanied by Qaanaaq's music man, Peter Q Sadorana. The day's excitement was far from over though. Everyone we'd passed on the snowy pathways had urged us to make for the shoreline.

We'd decided not to run the dogs that day as we'd been assured of plenty to keep us busy otherwise, with a large party and impromptu dancing contest which, through pure enthusiasm and zero skill I'd managed to win. Also, we had earmarked the start of the next week for a major step up in journeying ambition. The dogs would need to be well rested.

The culture surrounding dog sledding is unique in the High Arctic, and even more so in the handful of cultures where it is still used in place of more modern alternatives of transport. It is not Scandinavia, nor Colorado, or other snowy places in the south where dog sledding is a recreational pursuit – something optional and surplus to necessity. To the dog sledding Inuit, dogs are not toys or a commercial venture; they are the way to get from village to village, and to reach hunting grounds. Once or twice a year though, this pragmatism is put to one side and showcasing that most quintessential of Inuit mastery is centre stage, just for the sake of it.

On the sea ice was the largest congregation of villagers we'd seen since New Year. The sleepy atmosphere in Qaanaaq had vanished and the competitors lined up facing Herbert Island in the distance. It was the winter sled race – latterly held at Qaanaaq having been 'banished' from near the Thule Air Base for unclear reasons.

Games of strength and skill have evolved naturally in almost every society on Earth and racing is an obvious extension. This wasn't about efficiency, hauling in the largest fishing catch or taking family to visit relatives in a distant settlement; it was just about speed. The sleds brought to bear were the very smallest and lightest on offer. Short of a small canvas bag draped from the rear cross beam, just a caribou skin for comfort stretched across the small flatbed. Each dog team for the dozen or so hunters who were taking part was picked from the best-bred, largest animals in the region. Some were truly monsters and only six to eight were hitched to each sled. It was a perishing -32°C and twilight had again closed in on the landscape. Despite this, small children and the elderly of Qaanaaq had all come down to see the spectacle. Every competitor had his polar bear fur trousers on. One moment we were milling around, saying hello to Hans and raising an arm to Peter and Lars, a hunter with vast experience, who were beside their sleds, much like a racing car driver would proudly show off their million-pound machines, and the next they were off. There was no starting gun or horn blown; they seemed to just go. Some were caught off guard and had to leap onto their sleds and bark a single command to set off their lead dog.

Almost silent in the hazy blue glow of afternoon, the black silhouettes against the snow grew smaller as they began to duck in front of and behind small icebergs. The speed was gobsmacking. Anders asked a stranger standing nearby what the route was. Nearly thirty miles – a huge loop to the west, short of the edge of the sea ice and then back to the east towards Qeqertat before returning. It must take hours, I thought. Not so. The winner would most likely take little more than ninety minutes. This squarely put our proficiency, and frankly that of even experienced dog drivers, into perspective. We were watching a master class in the ancient art of driving dogs – the very best Inuit dog sledders in the world. A couple of dogs who had been cast aside and cut free for poor performance lolloped back towards the thinning crowd. They would be captured by their owner's family and taken back to a staking point – there was no room for slackers in this race.

We'd later learn the winner was Lars' son, a proud up-and-coming hunter. He was lifted aloft by a cheering crowd, sled and man, and flew a Greenlandic flag. The last time I'd witnessed such a scene was as a hunter unexpectedly brought back into Kulusuk (in the East) a polar bear he'd happened upon. He was like a Hollywood movie star winning an Oscar, beaming from ear to ear amidst the adulation.

CHAPTER 11: Death Trap

WE HAD DECIDED we wanted to access the ice sheet. Whether that meant a huge journey to the south and Ilulissat or even Isortoq in the southeast, a foray towards Etah and Inglefield Land to the north, or even mere local quests, would depend on the dogs, the ice and us.

The logical first step was to find a way up. The famed glacial access routes to the west, the Clements Markham Glacier and a couple of others, were hopelessly off limits past Siorapaluk. The ice ramp to the direct south called the Politiken Bræ (*bræ* is an older alternative to *gletscher*, meaning glacier in Danish), which was the other main way up, was notoriously unstable in recent years. Its local name was *Itugdlerriaq*, meaning 'valley'.

We drew up a list. From the most likely to least likely points of approach, we decided where we'd journey to and try. These weren't a stab in the dark though or just based off glancing through maps and satellite images. We had been invited into a couple of homes and enthusiastically shown routes and pencil marks on maps to indicate safe or known danger spots. The generosity of knowledge, hard won as it was, was incredibly endearing. Seemingly all that many people needed to hear was a rumour of our ambitions and plans before they would invite us in. Also, Rasmus had marked on our special rip-proof mapping with a pen where useful spots were – hunters' huts, dangerous headlands, likely ice edges, and the least steep and crevassed glaciers.

Top of our hit list was also the closest. 'Behind' the Piulerruup Nunaa peninsula was a wide glacial system. The vast, crevassed and fast-moving tidewater glacier, the Bowdoin Glacier, sat at the eastern extent of the ice tongues and at the head of the Bowdoin Fjord. That, obviously, was a no-go with dogs and would be most hazardous even on foot and with ropes. To the west though was the Tugto – a wide, slower ice stream with a lesser gradient. Without a sea terminus, the summer melt flowed into two large lakes on the lowlands, both of which were thoroughly iced up in the winter and only given away by their flatness compared to the surrounding snowy rock. In the summer they made for excellent *iqaluk* fishing – more commonly known as Arctic char. The Tugto would be our first potential ramp to the icecap and we earmarked the shorter approach to the east and round anti-clockwise, rather than via part of our Siorapaluk route and around past the frozen lakes. We heard that an abandoned, tiny settlement existed halfway up the fjord and so could be made use of.

Finn had turned up early to help move our gear to the beach so we invited him in for coffee. Of all the characters I'd met through years of travels, Finn was amongst the most inimitable and, it has to be said, surprising.

We'd not met his wife yet, an Inuit lady named Petrine, and he was rarely seen around town with her. He stood at around five-foot-seven and although not lofty by Scandinavian standards, was amongst the taller men in Qaanaaq. Finn had suffered for some years with knee problems and general ill health. He smoked heavily and had indulged in alcohol though his life, although relenting in latter years. In fact, before leaving Denmark in his twenties, he had worked at the Tuborg brewery near Copenhagen. This toll had meant he could only walk slowly and with quite a limp, and his resultant posture made him seem shorter yet. Even since the previous year when I'd seen him last, his mobility had deteriorated and driving dogs, of which he was inordinately proud in his younger years, was a memory. He still kept some of his older, trusty animals staked out to the east of Qaanaaq, short of the boggy area next to the cemetery.

It was hard to age Finn as, for him, superficial vanity was an unnecessary distraction. I suspected he was in his late fifties; with shortly cropped greying hair and a casual, unkempt stubble beard of similar length. He wore smart boots and had a stunning sealskin jacket, with a patterned fur outer side. Finn always wore a coloured beanie hat outside along with brightly reflective aviator sunglasses.

Finn sat down on our comfortable fabric chair – a deep sigh of relief as he rested his knees and gratefully received a hot mug of fresh coffee that Anders had brewed.

On first meeting Finn over a year before, it took me a short while to adapt to his manner. A stranger might mistake his dry humour and scepticism for coldness and patronising cynicism. We found him excellent company and his straight talking was both educational and often hilarious. There is no doubt about it – political correctness and tact, that had shaped the world to the south, had not reached Finn. Some of his viewpoints were endearingly old-fashioned and others, through a narrowness of life

John Ross meeting Polar Eskimos in 1818

Peter Freuchen and Knud Rasmussen in the 1920s

Robert Peary aboard the SS Roosevelt in 1909

Near Uummannaq - shortly before the trading station was created

A typical iglu in 1903

A husband warming his wife's feet in c.1908

Agpalerssuarssuk, having shot a seal in 1903

Polar Eskimos after a seal hunt near Kap York in 1905

Thule Air Base and 'Dundas' mountain in 2005

Navarana, as a girl in 1964 (left) and in 2016 (right)

Qaanaaq village in the spring of 2014

The team - Alex, Anastasia, James and Anders

Before a forty-mile man-haul to Qeqertat, December 2013

A basic, uninhabited home in Qeqertat, December 2013

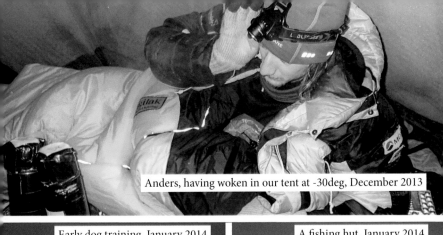

Anders, having woken in our tent at -30deg, December 2013

Early dog training, January 2014

A fishing hut, January 2014

Peter Duneq in full furs
during the winter of 2014

Dog sledding using only moonlight, January 2014

Below -35deg, Anders and Alex

Having failed on the Meehan Glacier

The day before sunrise, February 2014

A rest in front of the 'Red Cliffs' in early spring

James with Peter Duneq

Dave and Muffin, slacking

The ice cliff on our successful ascent

Thor, having broken his leg

Siorapaluk, March 2014

A house on Siorapaluk's hill

As the wind grew on the Robertson Fjord

New and old in 2014

An evening in Peter's Qeqertat hut

The breaking ice, April 2014

experience you'd never expect from a Dane still resident in Denmark, were beyond risqué.

Finn had abandoned the horror stories and tales of peril and woe that he tried on Anastasia, Anders and James on our arrival. He'd done similarly with me the previous summer; then dropped the defence and facade. He revelled in a mischievous pleasure regaling these exaggerations to the dropped-jaws of the handful of tourists in July.

Some unexplained aspects of Finn's life slowly became clearer as we spoke. He was vague at times and I could sense a real pain in his eyes when talk of home or family broached. He deftly deflected with dry jokes or topic changes. My guess was that, not unlike others in Greenland I'd met who'd immigrated, something had not gone well for him in a previous life back home. He spoke vaguely about a child, but Finn hadn't left Avanerriaq, let alone Greenland, for some time. Finn was a proud Greenlander now. The sadness prompted by this accidental nostalgia was instantly healed by speaking of his adopted home and his life in the North. He had been to some extent insulated from the outside world and the dramatic social changes and progress that we in the south are attuned to. Rates of cultural change are curious in Greenland. The country has accelerated in two centuries faster than Western Europe has done in over a thousand years. From Stone Age to the internet in ten generations – that's tough. Some aspects keep up, but the physical isolation and limited integration with the wider global community leave other facets stagnant. As a result, Finn could come out with a sweeping, forthright comment on a racial group for example, which we had to parry in the same way as you might from a conservative two generations your senior.

Finn with renewed energy and a caffeine boost conducted a summary inspection of our boxed equipment. Like a Polar Eskimo, he had little time for Boy Scout 'know-it-alls' and would have had zero qualms about pointing out issues. It was time to load up. He'd been having trouble with his left rear tyre on the truck, with a second deflation in a week. It was probably more than just bad luck, perhaps something on the truck damaging the tyre, but he was adamant we should just fit another spare wheel and see how it fared.

We eventually set out east and the days passed, covering dozen of miles, as we coaxed our dog teams around to the north. Alas, our first stab at glacial, and thereafter icecap access via the Bowdoin Fjord was blocked by an impenetrable moraine stack. Toil with tough conditions, albeit with beautiful views and lightshows from the ebbing polar winter, gave us nothing. Such is the Arctic.

The journey back, however, was something of a consolation prize. Little fair weather clouds had shaped the low, orange sunlight into beams that touched all facing it. It shimmered off the sea ice and snow like a gaudy crystal encrusted gown and the snowy rock across the fjord, miles away, had at last felt its warmth for the first time in months. The shadows were that unique polar blue, and those in transition a thousand shades of red and pink.

But, I began to realise I wanted to avoid generating an obsession with the icecap. We could spend away months in a quest for a narrow pathway up onto it, and then say "well, what now?"

Well, what then? We had our eyes set a thousand miles away but we'd failed even to ascend the Tugto via the Bowdoin Fjord. We wanted a series of targets to aim for – ways to measure our progress with the dogs. Perhaps we could get to Etah and Inglefield Land, or Kane Basin. Perhaps we'd be locked into the Avanerriaq region. The ice was king. Only it would choose.

Anders, James and I laid out my plan – keeping Anastasia updated, separated as she was, via an intermittent internet link. We still had the big unknown; the ultimate potential of our dogs. We could only commit once we had an answer to that question, whether we'd accessed the permanent ice or not. So, I proposed that we maintain our daily training and intensive feeding. Our smaller and weaker dogs had begun to catch up and we mustn't sabotage them. We could use our relentless forays to find a route to the icecap as our extended trips. If that came to fruition at some point, sooner or later, then we could make a serious judgement about the dogs, conditions and time of year – all of which would dictate our limits. At the back of my mind was that we could not afford to strand ourselves hundreds of miles from settlements with a 'broken' dog team, or get caught up in the annual melt.

So where next for our next stab at the ice? The Tugto via Bowdoin had been a tipoff from Rasmus, early on. He'd even mentioned we might ascend it on skis for the Dark Ice journey if conditions pushed the western glaciers beyond reach – as they had. We needed more inside knowledge.

Peter was our first point of call but was unsure of the best routes. It turned out that although he often travelled south with dogs in search of polar bear, and hunted muskoxen on the Inglefield Land coast in the summer via boat and kayak, he hadn't really made western or northern trips in late winter. He did know who would though – a friend of Mads Ole. His name was Massaanguaq.

In this scattered community with families dispersing across multiple settlements and with confusing naming conventions, we finally worked out that Massaanguaq was the Polar Eskimo-Japanese son of the 'old man Oshima' from Siorapaluk, and brother to Toku. Toku we'd briefly met as she, with husband Kim, visited our sled building extravaganza with Rasmus, which had become quite the talk of town. She had evidently riled Rasmus at the time by criticising an aspect of his sled design. Whether she was abrasive or just forthright wasn't clear, but there was a lasting atmosphere that I postulate may have roots in her refusal to comply with traditional gender roles.

Right next to the melt water gorge that split 'old Qaanaaq' from the newer area, was the small home where we were told we'd find Massaanguaq. The building, apart from the original 1950s huts on the foreshore, was of an older style. It had an enviable location. Its initially blue paint job had faded and flaked over the decades, and looked like it could do with a refresh. The timber and boarding was exposed in some areas, but so weathered and frozen so as to not be at risk of rot.

Outside, there were large drying racks for carcasses and pelts. Three fabulous, large, healthy male dogs were confidently sat atop the ridge on the near side of the gorge. They eyed us up with alleviated boredom and a hint of suspicion.

A lantern hung outside the front door, about eight feet up a wooden set of steps, and the whole home was raised off the slope on wooden struts. The warm glow from the lantern cut through the twilight and provided an oasis of orange against the blues of polar night. We shuffled up, line astern on the steps and knocked. Anders followed the rap on the doorframe with an "alluu!" We had slipped into a habit of relying on Anders' native fluency in Danish to initiate conversations, until we knew what was and wasn't spoken. Often even Danish was useless and so Inuktun had to be improvised with our few accrued words.

"Hi! Come," came a muffled voice from within. Massaanguaq smiled and pointed to the table as we strode into his single open living area and kicked our large boots off.

He was so enthusiastic to help that he was almost frenzied. We had no idea he even knew about us, but had not accounted for the sheer efficiency and scale of the Qaanaaq grapevine. He was disappointed we could not ski north, as our original ambitions were, because he was intending to follow our progress.

We explained how we needed to get up onto the icecap. A wry smile crossed Massaanguaq's face as he set down a large jug of hot water for tea and unfurled an old map. It was one I hadn't seen before, with lots of detail and was, the markings on the blue a give-away, a pilotage map for mariners. It turned out we weren't the only ones with that particular goal. Although the north, the western fjords and the landmass and settlements to the south were routine in the spring and summer for the Polar Eskimos, even this early in the year exploratory journeys were made. He shook his head in disbelief about the reports that had been spreading around town by word of mouth: aside from the concerns about the headlands between the settlements, a stone's throw in comparison to the distant extents of Polar Eskimo territory, woes spread further. The ice west of Siorapaluk was broken, paper thin or non-existent – knocking the series of small glaciers along the coastline out of action. To the south, the *Itugdlerriaq* route across the distant landmass and to Pituffik, Kap York, Savissivik and Melville Bay ultimately, was totally out of condition for travel. Only a few local glaciers, the Tugto being one, and routes into the dead end of the large fjord and Qeqertat, were consolidated and safe, relatively of course – you're still talking about long distance travel over a frozen skim of sea water in the darkness.

Fishing and hunting activity had appeared prolific, remarkable since the ice had not long been formed and previous weeks included the very darkest of mid-winter. We didn't have much to compare it to though, and the introspective nature of many meant that it was hard to differentiate a sombre atmosphere from one of contentment. We were no longer in any doubt however – the hunting situation was dire. We were not alone in feeling, travel-wise at least, imprisoned in a hundred-mile by fifty-mile rectangular polar penitentiary.

The Polar Eskimos have not proven themselves to be amongst the most phenomenally tough and resourceful survivors for their tendency to give up. They might admit defeat to a battle, especially one against the ice,

180

but the war lasts thousands of years and a temporary retreat and regroup is part of a sensible polar person's armoury.

To paraphrase Massaanguaq's advice: "If you want to go on the icecap, it can perhaps be done, but perhaps not yet and with large loads, maybe not possible. Once there, the routes to Etah and Inglefield Land are not as dependent on sea ice whims." In short, *ammaqa* – the famous Inuit 'maybe'. He pointed out some excellent pencil waypoints on his map from the region over towards Etah. "The inland ice (meaning the ice sheet itself) to the south – I do not know. We do not go there."

The ice sheet holds nothing of value for Polar Eskimos, or any Inuit really. There's no food there, no shelter, the winds are horrific for much of the time and distances from anywhere to somewhere are simply gigantic – that is if you can navigate accurately.

Luckily, that's where my own experience came in, having crossed the ice sheet on skis three and, well, nine-tenths of a fourth time. I'd made an attempt at the Norwegian speed record with a British teammate in 2011 and with a few miles to go and looking at a week or more of crevasse crossings to get to land, chose to shift our helicopter pickup spot – so a full crossing we couldn't claim. We had covered over three hundred and thirty miles in well under twelve days, including vast crevassed zones.

Anders, James and I had debated what we'd do after a hypothetical ascent quite enough and so concentrated on those access glaciers. Massaanguaq shared as much as he could, and as we were about to leave, his older friend came in and made himself a coffee. He spoke no English or Danish whatsoever. Having relayed the predicament in an almost lyrical few phrases of Inuktun, we received dejected confirmation, via gestures, of what we'd been told. We listened to pure Inuktun too seldom – much, much too little to have a hope of learning it to any serious extent.

We drew up a hit-list of glaciers. We'd try them relentlessly in turn, the Tugto having been the first. In between, we could continue to train and rest the dogs, and spend time in the community.

First, I earmarked a more distant glacier that had reportedly been climbed by a dog team. News was, as ever, uncertain and accompanied by 'maybes' and shrugs, which are usually code for 'no'. Avanerriaq had over the recent decades attracted a handful of Japanese settlers. Unsatisfied by life in modern Japan or elsewhere, they integrated well into the Polar Eskimo world. It was just another example of the intrinsic lack of xenophobia that typifies the people there. If you work, you listen, you integrate and you contribute to the culture, the people do not care where you come from or what you look like. Intermarriage then further strengthens the links. This is a stark contrast to the sometimes-bitter resentment between native and settler in North America.

A Japanese man, skiing solo, but with a dog for bear-security, was rumoured to have climbed the mighty Meehan Glacier. To a Polar Eskimo he was *allamioq* – from a far place. I'd seen the Meehan on maps before and earmarked it as a low-priority backup for Dark Ice's route, but it was somewhat of an enigma. The contours told us it was steep, not particularly long in miles as the crow-flew, and wiggled right and then left between rock faces to the icecap. The Meehan sat at the head of the Robertson fjord that also saw a large outlet glacier on the northeastern corner and Siorapaluk en route. Short of heading west and onto the precarious broken ice towards the series of access glaciers past Neqi (derived from the word for meat – *niqi*, an abandoned site originally of just four *iglus*), this was the most westerly routing point we could use to minimise travel distance to Etah.

We didn't know the name of the Japanese man, where he was headed, or why, but polar history has been peppered by a handful of eccentric, very tough, soloist Japanese men and so it was hardly an aberration. There was some concern, since he hadn't established communication with anyone to update on his progress or, more pointedly, his safety. In the old days of polar exploration contact was a luxury, but in the modern day it is common sense, even for me as a purist, to set up links to the outside world. Perhaps ultra-purists or traditionalists would disagree. The very topic of soloist travel is emotive. As the satisfaction an ego might enjoy from travelling alone ramps up, so does the level of danger. As Polar Eskimos often remind visitors, but don't always themselves adhere to, Peter Freuchen put it well: 'No one should be left alone in the Arctic, if it can be avoided. There are so many problems which can seem almost insurmountable to one man, though they would turn out to be utterly negligible for two men.'

It was decided. The Meehan it would be. We'd take enough supplies to keep dogs and us alive for a week or so – sufficient if we ascended the glacier to see us safely across the ice and down another glacier to Etah. There, we'd find a vast depot of food and fuel laid for us the summer before by boat by Otto. If worst came to the worst the muskox herds of

Inglefield Land were said to be vast and in fact perhaps too large, with insufficient predation to control numbers. I hadn't verified this, and was occasionally sceptical of local ecological theories, but we were encouraged to harvest lone or old oxen given the opportunity. I knew they make for adequate eating.

I'd been to the town store for supplies with Anders. On the way back, Troels came barrelling down the hill. With his distinctive greeting and insistent enthusiasm, he told us we must come to the ice. We were unsure of what he meant.

"The school is empty today. We all go to the ice for games," he said.

Sure enough, as we moved past a gap between the fuel storage towers, we saw a crowd on the ice. We'd collect James and wander down.

Almost everyone was there, noticeably and similarly to the New Year celebrations, apart from the older hunters. Rasmus, Lars and their ilk were busy elsewhere, or just not attracted by the crowds.

It was the adults at play initially. In a line behind a young man brandishing a homemade baseball bat were those in waiting. Both girls and boys, men and women were getting stuck in, although the males were by far the most vocal and swaggering. Some, but not all, of the girls, especially the teenagers, were shy – almost painfully so.

A pitcher threw a tennis ball and, with somewhat sporadic success, the bat was swung at it. The game was a mixture of rounders and baseball, with teams made up randomly – a mass of parkas, *kamiks* and fur hoods. When someone did well, the now-familiar call of 'huai, huai, huai!' filled the air as it did when the dog sled race winners were held aloft, sled and man, by a sea of hands.

One thing hadn't escaped my notice. Baseball is an import. Of course, most global games and sports are too - tennis into England, rugby into New Zealand. That's no surprise and I'd seen young children playing football in all corners of Greenland – often until late at night in the midnight sun or out on the sea ice in spring. Nationally, in the more benign South, it's a sport taken very seriously, albeit played on dirt and gravel pitches in summer. Originally a ball of walrus skin, grass and feathers had been a past substitute for a real football.

Unlike the traditional strength games through the festive period though, this emerged as the choice of the people – to play a North American sport (remember that despite European colonialism, Greenland is geographically North American and its natives trace their ancestors there too – European links are recent and superficial). Exposure to the south makes 'culture creep', and exchanges of ideas, inevitable. Inuit are famed for their crafts, and the brainteasers and puzzles these provide, and also their ingenuity and enthusiasm for original games and contests. Would these continue to thrive? Perhaps baseball was a sport 'borrowed' in past decades from the Americans who called Thule Air Base home. This open-mindedness and willingness to integrate is cause for optimism, but at what cost? In fifty years, will the children and hunters, if there are any left, still compete in millennia-old Inughuit tests of skill and strength? Back at home, does your nation still play the same sports and pastimes it did in the Middle Ages? Amalgamation is part of how the world, increasingly interconnected, develops.

It was the children's turn. Much to their delight, from toddlers to pre-adolescents, a sack of prizes donated from the store was laid out randomly on the snow-sprinkled ice. It was a flat area, devoid of sled tracks, ice blocks or the less-appealing, hard-frozen evidence of dog activity which graced much of Qaanaaq. Chocolate bars and cans of cola were obvious incentives. Washing powder and sanitary packs, less so, but a prize is a prize.

In a couple of hotly contested rounds, the young folk were lined up on the edge by a self-appointed referee, blindfolded with scarves and then released to the cheers of their families.

By virtue of the age range, sizes differed and the contest was fought without mercy; it was serious business. Mothers and older siblings were calling directions to their cohorts and aiming for the highest value prizes. One wasn't enough – the most proficient were collecting three or four – quite a haul. The one Polar Eskimo child in a custom-made fur all-in-one who had moments before amused himself sliding a small wooden sled repeatedly into James' leg, wasn't so good at the game. Disorientated, he turned away from the field of prizes and crawled at lightning speed in the opposite direction. There were no protests from the crowd as his mother turned him around and sent him back into the fray. It was thoroughly amusing for the audience but there was a serious slant. As so many games and sports are, whether for a young animal or adult human beings, these served as lessons in physical coordination, forming alliances and, of course, competition.

CHAPTER 12: Optimism

THE MEEHAN wouldn't just be a quick skirmish. Our dogs would need to be on their game, and so would we.

There's a danger, being based in a small community, of mental 'creep' towards assuming a safe refuge each evening. Alternatively, without opportunity for recovery, there is no respite. A full dunking in a haven-free wilderness, unsupported polar travel, generates so much stress it can truly separate wheat from chaff.

We had been primed for multi-months in a tent. If there were an injury, breakage or illness on the Dark Ice Project, there'd be no warm shelter to recuperate and work in. Expectations shift as a result and mindset is then all about sustainability. You end up being extra-kind in the way you treat equipment – in fact, the most evident indication that separates the seasoned professional and on-the-learn novice is how they treat kit. The latter tend to get through supplies at a rate of knots, dent and ding precious equipment and then expect replacement, not repair.

We had to shift back into that frame of mind. Whilst we'd make use along the way of whatever was available, we packed with extra checks and redundancy. I often talk about a 'skills or coping headroom'. If the basics – tent up and down, stove-work, securing equipment against wind, selecting a safe camping spot, navigation in fair conditions – fail you, then if you actually add in wind, whiteout, polar bears or medical emergency, then you're in trouble. In good conditions, we needed to be utterly at ease, whether man-hauling or travelling with dogs. In mid-January, the dogs were half under control. Now, with the sun up briefly each day as winter handed over to early spring, I primed the team to step up. In contrast, it took me two years as I began my polar career to feel adequate in facing the white wilderness independently. Our lives in Avanerriaq were an abrupt acceleration and presiding over a dozen dogs is certainly harder than grasping the mechanics of cross-country skiing.

At last, we were on the move. The shroud of winter blackness gave way to twilight as we grinded and slid our way west. Enrique did a sterling job, with Comedy, Garfunkel and team champing at the bit to chase.

We had all, as we often travelled along in silence for protracted periods in between calling commands or reassurance to our dogs, found ways to measure progress. We rarely used the GPS, as it should never be relied on as a crutch or replacement for traditional methods. James had been counting the undulations in the shoreline – punctuated by little mini-bays and points. This wasn't unlike the advice I'd been given years ago by Inuit on both sides of Greenland; in the dark or in the whiteout, count the cracks in the ice or the notches along the coast. That way, you can count yourself back, or just keep track in a sometimes-disorientating place. I had been counting major landmarks against a mental image I'd developed – three glaciers before the headland. Anders and I chatted about the landscape as we encouraged the dogs along, often hopping off to help them, unhook a leg (Odin got tangled regularly) or drive blood back to our feet.

I had, by the very nature of spending hour after hour bonding with my particular team of dogs, started to drift away from James' team. We'd decided right from the start to not share or trade teams – the dogs would react far better to a consistent leadership. It was odd in a way. In December and the early days, we'd trained one team at a time and I'd often ridden with both. Feeding was an all-dog affair, with only one person needed to dole out the vast quantities of meat and kibble they got through. That was now the only time we really had with each other's team. I missed the early days and felt sad that a distance had grown between me and Houdini, and Pinky and The Brain for example. They were charming dogs and I was missing out on their development, seeing them only at rest stops or on the chains at day's end. I recall being shocked at the leaps and bounds of confidence and physical tone Phoenix had gained.

Anders and I had a running joke about Dave and Muffin – the more amply 'insulated' of all the dogs. Recruited and overfed as a lazy fluff ball for polar bear defence, Dave still had an uneasy relationship with physical exercise and Muffin was just a plain chancer – seeing if he could get away with minimal effort from the start. They had, as a chubby pair, taken up a reliable position on the left flank of the team, the maximum distance from Thor, and pulling as little as they could conceivably get away with.

Instead of a thirty-mile sprint to Siorapaluk as an end in itself, we reduced the planned daily ranges to save the dogs. Although sixty-mile days are oft-quoted, and indeed boasted of, they eventually necessitate a major rest and 'refuel', and can cause very sore paw pads or lead to injury for the smaller or older dogs.

We'd stop just short of Ivnartalik, (Kap Cleveland to a Dane), the name given to that infamous, but now not as intimidating, sharp cliff headland which is the gateway to the MacCormick Fjord.

The dogs picked up an old track – raised on the surface, rather counter-intuitively. You might expect a track laid into the virgin snow to leave indented marks where the sled runners, skis or hundreds of paw steps once were. In the immediate aftermath, you'd be correct. But, when a track is laid, the snow is compressed by the weight into a hard pack. This makes it more resilient to the elements. If you then add the ingredient of wind or sun melting over a few days, the softer snow around the track is dislodged and even removed, leaving a raised track or mark. I'd noticed it with footprints and even latrine spots when on long polar ski journeys.

We clocked through the miles handsomely as the sun began its afternoon descent towards the horizon, now dropping behind Herbert Island. With some light still in the sky, a blessing for the chore of laying out dog chains and feeding time, I spotted something unnatural on the shoreline to our right. It would have been entirely invisible the last time we passed it in the total darkness. First a square shape – it must have been a hut and then a low, derelict shed was decipherable. Finally, an old wooden boat, listing on a block of timber, sat to the rear. It was the tiny cabin Rasmus had marked on our map with a large X.

We went through the standard routine: chain out, screw it into a safe pan of ice, dogs in their spots, fed, then we could grab our tent sacks and wander over to the shelter. We would save an hour or so of travel time by using the hut and not erecting the tipi. It was perfect – the quintessential hunter's shelter. Tiny, so easy to heat, and square with thick plywood walls, it was perhaps only eight by seven feet. To further retain heat, a loose-fitting door with ice around the edge was only four feet or so high and positioned as low down as possible.

The overwhelming benefit of the hut was its solid construction. Held down on each corner by a chain running to an oil drum full of rocks, it wouldn't only be safe in high winds, but quieter than flapping canvas too. It wasn't polar bear proof – nothing is, but it would buy you some time in an attack. Critically though, it enabled proper clothing care. In tent life, you cannot heat the tent properly (except if in the night-time sun of polar summer) and so drying lines are useless. The socks and mitts just freeze solid above your head. The only solution is to obviously keep them dry to start with, dry them on your body overnight, or actively over the stove if critically important and you've got them really wet.

In a hut, with the adequate fuel you're bound to have since you're within a hundred or so miles of a settlement, you can get the temperature up from minus forty to plus thirty in minutes. Drying lines can then be deployed to really set you up for the next day. It's a phenomenal luxury – it seems daft enthusing about a small, draughty wooden shack in the middle of nowhere, but in context it's like a palace – sooty and imperfect though they are. In a large one though, designed for the summer, there is more cold air to heat and more walls for warmth to leach through.

All piled in, we'd passed a packet of biltong beef around for a snack and set out our mugs expectantly for our evening hot chocolate. The routine is quaint when you look back at it, but was part of the comforting routine.

All of a sudden we heard dogs – barks, wails and howls. I thought they seemed too close. Our dogs were a hundred yards or so away. Had they got loose?

Having only just disrobed from our outer insulation layers into more comfortable and wieldy fleeces, none of us were keen to go back out as we exchanged jaded glances.

We needn't have worried. James poked his head outside the door – wincing at the cold as his hatless head felt the full effect of the Arctic air.

"Dogs!" he said. "Not ours."

Not one, but two dog sleds were arriving along the beach and ice foot from the west – our direction of travel. This confirmed that there were safe routes at least, but the excitement and novelty of coming across others was palpable. We threw on down jackets and clambered outside to greet the two Polar Eskimos.

They were not from Qaanaaq and were indeed unaware of our presence in the region; the pair did seem surprised – but instantly friendly. They were father and son, and both bore traditional local names. The length and pronunciation means that, to my shame, I cannot recall or spell these without half-guessing. The older, the father, was tiny, barely over five feet tall and certainly well over seventy years old. His face was weathered by an entire lifetime in Avanerriaq; back to long before modernity had began to alter Inughuit lives. He spoke not a word of English, nor Danish. We found out from his son, slightly taller and with a satisfactorily large, round belly, who spoke Danish, that they lived in Siorapaluk. They were going to hunt near Qeqertat, and would stop only briefly into Qaanaaq on the way. Both wore the full complement of wonderful sealskin kamiks, polar bear trousers, hand-stitched parkas, *natseq*, and fox fur hoods. This pair, I thought to myself and recalling the precious few books written of the Polar Eskimos between the 1940s and 1980s, were perhaps representatives of the very last stronghold showing how things were. Everything is relative. Nuuk, the tiny capital, is alien to a resident of New York, or Paris or Tokyo. Ilulissat is considered 'frontier' to the Greenlanders of Nuuk. Qaanaaq is, as the hub of Avanerriaq, again a world away from Ilulissat. Even beyond that, the old satellite settlements were a multitude of steps further still. This was **the** most original extant way of life in the Inuit world, and these smiling, welcoming people the living manifestation.

Far from being put out at having 'their' hut already inhabited, they seemed as happy to share as we were. We carried in a few of their belongings but kept an eye on what they did next. I realised, and elbowed Anders to suggest to him, that this might be a real education.

The deftness and precision, plus the ease, with which they worked was masterful in the true sense. They untangled in half the time we did, forwent ice screws in deference to cutting anchor tunnels into the ice with a small knife, filled their huge, ancient looking heaters and lamps with fuel and were inside in a flash. I realised, proud though I was of our progress, that we weren't a patch. Sixty years of practice versus six weeks or so.

It would be a squeeze.

There was a raised platform, like all shelters, which could take three, perhaps four people packed in like sardines. Also a lower, smaller one too that had been used as a table. A broken lantern, used matches, and scraps of paper were scattered across. We offered to decamp to our tent – it wouldn't take half an hour. It was their hut and we took up quite some room. They wouldn't hear of it for a second though – the pair actually quite excited by sharing with strange foreigners in curious clothing.

We shoved our things over and made space for the father, and his son cleared the lower platform, much to our relief. He was clearly a successful hunter and had the girth to prove it. We'd already got the hut up to temperature with our Colemans and as the half-light began to fade entirely, the younger Polar Eskimo fitted a tungsten filament net to a burner, creating a bright light. We wiled away the evening sharing incoherent stories in broken combinations of languages. Hung on the wall, on nails, were various outer jackets. Ours were huge, and garish – yellow and adorned with sponsor logos. Theirs were as if from another century – small, muted in natural shades and altogether far more attractive. They looked like they belonged – a fitting part of the polar world in which they were created.

We slept well that night, warm even as the heaters, now switched down to a simmer, gave way to the heat sink of the outdoors. They slept beneath a few old blankets, comfortable and warm, although heavy and bulky – I did feel thankful for my sleeping bag.

The next morning I woke to instant panic – roused from deep sleep to action stations in a split second. Apart from urgent-sounding voices, I saw the orange flickers of fire reflecting off the back wooden wall of the hut.

I span round to see two-foot-high flames running across the hut's floor. I was on one side of our four sleeping slots on the wooden platform, and was furthest from the action.

James was already tackling the blaze. He'd moved the stove, which he'd been as the earliest riser priming to get going on our breakfasts, away from the flames and cut the fuel supply off. Flames licked up the sides of the stove body and around his bare hands.

By now, our hut-mates were also awake. Thinking quickly, the younger of the two hopped off the lower platform to shuffle a container of five litres of naphtha fuel away from the path of the fire. Beyond that, the reality was that the appearance of the blaze was vastly more dramatic and spectacular than it was dangerous. A small leak from one of our fuel containers had caused a little trail of drips across the floor. Easily ignited when firing up stoves, this then caught light from one of the storm matches. The small amount of naphtha could be allowed to burn off harmlessly without needing to be covered or doused. It was all over in less than ten seconds, but it's safe to say it had the effect of more than one or two cups of morning coffee. Awake, we all certainly were.

Nervously at first in the ensuing silence and stillness, everyone exchanged glances around the room; our elderly roommate had also stirred by that point and sat up, bleary-eyed.

Then, a couple of chuckles became laughter, which echoed off the wooden walls. James and the younger man exchanged backslaps and the latter made a joke, gesturing about how he'd nearly burned down a hunting shelter and a sled-tent tarp when he was young. Joking aside though, it was a shot across the bows. Little things, attention to detail, slipping can lead to serious disasters in no time. Along with violent incidents like crevasse falls, falling through thin ice or polar bear attacks, fire is a nightmare for any polar traveller.

We went through a ritual exchange over breakfast: biltong from our side, and either *mattaaq* or dry fish from theirs. *Mattaaq* can also be slowly fermented and I have been reliably informed it tastes of walnuts and smelly French cheese – I will take their word for it! The spiced, meaty strips of dried raw beef biltong were a real hit with everyone we gifted some to. Our silver-foil clad packets of porridge and wheat oats also intrigued them; clinical and unappetising though they appeared, the taste and practicality more than compensated. Food is a real glue between cultures, proven again and again by a satisfied grin that follows an apprehensive first bite.

We were to go our own ways soon after, needing to make the best of the brief daylight. The skies were again mercifully clear and as such the pre-dawn glow appeared early in the tiny, dirty, square window above the low door.

They headed west, we east. Before though, the older of our new friends took the time to walk James and me out to the edge of the ice foot where the view was best, and advised on our route. Anders had begun the three or four shuttles needed to repack the sleds and in the time it took us to relay the advice, the Polar Eskimos were nearly ready.

We'd arrived on the fast sea ice, a few hundred yards out to sea, and then ducked into shore. They had approached on the ice foot and beach itself, meaning they'd rounded the acutely-angled cape headland. We'd planned to cut it out like the previous time, but apparently there was concern over some of the ice just off the cape and a little further on in the widest part of the fjord mouth.

With a casual wave to us and in close convoy, the men and their two dog teams sped off towards Qaanaaq. Unbeknownst to us until the final moment, the larger of the two held a precious cargo beneath the tarp – an already butchered walrus – *aaveq*, hunted north of Siorapaluk. It would be well received in Qaanaaq and Qeqertat. Hunting walrus is

191

highly dangerous as these vast hippopotamuses of the north have short tempers and fearsome tusks – a regular source of worry for family waiting patiently at home for a hunter to return. The Polar Eskimos can hunt them year round – ambushed and shot today and clubbed in the days before firearms, or in the summer harpooned from a boat and recovered with the aid of an *avataq* – an inflated sealskin buoy.

Our dogs were down on a large, flat pan of sea ice, so we had to coax them up to where the hut was through a pretty bumpy section of tidal ice rubble. From there we were very much committed. The wide, sloping beach up to the highlands and icecap closed in and we found ourselves running along a narrow path; ideal for our two lead dogs who were having a bit of a 'day off' – they couldn't stray too far left and right. To our south was the sea ice, and before long the ice we skirted along rose a good ten feet above it, separated by rubble a dozen feet in width. The slope to the landward side had been replaced with a precipitous near-cliff of disconcertingly loose rubble and small rocks. It must have been over a thousand feet high.

An hour passed, but the cape drew near faster than I anticipated. Our new friends had negotiated it the previous evening, so I wasn't concerned about it being out of condition. The challenge for us would be to control the dogs. If one of them got an idea in their head they wanted to head through the rubble and not stay on message, others would follow and soon their fate would be out of our hands. We would need, with one of us walking out ahead of each sled team with whip in hand, to use every ounce of authority, control and skill we'd learned through the dark winter. Although James' team were moving faster, they'd started off behind and couldn't overtake, courtesy of the narrow ice foot, so it would be Anders and myself first.

I stopped Enrique a hundred yards or so short of where I could see a large, intimidating section of hard rock, unlike the scree-like nature of the rest – it was the headland. He was reluctant to slow down and needed at least two or three more 'aeee's than on a good day. This wasn't a good start. Enormously fond already of the excitable ball of energy and amusement Enrique was, I needed him on side.

I laid the whip out in front of Enrique, lengthways across the ice foot, handle near the drop down to the sea and tail reaching the rock slope. This was partly so I could hold the team and chat to James for a moment before setting off again, and also to calm them down and assert good order in the ranks. James' body language was relaxed. He'd found the first portion of our day straightforward as he was following behind, and having agreed the plan of action, raised his arm with thumbs up.

The whip on the ground was a new addition to our dog-driving armoury. Being made of sealskin, the perceived wisdom was that they and dogs did not mix. We'd been warned not to leave our precious whips anywhere near in range of the chewing teeth of any dogs – they took an age to manufacture by hand, used the best quality dried seal hide and so lived safely stowed in cold boxes or hung from the back of a moving sled. Whips mustn't be kept in a warm building, as the skin dries out and can crack, eventually snapping.

In this case though, supervised, we found that the dogs' inherent trepidation towards whips, and outright fear in a few, had a use. If I had brought the team to a halt for a reason; perhaps to chat between teams, to see to a troublesome dog, to assess the safety of the sea ice ahead, then I didn't want to have to stand ahead of them, ready to prevent a runaway. That respect for the whip was such that we found, accidentally at first, that if laid out like a 'line in the sand', or rather, snow, then they would not cross it. Enrique or Thor, the most bullish of my team, might approach and sniff, but cross it they would not. It was like a handbrake – ideal.

It was time to head round into the MacCormick Fjord (Iterlaggaaq). The sun had risen and was casting our shadows long across the orange, sandy rock to the west. As I walked forward, the dogs followed obediently and closely. Every time I sensed them coming too close, I whipped left and then right to maintain order. I had time to glance out to sea. Indeed, it looked precarious, very much unlike the thick, quality first year ice we'd sledded over in the dark a few weeks before. Something had clearly happened – not wind as we'd have felt it near Qaanaaq – but maybe a tidal surge or a change in current. The end result was a large section that had clearly fractured, moved and then refrozen in an odd configuration. One large pan was grey and textured in a way that shouts at you 'thin – danger!'

The actual apex of Kap Cleveland was sharp and appeared as a large block of sandy stone – the sightline beyond, to the right, was blocked. As the ice foot had neared it, the ten feet or so of width we'd enjoyed narrowed to six, then five, then at the corner itself barely the width of a dog sled. One or two blocks of ice was all that separated this narrow ledge from a drop down to the thin, new sea ice.

I looked behind, slowed and gave Enrique a knowing look. "You'd better behave, young man!" I muttered.

My first view of the fjord showed that it was still shrouded in shadow. The angle and height of the sun saw to that. I felt a chill run through me, though of course the sun's radiation made little difference. The dogs confidently followed. Crazy stopped to glance out to sea with a look of intent. I sharply barked disapproval and he retreated back into the team. Anders was walking behind, a mitt on both the sled uprights. I was seriously concerned that the sled might get caught on the rock and sustain damage. Although the runners were planed and shaped to allow for maximum 'skidding' to change direction, a London taxi they were not and the turning circle would need a heave from Anders. Once round safely, with a sigh of relief, Anders could go back and help James.

I sat down and waited, squinting along the new shoreline that extended north away from me, and over the fjord itself. We wanted to cross the fjord as soon as possible. Every mile we sledded along this new beach to find a safe crossing would mean another added on the other side to get to the next headland. We wanted to reach Siorapaluk that day, if not further.

James too rounded the headland with Comedy at the fore and Houdini scalking at the side – I gathered that, contrary to his early cockiness and physical potential, James was having problems motivating and training Houdini. He just didn't seem to 'get it'. Most young dogs must learn the art of sled-hauling from the older animals, and are trained from soon after they turn six months – the rest of it innate to their genetics through centuries of artificial selection. Houdini had showed so much promise, but was a slow and lazy student.

The beach ahead looked good, so with Enrique aching to run unconstrained, I let them stretch their legs. Our two sleds shot down the icy beach in between the steep snowy hills and fjord. Most of it was totally hard-packed or clean sheet ice, so the pace was phenomenal – a real adrenaline buzz. We had to stay on our toes because there were obstacles; large ice blocks, boulders, and halfway along, a huge snowdrift, *agiuppineq*, blocking our path. It was about five feet high and I had no idea what was beyond. In a burst of enthusiasm, I yelled back to Anders, "let's go for it!"

He smiled back and then laughed. We'd take it head on but needed even more speed to clear it with enough momentum.

"Hak, hak, yee, yee, yeaaa, yeaaa," we called. The dogs took up the invitation, loving the encouragement and excitement, and surged up a gear.

The dogs sprinted up the slope, feet sinking slightly into the powder, summited, and then disappeared out of sight the other side. As hoped, we had the speed to get the half-ton sled up the slope too and then clattered down the other side. It was like a rollercoaster, great fun, and it felt like we almost became airborne. Unlikely.

To our collective relief, the ice in the fjord was soon passable. It was a strong, pure white colour, we could see no leads, fracture zones or screw ice, and so the likelihood was that the enclosed waters of the fjord sheltered the ice from disturbance.

We'd lost the tracks of the Polar Eskimo hunters a while back – perhaps they'd crossed further south, right on the transition from good to bad ice. Eventually though, James spied a gap down onto the fjord's ice and set off for the other side. Suddenly bereft of a narrow path to follow, our route snaked somewhat. Once two thirds of the way across, we reached the line that dissected the fjord – back into the sunshine once again.

The remainder of the journey was most uneventful – ideal for a polar traveller but easily omitted from an account. We found our way up onto the next headland, ahead of the lowland delta of Nûgssuaq, onto the bumpy beach again, around the much kinder, almost unnoticeably gradual headland, Kangeq, and into the Robertson, locally known as Hiorapaluup Kangerdlua. It seemed so daft that as we passed it in January, I'd been afraid of what the promontory might bring – the terror of the polar darkness and over-imagination, driven by sensory deprivation.

The lights of Siorapaluk were no longer a beacon for us, or the dogs, to aim for. In fact, with five miles of sea ice to cover before arriving, it was only the memory of how the cliffs rise above the village that gave away our target. The tiny settlement of nestled buildings on the shoreline and hill were imperceptible until much nearer.

Our welcoming party was far more subdued than when Peter appeared the time before. A couple of hunters, feeding their dogs, raised arms of recognition and a child ran up and asked our names, before shyly running back off. We were no longer a novelty in Avanerriaq, had met many locals, or at least their families and friends, so the curiosity had waned. For the few (it's luckily rare in the isolated North) local Greenlanders who saw foreigners - *qallunaat* - merely as a chance to sell the lower quality offcuts of local crafts and carvings for a fortune, we as semi-permanent residents were now off the radar.

Qallunaaq (singular of *qallunaat*) is a word that increasingly stimulates debate across the Inuit lands that use it. Some perceive it as equal and opposite retort to the umbrella term Eskimo, and just as pejorative, especially when used to describe 'white man' and not just a Dane. These words are descriptors, and it's torrid history that generates any offence, not the actual words. They are exonyms – *qallunaaq* an Inuit attempt to describe a foreigner – any foreigner – and Eskimo a Ameri-European attempt to describe a native north of the tree line – any native. Many southerners now adopt the endonyms of those they describe – Inuit, Iñupiat and so on, and there is a case for Inuit to do the same for them.

It was only mid-afternoon and conditions were excellent – we had enjoyed a clear, uninterrupted view the full length of the fjord to the vast Verhoeff outlet glacier and the smaller Meehan to the west. Towering above the tiny hamlet's handful of *ikaat* wooden structures placed on the beach and hill, steeper than most chosen as settlements, were the cliffs. Famed in folklore, in summer they play host to thousands of small migrating seabirds, little auks, which are caught expertly in nets atop a long pole. These are rotted inside a sealskin for months and eaten as *kiviat* (often phonetically misspelled *qiviaq*). Even locals frequently succumb to food poisoning, and the taste can generously be described as 'ripe'. Ultimately, an infection after eating *kiviat* killed the great Knud Rasmussen.

Despite seals, foxes and fishing stocks spanning the whole territory of the Polar Eskimos and the general sharing philosophy of their culture, historically villages didn't take kindly to overlapping hunting territories. This rule was however on hiatus for special hunting sectors – the bird cliffs were an example – a free for all and not just for residents of the Siorapaluk camp, and later the village there. Other special exemptions were in place for the narwhal of the Inglefield Fjord near Qeqertat and walrus near Neqi. Fox trapping was originally a female job, driven by a male belief that they were cowardly and fair game for women without the title of 'hunter'. Amusingly, after the chief demand from southern traders turned out to be for fox furs, male attitudes reversed to state that foxes were now 'cunning', and the valuable new commodities became fair game for male hunters. The furs were still chewed, boiled and dried by the women.

Given the favourable circumstances, we'd only spend an hour amongst the people, to greet and glean up to date information and then move on. I didn't want to impose on the residents either, for they would surely go to great lengths again to accommodate us, and we'd lose good sledding weather. We'd try and reach the Meehan before nightfall and camp at its foot.

Being daytime, those who weren't out hunting and fishing, or at home, were to be found in the central community building – the largest and most recently constructed. It contained a small store for food and provisions, an offshoot of the larger store in Qaanaaq. Also, a little room to store packets and letters brought over intermittently by helicopter sat off to the side.

Although half a dozen women and young people, ten per cent of Siorapaluk's full population, were either scanning the poorly stocked shelves for tinned food or just standing around, there was a hushed atmosphere. A couple of people we'd met before smiled, but were shy. Anders asked the storekeeper if any hunters were in town or whether they were all on excursions. Most, it appeared, were, but 'old man' Oshima, whose grown up progeny we knew in Qaanaaq, was home.

A young boy, perhaps ten years old, tugged at my arm. I was still wearing my down jacket as we only intended to be inside for a moment, so we stuck out somewhat. He wasn't being mischievous though, as we'd come to expect from most young children. He had heard the conversation and was enthusiastically offering his services as a guide to Oshima's house.

It's an observation I'd made since my earliest days in Greenland, myself barely out of my teens, about the children. School days are short and rarely progress into later teenage years. At home parents, especially the men, are often away working and hunting and so for want of a better phrase, the youngest generation, *kingudhiarruit*, have time on their hands. There's only so much time that playing games can pass and for those keen to learn the art of the hunter, the clothes-maker or the dog driver, their mentors could not always be available. Boredom and even a sort of winter hysteria, especially in the dark months, can manifest in many ways – depression and resentment of their situation, petty criminality can be another, but in others an enthusiastic desire to help anyone and get involved in anything. Malaurie wrote copiously about the 'malaise' and 'black thoughts' of the Polar Eskimos, which they overcame daily by keeping busy. We were led outside back into the cold, between a couple of abandoned homes and sheds, not far from the little green home in which we'd slept during our first time in Siorapaluk, and then up the hill. Snow had accumulated and we trudged in a line in snow up to our knees. The poor boy, galloping ahead, was up to his waist. Traversing a rocky ridge that led to a flatter section of earth and boulders, we reached the highest elevated house in the hamlet, originally yellow but now faded to a flaky beige and natural timber shade.

The only barriers to entry were a set of steps and wooden swing gate, to keep dogs away from his fish and meat drying racks, as his front door was open. Oshima had heard the footsteps outside and came to see what the commotion was about. The child pointed to us and spoke to him in Inuktun, then promptly ran off with a laugh down the hill, before we had a chance to thank him. Oshima motioned hastily with his hand to come inside.

He spoke a few words of English and insisted on employing them as we went through the familiar ritual of being shown to our seats, always the best in the room, and made coffee and tea. He was painfully quietly spoken and I had to strain to hear. He seemed to know it all already. Despite the distances that separated settlements, the speed that rumours, whether accurate or not, spread far and wide was remarkable. He had already found a map and, donning reading spectacles, he pulled it out alongside our own. For a minute or two Oshima studied them intently, comparing the markings and drawing his worn and weathered index finger across the papers. He seemed satisfied, and asked me more about what advice we needed most.

I was unsure about what language he wanted, so started in the simplest English I could. His nods occasionally turned to confusion, and Anders helped us through with some Danish vocabulary. Being Japanese to an extent I wasn't sure about – we did not know even if he was born here or had mixed heritage – I didn't want to assume anything about his fluency in any language. It turned out neither – Oshima had visited decades ago, and never left.

Our aims? The icecap, by any means. If successful? Onwards to Etah as a first objective, and testing of potential for extended journeys on the inland ice sheet.

He smiled. "Yes! You can do. Hard."

He once again told us of this enigma – the Japanese solo skier and his dog. He said there had been much discussion, and worry, about his plans and his fate.

Completely beside the fact he was travelling apparently alone, through a treacherous area of High Arctic wilderness in late winter and also without a full or even partial complement of safety equipment (like a beacon or satellite phone), there was the legality issue. He hadn't left any form of route or plan with a local, but the common sense and 'blind eye' often applied by those in power to some travel restrictions wouldn't extend to something this abstract and potentially reckless. You however may be on the ultra-purist side of the spectrum and believe it bizarre and artificial to apply any bureaucratic shackles to the activities of 'explorers'.

Although tweaked almost annually by a Nuuk government department struggling to keep pace with environmental change and foreign sports expeditions further south, the land laid at the time as follows: There was to be no remote travel between mid-September and the end of March – spanning the winter darkness and associated worst of the cold. Exceptions to this were areas around common adventure travel hubs in the South and East, and also sea ice outside of the unusually conservative three nautical miles of territorial coastline waters. In addition, the rocky Inglefield Land north of Qaanaaq was 'permit free' year-round (to ease logistics for summer geologists) and the national park, a vast northeastern chunk of Greenland, needed additional permissions beyond a travel permit. Also, no permits would be issued to soloists, and Inuit are of course exempt. One useful break in the rules were that out of a seven day period, you could travel into a 'permit' area for twenty-four hours without one.

I won't tread too far into my misgivings about the flaws behind some of the knee-jerk reaction to tragedies, so tightening regulations in Nuuk, especially the permit start dates creeping ever-later into the spring – dangerous and daft in my view. Early is snowy, cold and stable. Later is unpredictable and with melt water causing havoc to icecap routes.

The Japanese man was relying on the relaxed approach of northern enforcement and the common sense of local people. If he was lucky, this would be no problem, but in my view when operating on the edge of the envelope, your responsibilities to others increase yet more. He was travelling solo, and was highly likely to enter a 'permit area' of icecap for longer than a day. We hoped, for his sake and others, that he was on top of his game in terms of skills and would return unscathed.

Critically for our research though, he was said to have ascended the Meehan, proving it was navigable for a skier at least. We knew dogs were another matter.

Oshima drew his hand slowly over the Meehan ice tongue on the map as it snaked amongst rocky outcrops and cliffs. Contours waxed and waned in steep sections. His detailed knowledge was extraordinary, even though it was a mere 'backup' route to the inland ice for when the straightforward western ones were out of reach, as then.

We should climb the snow ditch on the left-hand side and follow it up the initial steep rise from sea level. Once on a flatter part, we'd cross over to the right-hand side and avoid the worst of the crevasses. Hugging the other side, we needed to snake around to the right before crossing the glacier yet again to avoid a violent icefall section. From there, the hinge region with the icecap itself would be crevassed, some snow shrouded (most hazardous) and some not. It was bad all the way across, and we needed to proceed slowly and test the snow ahead of us carefully. It was sage advice. We thanked him warmly and enjoyed the last of our tea. We needed to get on in order to not finish late. Besides, our dogs were temporarily anchored in full teams on the edge of Siorapaluk, not in groups. We didn't want to return to see there had been fighting.

On our way once again, we followed the coastline – the Meehan in sight for all but the final few miles where a small bluff obscured it. It was windless, the daylight turned to twilight and the teams were beyond reproach. This, I thought, was reward for our hundreds of hours of training.

We camped at the foot of the glacier, but slightly offset to one side. It would be unwise to be in the sights of a potential katabatic storm flowing down the gulley. Also, too close and we could suffer the effects of any ice collapsing at the leading edge, potentially cracking the sea ice too.

We doled out the chain and set the dogs in two parallel lines – one team on each. In the middle, protected from any roaming polar bears, we pitched the spacious tipi. The bear risk in reality was low. To get to us, they'd need to pass Siorapaluk, and would either get attracted to their rubbish tip or become an unfortunate victim of a Polar Eskimo hunter with a keen eye trained out across the ice.

Instead of the extremely quick camp set-up possible on a man-hauling journey – teammates in the past and I had gone from stopping skiing to stove running in well under five minutes – the dogs were quite the anchors. The normal order of priority is 'security, group tasks, personal administration' – now it was 'security, dogs, group, personal'.

I was placing the final ice screw as James was finishing up and Anders was carrying in 'tent bags' (essentially overnight equipment and a set of rations). It was slow work, as I had to clear compacted ice and snow from inside the screw. Without a clear tube beyond the teeth, trying to get them to bite into the rock solid sea ice was impossible. Our custom solution to this was a piece of wood, to be held down on the floor with one hand, and a nine inch iron nail sticking straight up from it. With a couple of sharp thwacks, the nail should dislodge the trapped ice and send it out the other end.

It was late and the only light, apart from our lamps, was from the stars. I glanced up, alone for once and quiet since the dogs were exhausted, to admire the stellar display only available in the true wilderness, entirely free from light pollution. The longer I looked, the more stars there were; it became almost overwhelming – a sensory overload. I almost forgot about the -30°C air for a moment.

The ice screw needed one final impact, and as I brought the metal tube down hard one last time, I felt it skip and miss. I held still for a moment, unsure what had happened. It finally dawned as I realised I could not move my hand, inside a thick down mitt though it was, that I really had missed. The pain came next. I had sent the nail straight through my mitt and deep into the flesh of my palm. Instinctively, I yanked back and with some resistance, my hand came free. I raised my arm to get a look and blood poured from the cuff of the mitt down my arm.

On closer inspection and having delved into a handy medical pouch, it turned out the hole was small, but deep. The bleeding subsided with pressure and I was able to clean the wound with iodine and dress it. The pain that persisted was a dull, thudding ache.

The other two hadn't really been aware of my lone, dramatic attempts to impale myself, and were visibly surprised when I told them.

Finally, medical mishap over, I pulled the tarps over our sled contents and ensured the dog food was out of reach. I checked for injuries, trimmed some of the fur between their toes to avoid icing up and resultant chewing, ensured that chains weren't twisted, but savoured a few minutes to just enjoy the beautiful evening sky. I gave Pinky and the Brain a good scratch between the ears and then joined James and Anders in our little canvas home. They'd got the stove running and a hot dinner wasn't far away – an expedition paradise.

Muffin and Zorro

CHAPTER 13: Rolling with the Punches

BLEARY EYED, but well rested, I stirred after a good six hours of sleep. I went through my normal wakeup routine when in a sleeping bag – rousing each limb in turn to get some blood flowing – and coming to terms with the day ahead. It struck dramatically at how having the dogs provided us security, especially in our heads, and therefore deeper sleep. When in a fragile tent with nothing but fabric between you and the polar wilderness and all that entails, it can have you slightly on edge - keeping an eye on where your gun is and listening intently to the faintest sounds outside. It's almost never a threat, but you only need to be complacent to the tell-tale sign of breaking sea ice or a predator once.

"Morning boys and girls!" hollered loudly was a standard greeting, partly to raise morning spirits with a light mood, and partly to make sure no-one could pretend to have not heard the infernal alarm clock. We knew that Anders' cessation of his extended renditions of snoring were indication of his being awake.

It could be our last morning on the sea ice before a foray onto icecap and highlands, with more unpredictable conditions that can accompany. I had to remind myself that although icecaps had been my apprenticeship and I found life on them very familiar, the others had different backgrounds – Anders in the Scandinavian hills and taiga, and James in the mountains. I didn't think much about the icecap in terms of trepidation and the unknown, more in just how we'd need to tweak our routine to suit.

We packed up and attached the dogs – the glacier front straight ahead of us, beautiful as it rose steeply from the sea and up into the rocky mountains. In a few weeks, the sun would be in the sky for much of the day, even encroaching into the night-time hours. It was sad to think that the beautiful palette of blues that the twilight delivered and the oranges, reds and yellows of the low sunsets and sunrises would become increasingly rare. So few, save its own people, have or will ever see the Arctic outside of the fleeting summer weeks or the contrasty sun and blue skies of the late spring. It seemed a shame. The unearthly, movingly beautiful side of this 'cold place' is really to be found in the darker half of the annual cycle.

The day would be staccato. The way to tackle the glacier, except if we were lucky and found an easy route or even some ski tracks, would be using a scout and then a number of concerted short efforts to climb with the dogs. There would be none of the monotony or rhythm of clocking up miles across sea ice expanses.

With the lightest whisper of "hak", in fact to the detriment of my dog control credentials I should probably admit it was just **before**, the hounds were off. We had less than a mile to go before we'd meet the vast wall of ice, so could afford to let them have their fun – sprinting much of the way. James wanted to do the same with his team, so let Anders and me almost reach the Meehan before giving chase.

There's no denying it – any major glacier is intimidating but we were presented with a fair prospect. Vast yawning crevasses (deep fissures), steep sections and slippery glassy areas of ice all contribute. In comparison to some I'd traversed in the past on foot though, I could see options. That was a start. The plan was simple. I'd ski up alone to get a better view of the middle section and James and Anders would keep order with the dogs, taking the chance to untangle and make a couple of running repairs to harnesses. I could take photographs of critical sections that might require discussion, but it was my assessment of the glacier itself that the yes-no decision would hinge on.

The right-hand side – the faster-moving zone of ice – was impenetrable. There are many factors that contribute to the behaviour of glacial ice as it flows unstoppably towards the sea with gravity and trillions of tons of bulk on its side. The ice sheet itself is nearly seven-hundred thousand cubic miles of ice – an unfathomable statistic. That is over seven trillion swimming pools worth. Speed of movement is the main controller of the ice's appearance though. If it moves rapidly, meaning there's a 'pulling' force (extensional tensile stress), then the ice splits hundreds of times across the width of the glacier, rather like the brittle chocolate on a bending Mars Bar.

That blocked side had a large ice cliff at its leading edge, endless sharp spires of aggressive white and blue ice, and it butted up hard against the rock cliff to the side.

The middle was steep too, but softened in appearance as it reached the shallower outside of the curve. The left was where I saw possibility. The rock that formed that side of the valley, or gorge, was more of a rolling

204

hill than a vertical wall, and that had allowed a characteristic ditch to form where ice met rock. Although snow cover was in short supply, it had accumulated in the ditch. What resulted was a ramp of soft, uncrevassed snow.

We'd long since foregone our technical climbing and glacier gear but kept some rope and pulleys handy, plus endless karabiners (useful for everything). We didn't know when we'd need to fish someone or something out of a lead or a crack in the ice, or have to lift or drag loads around. It might seem foolish to head up a glacier alone, but rationally it's little different in terms of danger than much polar travel. Someone would need to watch the dogs, so we couldn't set up a three-on-a-rope system to arrest any falls or accidents. Roping up two people is very dangerous as a violent jolt from the fall of one is usually enough to pull the other off their feet and into the same abyss. It's normal for pairs to only rarely rope up on polar journeys and soloists obviously don't even have the choice.

I was looking for a passage for dogs, not a climbing route, so my selection of routes was going to be conservative anyway. I wouldn't enter heavily crevassed areas and could test unknown snow the normal way – with sharp prods from a ski pole. With a plan to be back two and a half hours after I set off, it was time to test the Meehan.

Feeling liberated and rather at home back on cross country skis, I felt the snow glide under them with the familiar whooshing sound that can become metronomic. I swung my arms back and forth, only lightly tapping the snowy ice surface with the spiked tips of my poles.

Soon, I was at the glacier terminus. In summer, as it slowly calved icebergs into the fjord, the leading edge would be young and raw, exposed to the air for the first time in thousands of years. In winter, it slows down as the glacier can't calve and snow can soften the appearance – almost merging seamlessly into the frozen sea. Every glacier is dramatically different; the most majestic and sometimes terrifying place a polar skier plies their trade.

I made my way up the slope, perhaps only a thirty-degree angle, and curled right onto the snowy ditch. What I found was like a haphazard staircase of vast steps and landings. Some parts were steep, others flat as a pancake. The snow sat deep here and there, but ice poked through in others. There was no crevassing, but I had to keep in mind that the easy going was fine for a skier, manoeuvrable and lightweight as they are, but I had to adopt the mindset of a dog sled.

I picked my way up and up, out of sight of the team, and into the shadows, out of the line of the rising glare of the sun. It became cold and I added the nose and cheek section of my fabric balaclava. I needed to keep moving to stay warm, as I'd left my heavier insulation back on the sled.

Some of the 'steps' would definitely present a challenge for the dogs. Although underfoot it was snowy – perfect for dog paws to grip onto – we'd need to assist and even use ropes and anchors. I was optimistic, nonetheless.

It was time to attempt the crossing to the other side of the glacier. The ditch was filling with rocks and narrowed to a tapered end, so I couldn't stay there forever – a shame as I was making light work of it.

I had to clamber up onto the main glacier section – pulleys and throwing dogs up one by one would be needed, but still, do-able. Once atop the vast slab of ice, I smiled and rested a moment as the sun hit my face. I'd been gone nearly an hour, so assuming a careful and unrushed descent, would need to make a decision pretty soon, or risk worrying Anders and James.

It was there that my heart began to sink. The shape of the ice, limited snowfall, and I presumed a couple of windy blasts from 'up top' had exposed the glacier ice itself. Sometimes this can be rough and grippy, but otherwise is glassy smooth and slippery. I soon began to struggle to move. My skis had long since been removed and carried over my shoulder, forcing me to walk with both poles in the other hand. I could have stowed my skis where the snow ended, but what if I needed them later or had to return via another path? I wore not just my large polar soft boots, but also a set of microspikes that are tensioned using a soft rubber mesh over the sole. The aim is to create traction on icy surfaces whilst avoiding the discomfort of large, clumsy climbing crampons.

Hard packed and then pressurised over unfathomable stretches of time and with the huge weight and power of the ever-changing ice sheet, glacier ice is often as hard as rock. Even my microspikes were struggling and I had to select my foot placement with care.

I pushed on for another fifteen minutes, crossing much of the Meehan until I reached the edge of a large, open crevassed zone. This would be the extent of my eastward travel. I only saw more exposed blue and grey ice ahead with tiny patches of snow in the 'dimples'. Perhaps, with mighty efforts, patience and good luck, we could get the dogs up by walking them on leads. The sleds could be pushed up on the low friction surface by people. The deal breaker for me wasn't the way up though. I suspected a day or two of hard work would bring us the icecap via this route. It was the way down. We had to assume that, having completed our work on the icecap, we'd have to descend back down to the sea ice the way we'd gone up. Intuition, whether you're hill walking or driving dogs up an ice rink of a large polar glacier, says that going up is hard, and coming down the easy, fun part. On the contrary, going up is controllable and easy to stage in manageable chunks, as long as the surface is feasible. Going down, as a hiker, stresses joints and toes. Going down with dogs can be extremely hazardous, with a dozen things that can run out of control – the mixed blessing of gravity.

It was for this reason that I, with palpable frustration, wrote off the Meehan. The dogs would be nigh on impossible to control as a team and the sled, even with ropes or chains as brakes, would at half a metric ton be a behemoth with its own mind. If it were a slow, land glacier like the one flowing down to Etah, that might work, but the random and viciously open crevasses of the Meehan were death traps. If we allowed the sled to run out of control just for a split second, it would accelerate instantly, run over the dog team and drag them into the void.

Apart from the tales found once or twice in journals and very early books, we'd heard twice about the perils of mixing glaciers with dogs, and of Polar Eskimos losing their own lives in them. There was a reason the locals only use glaciers when absolutely necessary, and for minimal time.

One hunter, in a story retold by Finn, had been walking his dogs slowly and carefully up a glacier to the west, missing crevasses to the left and the right. It was mid-spring, so they were partially filled and obscured by snow. Something caught the attention of one of the dogs and, with their typical lack of a sense of self-preservation, the whole team bolted. Soon, they crossed a weak snow bridge over a crevasse and most of the team broke through. Although the sled was heavy enough and sufficiently far back to arrest the fall, a few of the dogs were hanging in their harnesses in mid air. They struggled and ended up wriggling out of their harnesses, falling to their deaths. Soon the hunter was able to yank the survivors back out by their ropes and regain control. He returned to Qaanaaq with only half his team, heartbroken.

A bystander might, and naïve visitors do, mistake the aloofness and practical approach seen day to day towards his dogs by a Polar Eskimo as disdain or cruelty. The truth could not be more different. A hunter will breed, raise, feed and spend years with his dogs, relying on them for his survival, risking his own life to feed them. A creation of a two-way bond of absolute trust.

To avoid such disasters, a trick used for some time now was to tie a loose cord around a dog's waist and run the hauling trace through it – this stops a dog being able to wriggle backwards out of a harness. An overtight waist rope is also a tell-tale sign of a dog owner who has been neglecting his dogs. As dogs grow and change shape from lean in summer to muscular in winter, the waist ropes tighten. A good hunter will ensure that the rope is slightly loose and isn't causing any rubbing or sores on the dog's skin.

I retreated, taking photographs and some footage as I went, and over an hour later hopped down the final slope onto the sea ice, teams and teammates in sight. They had been looking to me expectantly, so I skied as fast as possible and made a cutting gesture to signal 'no luck'.

Their reaction to the failure was remarkably chipper. It was as we half-suspected – fine for a skier and a dog, and suicide for a large transit sled, heavy loads and a full dog team.

We spent a short while relaxing with the dogs, had a snack, and then laid out the navigational chart on the lid of our sled box. Next glacier!

We had no options further to the west of Siorapaluk. The ice was thin or broken altogether even just a dozen or so miles down the coast. In fact, the whole fjord entrance was recently reformed. It would need another few days to thicken. Even the old meat storage and hut cluster of Neqi was unobtainable, let alone the series of glaciers beyond towards the main capes and Smith Sound. We'd go back east and try the next fjord – 'attacking' our old nemesis the Tugto again but via the Majortulerivviggiaq lowland plain and frozen Taherruit frozen lakes, not as before along the Bowdoin Fjord to the east of Qaanaaq.

Alas, after days of effort, the portcullis of moraine again blocked our path, even though we could see the Tugto clearly beyond, with glassy ice hummocks and previous little snow. We'd had to wrap up in some of the coldest temperatures yet, well below -35°C, and used skis on a fragile frozen river leading to the *taheq* – or lake. We retreated to Qaanaaq empty-handed.

On the journey back to Qaanaaq, we made use of one of the two hunting shelters en route – the other being derelict and filled with drifted snow. As the miles ticked by, I'd reflected on the distinctions between homes and shelters in the wilderness, and their meaning to the psyche of a polar skier.

Four walls say 'home' to me. A tent means 'expedition'. To bounce around from one to the other each day and then have the deceptive comfort of a settlement between forays was odd to get used to. Generally, if crossing an icecap for example, you set yourself squarely towards the realities of the weeks ahead and reset expectations of safety, comfort and luxuries. Small things take on huge importance and you become, for want of a better word, tougher. It takes a few days to flip from one mentality to another, making this existence in Avanerriaq confusing at times.

It shouldn't be assumed that a tent though is at the bottom of the pile when it comes to comfort. In many cases, a well-administered tent in skilled hands can be warmer, larger, cleaner and more pleasant than a hunting hut. What the huts could provide though, apart from not having to be pitched and collapsed, were security from predators and wind. Nothing is bear-proof and polar bears often break into caches, huts and cabins all across the Arctic, but the wooden walls buy you time and warning so you can wake and react.

There is something primal and wonderful about creating warmth and safety from amongst the cold and hostile. It is even more special to happen upon someone else's shelter when tired and in low spirits, and be invited in.

I squinted as I led the dogs around the final cape before Qaanaaq, the bright sun beaming straight into my eyes from above Herbert Island as it followed its low, early spring track. I nearly tripped as I whipped left and right, half-blinded, but Enrique wasn't in the mood for exuberant leaps for freedom that day, so we passed much of the southern shore at a leisurely pace. We owed the dogs a day off work but they didn't know that. I also thought about the psychology of dog sledding from their point of view, and we three had a few amusing reflections on it. The dogs loved to run, for sure. It was selectively bred into the type of dog as an innate behaviour. It's wrong to anthropomorphise animals, even if they show human-like traits, and thereby to credit them with self-awareness or the ability to conceptualise time, hopes or fears. To not know where the finish line was though, with the daily exertion of hauling a sled, could be enough to break the mind of a human polar skier. Not so the dogs. They did not care; perhaps they did not know to care – a kind of blissful ignorance. They did know when they were tired though, and a handful tried every trick in the book to try and get away with slacking without catching our notice.

Bump, bump, bump. We left the smooth, snowy track of the coast and entered the outskirts of Qaanaaq, still out on the sea ice of course. We snaked left and right amongst screw ice. The path opened up a little ahead, and I saw a dog team coming straight for us. I had no idea who it was yet, but the gap was closing fast – me to the right, and he to the left. Would my dogs rebel embarrassingly and his obediently stay on course? No idea. We had of course been routinely watched by other hunters, travelling with some too, but it was a high stakes test for sure. Twenty yards, then ten. Enrique stayed true – Thor glanced over, but made no lunge. Disaster averted! I tried to look nonchalant and unconcerned, draped casually across the front of the sled as we all did. It was just as well, as mid-greeting, I realised the driver was Mikael.

Qaanaaq, once again.

CHAPTER 14: Replan

ANDRÉ MALRAUX'S observation that 'risk alone does not qualify something as an adventure' is complimented by the geologist-explorer Conrad Kilian's succinct response to tiresome faux-motivational tales of explorer blood and toil, 'good enough…we've been through that. Now, tell me, what have you got to report to us?' What purpose? What value? These were inescapable questions for us.

After the weeks as novices acquiring the skilful art of driving dogs, we were able to concentrate on the journeys, the routes and the aims, instead of simply seeing getting the dogs running well as the end in itself. To begin with, merely getting them in order, in the right direction, and then settling into a sustainable rhythm was everything. Eventually that morphs into an afterthought.

Obviously we, and all of the inhabitants of Avanerriaq, were locked into our various inlets, fjords and sounds we found ourselves in, unable to link with those north and south due to a lack of navigable ice around headlands. Although not directly linked to the ice conditions far, far north on the Arctic Ocean, which had swayed my judgement regarding the viability of Dark Ice, our local ice was not an unrelated system.

The only way out (discounting airlifts of course) was inland onto the icecap. If able to access the freshwater glacial ice from the coastal halo, a traveller could then within reason end up anywhere.

In our research and brainstorming, the formidable glaciers we had attempted so far had stymied notions for traverses to the Far South, but much more so by the dogs' projected maximum range and the likelihood of ice breakup at the other end when we reached it.

As far as we could tell, even as the spring was approaching its last weeks, no-one had yet ventured north to Etah or the rich hunting grounds of Inglefield Land, and certainly not the southernmost settlement of the region at Savissivik, frequently locked off and at risk of abandonment.

These limitations could be disastrous for the settlements; a massively reduced caribou and muskox hunting season, and an inability to visit extended families in the remotest outposts. We had already heard stories of the tiny store in Savissivik running out of supplies and the infants of the families there struggling to eat enough. Their only stroke of luck was that being at the northern extent of the notorious Melville Bay, the area that separates the land of the Polar Eskimos from 'mainstream' Greenland, meant a large supply of polar bears. Some wander straight into the settlement and require no overt hunting; the limit on how many are taken is purely enforced by government quota.

The main route north is the Clements Markham Glacier, the same as we had earmarked for our ascent due to its gradual slope. This was entirely cut off from inhabited areas by open water. To the south, the only way in reality was the Politiken, which could actually be seen across the Murchison Sound from Qaanaaq in good weather. Another very steep route was marked on maps but didn't seem attractive at all. This main southbound glacier route then led to a small icecap traverse and a descent to the coast and islands beyond; perhaps a three to five day journey by dog sled. However, Finn had told us that it was most certainly impossible this year and had been getting progressively less accessible, icier and steeper, each year before. This story was confirmed when we heard one very experienced hunter with a light sled and fit team had just a day before needed to abandon his attempt and so returned to Qaanaaq.

The people of Qaanaaq, *qaanaarmiut* (the suffix –miut is used to show 'people from a place'), Siorapaluk and Qeqertat were trapped in the Murchison Sound and Inglefield Fjord. Looking now at the prospect of basing our journeys in the region rather than south, this shared problem in need of a solution became a focus for me. Could we find a new route to access the ice sheet? This could benefit both our own plans and more so, even those of the locals.

I had noticed a glacier the previous summer out of the small window of our plane, when I travelled up to arrange the cargo and equipment. It was south of Qaanaaq and in those snow-free weeks stuck out, mainly for its beauty. I saw a cascade of ice pour out from between two rocky outcrops and across the low gravelly coastline. Vast and wide, it looked just like wax would ooze out from a gap in a wounded candle's lip.

At the time I thought nothing more of it, apart from taking a few photographs and noting its lack of crevasses – a joyous sight. It was south and not north of our start point, and so at the time was irrelevant since it would be useless on the Dark Ice Project. Sat around our wooden table in

Qaanaaq, I mentioned it to the team, tentatively as even its location was somewhat vague. I unfurled a map and we crowded round.

Sure enough, along the long, narrow Olrik Fjord that flowed east to west around thirty miles south of Qaanaaq, was a glacier, amongst others, whose shape was unmistakeable. It wasn't large in comparison to some of the real monsters, the tidewater glaciers that act as major exits for inland ice to calve into the sea. Regardless, the bulb shape of this piedmont glacier made it the one.

It appeared unnamed, but we knew that some of the hunters must be aware of it. We headed out around the quiet village as the sky dimmed to twilight and knocked on doors. A number of affirmatives confirmed it as the glacier we were after, but stories were limited to its splendour during the summer when its whites and blues contrast against the brown rocky shore.

A number of hunters recalled isolated herds of caribou on the slopes to its north, just across the water. No one, however, mentioned using it as an access route or even setting foot on it. It appeared that some areas and glaciers of this region, which has been populated on and off for thousands of years, are to look at and not to touch.

We had time, quite a few remaining weeks, and the sea ice south and east appeared on the satellite images to be pretty amiable. We should commit to an extended journey to the fjord and to try and access the glacier. We could also head up the neck of the glacial tongue and double-check there was no crevassed hinge region as it met the icecap. Generally, in a given area, you get either crevasses or melt channels but not both together.

I looked out the window of our home with yet another stunning sky of an impossible number of colours reflected off the ice and snow from the sky above. Whoever said that the Arctic was a monotonous grey, devoid of colour, had clearly never seen this. I could see the Politikken, glimmering with foreboding snow-free ice in the sun and the headland to the east, my left, that we'd need to negotiate in order to make our way along the Olrik.

Although we'd travelled south and then east on our way to Qeqertat one time, we'd not ventured that far as we felt it held little interest for our early plans, our eyes then focussed north. We also knew the edge of the navigable ice wasn't too far away to the south. I had some more intelligence gathering to do and tapped into the seemingly endless knowledge banks of our hunter friends. Peter, Finn, Mikael and Otto all agreed that the route was good, but that we should beware of thin ice off the headland.

The standard tactic we had when nervous of a headland was to aim a couple of knuckles (a primitive but effective form of distance measurement which can be communicated easily) to the landward side of the headland, join the beach or ice foot there, and gingerly skirt our way around it. This would hopefully keep us on solid surfaces and our feet dry.

As an enormous boost to us all, we also had Anastasia back. She flew back up after her enforced hiatus back in London and we collected her from the airstrip by dog sled. She was the same beaming individual we'd missed, and it took time for her to take in the bounds with which we'd improved with the dogs. The last time she saw them, all was chaotic. James now had a co-driver, and we had tales to regale – months of lessons learned – and the bruises to prove it.

CHAPTER 15: Pushing Our Luck

WITH WEATHER CONDITIONS settled by stable high pressure, there was no time to lose, and we decided to leave the next day on our quest for a way onto the Inland Ice.

Finn gave us a lift in his pickup to the tide crack in return for a handful of lithium batteries and the now-familiar shuttle of supplies over the jumbled ice to the sleds took a little under half an hour. The dogs were at their rowdiest because they saw us come, then go, then reappear, a few times and must have wondered what on Earth was up. It was the tail end of March and we were ready to go, our little yellow home secured on the hill and everything we needed, nearly a ton in all, strapped to the sleds.

Then, Lyka appeared. Hearts sank. Dogs went ballistic. It wasn't a new occurrence, but her timing could not have been worse. The dogs were jumping about in anticipation of some exercise anyway but this distraction meant that their energies were aimed in any direction but where they were needed. Lyka darted in and out of the dogs, revelling in her freedom and teasing them for the lack of theirs. From one dog team to the other she bounded, leaving us to control them the best we could.

Lyka was no longer our dog. Unable to cajole her even remotely into running with a team, we had swapped her for a similarly aged young male. A dirty white and very much still growing, his flash of black fur across his face saw him named 'Zorro', but he often went by the name of simply 'puppy'. Lyka's new owner now had her on a metal slip chain in the centre of Qaanaaq. This had the opposite effect of calming her and the poor, frantic little dog spent all day and night barking and trying to slip her chain. Every couple of days, she succeeded, hence the unauthorised visits and repeats of her jumping and escaping behaviour. What she needed was a quiet staking point on the edge of town alongside a calm, older male to learn from.

As usual, to regulate the dogs' enthusiasm, especially Enrique's and to make sure they didn't dart off somewhere of their own choosing, one of us walked out each team in turn. Using the whip to flop to one side and then the other, it created a 'wall' in the minds of the lead dogs that they didn't want to cross, for fear of the whip. Taking the lead with my sled, each time Enrique got a little ahead of himself a short flick with the whip handle brought the long tail neatly down in front of him, sparking a retreat.

Usually as soon as we found flat ice, and the smells and temptations of Qaanaaq, the other dog teams and fish caches had ebbed away, I could stop the dogs, use an 'ah-eeeeee' command to keep them still, walk back and flop onto the sled. Then, in an almost theatrical moment of suspense that never grew dull, one call of 'hak!' was enough to unleash an indescribable release of pent up energy and off we went. If I had not laid down on the flatbed of the sled or jumped onto the back, I would have been left long behind.

Runaway sleds were something we were, thinking about it now somewhat over-anxiously, concerned about. The destruction and embarrassment of having a sled accelerate off at breakneck speed without anyone at the helm would set us back at best, and at worst result in a lost team.

One older hunter still on the ice each week was Lars. He was a walking encyclopaedia of Polar Eskimo history and practical day-to-day sledding and hunting tips – a real master of the Arctic reflected in his modest, quiet tone. This grey-haired and neatly moustached gentleman never inflicted his knowledge; he gently offered it. One story brought our paranoia about dog control firmly home. As a thirty-year old hunter in the years before much of what is now Qaanaaq existed at all, he was alone near Herbert Island in winter, save for his ten dogs. Stepped off the sled to the rear and coiling a rope ready for the journey home, something caught his dogs' attention in the murky darkness. One of them bolted in the direction of the island, and the ice edge a few miles beyond. The rest followed and before he could stop them, Lars' whole team, and sled, was gone. He stood there on the sea ice with only his whip, and by pure chance, had moments before donned his thickest fur parka. His rifle was slung over the rear of the sled, however.

Lars called his dogs, but nothing. He began to walk back towards Qaanaaq, which he could only locate through intimate knowledge of the land and ice, in those days lacking its dim glow of electric lights.

At some point in the next hour, he realised he was not alone. Ironically his quarry, a large male polar bear, had followed various scents and was now stood feet away, sniffing the air to try and identify whether Lars was food or not. The bear approached, and Lars commanded it sternly to stay back – a deep, confident voice can, remarkably, deter curious bears. This failed, so Lars used his whip and expertly planted a stinger of a crack on the bear's nose. Still it came, cautiously. In this manner, walking backwards much of the way so as not to turn his back, Lars retreated the miles back to his village. The fate of the bear was sealed. Lars had lost his beloved team though, his sled and many priceless possessions. Never seen again, he presumed they'd reached the thinner edge near the edge of fast ice, broken through, and drowned. If this could happen to Lars, what chance did we have?

Weeks later, our one close call with a runaway catastrophe did indeed come. Not yet with lead dogs under our thumb, my team bolted whilst neither Anders nor I were aboard. They made straight for Qaanaaq at breakneck speed. I rallied James' team and we gave chase, with nightmares of what pandemonium we'd return to. Through sheer dumb luck, the scent they'd caught was their own, and had reached their staking points, well short of Qaanaaq itself, and usefully tied themselves up in knots, halting any further advance.

Lyka had not been distracted by some other tasty morsel or group of dogs to taunt and so, we assumed these weeks later still thinking we were her humans, came bounding past us. She sprinted over to the other team, which had settled into a good six mile per hour rhythm, made them deviate off course by forty five degrees and then stopped, causing them to follow suit. What a start!

At least the weather was holding strong in terms of visibility and we could clearly make out the headland a long way to our south. A keen easterly breeze had built, lifting up some of the precious layer of snow off the ice and transforming it into drift. Their language having developed in such a bespoke response to the local geography, locals even had a word for this particular wind – *anilatsihoq* – the east wind from the fjord.

James had led his team in a wide arch past us, gleaming back proudly at us that his team were the fastest, and had consequently 'inherited' Lyka from us. This made him less delighted. After around an hour, Anders and I had tired of the amusing sight of seeing both him and Anastasia try and shoo the infernal little black dog away, and saw them finally stop with a loud "aa-eeeee!"

James got straight off the sled and, handing the whip to Anastasia, marched directly back towards us. I had never seen such intent in this normally reserved and peaceful teammate of ours! He had had enough of Lyka. Every time they got going well and the boys had got into a rhythm, their collective love interest appeared from a flank and veered them off.

"What can we do about her, short of shooting her!" James exclaimed from beneath his hood. Although one hundred per cent joke, it did cross my mind that that fate would be the likeliest if we were travelling with the local Polar Eskimos and a stray dog was causing disruption.

"I don't know," I said. "Tie her to an iceberg and hope that by the time she's chewed her way free, we'll be out of sight and she'll run to Qaanaaq?"

It was tempting, and we couldn't think of a real solution. We were too far from Qaanaaq now to go back and shackle her up outside her new home.

On we would go, twenty-two dogs strong. One too many. The wind grew to a fresh breeze and it was making its way down the wide fjord from the east. Enjoying one of the advantages that dog driving has over man-hauling, I turned my whole body to face away from the wind and pulled my hood up to form a microclimate of calmness around my face. I would need to glance at the dogs to check their lines were ok and that our heading was good, but otherwise I could watch as each face and ridge of the now-familiar Herbert Island showed itself.

The initial area of concern was the first headland, the one we were warned about. Sometimes the ice there could be absent entirely, making use of the precarious ice foot necessary, or chancing it on the ice further offshore and away from the turbulent sub-ice currents.

We could all see that the headland itself was near vertical and the ice jumbled at its foot. Apparently there was a tiny hunting hut on the corner, but we couldn't see where. Sceptical that an ice foot would be our best option, I suggested we aim for the headland itself cautiously and, if the ice looked poor, deviate to the west and skirt round.

The gamble paid off and instead of losing time and distance to a dogleg either left or right, we found the ice to be thick. There were even the remnants of seal nets on the thick but crack-strewn ice; this ice had been stable for some days.

Areas where currents meet and split, and the associated breathing holes called *aglut*, are favourite spots for netting seals, the primary hunting tactic in the dark winter months. In the spring and summer, harpooning a seal by ambush or shooting from behind a white canvas on a frame, pushed carefully across the ice, is often more efficient.

Each quarry requires its own technique, as one animal's strength may be its cunning, another its speed, and another a large set of sharp teeth. The ultimate prize is unsurprisingly *nanoq* – the polar bear.

Apart from the addition of a rifle to make a clean, safe kill, tactics haven't altered greatly since historic times. A dog team is used to search for and surprise roaming or resting bears, in past centuries teams were as small as three or four, although remarkable stories do exist of dog-less hunters working alone. They are trained to chase and attack the bear if allowed free from the sled traces, with the first dog often losing their life to the bear's formidable defensive efforts. Hunters could then close in to spear the bear and complete the hunt, but not without risk of themselves receiving serious wounds. Now, a well-placed bullet can reduce much of the risk and ensure the bear suffers less. As is typical, the hunter can then skin and divide the bear whilst still warm, and reward the dogs with a fresh feed.

A large number of the annual quota now hunted are those bears straying into human villages, but their distribution reacted as Polar Eskimo communities and their demands grew. Long ago there were so many bears in the Kap York region, near where Avanerriaq transitions into Melville Bay, that hunters let most go, taking only the prime specimens.

Finally we spotted the tiny wooden hut, precariously perched on the edge of the crumbly cliff, supported by wooden struts that I suspected wouldn't pass any form of structural engineering test. Still, it had clearly survived all that the Arctic had to throw at it over a number of years.

Anders decided he wanted to investigate and, as we rested the dogs, made his way through the ice hummocks and rocks and rumble of the headland. He emerged from the top of a rickety wooden ladder onto the 'veranda' of the hut, and poked his head inside.

"There is a little wooden chair, which I won't break by trying to use it, and…a halibut!" We all roared with laughter as Anders stood there on the deck with a solid-frozen halibut in one hand, its nose pointing to the sky. For us, don't ask me why but halibut, both their appearance and the word, had become a running joke.

We had a long way to go east before reaching our stop for the night, the final little hut in the area and our first miles on the dramatic Olrik Fjord were something I'd looked forward to. Narrow and long, it had always stuck out visually and was tantalising as its entrance could be spied from the hill above Qaanaaq. Along the southern side was an almost methodical succession of glaciers from the icecap beyond, and the north side was a long rocky scree and snow slope.

Glancing back at the 'no-go' Politikken and the aptly-named Savage Glacier to its left, we checked out the coast, hugging the north as we went. It did begin to drag by the time we began to look out for signs of our shelter for the night.

The wind had scoured the sea ice of much of its precious snow on the main crossing from Qaanaaq, but here it had gone a step further. One area of cliff to the northeast was, for want of a better word, missing, and this channelled the wind into quite a breeze. The last ten minutes, actually after we'd spotted the vague dark dot we hoped was another shelter, became a little race. The snow was gone, leaving bare and smooth ice below. Flat at first, as we approached shore, the ice began to undulate into regular, wave-like ripples. This was the result of the ice forming slowly over water being moved by both tides and wind; from a distance it was quite beautiful.

Close up however, it made the ride in quite the rollercoaster. The dogs got their second wind as the resistance of the sled dropped to nearly zero over the glassy ice and so began to gallop, seemingly forgetting the hours of work they'd already done. We were following the others in once again and Enrique became like a dog possessed, sprinting and looking back to the rest of the team with a frenzied look of 'Come on! Run faster!'

Almost as if made specially for us, the ripples of sea ice led up to a beach which had a covering layer of ice, a hundred yards or so either side of the rather new-looking hut. One team could be staked left, one right, and the distance to walk all of the gear up was minimal. As if to complete the perfection, the sun came out behind us to the east and offered half an hour of deep, warm light before it set behind a large mountain.

The dogs were chained up and fed first as always, and then we grouped up for a chat and inspected our home for the night. We were in a little enclave protected from the wind, so our few shuttles back and forth from the sleds could be leisurely. Just a few paces further up the hill though and the full force of this funnelled airstream could be felt.

Evidence of summer hunting was scattered around the hut; antlers, vertebrae, wings of birds. It still staggered me that caribou could survive on this isolated, cold, windy, almost vegetation-free expanse.

The hut was probably the most recently erected of any we had seen and sported an angled roof. Unsure about the wisdom of having so much headroom; the greater the volume of air, the slower it is to heat and harder to keep warm, Anders and I fiddled with the oil burner sat in the corner, which had a nifty pipe to direct fumes through the wall and out – luxury indeed. We quickly found though that all was not well with it. Despite our best efforts and after starting these primitive but simple heaters dozens of times before, we couldn't achieve a clean burn. New, clean oil, and checking for obstructions or contamination seemed to do little good.

Soon, belching from the sooty lid of the burner was a continuous stream of acrid smoke and small black carbon specks - *paoq*. Our eyes burned almost unbearably and as Anastasia and James came up the wooden steps and purposefully stamped inside, they joined Anders and me in a cacophony of coughing and spluttering.

This existence was unpleasant – but we could easily decamp to the luxury of our tipi tent if need be. It made me think about the way of life that pre-'Discovery' Polar Eskimos endured.

Ask anyone at home about what an 'igloo' is and you'll invariably hear about dome-shaped snow or ice houses in which 'Eskimos' or Inuit live. The inaccuracies here are plenty. Firstly, an *iglu* simply means house, and was most commonly a semi-permanent dwelling made from a combination of available resources, rocks, peaty earth in *issoq* slabs, dried and stitched sealskins and even washed up driftwood – an *igluigaq*.

What most people would envisage as an igloo is actually often a temporary and transient shelter on extended journeys when alternatives like hunting shelters (either in situ or dragged behind a dog sled) or a simple tarp aren't options. This 'snow house' is called an *igluvigaq*, rare in the dry Greenlandic North but something impressive settlements could be built from in snowier parts of the Canadian Arctic. Some semi-permanent ones had passages from one to the other, and the largest could house forty Inuit. There are many interchangeable terms between the closely related languages of the Greenlandic Polar Eskimo and Eastern Canadian Baffin Island Inuit, but lost nuance can lead to this slip of accuracy. These snow houses are not made of ice, which is far too hard and difficult to work and shape. Instead, deep compacted snow is cut into large blocks and constructed expertly into a self-supporting and heat-retaining, wind-excluding home. The caveat is that they need a good quantity of hard-packed snow. Unless a major snowdrift behind an iceberg could be found, this often takes snow houses out of the equation in Avanerriaq.

Coming back to the parallels I was drawing between our smoky hunter's shelter and the semi-permanent homes of the pre-1818 natives, I remembered a large, old book I chanced upon in the little wooden eave of polar veteran Robert's Peroni's home in Tasiilaq, Eastern Greenland (the region of Greenland known locally as Tunu), a few years before. It showed grainy and dated images of traditional dwellings from the earliest days of colour photography. Frankly, at risk of condescension, those depicted looked in a sorry state. The people appeared cramped and unable to stand fully upright, faces blackened from burning seal blubber and sharing the same space to live, cook, sleep and rest in. I became evermore grateful for my lot in life.

Only rarely would communities convene outside of an *iglu* when not out 'on the land' – indeed, the pressure to hunt was such that men were rarely home. However, between high snow walls to exclude cold and wind, a group might occasionally crowd around a central fire to boil meat from a nearby rack and share gossip.

Whilst many homes that the Polar Eskimos created from the materials surrounding them appeared to, by the reports of the first explorers and subsequent ethnologists, be more comfortable than the picture I just painted, with an entrance tunnel, headroom to stand and an *igliq* raised sleeping platform (albeit one which children and parents shared), it was still far removed from what other civilisations around the world were accustomed to. It is obvious that this was entirely down to the building materials available, a lack of complex tools for the same reason, and an inability to write things down – a limit to arithmetic, engineering and education. It was not due to a lack of ambition. This truth will be vital when we discuss their future later.

Having wedged the door open to release much of the airborne soot, hanging feather-like in the air, we had started to breathe a little more easily. Anders, who had been given the unenviable task of monitoring the heater, had succeeded in taming the contraption to some extent, in between moments of two-foot-high flames and a couple of accidental extinguishes.

I placed a small thermometer on a ledge next to a wall, partly for curiosity and partly to decide when it was worth hanging up some clothing to air and release any moisture it had absorbed.

It steadily rose from -20°C to -10°C, thawed, and then onwards to ten degrees in the positive direction, before stalling. In one of the tiniest six-by-six shelters, a single burner could send the temperature sky-high; there being precious little air to heat. In this more spacious one though, the heater was fighting a losing battle with the intense cold outside and the large surface area of walls and roof. The insulation they contained was some help, but the cold can rarely be overcome when it sets its mind to it.

At any rate, -15°C inside a tent is considered a comfortable working temperature, so we were living in the lap of luxury by comparison. No complaints.

With the dogs fed, scuffles out the way and the more timid dogs checked to make sure they'd eaten sufficient; we went through the normal meal-time and snow-melting routine in preparation for our push to the glacier. I was excited and wondered if maybe, just maybe, the glacier could be our key to a success of real significance. I took a final look across the little bay, past the dogs and to where the sun had disappeared behind the mountains. I scampered outside and behind a rock to answer the call, before retiring to bed. It is almost a habit, childish really, that this final trip of the day outside is done in a flurry of activity and with insufficient clothing – usually a base layer and a fleece at most, plus bare feet in boots or just Primaloft booties.

Good conditions beckoned the following morning and we got 'on the road' by around eight o' clock. It was a long slog to where we expected to intercept the glacier and the sea ice was again bereft of snow. The ice foot and beach served well as a route for a mile or so, before becoming so narrow that our wooden sled cross beams began to get stuck on the protruding rocks. A very smug-looking James and Anastasia overtook Anders' and my team having taken longer to cross the crack, thereafter finding their pace on open ice.

To the left, the north, were unusually low rolling hills, snow-covered of course, stretching up and away. These were where we were told caribou were to be found. It made sense to cross the fjord from the northern shore to the southern at some point, and I signalled to James that it was time as the fjord widened.

The sun had risen high in the sky and save for a few wispy clouds, it was a perfect blue day in the High Arctic – the wind was low and that made the journey all the more pleasant.

We took a break a few hours in to discuss progress and mastermind our route into the glacier, and James had built up a lead of a hundred yards or so; his team working like a dream and entertaining themselves with fresh sights and smells.

I saw both of them had got off the sled for a quick jog, perfectly usual to get the blood flowing into cold toes. All of a sudden, the dogs disappeared from view. Within a couple of seconds, so had one of the yellow-clad figures. The second fell down to their waist. My eyes out on stalks and instantly commanding the dogs to stop with an urgent "aa-eeeee!!", I could make out the dogs floundering in the water. Most alarming of all, I could vaguely see the sled begin to tip and sink down too. A thousand pounds of sled would not stay buoyant for long and it was attached firmly to the ten animals.

It was at this point that I lost track of events. I knew I had to help, but must not allow the same fate to befall my own team. It meant we had to check our own sea ice beneath our feet and stay put if safe. The only help I could be was on skis, so as not to add to the emergency when I arrived.

I asked Anders to stay with the sled – I would don skis and go over to the stricken dog team. My efforts to unlash the skis stowed horizontally on the front of the sled took my attention and in that minute or so, it makes sense to let James explain what happened first-hand:

'Deep into the fast-ice filled fjord we were happily sledding along, a hundred yards or so from the 'beach' when most of the dogs dropped straight through the ice. Looking around we realised we had strayed onto a large area of very thin ice lightly covered in wet snow, with almost no demarcation. We instantly made the decision to retreat. The only way to do that was with the dogs pulling, we couldn't just drag the sledge backwards and the dogs out of the water with it. Anastasia held the sledge while I went forward to help the dogs. I fell through up to my chest but managed to wriggle back on to the ice. We were very aware that if the sledge broke through it would sink and drown any dogs attached.

We readied ourselves to lose the sledge and release the dogs if needs be. The hole in the ice was growing as the dogs tried to climb out. We beckoned the dogs, both in and out of the water, over to one side ready to U-turn the sledge back to safety. Anastasia and I both broke through again but again managed to recover quickly. Just as the runners of the sledge broke through and the back of sledge began to sink, enough of the dogs climbed out of the water and were able to pull the sledge clear and follow us as we encouraged them back towards safer ice.'

Just as I was stepping into my bindings, James, Anastasia and the hounds were inexplicably hurtling their way back towards us. Stopping a sled's length short in order to not let the dogs clash, they both calmly sauntered over. The time for storytelling was later, and I flicked into objective-mode. I asked if either were injured, what clothing had become saturated and if they had sensation in feet and hands. The affirmative from both reassured me but we still had to work fast. The good conditions could change fast and a wet body in soaked clothes at -20°C can chill to dangerous levels alarmingly rapidly.

They wouldn't hear anything of it, then or now, but fast thinking from the pair whilst in shock and immersed in freezing seawater undoubtedly saved the lives of their dogs and also each other.

We quickly decided that James and Anastasia would remain in their existing clothing and change only socks and gloves. This would mean they would have to dry their clothes through exercise and body heat; in other words by skiing or hiking until they were dry.

It was not far to the shoreline where we were planning to divert off towards the ice tongue, a rise of around ten feet from the fjord. To speed things up and as we predicted a load of dead-ends in the extensive and steep pressure ice, I left the trio to finish their sock changes and regroup as I set off on skis to route-find, one of my favourite polar tasks.

I climbed a large block of blue-grey sea ice to get a better view and first, I glanced back to assess what had happened. Although we knew that a section of the fjord was often dangerous due to shallow, fast-moving sub-ice water, it was now clearly visible some way off; a darkened patch against the perfect white snow. The spot where the first sled and the dogs crashed through was stark; a now black hole in otherwise good-looking ice. Whilst it could be said that slow, methodical checking of the ice thickness could have served as a pre-warning and avoided the drama, we believed we were far away from the hazardous sections and there were no tell-tale signs on the margins. You cannot spend each yard of every journey painstakingly testing sea ice and snow bridges – you'd never get anywhere.

Looking forward, I could see a glimpse of the leading edge of the closest, western extent of the vast 'blob' of glacier ice that spilled out onto the lowland. More immediate was a sharp shoreline with a six to ten foot rise onto land, and then rubble and fractured ice between that and my vantage point. On skis I began to find an optimum route for the dogs so that I could bridge gaps in the ice, and I was soon out of sight of the sleds. A skier's ideal path could be impossible for the sleds so I had to not slip into 'automatic' and reminded myself of their limits.

I would find dead ends, for sure. Since I intended to progress a fair way onto land and to try and find a good approach as well, I could be apart from Anastasia, James, Anders and dogs for perhaps an hour or more. This meant no chance to exchange notes so I took advantage of the calm lack of wind and decided to write messages in the snow. If I found my path blocked and had to backtrack twenty yards to try another, I needed to avoid confusing them with which one to follow. A simple cross sign carved into the snow next to the 'do not follow' ski trail with my ski pole, and a smiley face next to the one I favoured should do the trick.

Left and right I wiggled through the ice, eventually finding the steep rise to land right in front of me. All that remained was to make a fairly committed leap across a four-foot gap and I made landfall. I quickly scouted to find a replacement crossing spot for that gap, which the dogs would fall in. Job done.

Fortuitously, a snow ramp to the mainland sat thirty yards or so to the right, so I followed that up. Once clear, I could make out much of the side of the glacier – quite a sight! From what I could make out, there was

226

little crevassing, one large melt river scar. Only the extreme western edge looked steep and uninviting.

I decided to forge on and try to see how a move towards the glacier itself would work – assuming that the sleds must be on their way by then and that I would soon be caught up with.

The terrain was very poor for skiing, even though I only had short 'kicker' skins on the bottoms for grip. Tufts of the dry, pioneering plants were pushing through a thin carpet of snow, but more irritatingly, so were stones and rocks. I winced as I felt and heard the scrapes of skis sliding over them. Avoiding the worst by snaking around, I was gradually gaining elevation and learning more about the mammoth ice wall we were about to tackle.

The sleds meanwhile caught up and we found an easier route on the lower sections of snow and ice. In no time the glassy ice shoreline was behind us and a neat triangle of near-sea ice-level melt channels opened out to large cliffs of blue and white ice – the glacier. Ten minutes of following smooth frozen 'rivers' gave us our first proper look – we were placed centrally on the glacier front.

What we discovered wasn't ideal. To our immediate front was a sheer cliff of ice at least thirty feet in height. To the right (the west) was a continuing cliff, with a gap of twenty feet or so before a steep slope of rock, moraine and the start of our lowland. To the left was a vast wall of moraine, easily fifty feet or more high, and it seemed to butt right up against the edge of the glacier.

These were not attractive options for a group of four humans and twenty-one dogs seeking to get a ton of sled and supplies up onto a glacier. The one incentive for us was that from our previous vantage, the glacier top itself was enticingly flat and navigable.

We needed to explore the leading edge of the glacier. Perhaps we'd find a way up in five minutes. Perhaps we'd need to reach the furthest part, miles away, before an opportunity presented itself. Of course, there was a chance of retreating again, disappointed. What we lacked most was an overview of where we were, so I went in search of 'over watch'. Leaving the three others, along with the dogs and sleds at sea level, I clambered up a steep snow and rock slope onto an area of high ground.

From my new vantage point I could see almost everything; up onto the gently sloping glacier itself, the vast melt scar down its belly, the moraine in the direction we were interested in and finally down to the small ant-like figures – the patiently waiting team. I gestured for them to move to the moraine as I saw a ramp to get half the way up and along a sort of shelf. It was rocky, but the runners could easily be planed smooth again another day. It was a one in four slope, so as the trio coaxed the dogs to haul up and pushing hard from behind the sleds themselves, I had time to scout ahead.

"Guys, it's not going to work that way. More of the same. Unless there's a ramp on the far, far side next to the mountains." I reported. "We'll have to find a way up around here, or call it a day."

Luckily, progress had been slow and I found the two sleds a third of the way up the slope and resting for a moment in between heaves.

A sigh of disappointment circled. You could almost sense the dogs could tell that their hard fought yards up the slope would soon be relinquished. They were on a flattish area, the sleds weren't going anywhere, and the sun gently warmed their little gulley. We decided to leave them there and go for a scout near the melt gorge exit point and the area where the moraine began on the left edge of the central cliffs. It was more for intrigue really, as we had written it off as a dog route.

First though, Anders said he wanted to see the ice from the top, even just for the sake of it. I agreed to head up with him, and James and Anastasia were happy tending to the dogs and doing some additional clothes-drying in the sun. Even at extreme negative-degree temperatures, the sun can dry and 'reloft' clothes by sublimation.

Moraine is hard to climb, aside from being mightily irritating as a barrier to progress or on the other hand a lifeline red carpet to salvation off dangerous ice. As made clear before, it is not rock. Like a mound of granulated sugar, it has no solid core or basis and can shift and landslide without warning. Our moraine here was fifty feet tall and very steep. Like an extreme scramble up a scree-slope and without ropes, we three-pointed our way up. At times, my foothold choices failed me and I had to sidestep urgently to not lose my position altogether. Anders was ahead. I could see from below that it was becoming very precarious. A fall would result in a serious tumble with plenty of rock to collide with and loose earth to bury us on the way down.

Anders had just reached the long ridge and shouted down he could see the ice.

"It meets the ice directly!" he said. If only we could get the dogs up. An impossibility.

Anders photographed a panorama for our benefit, and then came down via where I was embedded. Rocks and moraine rained around me in all directions. He was inadvertently and unavoidably kicking down fifty per cent of the surface he was skipping over. The whole slope was in motion. We scuttled down to the bottom as fast as possible, trying desperately to not lose footing.

It was time to check that scar in the ice. Anders went over to the main leading edge. It was the apex of the glacier – the furthest extent of its reach to the northwest. Like tourists in front of the Tower of Pisa, he stood aside this giant vertical cliff of ice and we took a couple of photographs. Just a foot away, he looked up in trepidation at the sheer bulk of it, and the striations of blue, grey and black, which were the result of sediment layers as the ice had creaked forward over hundreds of years.

We cornered ice blocks, boulders and the zigzag shape of the end point of the giant scar that ran down the main glacier. It could be mistaken for a vast longitudinal crevasse, but was a result of summer melting – carved by water just as it does to rock to create a canyon.

I think we must have all seen it at once. I'm certain that none of us seriously expected to find anything of real use to us here. We knew full well that in ninety-five per cent of cases, access to glaciers from the bottom is best found on the gentler edges, around the lateral moraine.

There was silence. Anastasia spun around and smiled. We all looked up, our necks craning and eyes straining to link spot to spot, ledge to ledge.

There was a way.

Around the rear of a large moraine stack that seamlessly assimilated with the ice, it was a mess. Dusty, loose rock and gravel sat amongst ice and large rocks protruded, with a distinctly unstable air about it.

We needed to climb up around twenty-five or thirty feet to clear the cliff and find the lowest slope to reach this holy grail of icecap-access glaciers. This, messy and difficult, could be it. With the gradient of, say, a staircase, the ice and rock led us up to the ice-side of the moraine stack. It was the glacier top.

We climbed and clambered after collecting ropes and other equipment. Stood atop our 'flight of stairs' and encouraged that we could, after a serious fashion drag up bags, boxes and dogs, and then pulley up a sled, I surveyed the scene. Extending to the right, and free from the oppressive shade of the cliffs, was a smooth, undulating glacier bathed in sunlight. There was precious little snow cover and only the dips caught drifts of it. Apart from the deep gorge, it was like a dream.

James stepped on a little way to explore. All of a sudden, my attention snapped back from the spectacular view to more immediate dangers.

"Hold on!" I called. James was already well aware of what I was about to say, as he gingerly walked one foot in front of the other, testing the snow and earth-strewn snow ahead of him. He was following the boundary between ice and moraine. Crevasses. With this level of snow, large ones would be open and easy to spot, but smaller 'slots' could be shrouded and lead to a bad fall or a broken ankle.

After three failed attempts to gain admission to the icecap, in a region where we knew it really **should** be possible, it was a relief too and that made the view all the sweeter. All glaciers differ – beautiful and daunting in their own ways, whether a flat snowfield, a glassy hummock-strewn ramp or a crevassed-monster.

We decided to head up and have a look. We knew it should flatten off and provide us with a view of the miles of gradual, navigable slope heading up to the mile-high elevation of this outcrop of the ice sheet. Eventually, the ice sheet rises up to three times that – a scale hard to grasp.

Anastasia, ever the fearless volunteer as evidenced whilst training on a seriously hazardous crevasse-field and icefall in Iceland the year before, was first up. With the odd call of "left a bit!", "try a bit to the right?", on we went. We took turns to scout, some of which on quite steep sections of ice less obvious when viewed from afar, but so far so good.

It was great fun. Freed from the shackles of dog sledding or having to haul a sledge ourselves, we explored. There was no evidence of dangerous crevassing. We finally needed to remove some ice screws that we'd placed as safety anchors, and it gave me an opportunity to step back and photograph Anders and James as tiny specks against the enormity of ice.

Enjoying our little adventure and relishing the stress relief of having finally 'done it', we walked a long loop. We once again met the moraine, but where the ice and moraine descended into a steep ditch in a sort of V-shape. The sun was blocked and a chilly breeze flowed along. For the first time in hours, I had to reach into my outer jacket pocket to don my neck gaiter, which could protect part of my face from the cold. As a reminder of the seriousness of the place we were immersed in, I spotted a horizontally orientated, isolated cloud in the sky. I'd seen it before, especially on icecaps. It meant wind.

As our jubilant team had checked all the ice protection and ropes were collected back in and hopped back down to the estuary floor, I wanted to check on James and Anastasia. Some of their clothing was, although warm, still damp and that worried me. We made a few tweaks to mitt choices and so on, and the hardy pair promised to regularly get off the sled and rewarm by jogging as we sledded back west.

Anders and I had a cold ride back. We had set ourselves alongside each other, slumped on our sides with our backs to the steadily growing wind. The sun had become obscured by a large hill, so we had lost what minuscule warming effect it had. The shadows intensified the colours though, so the entire valley and frozen sea within was a picture – every texture and shade of blue had its place. I snapped back to reality as I realised my nose was cold. I held my mitt in front of it, allowing the polar bear fur to insulate and exclude the wind.

The other pair were regularly getting off to jog, and the miles suddenly couldn't pass fast enough.

That evening in the hut, we shunned the problematic heater in deference to our two Coleman stoves running on some locally sourced petroleum we were testing and had in abundance. It was horribly dirty and contaminated, coughing and spluttering through our fastidious stove jets with yellow flame amongst the blue. James had noticed a little demarcation on his big toe, so carefully dried his boot liners and socks over the heat to make sure it couldn't deteriorate the next day. There are so many levels of cold damage to human tissue, and his was very slight and easily reversible. It needed to be watched like a hawk and nursed back to health, otherwise the compromised blood flow could move to stage two, then three and so on alarmingly quickly.

'Puppy', Zorro, had been flagging for some time and had sore paw pads. The prevalence of barren sea ice without even basic snow cover on previous days had clearly taken its toll. After long journeys on all but the 'softest' pack of snow, dogs can get sore feet. Usually the solution is rest and if available, lotions or specialist dog paw waxes.

If a dog slacked off and started running half a body-length behind the main pack, it usually wouldn't be tolerated. In this case though, and given that we felt extra affection for Puppy who was still a few months from being fully grown, we made an exception. The extra effort of hauling might prove too much for the poor animal. I empathised with memories of forced marches in military training with sub-standard clothing. We'd also been trimming the dogs' hair between their toes to avoid discomfort from ice balls forming underfoot – eighty canine feet to treat every few weeks.

Deep snow now made the dogs have to step with more care, instead of neatly flowing along with efficient gaits. At around -15°C or -20°C, the snow would actually be at an ideal temperature – warm enough to not suffer from unmeltable ice crystals and cold enough to not become wet and 'clingy'.

Some hours later, we reached the headland, with precariously perched hunting shelter, complete with halibut, still reliably atop the rocky face.

We needed a rope detangle and were making slow, if reliable progress, so stopped to take in the view, shelter from the wind and have a chat. I'd been thinking. Not just about the glacier, the dogs, the snow, the wind or anything so immediate. I felt a tinge of déjà vu from that horrible December evening in Hans' guesthouse, post-satellite image appraisal.

"Chaps, let's talk dogs," I began, diplomatically. "We had no idea of how we'd get on with them, if they'd run well or if our skills would accrue fast enough. We had our eye on doing an extended journey over the icecap to the south. I have to be honest – I don't think in the deep snow we'd find up there and with heavy supplies of food, that we'd reach either hypothetical target."

There was little retort. None, in fact. The elephant in the room had been stomping around for some weeks. I suppose we had all been appreciating the improvements the dogs, and we, had been making, and expected it to continue. But, when would the stamina and control advances plateau off? When would we reach our zenith? We didn't have unlimited time and needed to make a call either way soon. I knew that 1000-mile plus journeys had been achieved in the past with dogs. Most were with resupplies, an impossibility for us. The few that weren't, were truly mammoth and by veteran dog drivers. Some relied on the destruction of animals to feed the rest. That was one way to get around the problem with ultra-long distance dog travel – the other is to just load up. Yes, dogs can run faster than a human, and further in a day than a human. But, you need to feed ten or twelve mouths, not one or two. Their daily feeds more or less match a person's in weight. The problem is therefore obvious and their 'ultimate potential distance' is defined by how much food could be pulled on the sled.

Would it be in some way a failure to stay in the wider Avanerriaq area and do large mileages there? It would certainly be more technically demanding, instead of just a long slog over a featureless ice sheet. We also wouldn't have to contend with spurious surface melting or uncertainty about selling dogs the other end. It did seem on one hand unimportant where we ended up, but a sort of cop out to not head south. I struggled with it and it was clear I wasn't the only one.

"I can't honestly say I think we'd make good progress in heavy snow either," James said.

Anastasia agreed. "What would we do if we ran out of supplies or got stuck?"

To that question, the answer was simple, and horrendous. We would need either a bank busting resupply by ski plane from Iceland, or be evacuated from the ice sheet. We could reasonably abandon the sleds, but we, plus nearly a ton of dogs would need to be shuttled by helicopter to the coast. Without a medical need or emergency to initiate an insurance claim, it would cost tens of thousands of pounds and make us a laughing stock. We mustn't begin unless we have a definite means to turn back, or fair certainty of success.

"I think we need to put the icecap idea to bed then," I said seriously. "We can make more certain plans around here, plus there's so much more to do. We went into this without expectations, as it's all so new to us. There's no shame."

Our group of four nodded. We were a little sad, but it was the right decision and I felt content – the coast held for me more novelty and challenge. We had made huge progress socially – perhaps as small catalysts to change local views towards outsiders and especially those from formerly colonial nations. Selfishly, I knew the extended icecap journey would have been more for my career than my heart. I had made four journeys on the icecap in past years and so repetition could start to eek in. The only purpose would be to create a headline or more impressive CV entry. For that reason, I put education ahead of ego.

Onwards. The dogs had enjoyed their brief rest by lying down and having a leisurely pee. They would never fully appreciate the beauty of the landscape they lived in – a vast 'loo with a view'.

It took three hours or so to cross the main fjord. The dogs had Qaanaaq in their sights, little black dots on the horizon that began to morph into twinkling lights as the evening drew in, fast and unrelentingly as ever.

I wanted to direct the dogs left, so we would seamlessly pick up some tracks to the west and then slide into our staking area where we had our dog camp. The dogs had different ideas though and kept steaming straight ahead towards the sights and smells of the busy sea ice just off the shore at the centre of town. All the other teams, seals, fish, meat and other scents must have been irresistible for a curious dog. Considering halting the team and manually walking them left, the slow option, I hesitated.

"Let them run in?" I asked Anders. He smiled and nodded a mischievous affirmative. We were almost side by side with James and Anastasia's team. The excitement of Qaanaaq needed no additional motivation for the dogs so needn't run line astern.

This seemingly innocuous decision was so indicative. A couple of months before, I wouldn't have dreamt of it. Our control was too poor, as was our confidence, and premonitions of chaos and destruction would have necessitated the 'safe' option. This time, I had confidence in the team and confidence in myself. We could enter Qaanaaq via the front door at speed and deal with whatever came our way. Assertive dog control would steer us clear of staked out dogs and ultimately, stop us when we needed it.

The bumpy ice began – a sure sign we were nearly ashore. Directly in front of the centre of Qaanaaq, where the oil storage tanks were, the pressured screw ice progressed the furthest out to sea of any area. There was nigh on half a mile of it. Hanging on tight and encouraging the dogs with calls of "yip, yip!" we were racing in. Soon, they would be able to rest and lick their sore feet.

Bang, bang, bang. The runners of the sled bounced along over the rock-solid ice features and the lashings creaked as they flexed. The two main runners were rising and falling independently, just like the advanced suspension you'd expect on a 4x4 truck. Between bounding and a fast trot, the dogs' speed made the blocks of ice pass either side of us in a blur. It was great fun.

I whipped to the side and shouted to get Enrique's attention. "Haruu, haruu." Left, left. We gently erred to the side and met a direct track I'd eyed up for our route in. As a straight race, we had pulled gradually ahead of the others and so they pulled in behind to follow. I could make out figures on the beach. We had an audience. Don't mess up now, I thought!

The impacts with the ice were bone shattering. We had reached the tidal zone with the tide crack itself not far ahead. Hundreds of sled tracks in and out over past weeks had marked the path with scars carved into the ice and hard packed snow. The final rise was ahead – beyond it the smooth icy beach. We leapt over it and the bow of the sled shot up in the air, slamming back down. Anders hopped off, once the flatbed was horizontal once again, and we both called a stop, trying to sound as nonchalant as possible. I even managed a friendly wave to the group of men a dozen yards or so away, which they duly returned. The dogs had been as good as gold and I was beaming with pride.

All that was left was to walk them calmly down the beach, unload gear at the bottom of our hill, quickly re-cross the tide crack to our spot and then stake out and feed.

Our success on the glacier was news we wanted to spread. We no longer ourselves **needed** icecap access routes, but the local people badly did. Short of buying exorbitant helicopter tickets that were often delayed or cancelled due to questionable weather concerns, their option was dogs. With the Politikken out of action and the ice not extending past Siorapaluk, the Polar Eskimos could astonishingly now, mid-spring season, still not head north to Etah and the muskox of Inglefield Land, or south to Savissivik.

It would be a daft and very indirect horseshoe of a route to try and head up our glacier and then a couple of hundred miles all the way back west to Etah, but it was only a minor diversion for someone heading south past Pituffik, where Qaanaaq was relocated from to make way for the Thule Air Base. In that sense, I really felt that we had something to contribute. Of course, everyone knew the glacier was there, but we could now recommend it as a viable route.

The following days, as April loomed, passed by resting and then training the dogs, and dedicating time to shooting photographs for our sponsors, as has been a necessary aspect of polar travel for the past hundred years.

We needed an evening off and realised we'd been a little complacent in so much that as we'd made friends, had made less effort to meet new people. Tipping a hat, waving or saying 'alluu' to a stranger in the local store isn't quite the same. So, to the bar - *taffi*.

Thor

CHAPTER 16: Part of the Gang

W E KNEW THAT the bar was a far cry from what you'd find outside Greenland or even in the larger southern settlements. A disused former home, barely maintained, that had a bench installed as a 'bar' and a few tables along one wall, it was a social hub for young and old. And a place full of surprises.

We rationed our depleting stash of kroner notes as the cans of beer, merely moved over from the town store a few hours previously, had nearly doubled in price en route. Our cash was for important purchases from, amongst other places, the hunting union and timber yard. The store could theoretically accept a credit card but that could be temperamental. As such, cash was king and couldn't be endlessly flittered away on socialising, no matter how integral to our time in Qaanaaq that was.

We'd been in the bar, debating amongst ourselves the pros and cons of Green, Gold and Classic varieties of Tuborg beer, before more people arrived. As normal, it was quiet at first as people ate and began to drink at home before gravitating towards the bar or alternatively to get-togethers in friends' houses. We decided to play darts.

Stood in the middle of the bar, it was a sure-fire way to attract attention, which we'd learnt could be a mixed blessing when alcohol was involved. Most people sat in small groups of two or three. Some came in not to drink, but to chat to the man behind the bar, a friendly Polar Eskimo in his early twenties.

Initially, with a fairly empty space, darts were easy to play. We wanted to get our games over and done before flying darts and inebriated revellers could become a hazard.

We did draw a small crowd. An awkward theme developed – generally a solitary middle-aged man who, after a drink too many on a Friday when social security pay-outs are made, would grow a little invasive of personal space. Harmless, but a sad indication of the way of life for a subset of most Inuit communities, even those 'officially' dry. Qaanaaq enforced a short-lived alcohol ban a decade ago and Siorapaluk still does, on paper anyhow. No-one can deny alcohol being at the centre of so many societal problems in small, transitioning communities, especially in the Arctic. The blame for it is shared – those who clumsily introduced it and those who, responsible for their own behaviour, succumb to and abuse it. Whether in an inner-city chain pub or a makeshift bar in the wilderness, human beings are universally-levelled in how they behave after one too many.

Merete and Troels arrived through the iced-up doorway. We chatted about how we'd fared in the Olrik Fjord and about James' and Anastasia's close call with the thin ice. Troels played it down with his characteristic nonchalance but Merete looked alarmed. She appeared almost maternally protective towards our pair of swimmers.

Merete was a lovely woman, and more obviously so as we got to know her. She was a talented cook and ironically the first time any of us tasted the most exotic of Arctic meats, polar bear, it was at a small gathering at her home. A by-product of the strictly quota-limited hunt for bear furs to supply local people, the meat was fatty and uninspiring, but Merete's skills made the best of it. We had been advised to chew on the meat whilst frozen and raw, but prepared most of it in a thick broth.

Behind a wall of authentic humility, it turned out she'd led a fascinating career across the globe – from acting as independent observer for UN humanitarian missions to nursing in Africa, where she adopted her daughter, Babette. Babette studied back in Europe, but briefly visited Qaanaaq in the spring. Very circumspect about the cold, she was nonetheless adamant about a dog sled ride. We obliged gladly and one morning, she and Merete become our latest opportunities to practice *alupaartoq* – having passengers. The first, two weeks before, had been Troels and later some of the visitors from Nuuk. As a sharp reminder of the pitfalls of lapsing concentration for just a moment, Merete had been stood in front of one of the sleds as it set into motion, running her down as the runners passed over. Even the bruises couldn't dampen her enthusiasm for getting out onto the sea ice and out of Qaanaaq, but all our hearts certainly skipped a beat.

Back at the bar, by around eleven o'clock the party was in full swing and as it got to the point where darts needed to fly over peoples' heads in order to reach the dartboard, and one or two people starting to dance strayed suddenly into the firing line, we stopped. Disturbingly, our relinquishment of the darts only allowed another group to begin. Their growing collection of empty cans encouraged us to stand well behind.

During a typical day, the people of Qaanaaq appeared so far from the overtly partying type that, increasingly well oiled, the scene was far removed from what we'd become used to. It was almost like home – inebriated people dancing around to modern tracks, and also some classic rock music. Western music has been a slow sell on the Polar Eskimos – in the nineteenth century even classical music was shunned and mocked in deference to local chants. Slowly, Lutheran hymns promulgated, and now there is a more or less total adoption of modern southern music.

Apart from a couple of sparring old ladies, neither of them much over five feet tall, who needed to be separated and calmed down, the night was one of intrigue as much as of fun. We'd met almost everyone, particularly the younger locals. Far from coming across as disjointed from the community or even aloof, we were increasingly part of it and urged by people to get more involved. At least two young men were disarmingly honest with me as they sat across the table; when we arrived, they were sceptical and wondered what we wanted. Now, they realised: to learn and be part of Qaanaaq. Our approach was working. With that, it was time for home and sleep with more than a slightly heavy head – even the cold outdoors could not heal that.

I reflected on the response we'd received having arrived. It was always going to be hard to predict. Complex histories shape the ways outsiders are accepted, or not accepted, into communities, especially aboriginal ones. We had struck gold. Others, for example a British language academic who recently stationed himself in Qaanaaq, reported torrid experiences. To me it's clear that these were a result of a combination of his hubris and ineptitude in the environment, despite learning Inuktun.

Batman

CHAPTER 17: Judgement

NOT ALL DOG SLED journeys are to link village to village. If we had decided to become fully active in hunting, impossible for reasons of legality and respect to hunters, then that would be far and away the next most popular purpose. Unless a child or young teenager learning the art of driving dogs, or for one of the couple of races every spring, the Polar Eskimos do not head out for fun or purely for training, as we did. They cannot see the point – it's a waste of resources and time. Hunters who cannot travel, or choose not to, be it due to weather or poor game opportunities, stay home or make repairs. They relax and enjoy the trappings of their ever-increasingly comfortable and well-appointed homes. I can't say I blame them. An example sticks in my mind particularly.

Peter told us that his friend, Toku Oshima, (Kim Petersen's wife, the Japanese lady who'd locked horns with Rasmus in the shed in January), had been fishing far, far out on the sea ice, more distant than any we'd encountered so far. A rare case, usually women were dog sled passengers and at most required to make a transit camp homely, she was locally known for her ability to select productive fishing spots. Peter himself had been preparing, along with an older friend of his, to head south in search of polar bear. He was one of the hunters legally allowed to take one of the small quota of bears annually allotted to villages.

The weather was unchanged – with little cloud, almost no precipitation and with temperatures cold but not brutal. The calmness though was no guarantee. We'd seen a handful of breezy days, but by no means anything remotely stormy. For me, a veteran of some truly violent winds, it was rather wonderful. In fact, the general attitude of an experienced polar skier would be that if out in the wilderness, wind is dangerous only in the fact it can destroy or damage your tent. Skiing can continue, within reason, in high winds as long as you can navigate, are well clothed, and can handle it mentally. Camping is the hazardous part – when you're most vulnerable. The Polar Eskimos don't see it that way.

Inuit motivations differ from someone like me when making a human-powered journey. I might want to travel from A to B via a resource-sparse route, usually against the clock and in some senses for the sake of it. They, Inuit, are far more likely to use a course with resources available en route, and with a purpose greater than 'finding' B. Incentives might be to migrate or find new hunting territory, for hunting itself, or to visit another settlement.

This manifests by making daily mileage of greater value to me and therefore camping in borderline conditions more common. An Inuk might instead care less about schedules and racing around. As long as they arrive safely in a reasonable time, fine. They benefit from robust shelters too, with pre-laid hunting huts, hamlets en route, or sleeping structures pulled along by dogs.

The result is that Inuit typically take far fewer risks. It's all about playing the long game. This is where, I believe, their pan-Arctic famed patience comes from. 'Maybe', a favourite word of theirs, and namesake of my second book, reflects, a reluctance to tackle questions head-on. Frankly, whether you get 'it' done today or tomorrow, or next week, doesn't matter. They rarely become angered by weather, as we might. Of course, I generalise, but it's undoubtedly a cultural norm.

Peter was supposed to have headed out a few days before, but some comparatively moderate winds had picked up, perhaps twenty miles per hour or gusting to thirty. This is nothing objectively dangerous, but will slow progress and make doing things, like fishing, difficult. It would be well beneath the threshold at which I'd choose to halt skiing and seek shelter on a man-haul.

I must admit, I was surprised. The reason he'd mentioned Toku to us was that apparently she had a large surplus of fish bycatch she didn't need. She had offered it to us, and Peter mentioned he could, on the way back to Qaanaaq, go via Toku's fishing spot and bring them back should he not have a large catch of his own on the sled. It was all extremely generous.

The curious thing though was the inconsistency between his, and the general, assertions as to the impervious and macho image of 'the hunter', and the willingness to venture out only when conditions were calm.

On my 2008 Long Haul with George Bullard, I went on and on about sustainability. He must have got sick of hearing about it, but it was critical to our success; don't rush, make mistakes or prioritise a mile over survival. The mindsets were similar – you have an aim and its completion is all that matters. How, and when, is almost immaterial.

So, my initial confusion about why a proud Polar Eskimo hunter would be afraid of the wind was misguided. He was not afraid of it. He, and hundreds of successful ancestors before him who guided their tiny communities through the most horrific conditions with scant resources and zero outside assistance, was an arch-strategist. There is nothing to be gained from taking a risk or just compromising yield (fishing in the wind would doubtless harvest a smaller catch) for no reason. If you're out of supplies, injured or otherwise forced to, sure, push. If not, you must play the waiting game and do so intelligently.

Back to our fish, though. Peter was very sceptical about going onto the ice and after three daily visits, we decided to wait no longer. We felt happy about sledding in the wind and were proficient with equipment, and more importantly not losing it to the force of the wind, so would fetch the bycatch ourselves.

Later, Peter did indeed head out on his hunt, but he and companion returned empty-handed. The geography of the region made Qaanaaq, north to the Smith Sound and south to around Pituffik, not free from bears by a long shot, but not prime territory for them. Bears require large tracts of broken ice on which to hunt seals and also areas free from larger human habitations. This is yet another reason why the forced relocation to Qaanaaq was a severe problem for the Polar Eskimos.

Peter had offered us rough instructions of how to find the fishing spot, not too dissimilar to the southbound path that led to the Olrik Fjord. We'd need to navigate with skill and keep eyes peeled if we were to not miss it, a tiny sled-mounted hut and hole in the ice amongst a seemingly endless sea of white ice. Toku herself would not be there to greet us.

It was three hours before James and team, again running ahead with Comedy the lead dog, glimpsed a little dot in the distance. It was significantly off from the direction we'd been assured the hut was to be found. On another day with poorer visibility we'd have missed it and ended up having to grid search the ice or turn back. It was particularly lucky since it was to the left – into the wind.

Sure enough, it was as described. Toku's little mobile shelter was similar in size to all those we'd seen before, prescriptive due to the standard 'gauge' of a sled width. She had clearly had some spare time, access to Kim's store and a moment of house-proudness, as it was painted brightly with 'TOKU' written prominently along one side – there was no doubt that we'd happened upon the right place.

Also, in a huge pile, perhaps four feet high, sat dozens of frozen fish and rays beside the refrozen fishing holes. We were not disappointed. The fish would last our teams for days.

However, we did make an unexpected discovery; one that could not have been missed. Laid full-length beside the two rectangular holes was a vast creature. Dark-grey and black with a smooth, now frozen skin and a peaceful expression on its lifeless face, it elicited both my sadness and respect. It must have been around ten feet long. I imagined the hours and hours of struggle and eventual defeat as it was hauled in by Toku and perhaps her companions some days before (sometimes dogs are enlisted to heave also) and then being allowed to freeze, due to be sledded back to town and butchered. That, in fact, did puzzle me. Due to the extreme cold temperatures of the High Arctic, the Polar Eskimos tend to save time and effort by butchering large catches immediately, before they freeze solid. In contrast, caribou and oxen are generally summer quarry when temperatures can peak just above freezing, so there's less of a hurry.

A Greenland shark – *iqalugguaq*. I had seen one a couple of years before, already butchered and ready for dog food on the east coast. They are a fascinating part of the folklore of Greenland and its Inuit culture, as almost all animals are – occupying roles as creators, providers, kindred spirits with human brothers, or bringers of death and disease.

This one was never destined for human consumption and catching it at all was as much a product of good fortune as skill. As such, there seems to be very little impact on the species' ecology by occasional fishing successes.

We took a few photographs, unlikely to see another during our time in Avanerriaq. To get an idea of the scale, we also lay next to it and took a couple more. This sparked a huge conflict of emotion, as both a passionate polar traveller and realist as to the ways of the Arctic, and a biology graduate with love for the natural world.

Reflecting on the photographs, there was an eerie similarity to the sorts of trophy hunting photographs so vilified in recent years. Was this any different? The initial motivation was to show the animal's incredible scale. I hadn't fished the magnificent, if aesthetically challenged, shark myself. It was fished for a purpose, in as fair a fight as you can achieve, and is not listed as IUCN Threatened. Really, it wasn't any different to smiling in a photo next to a beef burger. It did though make me think more widely about the ethics of harvesting animals, trophy hunting (to which I'm thoroughly opposed) and the dignity we should afford fallen animals.

It took some time to load up the fish. We needed to keep the dogs well clear – it wasn't their feeding time after all. It turned out that the mishmash of large rays with serious-looking tail spines (removed before feeding to dogs), smaller halibut and lots of miscellaneous species I could not identify, were still slippery, albeit frozen. Keeping them on-board would be tricky, rather like averting a landslip hell-bent on fulfilling its destiny. Finally, having loaded up both sleds to capacity, strapping down with a tarp and finding a small gap to place ourselves, we were on our way. I suspect we might have jettisoned a fish or two en route.

We must have been a few miles out from Qaanaaq when we entered a zone of bumpy ice, and had to weave in and amongst a collection of small, but quite beautifully shaped pyramid-like icebergs. The surface remained fast by virtue of the iciness and lack of drifted snow, but was cracked and fractured, albeit with no large open voids.

All of a sudden, whilst I was casually mulling over our evening schedule with Anders and how to divvy up the huge haul of fish, chaos.

The screaming was like that of a banshee. The pain was apparent in every balling wail and outburst. I shot forward to see what on Earth was going on. The dogs had without warning and command from us, stopped.

I couldn't work out what was happening at first. The dogs were running about and mobbing one of their number, more out of panic and curiosity than anything else. The dog at the centre of the mob? Thor.

The noise hadn't subsided one bit. Thor was still screaming his head off. He was holding his front left leg off the ground, and then rolled over onto his side. I jumped off the sled, shouted to James and Anastasia to keep their team well away, and to Anders to pull some of the more insistent dogs away. I knelt down next to Thor and he looked straight at me in horror. He simply would not stop screaming and the noise pierced every inch of me. It became obvious what had happened. One of the tiny cracks in the sea ice, formed as a pan undergoes tension and splits in two, was next to us. The dogs run over these and hop the three or four-inch-wide gaps hundreds of times per day. Today though, Thor had made a mistake. Apparently, he had stepped into the deep crack and then been forced forward by the momentum of the team. He had broken his leg. It wasn't a bad sprain or a dislocation as the site of the injury, now fast swelling, was nowhere near a joint.

What should I do? I tried to think straight – near impossible when you can't hear yourself think and time is clearly of the essence.

I relayed to Anders and we came to a conclusion – we had only two options. Either we manage to calm Thor down and see if we can stabilise or treat him, or we shoot him. I glanced back to the sled box where we stored the rifle as my heart sank. Logically, it wasn't looking good. A local hunter would immediately choose the latter – injuries weren't commonplace, but they did happen, and even old, 'past-it' sled dogs weren't safe from being euthanised. There were no veterinary services for thousands of miles. We were still way out of Qaanaaq.

I lamented to Anders that I couldn't see what we can do for him. Thor's eyes were wide in panic and he wouldn't let me touch his leg. All I could do was try and keep him on his side so he couldn't hurt the leg further, and try and reassure him. It was desperate.

"I think I have to put him out of his misery," I said despondently. "We can't get him back like this, we're in the middle of nowhere, and no one in Qaanaaq can help."

I got up and began the ten-yard walk to the sled box. It felt like a mile. As if he had heard us speak, Thor began to quieten. I'm not sure whether the endorphins had begun to flow or the swelling had immobilised the break and lessened the pain, but something changed, for sure. I had the rifle in my hand and was about to chamber a round from the magazine.

I looked at Anders and he shrugged, agonising as I was over the most horrible of decisions. Thirty seconds later, Thor was quieter and was just lying on his side, breathing fast and deeply. That would be his reprieve.

"Let's put him in the box," I said. "We can see what we can do for him back at the house. It hadn't broken the skin, I can't find a dislocation and we have human drugs. We can ask a vet back home if any might be of use."

With that, I drew in and released my own deep sigh of relief. I put the rifle down. Looking at Thor, we held eye contact for a few seconds. He had no idea how close he had come.

Getting Thor into the box was a nightmare. James and Anastasia were some distance off, still confused about what was going on, so James had walked over. We moved a lot of supplies from our box to his, to make space, and James kept our team calm as Anders and I lifted Thor carefully. Anders had a soft spot for Thor from day one. He was visibly moved by the whole experience – locals would condemn us for this sentimentality. After all, Amundsen had essentially succeeded in the Antarctic in 1911 due to his willingness to put dogs down to feed the rest. Scott and team perished for a number of reasons, not least due to their distaste for killing dogs – shunning them as a means of transport.

We lowered him in as slowly and gently as possible. The urge to escape this strange prison overwhelmed the pain from his leg momentarily as he tried to leap out, then the screaming and wailing returned. The poor dog was having a terrible day. We could do little to calm or console. Certain that we needed to get back as soon as possible, the other sled led off and we followed. The route was bumpy and with no suspension of course, Thor was being bounced around. The only saving grace was that the dogs worked well and didn't compound our problems. We tried the box lid on, hoping in a common tactic for settling down distressed animals – shrouding them in darkness. This didn't work. Thor was just about tall enough to peek out of the box, and combined with the pain in his leg, the terror of being somewhere so unnatural and totally out of control must have been unbearably stressful.

We set aside a staking point on the uppermost section of the hill, nearest the house. From there we could see to his needs and give his leg a chance to recuperate and heal. We decided he should be kept away from the other dogs, but he couldn't end up tied to our house due to our proximity to neighbours, who wouldn't appreciate Thor's highly vocal nature.

A closer inspection of Thor did suggest we'd made the right decision. Whilst still very uncomfortable, and stressed by the fact he was now apart from the dogs and not going out on the ice, his leg couldn't have broken more cleanly. It was clear from joints and seemed to have remained 'straight'. If he healed, with lots of food, rest and if we suspected an infection, antibiotics, then all would be well. If he didn't, it would be horribly sad but at least he would be given a fighting chance. We were somewhat against the clock though. We suspected we'd only have a month or so remaining in the North before the ice began to thaw and our purpose waned. Since we were no longer leaving Thule with the dogs, they'd need to be sold locally. We wouldn't be able to sell a lame dog. He had better hurry up.

Odin and Enrique

CHAPTER 18: Learning to Share

ANASTASIA HAD NEVER been to Qeqertat. The other three of us had visited the tiny outpost twice; once on foot and once on a fledgling and fairly unimpressive dog journey. Of the entire district, save perhaps for the abandoned settlements such as Etah or Moriussaq (whose final two occupants left in 2010), it was the most traditional. We had found the welcome there to be warm, and the way of life fascinating. There was a timeless and utterly charming atmosphere about the place.

As part of our final few journeys, we earmarked Qeqertat once more. This time, with spring well and truly upon us, we'd also be able to see more of it.

We decided to take the accepted route this time, following the breath-taking, sheer, rocky-orange cliffs along to the Bowdoin Fjord, past a few glaciers and then at the end of the headland, making a beeline for the rocky islands that Qeqertat sits on the edge of. The ease with which we covered the early miles was testament to how far we'd come. We only needed to rest and detangle the dogs once or twice. Harking back to our training days, or rather weeks, in the pitch-blackness, the comparison was stark.

After a few hours, I could see the gap in the cliff – *innaq* – at last: the Bowdoin Fjord, and the scene of our very first glacier ascent attempt. We'd passed the vast pillars and slabs of rock close up for the first time. The light dimmed rapidly as we went, but what remained still did justice to their sheer size. Nigh on a kilometre high in parts, rising vertically from the frozen sea, they were as intimidating as they were mesmerising. At the base typically was a short scree slope comprised of the tons of loose rock and rubble that fell from the cliffs – these were not a climber's paradise – far too crumbly. Most were a ferrous red or orange, although stripes and diagonals of other rock types, sand colours and black, ran through them like a painter had casually drawn a giant brush across them.

I could just make out the specks of black, someway up the fjord – a cluster of three huts we'd happened upon those months before. They were most certainly long abandoned as a settlement. A neighbour had told us though, when he heard of our Bowdoin plans, it was not used only as a temporary camp in the summer for fishing excursions, but had long ago been a settlement larger than the almost non-existent Qaanaaq, and called Kangerdlugssuak.

I began to reflect as the dogs pushed on in good order, the smile on my face hard to conceal as we passed a vast gap in the cliffs, invisible on our previous passes of the area. The reason? My team. At the same moment, I glanced into the void in a cliff and a crevassed glacier flowing gracefully yet steeply from the mini-icecap atop the peninsula down to sea level.

Anders, my sled-mate and the last addition to the team, was everything I hoped as I took the last-minute risk on him, untested. He'd weathered the change of plans with the flexibility that reflected a love for the place, the people and the environment, not the trophy. His wicked and at times risqué sense of humour drove the lighter moments of our daily efforts but could instantly switch to seriousness when the situation demanded.

Anastasia had endured much. Not least her extended hiatus from the expedition, that was due purely to her nation of birth, but she had shown that gender meant little against the importance of skill and resilience. We had experienced tense moments, that's for sure. Her need for time to herself and occasional differences in outlook made them inevitable, but nothing ran deep. We had missed her and it felt like a quarter of our machine was absent for those weeks. Her return to our little home once again felt like a sort of completeness, snags or not. I felt a sense of responsibility over the effect the loss of Dark Ice had on her. Her commitment to lose not only her hair (which she'd cropped for practicality), only second to wanting to immerse herself in the wilderness for her own internal transcendent needs, was utterly admirable. To lose our initial purpose was tough, but she remained positive right up until the final weeks, on the icecap or locally – whatever the Arctic allowed.

James' quiet nature and introspection that gilded a phenomenal physical ability and strategic mind made him a natural ally for Anastasia. She particularly identified with him and I suspect would have found just being around Anders and me, louder and more forthright as we were, tougher in isolation. This completed our circle of skills and personalities all differed and filled the fissures others left vacant. Consistent though was a basic decency – the lynchpin of good polar teams from the eighteenth century to the present day. James was so focussed on the mammoth man haul journey north that I feared initially the change to dogs, amidst Polar Eskimo culture, would throw him – a loss of motivation that might prove contagious. It couldn't have been further from the truth though. And, whilst it could take a little time to coax direct views from him, I always knew what emerged was well-considered.

James had built, at times single-handedly, a genuinely functional dog sled team almost from scratch. Sights of him sprinting across the ice to avert a disaster, over-loaded jacket flapping open wildly, were hilarious. And, after all, we shared a love for white chocolate – a bond that cannot be broken. Unless there's only one square of chocolate left…

The Bowdoin Fjord was in our rear-view mirror by the time my drifting thoughts snapped back to reality. The temperature was perhaps -20ºC and the wind was noticeable only when stationary. There was no need for overt face protection, the sun was high in the cloudless blue sky, and I even made do with thinner gloves.

The final ten miles or so were undoubtedly slower going as we ceased shadowing the headland. Out 'at sea' once more, blowing snow from previous days, perhaps originating from high up on the surround ice sheet, had built up a little. It could have been nearly a foot thick – unusual for our little corner of Greenland.

We heard James ahead calling "hak, hak" to encourage his dogs. We'd not had to do so continually for a few weeks. Anastasia, far away enough to only be discernible by her gait, had hopped off and was walking – then pushing. Before long, we were doing the same. We were sledding through virgin snow and consistent direction was once again somewhat defeating Enrique and Comedy.

I volunteered to run off ahead to give them something to chase. Anders magisterially waved me forward to do my duty and before I had a chance to get half a mile ahead, was being chased down. It was fun, and I pulled out my pocket camera to film the sensation of being run down by not one, but two affectionate dog teams.

To the north, my left, was a vast coastline – the scale of which was hard to comprehend, so few points of reference that there were. 'Moving past' in front of it was an island. I recognised this as the small, steep sided mass named for Robert Peary's wife, Josephine, who came to the region with her husband on an early expedition. She had, remarkably for an American woman of her time and standing, travelled hundreds of miles on the ice with her husband. The historical importance of this, the ancient gateway from Canadian Arctic lands to Greenlandic, was intoxicating.

The dogs made a good job of the final push to the now familiar foreshore. We were helping by pushing from behind through larger snowdrifts or isolated bumpy sections. It was the first time we'd homed in on Qeqertat by picking out little wooden homes on the near edge, rather than using the twinkling lights. The sun was about to set and the whole fjord was for half an hour bathed in warm light.

Spending most of our time out on the ice, working or relaxing at home, or with our local newfound friends, we'd grown a little distant from Hans and his guesthouse, although we saw him regularly at his home and around Qaanaaq. It was no longer the winter. The specialness of the polar darkness and the inherent exclusivity it generated was stark. In fact I suspect part of why we'd experienced such acceptance was down to our enduring the dark. Now it was April and spring was itself halfway gone, change was afoot. It is not a tourist haven – perhaps rightly so but there were a handful of visitors from the south, most staying for just a week until the next flight. A scientist or two, a government worker wanting to see the North, or even a very wealthy couple who craved a brief snapshot of a place most will only read about. We were mostly unaware of these comings and goings.

We staked out our dogs in a secluded bay out of sight of the village, as we'd now done elsewhere dozens of times before, and collected a few large sacks of food for them.

The dogs went ballistic. After a long run, probably the furthest either of our teams had completed in one push in weeks, they were ravenous. Leaping and lunging at the end of their chains, all aimed directly at me as I carried the sack on my shoulder, the main chain line moved across the dust-like snow to the full extent of its slack. An ice screw had been placed at each end to secure it. James and Anders turned their attention to the sleds, strapping down the supplies for the night having collected our grab bags to drag up the steep ice waves into Qeqertat.

I had moved onto the third staking spot on the first of the parallel chain lines.

"Alex! Dogs loose!"

252

I looked up from the small pile of kibble pellets I'd poured to see an entire chain's length of dogs sprinting towards me. I had to get the dog food out of the reach of both teams before even attempting to sort out the mess or make sense of what was going on. Anders and James were running to help as I hurried away and set the bag down.

It turned out that one of the ice screws had snapped, straight across the main shaft. The combined strength of the dogs had fractured the metal which was placed in the ice but with an inch protruding – a fatal error which weakened these normally bombproof anchors.

It was chaos; the whole line of dogs had rotated round and collided with the surviving chain line. Dogs were barking, leaping around, fighting and diving onto every speck of food in the snow. Chains tangle horribly at the best of times, and the end result was like a sort of writhing, deafening spider's web. We ended up unclipping all of the offending team and reattaching them to the sled, before placing a new ice screw. There was no way on Earth we could drag the chain back into position with the dogs in such a melee. Forty very determined legs were more than a match for us. Doing the best I could to divvy out the rest of the food fairly, we walked to the nearest sled. We sat down exhausted with a theatrical thump and started laughing. Never work with animals.

As the glow in the sky was beginning to fade I walked up towards the little collection of structures. Ahead was the community building, impressive with its sloping roof that nearly met the snow on both sides. We had assumed that we could, having checked with whoever was in charge at that moment, make a little space for ourselves inside once again. We weren't sure of where Peter was, so couldn't ask him if we could use his hut, which stood on the edge of the village. He could be in Siorapaluk, off hunting to the south, having a go at the Politikken ice ramp, or anywhere.

The other three were just finishing off moving the sleds out of the way down the sea ice when I'd carried a bag or two up to the building. I piled them next to the old wooden steps so as to create a temporary stash until we'd sorted out plans. It was as I stood up again and leant back with arms out to stretch my back, much as you would after a long motorway drive, that I heard a man speaking Danish. He didn't sound like a Greenlander, whose accents tend to be softer and less hectic.

I finally caught sight of the owner of the voice who was walking purposefully towards me. He didn't seem happy.

"Hej - jeg er engelsk," I offered. Hello, I'm English.

"You cannot go in there. Who are you? We are in there," he said gruffly. I was taken aback. In such a thoroughly polite society, I wasn't used to rudeness.

Now with Anders and Anastasia arriving just behind and both oblivious to the odd start to the conversation and therefore disarmingly friendly, I explained. I told him who we were, that we'd been in the region since the early winter and were here in Qeqertat to see people and rest our dogs. He wasn't having any of it. He took my explanation as an escalation.

"We have been here in April three years now. The building is for us," he said, staring possessively at it. "We have authority to be here."

It did cross my mind to point out that we'd merely walked into the hamlet and placed a few bags down. We haven't behaved at all presumptuously, hadn't raised a British flag over the building to stake our claim and frankly, could just camp if necessary.

At that moment, the creaky door to the one-room building opened and out came two men dressed head to toe in furs. It was Rasmus and Lars. They both beamed at me and joined the circle. The Danish man seemed to have the wind knocked out of his sails as he was joined by, we assumed, a colleague, who seemed more friendly.

In minutes, it was made clear by Lars that of course we'd come into the building. A frostiness grew towards the first Dane that an issue had arisen at all – it wasn't 'their patch' after all. I smiled and outstretched my hand to the two newcomers. It was duly grasped and names were exchanged – Steffen and Gorm. Diplomatic incident over.

James, oblivious to the early exchanges and conflict-immune as ever, sauntered up and placed our stoves down, a smile from ear to ear.

We headed inside. The heat was oppressive – someone, we assumed one of the Polar Eskimos, had turned the burners up to full blast. This overt desire of Polar Eskimos to be warm, even sweating, is a legacy from the past days when *iglu* life was spent near naked and beholden to the heating of blubber lamps. We wondered why they would stay there with their clients (we assumed they were hired to provide dog transit), when there were homes nearby. It turned out that they didn't have close family in Qeqertat, so just made do as we did.

We needed to check on the dogs, and having settled them down heard a familiar noise from atop a rock to the left. Déjà vu.

"Kammak!"

Peter was outside his hut.

It turned out that he had arrived the previous day along with three other dog drivers as guides for a small group of Germans. They were bone fide tourists – an organised tour of moneyed Arctic novices simply in the North as passengers on dog sleds and see the icebergs and scenery. They, apart from Peter, had made use of a disused green home up the hill and seemed to want to keep themselves to themselves. It was an odd lack of sociability I'd seen before in insular groups touring parts of the Arctic. They seemed to crave the security of the crowd and rarely looked outside of it.

Peter seemed a little offended that he didn't know we were coming. I tried to tell him we had no idea of his plans, which began to placate him somewhat. Peter had this strange alternation between moments of real self-assuredness bordering on the macho and then what could almost be called neediness. This wasn't his personal idiosyncrasy though – every single account I researched from authors of all nationalities and points in history reported unexpected diatribes from those they'd befriended – often punctuated with self-pity and faux-modesty, or even a shock decision to retreat from a journey. Some appeared to be merely for effect and others perhaps more deep-rooted. Those who truly made friends in Avanerriaq were in a position to chastise or mock these 'phony theatrical fits of panic', as Malaurie put it. To do so with a Polar Eskimo hunter you do not have the respect of, and your dealings will be instantly at an end.

Peter was adamant that we'd all, five of us in total, stay with him in his hut, but we knew of its diminutive proportions and politely insisted we'd stay put with Rasmus and the others, but would come by for the evening and to share food.

That evening, having got back quite late from Peter's ramshackle yet cosy candlelit hut, and heard about his at times hapless clients, eaten copious seal, noodles and dry fish washed down with gallons of tea, we found out more about the Danish marauders. They were research scientists from the Danish Meteorological Institute. It was also time for me to eat some humble pie.

I had forgotten my spoon. It seemed that on every excursion, one of us left our spoon behind and this was my first time. The ribbing began. And, it wasn't just any spoon; it was my special extra-long titanium alloy one. The running joke had come full circle and I was the butt of it. Trans-European diplomatic relations were instantly mended as Steffen handed over a spare one from their vast catering box.

Conversation moved onto their work. I felt bad for the poor dog teams who'd had to haul out all the huge reinforced metal boxes packed with technical equipment, laptops and cables. Collecting sea ice thickness, salinity and other environmental datasets were their aims each spring before the ice breaks up for summer. Quite refreshing, and given the academically and politically loaded nature of what they were researching, I didn't sense an air of environmental preaching or taking sides beyond simply doing their jobs well. They were passionate about the science, the rigour of doing it properly and were keen to make sure that very expensive equipment remained intact, understandably so. We all sat around one table and I noticed an initial embarrassment from the shorter of the two, my confrontational welcoming party, lessening as he realised I bore no grudge.

Rasmus and Lars were sat a few yards away. Lars had taken up residence behind the wooden desk, presumably used for both little church services and teaching the handful of local children. Rasmus was sat, only half-derobed of furs even at this time of night and in the face of the roaring heater next to us. Sat further away but on the same bench, was Mads Ole. We hadn't seen him in some weeks and supposed he had been on an extended hunt. None spoke to each other a great deal and we kept the noise down as they sat, each with hands clasped around a mug of tea or coffee.

The curious trend of mixed modern and pre-Contact equipment continued apace. Mads Ole had an old but apparently functional inflatable sleeping mat and a sleeping bag. Rasmus had foam sleeping pads and a caribou hide to place on top. His own sleeping bag was vast, not unlike the heavy, rather lacklustre green monsters issued to military recruits in the 1990s. Lars, the eldest of the trio, had gone traditional and changed into wonderfully comfortable-looking woollen pyjamas and then, along with a caribou pad, a *qaaq*, just pulled some coarse-weave blankets over himself. Traditional skin *qipik* blankets or *kiviggarvik* sleeping bags had become rare even by the 1950s – previously in the worst of the cold, hunting groups or families would huddle close for warmth. For us, it was time for bed.

There was no need to spend an additional day yet again in Qeqertat, and besides, the other two groups were heading off the next afternoon too. Peter and his cohort were planning to tour the southern shores of the fjord, via a couple of hunting shelters and then curve back round to Qaanaaq a few days later. The weather was forecast to stay fine, so he and the other Inuit guides were comfortable taking passengers far from easy help. With Rasmus, the Danes et al, we had a rather fun race on our hands. They intended to collect a couple of samples at pre-designated GPS locations in the very middle of the fjord as soon as they had set the machines up in the warm, and afterwards to make a direct beeline for Qaanaaq. They were based in a meteorological shack we'd not been aware of, and had promised to visit on our return. We, however, would follow our coastal route back to Qaanaaq and we estimated, given the time they'd lose, our longer path, and the hunters' greater skill, that it could be either of us home first. Honour was at stake. We decided to give the dogs an extra feed and some buoying up to motivate them.

Our morning had passed slowly as we'd had some time to ourselves before agreeing to meet back around midday. James and Anders went for a walk to the highest rocky point above the hamlet and Anastasia had found quite the task to occupy her time. Near the top of the slope and just beyond the easternmost building, near the little store, was the flat area of snow beneath which was the lake, a freshwater source. We had found the little pipe that had been installed to draw out unfrozen water for use by the inhabitants and next to it, just under the blanket of snow, was an seemingly endless thin blue rope. It was desperately tangled. Anastasia proceeded to spend the next hour or two drawing it out and untangling, no matter how much more appeared. It seemed cathartic, and perhaps was just a background to having lone thinking time.

I casually wandered down towards the shore.

Zorro

CHAPTER 19: The Old Boy

I GLIMPSED THE low sun straining to find its way out from the bank of cloud hanging over the mountains fifteen miles in the distance. Even though the sun had been with us for a few weeks now, I still welcomed it and found myself staring for unnecessarily long at the spot where it might appear – from behind a cliff or island – to warm my face just a little.

Stood on the edge of the ice crack on a particularly prominent block of frozen seawater, I could see the full spectrum of landmarks that populate the Polar Eskimo's home. To my left, the cliffs and mountains ran low along the horizon, as far as I could see to the west. To the right, the main basin of the Inglefield Fjord looped around from where we had come the day before, with three mighty glaciers cascading down from the vast icecap beyond into the sea. Directly in front lay the openness of the sound. Apart from the disturbances near the coastline and a handful of towering icebergs, it was a perfectly flat blanket of white snow stretching all the way to the far distance. I could just make out the marks of two sled tracks winding their way across the snow; one to the right towards likely fishing spots and one straight forward to the cliffs near Qaanaaq.

Behind me, Qeqertat. You could miss it if not purposefully seeking it.

Immediately beside me was a collection of fuel drums, strategically left there from the summer before to tide them over until the next brief break in the ice in July. To the other side a couple of dogs slept silently on the snow, ears pricked up and reacting as my feet shifted on the ground.

Just as I glanced away, the sun was stolen away by another cloud and I noticed a dog sat alone on a patch of ice in front of the fuel drums, and next to a small, open wooden boat hauled out for the winter. He was light coated and although not alongside another dog for comparison, seemed tall and well built. He sat calmly, staring out across the sea ice in much the same way as me.

Wandering towards him, I could see this dog was fairly old, perhaps ten years, which is geriatric for these hard-worked Thule dogs. He barely looked over, as if mesmerised by what he was watching, perhaps scanning the ice for the return of his master and team of dogs. Why was he on his own?

So much of our time over the past few months had been pressured by deadlines, by impatient dogs, by weather, by the need to cover distances fast. In this rare moment to be along, I sat down next to the dog. He acknowledged my presence by turning his head to the side and looking up at me. I could now see the reason for him being left off the hunt and for his lack of typical enthusiasm. This dog had widespread cataracts across both eyes. I could not quite understand. Why was he kept at a team's staking point but not run? Why was he kept if he had poor eyesight? Surely not for breeding as it is a trait they would not want passed on. Most injured or ill old dogs would be put down. Was he a favourite of an old hunter who felt an uncharacteristic softness towards him and so kept him? I put my questions to one side; I would never find out.

I remained with my new companion for over an hour and we quietly sat, watching the horizon, mulling over thoughts. I occasionally gave him a scratch between the ears and a back rub. He looked up at me periodically, eventually shifting his bodyweight to lean against my shoulder.

The things he must have seen in his time.

In a place fabled for centuries by both southern Greenlanders and by the wider world once explorers made contact in only the nineteeth century, I had found a rare time for reflection, timelessness and very real happiness. So much else was about pressure, pain, frustration, fulfilment and elation in equal measure in my chosen path of life that I found myself involuntarily grinning. Happy. Glad to be where I was and doing what I did with the people I chose to be around me.

I hoped this dog, who I knew when I left the next day I would never see again, had been able to see at least a little of me, bearded and hooded up as I was in the cold, and felt a little companionship and contentment too.

The Old Boy of Qeqertat.

CHAPTER 20: Hidden in Plain Sight

OUR RACE to Qaanaaq was fiercely contested. We shimmied the dogs along and regularly detangled, rather like a Formula One pit stop, to keep their labours efficient. Incredibly, given that just a few weeks before we had welcomed the sun back from the dark polar winter, the extreme latitude we found ourselves in had a dramatic effect on the solar cycles. At midnight it was no longer entirely dark – a soft glow instead hanging around to the west. As the evening drew in then, it did so slowly and with the beautiful and colour-overloaded, lingering sunsets we'd grown to love. We had been guessing where our adversaries were in relation to us. I had been guesstimating their progress and enforced science stops, and hoped for a close finish.

As the light dimmed more and more, we had reached the final terrace of high cliffs. Perhaps it was only six miles to go – an hour or less from Qaanaaq.

I realised it was now dark enough to see artificial lights. With some spurious ice blocks on my eye level as I lay on the sled, I stood to get a better look, careful not to lose balance and tumble off. I hoped that one of them, most likely one of the Danes, had a light on. Nothing. I tried again five minutes later and sure enough, spied a twinkle to our left and thrillingly, to our rear. It could be another hunter, but I could make out three elongated shadows in convoy. It might be them.

I spread the word and everyone rallied their dogs as best they could. They'd never run better and were clearly loving it – ears up, heads up, no fidgeting and with confident, proud gaits.

We drew up onto the first section of beach, far from our own little spot on the western side. No other sleds were in use and we passed numerous teams of staked out dogs. There, we waited, hoping to jokingly rub in our 'victory'. It wasn't long until we saw the three sleds, heavily laden and one with a tandem flatbed pulled along behind, perfectly threaded through the pressure ice and onto the beach behind. The dogs stopped immediately, well mannered and calm, although they were clearly tired. We exchanged back slaps and teased Rasmus about his shocking loss of the race, which he took well. Perhaps the senses of humour across the seas between our homelands weren't so different after all. With a wide grin he mimicked placing his hands around my neck and shaking, before tapping me on the arm. Actions can so often replace words. In a fair fight, of course we'd have been left in his tracks.

Steffen gave us instructions of how to find their shack and we agreed to head over the next evening for a can or two of beer. It was apparently behind the bar building; no wonder we'd never found it.

We did still have to settle the dogs down in their normal spot offshore before we could retire for the evening. It was be the same as ever; one dog gripped by the harness or collar in each hand and quickly clipped onto a neatly laid out chain 'branch' coming off the two trunks; one for each team.

We found the Danish hut easily the next day and felt daft we'd not come across it before. Qaanaaq is hardly a large place and it takes just a day or two to become familiar with the layout.

The prefabricated building was roughly painted with sombre green-blue colours. It resembled a Nissen hut with cylindrical parts and was perhaps as old as Qaanaaq itself – from the 1950s or 1960s. It stood apart from a typical modern-day Polar Eskimo abode.

Most fascinating for us were the shoreline huts. They were in place since the forced relocation in 1953 and the Danish government Nissen huts most likely followed soon after. The population of Polar Eskimos near the Thule Air Base, Uummannaq (not to be confused with the extant settlement much further south of the same name), lived in very basic dwellings then. I've delved into lifestyles in that period elsewhere, but that time was towards the close of their truly independent era when it came to housing. Raw materials had been, as they had since the arrival of Rasmussen and his trading stations, bartered and paid for in kind, and makeshift homes were self-built.

After the unfortunate refugees were designated their new home, though of course known to them on their travels and first settled by ancestors centuries before, on the beaches of Piulerruup Nunaa, it must have been a culture shock. They were given little time, were in an area of far poorer hunting potential, and had to start from scratch. Some assistance was grudgingly given by the Danish and American governments and these huts, half a dozen still surviving, are the last signs of that time.

When I say that many basic homes are one room or perhaps two, I need to convey that they can provide a remarkable amount of space, and areas can be partitioned for different uses. They don't feel cramped, whilst clearly far from palatial. The old huts were another matter. They were really a gradual, hard-walled step up from tents or the more permanent *iglukut* turf and stone structures the original Polar Eskimos erected on beaches. They were only marginally bigger and had no provision for properly installed oil burners, let alone water or sanitation. Some used old packing timber or boxes as walls.

In a settlement where even today a few lone men live in converted shipping containers at the top of the hill, which back onto a shed built to house an earth-mover, it is perhaps less surprising that these fifteen by ten foot shacks are considered suitable for habitation. Of the half dozen, I surmised that two were structurally unsound and were dilapidated – used for random storage. It was a shame as they had prime beachfront locations but rumour told that demolition was not an option; perhaps a sort of Greenlandic 'historical conservation area'. One other was the hunting union that Rasmus headed, and had been neatened up inside with a ubiquitous oil heater. There was only room though for a table, a few chairs and a coffee machine.

The other three were inhabited. I can't lie – they appeared squalid. The bare wooden planks and beams were rotten in most areas with flaked blue or red paint in the few other spots. The front, south-facing sides had one or two small windows built in – only a couple of panes remained intact. Those that had succumbed to time and decay were blanked out with hardboard and gaffer tape.

We didn't know the occupants. They did not appear to be hunters and on the rare occasions we saw them venture in or out, it was clear that poor personal care and alcohol were daily troubles. It was sad and a simple illustration of how some parts of Greenlandic society struggle to come to terms with the acceleration of modernisation that is thrust upon them.

263

Anders banged loudly on the huge, reinforced steel door. It echoed and resonated with a sound that shouted 'old, industrial and government-made'.

No answer.

We all gave it a go but still nothing. It was a surprisingly long building which, contrary to a small façade that faced the rest of Qaanaaq, continued back over fifty feet. Perhaps they were in the back and couldn't hear.

I rotated the large steel bar lock clockwise and pulled to swing the door open. Inside, it reminded me initially of the innards of a warship – lots of robust pipework liberally painted white. A corridor led forward and we put our jackets and boots (we all had smaller hiking boots for around Qaanaaq now that temperatures were ten degrees warmer than in winter) next to ones already hung up.

The décor abruptly changed as we passed another doorway. Dated retro wooden panelling covered floors and walls right to the ceiling. Drawings, maps and memorabilia from decades of research in the Far North adorned the walls. It was so out of place at nigh on seventy-eight degrees North in an Inuit community to find somewhere so familiar and European. It could easily be in Copenhagen or aboard a research ship.

"Hello!" Anastasia called.

A door opened and our Danish hosts emerged, apologising for being out of earshot.

It was fascinating to glimpse prior to the cutting edge plans they had to track and study ice and climate up in Avanerriaq, and see how many of the historical aspects had been preserved. It is not unusual for the Arctic to keep centuries items preserved in tact. All around the Arctic long-abandoned stations and encampments still survive as if held in time.

We had anticipated a catch up over beers. We were right for the former but a little off-target for the latter.

It turned out that Gorm and Steffen had misjudged the store opening times and had a somewhat bare cupboard – so we were told. We'd brought six cans from the last of our personal stash as a contribution. It became the entire party. Over carefully rationed beer, we learned how the DMI worked with universities and funded annual research in various parts of Greenland. They had drawn the long straw (some would perhaps consider the short straw) and worked with the Far North.

There was, despite the more relaxed atmosphere we'd fostered since first meeting, slight reservation in their manner with us. Initially I interpreted it as suspicion or even irritation at having their patch encroached upon – wondering what on Earth we were doing in the ultimate 'remote corner of the world'. As time passed though, I got the feeling it was more a case of slight emasculation. Gorm in particular seemed a little put out when we had told them of our independence with travelling and how we'd developed our dog team, let alone as we spoke of our past epic journeys on ice.

Steffen seemed more comfortable, and actually shared a story from the previous day with Rasmus. He admitted, a little unsurprisingly, that they had quizzed Rasmus and Lars in some detail once we'd set off and were out of earshot. Who were these tourists? What were they doing there? I imagined they had, as scientists, routinely looked a little down their noses at small guided tour groups they occasionally came across – lower down in the 'worthiness' hierarchy of polar travellers.

"They are NOT tourists," was the retort that he said Rasmus had responded with.

We had such a limited window into the thoughts of a man so reserved as Rasmus, with his perfect poker face. Even his smiles gave little away, so this was news.

We laughed and palmed it off, but secretly, I was beaming inside. It's silly and insecure to crave validation from near-strangers, but it was hard not to feel a little pride. Europeans, especially the British, are the last people who'd be expected to transcend the 'outsider' status so fast. Our efforts, and I hoped our outdoor proficiency, had driven this nod of acceptance. It was a surprise when I found the same sentiments expressed by Freuchen, Malaurie and even Rasmussen at times, from times when such vulnerable expression on paper was rare.

Our new Danish friends took us to see the workshops, the purpose behind the whole building's existence. If the living area of the Met hut had a slightly retro feel to it, the workshop was like entering a time warp. It was full to the gunnels with equipment, machines and supplies. Nothing appeared to have been thrown out in decades. As such, the new simply sat in front of the old, or on top of it. Rack after rack of ancient boxes of bulbs, fuses, bolts and even valves (from pre-transistor days) covered

265

the walls. A small bench lathe sat in front of a small, dusty window, with ribbons of metal swarf messily surrounding it.

Gorm and Steffen were very open about their lair and proudly explained the history of and uses for most of the gear. Coming from a family of engineers I was particularly drawn to the tactile nature – it's something that gives me huge pleasure when travelling and on expeditions. When home in the UK and in 'planning mode', it can be easy to only operate in the more cerebral spheres – talking, thinking, research, typing, reading. I'm convinced that this hands-on attraction is something that we all share as humans – our ability to manipulate and create the world around us is central to what sets us apart.

At the rear of the maze of gaps between benches and shelving we made most intriguing discovery. It was the only item that they were ever so slightly cagey about.

The Danish and American governments cooperated on-and-off through the Cold War in their use of Greenland for defence projects, but these have since downscaled and diverged in the different political times that followed. American activity is limited to the Kangerlussuaq airstrip and practice landing near the mid-icecap abandoned radar station DYE-II, plus the Thule Air Base. The Danish have a limited military presence including summer warship patrols and the Sirius Patrol of dog sledders in the Northeast, based around Daneborg and Station Nord.

Aside from this though, and given the opportunities the remote High Arctic has for more shady activity, some undoubtedly mere folklore, there is without doubt more going on. Much-like the highly secretive Canadian 'Alert' station on the extreme tip of Ellesmere Island across the water, advanced communications, listening and detection technology are at play. Stories of sub-glacial military stations and nuclear weapon launching sites on the ice sheet itself are now stuff of historical fact, not myth, and the lure of Greenland's wilderness remains for secretive government projects. One such was the US's 1960s *Project Iceworm*, unbeknownst to the Danish government and only uncovered in the 1990s when the B-52 crash inquiry into contamination and its health legacy began. It sought to create a nuclear-powered, James Bond-esque sub-ice storage and launch facility for ballistic missiles, but was shut down due to unexpectedly rapid movement of the ice.

The machine was white, kitchen appliance-sized and displayed a few red readouts on the front. Data was being streamed to a laptop beside. Apparently, we were looking at a highly sensitive seismometer. There is cooperation around the globe between institutes and governments to share geological data and record earthquake activity, through the mantle of the Earth. This though, apparently, would also have the ability to detect and identify any surface or subterranean nuclear testing, made illegal under international treaties. We suspected that there was a little more to it than that. We were in one of the most truly isolated and extraordinary places on Earth, and amongst a Polar Eskimo settlement there was all this.

It had been good of our Danish friends to take time out for us – they were on a strict schedule and were to fly home in just a few days. Finances and deadlines are always a factor and I imagined how frustrating it must be to shoot in and out of Qaanaaq sporadically, only fleetingly settling in before being wrenched away back to Denmark via the familiar chain of refuels in Upernavik, Ilulissat and so on. They seemed quite bored and restless in their time off work, and we never saw them around the settlement otherwise – not even with the handful of other Danes. They seemed to hide away in their science-cave on the edge of civilisation.

CHAPTER 21: Breakup

OUR TIME with the dogs was inescapably going to be constrained by the annual sea ice window. As winter slowly draws in with the disappearance of the sun, it's often too dangerous to venture onto the forming sea ice with dogs, for fear of involuntary swims. The fleeting summer is for the most part a mixture of controlled starvation and relaxation for the hundreds of Thule dogs. They aren't of use to their owners, since the rocky land and open water negate all sledding options, so aren't trained or bulked up with precious, costly meat or kibble. Efforts are made to rotate staking points and give the poor animals a break in the monotony of their enforced summer holiday in the twenty-four hour sun, but it's tough to understand as a summer visitor. Particularly galling is the frustration many so obviously display when denied open affection from humans. The sight of free, unchained pups and the occasional taunt from an unpleasant youth compounds matters.

It is with that, presumably unaware of the implications of the first signs of the breakup of sea ice – the Polar Eskimo highway network – that the dogs have to face up to the end of their season of exercise and stimulation. Sometimes it comes in June, but more frequently in recent years, May or even April. The local hunters will eek out the final days of viable dog sledding and hunting time by hopping across and around melt pools on the ice surface and from floe to floe of cracking ice.

Our own personal 'last day on ice' was impossible to predict. A period of mild weather, a swell on the ocean or a storm could push it over the edge, the ice unable to reform again. It was only April and dark days of winter were already consigned to memory. We'd willed the light to return, as had the whole community, especially in the final week of tantalising twilight to the south. But, something had without doubt been lost; a specialness that ninety per cent of the comparative handful of visitors to the Arctic will never experience. For them, as we were lamenting, the light is bright, contrasty and stark. The sky presents as either blue or overcast and the sunsets and sunrises disappear in a flash. The sun brings energy and life to the Arctic on its annual return, but it strips away much of its subtlety. Winter truly is the jewel in the already exquisite Far North.

Would we have good sledding into May? June was beyond any of our schedules or sorry-looking expedition budget, but we vowed to stay until it became futile. We'd need a week or two to sell the dogs, redistribute unwanted supplies and sleds in a sort of fire sale, so would be settlement-bound from then. I was nervous about the fate of our dogs. Only time would tell where they'd go, and we all agreed earnestly that we'd do everything imaginable to ensure they found secure 'homes' and decent new owners. If forcibly rehoming a pet dog can be utterly devastating, doing so with twenty animals who'd strained, worked and toiled for months for your benefit might be even more of a tug. We kicked the can down the road and looked forward to our final weeks.

The rumour mill of Qaanaaq, for all its idiosyncrasies and questionable accuracy, did have some redeeming features. In just a few hours and not even making use of the town's recent technological adoptions, news of routes, hunting opportunities, weather and ice would reach every corner. Almost in synchrony, we'd picked up mutterings from the hunting union, Mikael, Finn and Peter that Siorapaluk was once again cut off. In the small porchway to the community shop where incoming post and packages were sorted and distributed, at least three separate discussions involved shrugs of shoulders and sad, resigned conversation. This was significant as we'd set our eyes on Neqi, beyond Siorapaluk, as our last hurrah.

Back at our home, James downloaded the latest remotely sensed satellite feeds from our meteorological source. Much of it was cloud-obscured but the infrared alternative, harder to interpret than 'real-colour visible light', did add some weight to the rumours. Cracks and dark grey, rather than light grey of consolidated ice, criss-crossed the fjord and across to the Smith Sound.

After much head-scratching and hopeful, but perhaps meaningless squints out of the south-facing window to assess the sea ice as far as our view stretched, Anders was the first to voice common sense.

"Well then, we must get out and travelling to make the best of what is left!"

He was right; the ice could be here one day and gone the next. Before we set to pouring over maps and drawing up supply lists once

269

again though, I stayed at the window and looked not at the distant sea ice, but our much-nearer 'dog city' beyond the tide crack. It amused me how different our reactions were to absenteeism than back in December – then, it was an instant call to action stations.

"Yeah," I said with a casual jadedness. "There's two missing. Never mind." We knew we'd get them back one way or another.

James had been dropping hints about wanting to climb the full height of the hill that rose behind Qaanaaq for some time. Thus far, it had not been practical or fitted into our pretty hectic routines and journeys. Now though, it made a lot of sense. I remember the previous summer climbing it solo myself. The views were, if they were impressive from the rising slope of Qaanaaq, simply jaw-dropping from the full thirteen-hundred-foot elevation of the hilltop. Just beyond was the edge of the mini-icecap. It was possible to see far beyond Herbert Island, to the west and towards the pair of now-familiar fjords. Perhaps the state of the ice would be evident. I had no craving to repeat the climb and the others wanted to get stuck into equipment preparation, so I walked outside and pointed out roughly the route I'd taken the last September. It was a deceivingly steep climb and some flatter sections lured you into dead ends or very loose, sheer rises.

James was off, raring to go in the manner of a mountain goat I'd become in equal parts used to and impressed by as we trained in the Brecon Beacons the previous year.

After nightfall, as we settled into a final warm evening in the yellow house, James banged the wooden front door open with a 'good shouldering' – something we'd needed to do more and more as weeks passed. The frame's fit was approximate at the best of times, and the ice that builds around the sills of doors between the cold and the warm added to the snugness. I still found it remarkable these scattered, modern mini-oases of relative comfort and warm refuge could survive the ravages of loose ground, permafrost and the High Arctic climate.

The news from atop the hill, although not overly optimistic, was at least consistent with the hum of rumours about Qaanaaq.

The ice, James reported authoritatively, was ok to the headland and then looked 'odd' beyond. The most likely scenario was a patchwork quilt of older thick ice, leads, half-heartedly reformed new ice, and open water zones. It would require care and skill, but it was no disaster. There's usually a way through some way or another, even with dogs. Critically, we'd have to keep an eye in our 'rear view mirrors'. It's so easy as an ice navigator to fixate on the way ahead, neglecting to realise your way back is being cut off, ever-changing as the conditions always are. Overextend without a glance back, and you might commit you, your team and your faithful dogs to genuine peril.

With our final 'Finn shuttle' down to the foreshore complete, it was a poignant moment – our last journey – and we had been greeted with an utterly flawless early morning. The sun had risen early and the sky was a uniform summer blue from hill to horizon. There wasn't a breath of wind. It was the sort of Arctic panorama that, if viewed in isolation, could hoodwink one into mistaking it for benign.

The way the human psyche interacts with the Arctic, and the wilderness in general, is complex. Our culture: that of an urbanised society, accruing much of our knowledge of the wild via books, film, photographs and now the internet, has been encouraged to view it in certain ways. For some it is a place of unimaginable beauty and charming wildlife, and the idea of seeing cold nations as a home is simply unimportant and irrelevant. To others, it is the earthly manifestation of brutality, natural violence and human survival against vast odds.

Painting extreme pictures enhanced the careers of the early explorers, reporting their adventures to a largely ignorant home audience. These enhanced their 'greatness' and macho status amongst 'mere mortals' who dwelled in comfortable, heated homes. Nowadays, hoaxes and crass exaggerations are more easily debunked and the charlatans exposed, but the underlying business model persists stubbornly in our time as it did in Peary's.

An example from history is the matter of Vilhjalmur Stefansson, who set himself in effect versus the polar legend Fridjof Nansen – a figurehead 'Norwegian polar hero'. Born in 1879, Stefansson was an Icelander who grew up in Canada and took an interest in native ethnology, especially of the North. After one Arctic expedition from 1913-18 that saw his ship crushed, the crew split up and many deaths, he lobbied both Canadian and British governments, unsuccessfully, to support his claim to Wrangel Island. Acknowledged as a territory of Russia even then, the barren island north of the Siberian mainland became an obsession of his. He wished to counter the machismo narratives by the hardened explorers of the time, notably Nansen, that the Arctic was formidable – uninhabitable by all but the special few. Stefansson wanted to show the Arctic as benign, fertile, and land ripe for families of settlers.

The handful of hapless settlers he eventually recruited were woefully underprepared and all but one perished within months. Stefansson's reputation was left in tatters. In trying to deconstruct a complex truth about the nature of the Arctic – its challenges, opportunities and dangers for human life – he had complicated the picture and left many with false perceptions. The Arctic was reinforced in minds as deadly. The truth, of course, is that the Arctic is neither friendly, nor irrationally violent.

Every ritual and well-practised drill we went through to ready us for a journey, from moving supplies through the tidal ice to checking sleds for cracks, would be the last we'd work as a team. All four of us were utterly in love with this peerless region of the Far North. We'd miss it. As a symbolic final passage with the dogs. I promised myself it would be our best, our most professional, and we'd savour it.

The two dogs were still missing.

Both escapees were from our southern contingent of slightly leaner-built, white-coated Greenland dogs. By process of elimination, they turned out to be Garfunkel and Pinky. Not on the same staking point, they'd nonetheless used the same tactic, not consciously we were certain, to spin the chains around each other so many times that they shorten and the clips unhitch. Hey presto, free dog.

In December, this would have been a cancelled trip, a minor panic, and a whole day of hopeless dog chasing, all the while trying to act as nonchalant and in control as possible. We'd get them back, after a fashion, but every few days we used to find ourselves updating our staking and chain system, down to how we sealed the rope knots with a flame, to try and reduce the escape rate. We weren't the only ones, and had on a few occasions helped other hunters to reclaim their own animals. The concern was, aside from a potential risk to children, that stray adults 'at large' for more than a few days tend to be put down, without warning, by a member of the community.

The moral quandary of our, and my, attitudes towards dogs, be they working dogs or domestic pets, hit me square between the eyes a week or so previously. We'd picked up a stray female dog who'd, entirely wild and unapproachable, been scavenging near our dog headquarters. She'd become increasingly hard to ignore, sometimes stealing Zorro's food and on two occasions chewing and destroying one of our foam sled pads. She was losing weight and had mated with a number of our staked dogs during her days of heat. We knew something had to be done, as we couldn't allow the pups to be born – they'd never survive, and we asked for advice from friends. Their response was both nonchalant and final. The final straw came as we found her with one of our dog chains twisted around her neck – she bit us as we released her, and had a deep, nasty wound caused by struggling to free herself.

That afternoon, knowing it was my role as leader to do the deed, I shot her.

The first round was more than enough, but more for my own sake, I rushed nearer whilst chambering another round and placed a second, which halted the involuntary twitching. Before she had a chance to freeze, I separated the various limbs and distributed them to the dogs – it would not be a total waste, I was determined.

Through evening, I was distant and humourless, and the team knew to just let me mull it over, rationalise, and get over it.

Regarding escapees, things had changed. The next day, within five minutes of us reaching the teams of dogs who still remained, the volume had reached typically raucous and discordant proportions. Ever in hope, the dogs thought it was dinnertime, or at least a cause for some excitement or other. This acted as a wide-reaching broadcast.

Without any coercion, first Garfunkel, then Pinky, came bounding happily through the broken sea ice towards us. Both had been hand shy in the early days. Now, Garfunkel was at least partially amiable, and Pinky was an irrepressible bundle of affection now that we'd gained his trust. Having been quickly reacquainted with their ropes and clips, we were able to pack supplies and get under way. We had a fair stash of the fish left, most of which I'd already 'tailed' so as to be safe to eat, and laid them under a tarp as the rear of the sleds. Houdini made a dash for one that was sticking out, but only managed a single bite before being reprimanded.

We'd been using the frozen, icy 'path' that ran the full length of the beach, land-wards of the tidal crack for quite some time. The surface was hard, covered in tracks from use and so made for fast, albeit bumpy sledding.

In a matter of hours we'd negotiated the undulations of the peninsula's south coast, most of the time bathed in rays of warm sunshine. It was still ten or fifteen degrees below zero, but the winter was well and truly over. Our clothing retained heat without the relentless, losing battle against bitter cold of the early days. The sun, weak by temperate standards, was still the sun, and I enjoyed angling my face and torso to face it, rather like a basking crocodile trying to claim its maximal share of solar warmth.

It was, as we again passed the precipitous scree cliffs, signifying the headland was near, that I first noticed something was odd.

We had stopped for a detangle of the dog's traces, and Anastasia clambered up onto some raised blocks of sea ice as James was completing the job and tying off the ropes, again ready to sled.

"There's broken ice, for sure," she said. "It is completely open in front of the fjord, but I cannot see how far it goes." We knew what we needed to know – that we'd round the headland and once again take a route, hugging the coast and deep into the fjord until we could cross the three or so miles to the other side. Whether it was a small break in the ice caused by the headland under-ice currents or a vast ice-free zone, it made our decision for us.

It wasn't the ice that was the surprise though. Some small pebbles were bouncing quietly down the scree and every now and again, a light, crystal-like snow shower harmlessly enveloped us as we sledded. I gazed up to the top of the cliff to see what was afoot. Although it was still quiet and calm where we were, I could see wafting white drifts at the summit. Wind – *anori*.

An hour later and now deep into the MacCormick Fjord, the game began to change. We had to step out from the relative protection of the shoreline, take advantage of an area of flattened tidal ice leading onto the fjord's consolidated, thick ice and thereby give us passage to our next stepping stone of land.

After I'd pointed out the tell-tale signs of wind up at higher elevation, we shifted into 'action stations'. Everyone was aware that we could get hit, and get hit hard. But, when? It was curious. We now had a good view of the high ridge and a few small peaks to the east, and hell was breaking loose up there. Huge swirls of snow were being picked up and thrown from the rock. Down where we were though, the air remained still. More eerie yet, it was silent. We could see the wind, but not feel or hear it. I warned the team that we mustn't allow any gaps to appear in our skills now, and it was inevitable that we'd have a seriously blowy period sooner or later. Extreme protection clothing was moved within grabbing reach in the sled boxes, and we double-checked everything was strapped down securely under the tarpaulins.

Soon, beautiful drift snow moved low over the ice surface like it was a liquid, flowing to the west and glistening in the sun. It grew yet further, perhaps in excess of twenty miles per hour, and I tilted my head in my oversize down-filled hood to protect my face.

aghuqtuq – goes against the wind

About a mile from the other shore, it hit, tripling in ferocity. Wind can be very particular in the path it takes and is of course controlled by its source, where the high pressure is, and the landscape shaping it on its route to either low pressure or another elevation. The steep cliffs and mountains of the region had shielded us thus far, but we were now beyond their protection. It began as if with a switch, and if the wind were visible, the shapes its path and eddies would carve across the ice would have been fascinating to see. One saving grace, at least at first, was that it now blew from our rear quarter, saving both us and the dogs from a head-on onslaught.

Those with some awareness of the challenges that have famously plagued polar travellers over the centuries may be familiar with the words katabatic and *piteraq* (one of a number of spellings – although of Eastern Greenlandic origin). As is often the way with dramatic legends, there has been quite some 'spread' in how the words are applied. A storm or a windy day can automatically and erroneously become '*piteraq*'.

Most familiar for those who venture across icecaps, and for the few hardy Inuit Greenlanders who perch their villages on the jaggedly mountainous southeast coast, are katabatics. Literally from the Greek to 'flow downhill', these winds are gravity driven. Heavy, cold, dense air up high on the icy plateau can slowly trickle down to the sea, or on occasion, release in a mighty, violent torrent if low pressure passes the coast. In their most brutal form, a true *piteraq*, of which I've only experienced two, wind speeds can enter into triple digits and wipe out whole settlements. They can catch out the inexperienced and ill prepared. A 2013 *piteraq* killed one Briton and nearly two others as they attempted a charity trek with minimal prior experience.

What we were experiencing now wasn't a katabatic. It wasn't an instant release of cold air, and my knowledge of the local geography suggested that our area wasn't prone to them, although there's never a guarantee. Instead, the wind best known to break the generally calm air of Avanerriaq was another famous phenomenon. The give-away was the bizarrely mild temperature of the wind, and the mountainous region between us and the inland ice.

Feared and respected not just in the Arctic but all around the world, they take on the names Chinook, Zonda and Bergwind. They are the foehn winds (or föhn) Freuchen endured and wrote of. Polar Eskimos have specific words for each type of wind. To them, these could have been the *pikannaq* (from the mountains), or *avanngaq* (from the north). The latter had killed three scientists atop a cliff a few years before.

Unlike the unceremonious katabatic dumps of frigid high elevation air down an ice slope to a lower level, foehn winds are more nuanced, but no less intense. They still flow downhill, unlike an upslope anabatic, and are driven by a precipitation shadow effect over mountain peaks. The result is an unusually warm blast of air down onto outlying lowlands. This might seem a little more amiable than a *piteraq*, but the wind speeds can too be vicious. The thaw then freeze effect likely wiped out large muskox and caribou herds in the past – the wet snow freezing hard into their coats like a solid 'armour', disabling them.

The wind we could feel cutting through any tiny gaps in our clothing was comparatively mild – perhaps nearing -10°C. The dogs just motored onwards regardless, albeit with slightly indignant expressions on their faces and a reluctance to look directly into the wind.

To make landfall some while later, we needed a serious run up and all the momentum we could muster. The ice had shifted and large blocks were making life trickier. The dogs, we'd noticed from past hiccups, tended to lose concentration at the critical point in tidal crack or pressure ice crossings, leaving us stranded atop a block of jagged ice or the sled jammed in a crevice. With lots of shouts of encouragement and pushing from behind, we got through eventually. Enrique, whose enthusiasm could never be doubted, used these moments to highlight his lack of intellect, and could be more hindrance than help, especially as a lead animal. Dave and Muffin would usually take the opportunity to have a lie down.

We were feeling the brutal force of the foehn; nothing in the way moderating its fury for over six miles. It was a case of hoods up and pulled tight, and yelled commands and hand signals amongst the team, but there was no overwhelming sense of danger. We were on land once again and the visibility was ok at head height, with spindrift and blowing snow obscuring vision up to knee level. It was just fairly unpleasant – no reason to stop sledding yet. I estimated the wind to be around fifty knots.

This beach was entirely different, not only to those on the opposite shore, but to when we'd sledded it before. Every detail of the Arctic landscape is in an irrepressible, minute-to-minute state of transition. There's barely a chance to become familiar with anything – before you know it you're faced with something new. Scoured of snow, we now found head-sized rocks and spherical icy formations that might as well have been rock. The dogs deftly sidestepped and leaped them with casual skill. The sled rumbled on with no regard for its own wellbeing and every time we collided head on with or side swiped a block, I felt for the poor wood and lashing. I hoped they'd hold together – designed by the experts though they were.

James, on the other sled, and I had endured enough and set to avoid the endless knocks. As the wind raged from the rear and the dogs ran along apace on the low-friction ice, we leapt onto the rear planks and held on for dear life as Anders and Anastasia kept the show on the road from the front with the whips. Every time we clattered at speed towards another potentially wood splintering obstacle, I flung my bodyweight out to the side, each mitt on a stanchion to steady me. Rather like a sidecar passenger in a motorcycle race, this managed to shift the sled's path to avoid impending disaster. I turned to face James with a wide grin on my face, just visible amongst the yellow fabric of my hood and black neck gaiter. He laughed back and we both yelled "wahoo!" in unison, spurring the dogs on yet again.

It was a mad time and possibly topped the lunacy of much of our experience in the High Arctic. Travelling at nearly fifteen miles an hour, although it felt a great deal faster, with swirling snow everywhere and storm force winds flying past us, it was magic. For well over an hour we weaved left and right towards the rounded spit of land that separated fjord from fjord.

The wind grew. Having left a slope of rock and snow behind us to one side and the frozen sea to the other, we now faced low, snow-covered gravel for hundreds of yards before the land rose up into hills. We were in the funnel that millions of cubic feet of furious air was trying to escape through. I got out the windmeter and, struggling to hold it still and steady enough for a reading, conservatively registered sixty-seven knots. It could have been gusting another twenty knots more.

We hadn't committed to reaching Siorapaluk that day, as we had no idea of whether we'd need to negotiate tons of fragmented ice pans or divert deep into the fjord to find thick ice. We were content to camp around the first headland, on the thick sea ice in the MacCormick, away from the swell fracture zones, or anywhere until the final crossing to Siorapaluk, after which time we may as well push for the settlement. It would serve as a waypoint from which to learn of what might lay ahead towards Neqi.

We didn't have snow worth speaking of to build into a protective wall, so I had to think ahead regarding our evening arrangements. We wouldn't be able to pitch the tipi in this melee, or even if we did, it probably wouldn't survive solo in the wind even with storm cords out. We'd need some form of windbreak. Stones and rocks would work, but could take hours to assemble into a reasonable wall.

It's often been suggested to me that when travelling on coastal sea ice, icebergs (some of them the size of a car, but others vast and the size of large buildings) could be perfect shields from the wind. It's not illogical. They're large and rock solid. If you can find a spot in the lee of one where spindrift isn't a menace, and that is grounded on the seabed, you might well be set to benefit. An extra hour of sleep instead of having to construct a wall can be a mental victory. However, icebergs can be very dangerous. Even when locked into sea ice for a winter season, the relatively warm water (which is around freezing point) eats away at the much colder glacial ice. When this reaches a crucial tipping point, the berg becomes top heavy and can spontaneously erupt from amongst the sea ice and invert. Anyone caught nearby would be obliterated by thousands of tons of flailing ice, or drowned.

There was a better option. We weren't going all the way to Siorapaluk that moment, over concern for finding broken ice in the midst of a blizzard, not being able to turn back and then not having anything to shelter the tent with.

There was a vague question mark in my head about whether a hunting shelter might be in the vicinity. I noticed James furiously pointing his arm out to the right – chopping up and down to get my attention. I squinted through the chaos of snow and held my hood in place to stop it blowing in front of my eyes. Sure enough, a box shape was in the distance. It was set over a hundred yards back from the shore, which was unusual. Most shelters we'd happened upon thus far had been right on the foreshore or fixed to rocks on a cliff-edge. The novelty of a low friction surface had worn off for the dogs too, and they were decidedly unimpressed with the wind. I had to remember that the blowing snow was at their head height.

It was all hands to the pump; we needed to get the dogs chained out and able to curl up in a ball to cocoon themselves in relative peace. In the meantime, they huddled together, facing away from the wind, fur puffed up – quite a sorry sight but without a bark of protest. By now the wind had grown to match some of the most relentless I'd encountered. Anders was nearly blown off his feet as he returned to our sled having delivered the last dog to its staking point. We had to walk with slow, deliberate steps and half bent-double. To my disbelief, the half-ton sled I was stood next to started to move. The wind was catching the flat sides and pushing it. Both sleds were in motion. To avoid them ending up a mile down the beach or in the tide crack by morning, we had to drag them onto a snowy gravel patch. It would scratch the plastic runners, but as is so often the case, it was a lesser of two evils. With that, we retired to the cramped shed, again thankful that it was held down at each corner with a drum of rocks and sturdy cable.

The din made sure that we'd have precious little sleep, and it hadn't abated a great deal by the end of our bleary-eyed, protracted breakfast of packeted porridge. We took turns to put on our windproof (a more hopeful than expectant claim in the circumstances) trousers and down jackets and go outside to 'test' it out. It's an old adage that weather always seems worse from within a hut or tent, so going out to get a real feel was important. It also gives purpose to a team, needing to get out of the wonderful, warm sleeping bag oases, and gets the blood flowing. It reminded me of the leadership trick employed by the Norwegian Roald Amundsen as he and his team overwintered prior to their successful world-first journey to the Geographic South Pole in 1911. Keen to not allow his cohorts to become stagnant or soft in their ship *Fram* or ice-top expedition hut, he had his men guesstimate the outdoor temperature and wind speed, thereafter making them layer up and venture out to check the instruments and find out for sure. It became a game, but one with a purpose. Amundsen's tactics would ultimately result in a typically drama-free and Scandinavian success in reaching the Pole in a season when Robert Scott's British team would all perish.

We were all but seven miles from Siorapaluk – essentially just a headland 'rounding' and fjord crossing to go, so became impatient and decided to get back on the trail – wind or no wind. Our dogs seemed to have rested well and were in high spirits as they once more took up positions ahead of our sleds, which had survived the night.

The next few hours were a constant battle against side winds, which put the already faulty inner-compasses of our dogs to the test. We needed to regularly correct them, but at least we didn't have to follow the land too far up the Robertson Fjord before making for the cliffs beside Siorapaluk. Above the swirling, almost-alive drift snow were clear, perfect blue skies. Only in the Arctic.

Siorapaluk was in the full blast zone of the wind. The whole village was in lock-down and no-one came outside as we happily bounced our way across the worn-smooth track through the tidal ice and onto the ice-beach. Selecting an area partially wind-broken by the few larger wooden structures on the lower slope of the settlement, the dogs got a good feed after a short but eventful day of sledding. We hadn't dared try and feed them the night before, for fear of the precious food being lost to the elements.

We hid behind a derelict home and sorted our gear out in the relative calm. We would certainly find a spot to pitch the tent and ride out the foehn, but the legendary hospitality of the Polar Eskimos once again rendered that plan obsolete. Another multi-talented local lady, Juana, who served as priest to Siorapaluk and also as the administrative link back to the community office in Qaanaaq, emerged in a huge fur-lined parka to greet us. She had a spare one-room home in town that was hardly ever used, so was engulfed in a snowdrift. We could stay there overnight before moving on, but she did ask for some remuneration for the trouble of opening it up and connecting it to a power source. This was broached quite some time after we'd gratefully accepted her offer, so we could hardly then back out, and it did not seem unreasonable in any case. It was a very neat tactic though, securing an agreement and moral obligation, and then levying a charge. We ended up meeting in the middle with a barter.

It did dawn on me days later, and I kicked myself for letting my memory fail me so inexcusably, but she and I weren't strangers. We'd met during a period of bad weather and helicopter malfunctions over a year before, when a group of Siorapaluk residents were waiting for a few days to get back to their homes and sled travel was impossible. We were both enjoying an evening meal prepared by Birthe Jensen. The kind lady invited me into the conversation and said that if I were ever in her home village, I should make contact.

The storm went on and on. The house was spacious but draughty, making any attempt at heating pointless. Instead, we compartmentalised as much as possible into warm and cold zones, and then burned some fuel to heat the former. Otherwise, it was a case of wrapping up warm and making practical use of our time. There were some 1980s copies of National Geographic on a shelf, which provided some distraction from the whirling outside that made the whole structure flex and creak. Rather ungallantly, I took a photograph of James sat on a wide seat, dressed in a combination of expedition clothing and a blanket we'd found, wrapped around his legs. He was nursing a mug of hot chocolate and thumbing bleary-eyed though a copy of one of the magazines. It probably wasn't a flattering look.

By the looks of it, and from the few trips we took outside to check on the dogs, untangle chains and film the storm up towards the head of the fjord, our fellow Siorapaluk residents were riding it out too. I saw no-one outside and some doors were barricaded with old shipping pallets.

By the following evening, the foehn has lost much of its bite and was more of a gusty breeze. The skies had remained clear.

We'd experienced a strange jumble of emotion that I'd become accustomed to in wind-enforced breaks. It's inhuman not to feel a primal rush of adrenaline and relief to be out of a violent storm and to be able to hear and watch it from a place of relative comfort – rather like watching a warm summer rainstorm from underneath a large tree. Counter of course, is the frustration and cabin fever of being cooped up.

It was Anders' turn to feed the dogs so he and Anastasia collected a forty-kilo sack and the remainder of our flatfish cache. They ran the gauntlet of leaping and lunging dogs forever acting as if they'd never been fed.

James and I meanwhile were in search of intelligence – of the ice thickness variety.

Etah had certainly been on the minds of many hunters – both in Siorapaluk and further east in other settlements. Spring would sooner or later give way to summer, and hunting opportunities would shift accordingly. There were a few shelters along the coast, but Etah was the established temporary camp in the north.

A few mugs of coffee in a succession of houses helped a great deal to flesh out what we already suspected, especially after the wind. No-one had climbed the Meehan since we'd tried, and alarmingly, still no-one had heard anything from the mysterious Japanese solo skier. This left only the succession of small glaciers along the coast as conduits to Etah. The Morris Jesup Glacier (named for one of the most prolific early donor-patrons of white explorers but locally named *Neqip hermia*) was the first, but the most oft used was the third in the row; the Clements Markham. Markham was in a sense Great Britain's answer to the United States' Jesup.

Those glaciers, our quarry of Neqi, and ultimately, Etah many miles to the northwest, all demanded the negotiation of yet another headland, Tuloriak. It had been our, and the Polar Eskimos', general bugbear all year. The ice around the headland, or lack thereof, wasn't the only problem though. There wasn't a particularly good beach or ice foot between Siorapaluk and Tulariaq, so travel on the sea ice was compulsory.

"Neqi?" I gestured to an elderly hunter who had shown great interest in our plans, jabbing my finger helpfully on a map. He seemed fairly disinterested by it, being from a generation before mapping was first made of the region. Whilst he might have benefited from advances in forecasting and aerial ice charts, it would have been very much via the famous hunter's rumour mill, not direct.

All Polar Eskimo hunters primarily build an encyclopaedic mental awareness of every detail and landmark of their wide territory. Charts and coastline mapping have, naturally, been a part of their life since explorers traded canvas and paper, and introduced cartographic skills, but they aren't a crutch. Evidence does also exist of basic directions being carved into driftwood or bone. Most recently, satellite feeds are accessed by very few, the younger hunters usually, but the wisdom can be liberally shared by word of mouth.

"Na'aa……nej nej," he replied gently, looking at me with a sorrowful gaze and a shake of the head. He acted out the process of sea swelling from beneath and then the ice breaking. Finally, he made a wind-like whooshing noise and all the ice was gone.

This was a huge change. Not the lack of ice; that degradation was something we, and everyone, had become jaded to. Instead, it was the man's certainty about the hopelessness of a journey west and north that struck me.

I spoke about the tendency of Greenlanders, in my experience and that of others from the eighteenth century to today, to answer yes/no questions with vagaries. The answer 'yes' can be just as common, even when known to be untrue. There is good reason for this and it has a great deal to do with the unspoken dynamic between Polar Eskimo, or other Greenlanders or Inuit for that matter, and visitors from overseas. Generalisation notwithstanding, from the earliest days there was a gulf of status between one and the other. It was driven essentially by power – through belongings, technology, access to food and transport, and at times even just physical height. Although, from then until this day, white southerners often serve as the butt of jokes or even mockery when behind closed doors, a reverence pervades in some circumstances. It can actually be very unhelpful practically – a colonial remnant.

This reverence manifests in many as an eagerness to please – telling someone what he or she wishes to hear, regardless of whether or not it's the case. False positives are rife. Only having spent months with these curious and entertaining exchanges can it be possible to decipher a real yes from a no, or a maybe from a yes, and still often you may flounder.

The very earliest relationships between explorer and Polar Eskimo local must have been a maze of misinterpretation, with an internal conflict in attitude combining pride and mockery with a very real element of fear of what power the newcomers may choose to wield. Then at other times, oft-reported was a more benign, authentic 'affectionate concern' by Polar Eskimo for their visitor.

Here though, we had a clear, emphatic negative. No ice. Don't go. We were only partially surprised. There had been no access along that route all winter, and the thaw was progressing resolutely with every passing day.

We'd explore a little way west nonetheless, as a minor deviation from a straight route home. I suppose it was dawning on all four of us that time was nearly up. Our lives there would vanish, much like the ice we stood upon. Instead of aiming for the shortest path, the most efficient or most sensible, we now favoured intrigue just for the hell of it. I wanted to savour it, the changes, the ice, the skies, the people I might never see again, the spots I may never set foot on again. The dogs were, I won't get ahead of myself and say flawless, but hard-working and a dream compared to just a couple of months before.

Our goodbyes and thank yous in Siorapaluk had to be brief; the wind had been gone for just a matter of hours and it might return. Its effects on the ice – our way home – might still be developing for the worse. Also, we heard that the first westbound tour of a handful of tourists from Europe was headed our way, most likely one or two on each of a convoy of dog sleds. I had a concern that they might end up in a dead end, trying to sled from the first headland directly to the next, and find an area altogether missing ice. Without knowing exactly what the wind had done, I couldn't be sure, but I had a suspicion that the initial going could be quite misleading. The group of Polar Eskimo dog drivers, including Peter and Rasmus, were utterly aware of dangers and were expert in every aspect of safe sea ice travel in their own 'back yard', but even they weren't psychic. Anything we could relay to them before entering a hazardous zone could only be positive – at least to avoid an irritating detour and perhaps to avert taking novices over thin ice.

With that urgency, and a few solemn yet eminently warm handshakes with our newfound friends plus a hug from Arnannguaq, the dogs burst into a well-paced gallop toward the other side of the fjord, one final time.

It was the last I'd see of this most northern band of native people on the planet – perched on the snow-clad hillside with the beautiful cliffs towering above. We took it all in – a moment for pensiveness and neither jokes nor chatter.

The lee of the hills had protected the beach well from the winds. Under cloudless skies but a still not-inconsiderable breeze, we'd crossed the fjord in about an hour and clambered onto the beach. So far, so good. It wasn't until we'd rounded the gentle headland that the legacy of the mighty foehn revealed itself. Any remnant of surface snow had been ripped from the surface and carried far, far away. The beach was like a narrow ice rink sprinkled with rock-solid boulders of ice; determined to collide with our sled runners at every opportunity. To the left was the gravel and barren ground that rose up to the highlands. To our right was a view totally unlike any we'd seen so far. The sea ice had ruptured and dispersed as far as the eye could see. On the sled ahead, Anastasia and James were jabbing their mitt-clad hands out to the side, gesturing to each other as they made sense of it.

When we stopped for a rest and trace detangle, I took the chance to properly photograph and document. It was like the illustrated page of a polar oceanography and sea ice 'stages of development' book. I could see every gradual progression that spawned from the windy break up. There were totally ice-free patches, ocean blue with gentle waves across their expanse. It was the first time I'd seen a wave in over half a year. There was the reflective and surprisingly bouncy first stage of refreezing and then one step further, a crystalline covering on the surface that was a quarter of an inch thick. One large swell and it would be gone, left to try and form one more time. In the more sheltered areas closer to the shore were vast zones of pancake ice, so-called due to its intricate tessellations. At this point it was turning lighter to a deep grey – a sign of thickening – and could at another time consolidate into the makings of a thin first year pan of sea ice. It was quite beautiful, but deadly to anyone who found themselves having to negotiate it on skis, foot or dog sled.

Our beach narrowed into the next, and final fjord. We soon found out where the snow was hiding. Formed into vast, compacted and hard drifts up to ten feet high, snow ridges stood as barriers from the hillside across to the drop into the water. All we could do was barrel our way through as best as we could – encouraging the dogs with yells of support, pushing from behind and trying to build up speed and momentum before encountering each. At times the sleds were tipped over to near forty-five degree angles and I was waiting for something or even someone to slip off and bounce across the beach.

Unable to use any form of track, all having been obliterated by the past two days of mayhem, we needed to route-find from scratch to get to the other side of the next fjord and then complete our final 'lap of honour', or rather 'stretch of coast', into Qaanaaq. This was a simple balance of guts, holding nerve and impatience. Too soon and we'd stray into perilous, brand new ice and even find ourselves without means of escape by going back. Too late and we'd waste hours – covering unnecessary miles of wearisome snow ridges.

James was the de facto 'commander' of his sled, and even though Anastasia was a fast learner and assertive with her dog team, his experience with the characters on his team and months of sledding counted. His reaction to risk and danger was something I'd realised I couldn't fully predict. His non-dramatic nature meant that James brushed off near-death experiences and erred towards de-escalation. He would never be one to show that he was fearful, either in the face of danger or when presented with a risky plan. The fact he was the youngest of my team was something I couldn't afford to forget. His youthful verve was easily masked given his maturity being far beyond his years. But, James could then be very cautious and conservative at a decisive crux; a quiet, thoughtful facial expression was the give-away. This was one of those occasions. When do we cross?

I stopped our sled so that Anders and I could climb atop an ice block and scan out to sea. The dogs duly curled up into eleven balls of fur for a rest, occasionally peering over to see what we were up to. James and Anastasia had kept on going, halting half a mile further along. The ice directly in front was white, indicating at least some strength, and although cracked regularly across its expanse, seemed stable. It wasn't the old consolidated fjord ice and some areas were clearly new. Anders and I concluded it was worth a try. The route to the opposite shore must be as narrow as possible, minimising our time 'at sea' and we could always bear left if the ice ahead and right looked thin.

Having only stopped a few moments before, the dogs were confused as I rallied them up and ready to go again. I felt a deep sense of respect at the uncomplaining nature of these animals who work at the behest of human drivers and cannot possibly be informed of where to, or how long for, or even why. They just do and for that we, and all those who've worked animals before, have a responsibility to do our best for them in return. Having said that, Dave and Muffin did stage a brief sit-in protest against the decision to undertake further physical exercise, but were soon carried along by the rest. Enrique was missing his usual motivational supporter in the form of Thor (still on home rest), but Crazy and Odin were never far behind.

With eye-watering thumps and bangs, we dropped the six feet or so onto the sea ice through the tide crack and halted again. Enrique sang his heart out with excitement.

I held the dogs as the designated whip-man and Anders took a look around; inspecting the hummocks of ice, stamping my feet on greyer areas. We needed to keep our eyes peeled, but the coast looked clear. I signalled to James and Anastasia back on the shore, further along, but they seemed hesitant.

The only way to find out was to try, and beyond pointing there wasn't much we could communicate out of earshot. Giving me just half a chance to hop onto the standing planks at the rear, Anders launched the sled with a "hak" and "yeehah!", the latter a rogue addition we found spurred the dogs on like nothing else. We'd hope James and Anastasia would follow us down and join the trail. They'd been for a swim just a few weeks before and didn't want a repeat.

Although we spied shadows and a blue haze out to sea, with a little mist that indicated broken ice, the fjord crossing looked safe. The other sled, with its better pace and something to chase, soon caught up. James, naturally, had long insisted it was down to superior driving skills.

"Sleds!" I heard Anastasia call suddenly. I looked ahead and behind. Nothing. What was she talking about?

It took Anastasia to point them out, but to my dismay, sure enough there they were. Eight slow-moving dark marks were moving along the horizon, past the areas of grey ice. In a long procession, four sleds and four dog teams. The hunters and their cargo of tourists.

We couldn't work out how they were out there. The zone of sea ice in the widest part between two headlands was most likely to be exposed to the swell, currents and wind. I'd hoped that we'd meet the convoy in Qaanaaq before they left, or on the beach on Piulerruup Nunaa. We'd been too slow.

I couldn't understand why they chose such a risky route. Everyone knew the sea ice was thawing and news must have reached Qaanaaq that the foehn had blown through, even if other villages were protected from the full blast. What did they know that we didn't? We'd taken our dog teams partway down the fjord in search of thicker, fast ice. I couldn't believe that any satellite images had been recent or detailed enough to show a 'path' of unbroken, thick ice that survived the breakup. There was no way to communicate with them and we were miles out of earshot, so could only press on and hope they'd be ok.

We threaded our way across the final yards of sea ice and through the now-familiar succession of tide crack, beach ice 'surfing', headland negotiation and counting down the miles on long, undulating sections of frozen beach and ice foot. The only hiccup this time around was an overzealous line we took around the headland outcrop – the collision with the sled relieving the million-year-old rock feature of a few pounds of its crumbly bulk.

Back behind the protection of the cliffs, the cold breeze that persisted since the death of the foehn wind was finally gone too. A few fair-weather clouds were all that could spoil a perfect run back into our adopted hometown. I doubt that the dogs sensed anything was different in those four hours or so it took to bring the airstrip, the dump and finally Qaanaaq's western edge back into view, but they didn't put a paw wrong.

naggammik – for the last time.

Our one final detangle on the inland extent of one of the mini-bays needed no rush. Usually we'd be impatient and even slightly irritable if we felt the tangling of dog ropes was avoidable – if a particular dog was fidgeting and wrapping all the others up by endlessly weaving left and right, over and under. It was cold, frustrating and unpleasant work. Dexterity was needed to untie tight knots, calling for mitts to be removed, and the lines were often coated in frozen dog mess.

This time was different. The sun was still up in the sky, now to the right of Herbert Island and we'd have no difficulties reaching the settlement before dark. There was a calm in our wind-broken locale. In January, in the dark, we'd been constantly thinking about what needed to happen next, watching the dogs without a moment to relax. We were now at ease with the dog teams and could enjoy the Arctic environment we knew so well – a windless early spring afternoon as idyllic as the cold North can offer.

Having neatened up the dogs and their web of green ropes, we gave them a rest and sipped at cool water from our insulated bottles. Anastasia and James' team were basking in the sun, splayed out on the ice. Meanwhile, Anders and I played catch with Enrique. Not a dog prone to taking a moment to relax, he was having a whale of a time sat in front of the snoozing dog team catching the snowballs we were tossing his way. He wasn't what you would call coordinated, but snapped up a fair few and nose-butted the rest. We finished up with a few nuggets of precious biltong as a reward for being a good sport.

I don't know whether Anders had been secretly practising it, or whether it was a spontaneous moment of luck, but all of a sudden he let out a casual trill of a whistle. All the dogs sprang to their feet. Enrique glanced over to us, as if awaiting further instructions. We were both stood ten feet or so to the side of the sled, but it was laden with supplies and so wasn't at risk of accelerating away without us.

Anders whistled again. Enrique, followed by his cohorts, took up the rope slack, creaked the sled into motion and trotted off. Anders slumped onto the front section of the sled and I hopped over and mounted the planks, holding onto the stanchions. It was the final proof that hounds and humans were truly on the same team.

It wasn't until the airstrip passed by to our left that the beach totally cleared of snow and left us with an ice rink – it was the slipperiest I'd seen yet. A red light and a broken-down fence was the only indicator of the end of the gravel landing strip and by the time we reached the small building, the dogs were at a strong gallop. Dog sled traffic over the weeks had polished the route into a highway.

"Yip, yip!" we yelled. Even faster we went. The municipal truck honed into sight around a bend near the dump, which was high enough to obscure our view. Vehicles were rare, and most were for the few local government contractors. There was an unwritten rule that powered vehicles give way to the predominant form of locomotion, dog sleds – much like the maritime law of 'power gives way to sail'. This assumed that dog drivers had full control over their teams, and in our early days the prospect of oncoming traffic would have raised at least an inner panic.

Now though, we just called a reassuring "da, da" and the truck slowed and passed.

The familiar shape of the tide crack stretched along to the right and I laughed as James and Anastasia stood side by side on the flat bed of their sled and did an impromptu jig. The dump had past, our old staking hill too, and we were home. Up the hill our little yellow home reflected the setting sun and the pile of wooden pallets indicated journey's end. We unloaded the sled, negotiated the tidal ice for a final time and staked the dogs out in their teams.

Enrique

CHAPTER 22: Centre of Attention

HAVING SPENT a day, somewhat reluctantly on my part, celebrating my twenty-eighth birthday, by the early evening many of the younger local families had begun to gravitate towards home and Merete had been able to visit after coming off-duty at the health centre. Still with the four of us and Troels were Marius (a friendly Greenlander we'd met from the northern West Coast, but an adopted 'son' of Avanerriaq), Finn, Karen and a half a dozen of so of their assorted family and friends. I had been presented with a collection of inventively wrapped gifts as people drifted in and out. Marius handed me his with a wide, slightly tipsy smile (our table was nearest the small collection of beers) and said "Happy Birthday". As if to compound my, now lessening, unease with the whole shebang being for me, they sang Happy Birthday in no fewer than four languages: English, Danish, Inuktun and finally thanks to Anastasia, Russian.

It was time to see what the small packages contained. At home my friends and I have long since replaced gifts with evenings out and meals, and my family and I make gift giving comically token. Usually we buy something for ourselves we need anyway and then hand it over to the 'giver'. They wrap and present back to the recipient, which elicits great 'surprise and elation'. Really, it's all about spending time together and having an excuse for eating good food.

One by one I ripped away the paper wrap and placed them in a row on the table. All eyes were on me, with the first hush in hours. A series of handcrafted figures and craft pieces sat in a row – all made locally and each taking hours of care and proficiency to create. I think my waning interest in gifts is to do with how personal they are. We can even have Amazon gift-wrap our presents for our friends and loved ones and never even set eyes on them – a perfunctory gesture. These were anything but – they required forethought.

I knew that local crafts were a Greenlandic micro-industry. Far removed from fishing and more recently, mineral exploitation, the small trickle of midsummer sightseers and US service-people creates a demand for authentic souvenirs. Making figures and decorative pieces has long been part of Inuit culture, but expanding in breadth after European arrival. There is now a limit though. The CITES convention that governs the international trade in goods, clothing and meat of endangered species restricts what hunters can do. The debate on whether threatened wildlife should be hunted at all, by anyone, is a tangent too far for this book but, a brief moment now on how the law is applied.

It's become clear that European laymen cannot equate a seal with the cow they eat as beef and use for clothing as leather – purely on emotional grounds. The trade in sealskins to the European Union dwindled with new laws in the 1990s following a Greenpeace-led campaign, and an import ban was in place in 2009 – latterly though with an 'Inuit exception' which allows for some trade in seals hunted by indigenous people. Indeed, there is now a nationwide paranoia about Greenpeace and whether white visitors to Greenlandic settlements are some of their spies.

Fair-trading is to me a precursor for securing a future for Inuit. The only significant trade in seal meat is to Korea and the surrounding area. Regardless of your view on this, understanding that subsistence seal hunting bares no resemblance to commercial seal hunts elsewhere around the globe is essential. This loss of income hit small Inuit communities hard.

Today, all that can readily be taken out of Greenland is the bone or antler of legally hunted caribou. In the modernity of the airstrip terminal at Kangerlussuaq in the South, a little shop sells large caribou carvings for eye-wateringly exorbitant sums, alongside trinkets and polar bear or narwhal image-adorned T shirts and mugs; most likely made in the Far East. It is one of the few spots in Greenland that has succumbed a little to commercialisation. Sad in some ways, but isolated.

Up north, things are different. Spectacular spiralled narwhal tusks, actually overgrown canine teeth, and at times over six feet in length, are worth a fortune. However, like polar bear skins and other side-products from hunts primarily aimed at collecting meat, CITES halts their export. Hans in particular had a small stock of tusks and more exotic carvings and figures, mostly destined for locals or very occasionally back via Danes under strict rules. My gifts included a whole range of local ornaments, all of them beautifully shaped and then polished. A little polar bear, a *tupilak* (a slightly grotesque avenging spirit from the days of the shamans) and wonderfully given our running team joke, a halibut on a sealskin necklace. Materials used ranged from walrus tusk to narwhal tooth.

Touched, I thanked my friends, new and old, and we ate, drank and chatted until the early hours of the morning. Anders had even sourced craft ale not normally available in the store and proudly handed it to me. We also ate walrus from a recent hunt to the north, finding it best for eating when boiled to tenderise, and then pan-fried with a dab of hot mustard.

CHAPTER 23: Coming to Terms

ANDERS HAD TRANSLATED a handwritten advert of mine to affix to the wall inside the shop's entranceway. It was an inevitability we'd put to the back of our minds – much like the ice breaking up. We had to let our dogs go.

Long before we had a clue as to the potential of our dog teams – daily ranges, ultimate potential distances without resupply, or even if we could drive them effectively at all – selling was part of the plan. Whether that took place on either side of the ice sheet in southern Greenland or right there in Qaanaaq, we couldn't foresee. But the day that we had to say goodbye to our unlikely band of canine rogues was inescapable. Our responsibility was two-fold – first to train them hard, consistent with the local style, whilst applying the standards of animal welfare we knew to be right, and second making sure they had bright futures.

It would be unlikely that we'd be able to sell dogs in quantities any greater than three or four to each hunter – limited demand and cash would see to that. Some wouldn't do well apart, and so we kept that in mind. In particular, and I have already touched on the awkward topic of dog treatment and new law-compliance in the Far North, we knew who to subtly not sell to. We, and others, were aware of the handful of hunters who did not care for their dogs, who were poor hunters, known as *heqajuit*, and brought in little fresh meat, or drank too much and couldn't provide for them. A couple of our dogs were liberated from these hunters, and we'd done our best to rehabilitate.

We'd been spending a lot of time at Troel's house. He enjoyed the company of people nearer his age, and who spoke conversational Danish and English. We had to clear out of our little yellow house a little earlier than anticipated so bunked on his floor space.

It was from here, birthday celebrations and all else settled, including shifting boxes of freight to the shore-side shack in anticipation of the sole summer shipment south, that we planned the great dog sale. It was nerve-wracking. What if no-one came and showed no interest? What if the local people had just been polite for all those months and had secretly been horrified with the state of our dog driving? What if they thought we'd ruined the dogs irreparably? The consequences for the dogs didn't bear thinking about.

Our concerns were short lived. Peter Duneq came up to the house with Else. He was very anxious that he had missed the train. He made us promise not to let go of 'Gouda' (Comedy) until he could come down after a fishing trip and see what was what, which we of course assured him. Within hours, Rasmus had visited and booked an appointment for the next morning down at our 'dog city' headquarters on the ice. This was unusual for him – he rarely veered from his own routine. He was a real 'elder', a respected hunter and reservoir of knowledge and wisdom. I place the word elder in inverted commas due to the different, perhaps lesser, reverence that the Polar Eskimos place on their older men compared to other native peoples. We usually only saw Rasmus at his home, tending to his dogs, at the hunting union shack, or out in the wilderness. He rarely attended social gatherings.

By the hand-scribbled notes and a handful of other visits, far from having a demand drought, it became clear we were going to have a queue. We joked over dinner that night, with a precious bottle of wine, about which dogs would be snapped up and which would be left to last – the unpopular kids picked last for the school sports team.

By the time the next morning we trudged reluctantly down to feed the dogs, nearly an hour before 'sale time', hunters were already there. We'd hoped to have some time with them and give the teams a good 'send off' meal – also to calm their barking and over-excitement before strangers arrived. It wasn't to be. I actually didn't recognise a couple of the men and wondered where they'd been hiding all those months, but we knew that some did keep themselves to themselves. They spent all their time either on the ice or at home – evading community events and especially those with a Danish contingent.

We went through the routine of crushing handshakes, shy smiles and testing out which of three or four languages got a little traction.

The dogs were inspected one by one with care, much as we'd done in December. Ribs, eyes, teeth and paws all got a thorough medical. They, albeit without lavish affection, also tested the dogs' confidence and friendliness with an outstretching glove and pat on the head. One hunter had brought his entire family, who were instrumental to the decision-making process and authorising the purchase. His wife stood back, shyly, holding a wodge of Danish banknotes.

The dogs started to sell. Houdini, and Pinky and the Brain were first. Predictably, by a rule that seemed well adhered to, it was the handsomest dogs first, not necessarily the best.

Rasmus slowly approached with a smile. He wanted Dave back, which pleased me as I felt he should return to who bred him, and Enrique. Dave was of course a large, impressive animal, but a reluctant runner. For breeding stock, Anastasia and I wondered? Then, he met Crazy, and pointed to him too. Peter hadn't mentioned wanting Crazy, one of his dogs, back and so we agreed. Rasmus couldn't collect until the next day but paid us up front. We'd advertised the dogs at below the cost we'd paid in December – partly to ensure they sold, and otherwise as we felt it appropriate to not see it as a financial incentive. The dogs mattered more than the cash.

With three-quarters of the dogs paid for and collected on that first morning, our dog city seemed empty. It was a little sad. Incredibly the Hitmen, possibly our best dogs but not 'lookers', were still left and so was Comedy Dad, who we held for Peter.

Rasmus turned up on time the next morning to collect his acquisitions. A friend, the very tall hunter we'd met once or twice before, was his second pair of hands and after letting us say farewell, he walked off with Crazy and Enrique, controlling their enthusiastic bounds with skill.

Rasmus and I remained in the gloomy morning half-light, as I'd asked the team if I could do the handover alone. Dave held a special spot for me, his shortcomings rendered irrelevant. I wanted to say a proper goodbye to the dog I'd first met on a cold, dark hillside in 2012 with Hans and Rasmus as I sought a bear dog for Dark Ice. A dog we'd seen build in confidence of over months of work, and who exuded a certain idle charm.

Rasmus was probably the most reserved person I'd met in my life. Whilst far from one to wear my own heart on my sleeve, I knew I was going to find the handover difficult, especially with potential disapproval as Rasmus stood silently beside us.

I knelt down and had a quick chat with Dave, gave him a good belly rub and head scratch. Then, before getting back on my feet, said my 'thank you' and planted a peck on his forehead. He gazed back amiably but somewhat vacantly. To my surprise, I heard Rasmus' quiet voice behind me.

"Hard thing." Then a pause, as if choosing his words with care. "Good dog," he said slowly and gently patted me on the shoulder. The way that we, and they the Polar Eskimos, express their affection, reliance and devotion to our dogs differs more than you can imagine, but at the core we both understood each other.

With that, I changed over Dave's collar, swapped the light chain for a walking rope, and handed it to Rasmus. We shook hands, first taking gloves off, he gladly adopting this most European of customs. Then, he walked Dave over the cracked and buckled sea ice towards the centre of Qaanaaq's beach line, and I retreated towards our hill, past our old home, and met back with the four at Troels'.

The Hitmen did sell, thankfully, and so did the rest. We were dog-less, and as such, confined to Qaanaaq unless we hitched a ride on a friend's sled.

At Marius' home where we spent an evening, knowing we were soon to leave, we chatted over the sale of the dogs, in between trying on his store of polar bear furs and *kamiks*. He let us in on the gossip through our months of dog sledding, and the fate of our dogs. At the beginning with our fledgling and occasionally hapless training in the dark days of winter, especially our initial habit of standing up which provoked much amusement, there was little confidence. Many expected us to begin returning dogs to previous owners, or make such a hash of it that we'd irreparably ruin them. I read tales from early interactions between white visitors to Avanerriaq and local hunters when the shortcomings and unfamiliarity with the polar conditions were greeted with real cruelty and amusement at the loss of dogs through inexperience, and even visitors suffering frostbite injuries. This flew in the face of the inclusion we'd enjoyed. With some verve, Marius recalled what had grown in place of their initial scepticism.

"People have watched you. They have seen your dogs running. They run very well. Your journeys on the ice have made people notice," he said. Smiles grew. "Everyone had decided that your dogs were strong and people would buy them. Perhaps you were sometimes too soft on them."

We accepted that final caveat and were comfortable with it – our upbringing shaped our attitude towards animals and whilst we could adapt, we wouldn't entirely change. Though, in a nation where appearing openly impressed or surprised can be seen as weakness, this was hefty praise indeed.

Our final week or two lodged with Troels were a strange half-life. We were once again considering the outside world – booking space on aircraft and sorting paperwork. We had dozens of loose ends to tie up, and people to thank and bid farewell.

Sat on Troels' table was the little fabric sewing kit we'd been loaned all those months ago by the elderly hunter from the far side of town. He'd insisted we keep it to the end, so under the blue skies of the Arctic spring evening we paid a visit. Beyond a broken wooden fence, which would have kept roaming dogs away from skins put out to dry, were a few steps and a front door left ajar. We walked in with a loud greeting – to pre-warn any occupant. This hunter was from the old school – living by subsistence and without the faintest interest in becoming involved in industry other than the one he knew as a boy. His home reflected that. There were none of the modern comforts we'd seen elsewhere. Even Rasmus had a smart new television the last time I visited him, yet with two-hundred pounds or so of walrus thawing in front of the stove.

Cigarette smoke hung thick in the air and it was dark – entirely so in the small porch and then as we parted a drape that separated the main room, lit only by a lantern in the corner and a flickering old television under a small window. Our old friend was sat, dozing, with a mug of steaming coffee at his side. He roused and without showing any surprise, found everyone a spot to perch on. We chatted briefly but with such limited common language it was somewhat stilted. James stood and placed the precious sewing pouch, which we'd replenished with some of our nylon and Kevlar threads, into the hunter's weathered, oil-marked hands. He smiled warmly and shook it in the air as if in triumph. We bade farewell soon after and reached home just in time, for we had a visitor.

A young man in his thirties and dressed in modern, but dirty and worn, outdoor fabrics, had been looking for us. The fabled solo Japanese skier.

Somewhat shell-shocked that he actually existed at all, and in fact a little relieved he was alive and well, we made coffee and sat him down. His English was good and, with impeccable politeness, the man introduced himself as Yusuke Kakuhata. I instantly began to connect the dots. I'd heard of his super-purist journeys in Arctic Canada from previous years and this turned out to be a training and planning season for his latest project to travel from Canada to Greenland across the Nares Strait much further north. He had long-since opted to travel without resupplies or any form of radio, beacon or satellite phone whatsoever, the fatalistic end on the spectrum of pure polar travel.

He was fascinating and told us of the difficult conditions on the Meehan and north. Finally, he asked for my permission to have the location of our resupply depots on the northern coast of Inglefield Land as an emergency insurance, which I of course gladly provided but warned him may have been raided by polar bears. The sharing of food caches is a proud tradition. Ours was laid in the summer of 2013 by a French friend who lives with his family on a polar-modified yacht – at a place called Inuarviggiaq (Marshall) Bay, the northern extreme of Polar Eskimo camps. The word itself means great massacre, and legend tells of an entire community descending into frenzied violence leaving not one soul alive. It countered the measured attitude towards violence that typified many Inuit groups.

This brave and solitary polar traveller, motivated by the love of the challenge and without pretensions of grandeur or fame, reminded me of Naomi Uemura. Uemura was lost in the winter of 1984 on Denali in Alaska, but not before completing world-first polar journeys and securing himself a reputation as a unique, gentle, driven, but lone traveller. Their manner of living will always attract confused questions of 'why?' but I respected both men enormously. With that, he thanked us for our hospitality and left.

Our travel date was looming.

We'd begun to get itchy feet anyhow without a set purpose or our dogs, so had spent time with friends and creating final batches of photographs for our stable of sponsors. We'd also at the request of some of the villagers, spent time with a group of teenagers and young adults for a sort of 'exchange of ideas and stories'. Much of my optimism for the young people of Avanerriaq laid with the group's leader, David Qujaukitsoq. He tirelessly strove to encourage them to look outwards, consolidate their local heritage and skills, and look after their health.

On the morning of our southbound flight, having been delayed and cancelled no fewer than five days running, we were ready. Mindsets had shifted south. Life in our Arctic home, a place we'd all utterly fallen in love with, was over. We had to think of flight times, hotels, train schedules, bank balances and all that indicated a return to our 'real worlds'. It would always be feasible to stay longer – a year, a decade, have a family and settle like Freuchen. We simply had to absorb as much as we could in the time we had.

As news spread we were to leave, one response was consistent. "When will you return?" They were sorry to see us leave, and after all – the turmoil of the Dark Ice postponement and every trial since – it was that which mattered. We'd become, for a time, truly immersed in an extraordinary corner of the world and begun to really know its people. Perhaps we might have added a stone or two to building a bridge between cultures that have too often refused to try and understand one another.

We knew where most of our dogs had ended up – either on staking sections of hillsides, on the beach or out on the sea ice. We'd visited them regularly to slip them a treat or two, and to ensure they were okay. One new owner had staked together a couple that didn't at all get along, and he willingly split them after we'd broached the issue, hopefully with tact. Odin, Dog With No Name and BS had already been enlisted as a training trio for a young child learning how to sled for the first time – that was particularly touching for us to see.

I walked down to the beach, now dressed in travel clothes – jeans with thermals underneath, a t-shirt and a fleece, plus my down jacket – to say a final goodbye. As Anders and Anastasia had before me, I found each one, had a one-sided chat, gave them a pat of thanks on the head, and walked back, a little misty-eyed, to the waiting truck with Finn and Hans. James hadn't been able bring himself to go at all and was visibly moved by our leaving the teams behind. From someone who'd been ambivalent about dogs initially, he was now as fond of them as anyone.

The flight, due to be chock full after the endless succession of weather delays, breakdowns and lack of pilots, had landed following its approach from Upernavik to the south of Melville Bay. Seemingly, all of Qaanaaq had made the two-mile hike or ride along the snowy track to the airstrip. Families were reunited, visitors from settlements in the South were leaving, and a couple of municipal staff were swapping over their rotas in the North.

With all of our supplies and equipment either boxed up for the summer voyage south by ship, in the plane's small hold or passed on to friends and Qaanaaq residents, we had just our rucksacks and some food for the flights. I thanked Hans for his peerless assistance and we exchanged warm pats on the shoulder – he was not a man disposed to hugs – and shook Finn's hand firmly, promising to visit in future. I would never see Finn again. He died the following year after battling various cancers and other ill health – a real, and premature, loss for his wife, Qaanaaq and the North.

As James, Anastasia, Anders and I walked out of the door and across the gravel to the small, bright red propeller plane, the contrast to December was stark. Snow had retreated from the landing strip, and the sky was cloudless and blue. I felt the feeble attempt of the sun to warm my cheek and remembered the cutting chill of the pitch black, -30°C air those months before. I looked out over the beach and sea ice to the far horizon. What an extraordinary privilege.

From a world of ice, cliffs, dog sleds, fishing, and modest one or two-room homes, we were hurtled back into one of modern aircraft, tarmac roads, and multi-story buildings.

Via Ilulissat and Kangerlussuaq we wound our way bit by bit to Europe. From Copenhagen, Anders returned to his family briefly and then worked for a few years in Greenland's West, then briefly as Troels' replacement in Qaanaaq. He and his girlfriend originally had ambitions to stay long term, but commitments in Denmark pulled too hard. James, Anastasia and I flew on to London with plans for the future. She took time away from the cold and studied yoga in eastern Asia, before settling back in London to work in property and raising a Utonagan puppy.

James and I stayed based in London too until his ambitions led to a move to Sheffield, England's mecca for young climbers. We continued to work together and made a near-hundred-mile journey on Iceland's Vatnajökull in the mid-winter of 2016.

Every time we speak, whether over a beer in a pub or a web chat in a far-flung part of the world, it doesn't take long for tales of our time in Avanerriaq to surface – 'no regrets'.

EPILOGUE: An Essay on the Polar Eskimo Future

'This severe and beautiful country became my home; with all my heart and soul I came to love it and its people.'
Peter Freuchen

THE PEOPLE of the extreme Far North, the Polar Eskimos, have had one of the most unique, isolated and accelerated histories of any on Earth. The earliest reports of their way of life, languages and culture by explorers were instrumental to our early understanding in the temperate lands to the south, albeit prejudiced by colonial ignorance. A few subsequent twentieth century studies by Rasmussen, Malaurie and others went into microscopic detail; quickly recording disappearing traditions before they succumbed to modernity. By the close of the century foreign attention was less ethnographic and more concerned with wildlife, vanishing ice and environmental concerns. From the perspective of the south, Inuit as a whole fell again into the shadows.

In the early and mid-nineteenth century, after their contact with Europeans, the Polar Eskimos numbered around two hundred. Their way of life was tough; they had fire, but lacked basics of that time – formed metal or wood – in any appreciable quantities. Life expectancy was low, and the survival of the weaker members of the society depended much upon the successes or failures of the previous hunting season. This now is how we might view the ecology of other species, and this survival-based-on-raw-nature was something that had been widely overcome elsewhere on Earth. Accidental death on the sea ice was regular and ritual suicide by the elderly and others was commonplace. I do wonder how they would have reacted if in an instant shown the way resource-rich civilisations were living in 1820s London, Moscow or Beijing.

It could be said that the people of Etah, Neqi and other sparse, transient settlements were content. At the very least, they were getting by and their population was stable. Without knowledge of what is around the corner, or thousands of miles away, it can certainly lead to a blissful unawareness. They simply did not know about ships, guns, radio, coffee, vegetables or most of the things others around the world used daily.

Upon the arrival of *qallunaaq*, everything changed. The Polar Eskimos were now acutely aware that they were a frontier of a much wider world. They knew that their lives would never be the same. Critically they knew that these foreigners were more powerful, and also had things that they wanted, and later needed.

From the early ships of Ross, Nares and the Scottish whalers until after the early visits of Cook and Peary, unequal trading pervaded where valuable local resources, especially abundant fox skins (worth ten times more than a seal pelt) were bartered in return for small quantities of goods the Polar Eskimos were keen for, such as firearms and timber. Reliance developed and there was no going back. It was rarely a fair trade and no allowance was made for lean periods in between visits by ships. It represented, nonetheless, a technological revolution of gigantic significance for the Polar Eskimos.

With metal and wood, coffee and tinned food becoming increasingly part of the Polar Eskimo way of life, kayaks became stronger and seals or walruses could be shot, not harpooned. Hunting was safer and more efficient and even the sealskin *iglu* made way for larger, more spacious shelters. Some southern imports, particularly carbohydrate-based foods like bread, and the bitter taste of tea, were acquired tastes and took time to catch on in the mid-nineteenth century.

After the dubious 1909 'claim' of the North Pole by Robert Peary, his siring of a number of half-American, half-Polar Eskimo children, and the distractions of a World War, the Polar Eskimos found themselves mostly ignored until long after the arrival of Danish-Greenlander Knud Rasmussen, the 'father of Eskimology'.

Rasmussen, perhaps the first to consider the welfare of the Polar Eskimos, set up his trading station in 1910. With him, concepts of value-based trading of commodities and actual currency finally came to Avanerriaq. Over ninety years had passed since John Ross first visited, and change had already been visited upon the Polar Eskimos. Indeed, Rasmussen chose the location Peary had used for an expedition camp for his trading station, as people had begun to cluster in the area instead of moving camp quite so often.

The twentieth century passed. The First World War and financial turmoil of the 1920s were distractions from Arctic exploration, but by the 1930s Denmark officially deemed the north of Greenland to be their property, receiving little in the way of protest from overseas. The American military showed increasing interest in the Avanerriaq, as their quarrel with the Soviet Union deepened, but behaved mostly as if the land was uninhabited. Denmark rejected a post-war $100m purchase offer, but their senior politicians conceded that Greenland was under a de facto US occupation throughout the Cold War. The 1980s and 1990s finally saw the earliest buds of Greenlandic global ambition and self-determination.

Over a decade into the next century, where are we? Environmental campaigning and attention for the Arctic has lost none of its column inches and in an era packed with information, yet also hypocrisy, sensationalism, agenda and bias, the Arctic is firmly centre stage.

The future for the Polar Eskimos is not as uncertain as you may assume. Trends have been established, political positions made clear and in many areas wheels are already in motion. It's a tale of great power imbalance, lack of outside awareness and often, apathetic resignation. But, it's also a cause for optimism, of resilience and of decency and pride for historic aspects of life proven to be workable in a modern world.

Today, there are fewer than a thousand people who live in Avanerriaq, from Savissivik in the south to Siorapaluk in the north. A small proportion of these are Danes, permanently settled and running businesses or on government contracts, and some are Greenlanders from the South. Contrast this to the 56,000 other inhabitants of Greenland, the 32,000 inhabitants of Canada's Nunavut (25,000 of them Inuit), those in Alaska, Russia and so on, and you have only a flake in a snowfield of native polar people.

A common perception is that the Arctic environment is in a state of human-inflicted change, perhaps a decline, and the people who live there are powerless in the face of such might. The truth is far more nuanced and complex.

The Polar Eskimos are a tiny minority and subtly different to other Inuit and northern people. They, not to say others do not, proudly defend their history, traditional skills and as a group are conservative politically.

Speaking to dozens of people in both the larger settlement of Qaanaaq and the tiny hamlets surrounding, what the locals want is simple and rarely deviated from. They want to be left to live a traditional way of life without strict rules from the South. They want to interact with the rest of their nation, and other states, with fair terms for trade. But, they want to benefit from the modernity of the wider world to an extent that suits them but doesn't drag them away from their roots. Whether you think these are reasonable or globally compatible is a separate matter, but they are what I gleaned.

Qaanaaq, as the hub, naturally attracts the majority of investment and amenities. There is a basic health centre, school, heated hall for sport and community gatherings, a store and centrally-generated power. Other communities have some but not all of these and of those, most are basic. Naturally, year on year families move from the satellites to the 'bright lights' of Qaanaaq. Life is without a doubt easier there and with more opportunities. A region's people which historically comprised a number of family groups and hunting alliances spread super-sparsely across hundreds of miles of beaches and cliffs, for reasons of resource availability, is clumping together. Why is this?

In a sort of self-fulfilling and reinforcing prophecy, Polar Eskimo families want the benefits of Qaanaaq. So, the dwindling populations where they move from give the government a shrinking reason to invest in those pockets of survivors. Almost the entire municipal budget ends up in Qaanaaq. It's more efficient and easier to control, for better or worse. Building a new school for six hundred people makes more sense than for thirty. There is a threshold that the government has set for complete loss of official subsidy or support for a community – I heard that this is around twenty people. Below that limit, there will be no ship resupply, no helicopter shuttles, no water or power maintenance and no schooling. Also, no resupply and no store either, so it breaks down. Unless, of course, locals accept a **complete** return to the ways of the past with all that entails.

I've not met anyone who explicitly seeks this purist path to return to pre-Contact conditions – and those who appear to, initially through nostalgia, quickly backpedal when they realise the implications. There must be no illusion that pre-Contact Arctic life was a utopia – the centuries of survival prove it worked, but it was a serious struggle. Conveniently forgotten today is the fact many Inuit at the time of first Contact were enthusiastic about what opportunities it could bring – the tragedy is that sometimes they were badly let down. There are pros and cons to the influence of the South. Diseases were introduced, but life expectancy rose from fifty or sixty in Peary's time to even beyond eighty. Dental care took a tumble as sugar arrived, and alcohol has impacted on the Polar

Eskimo pride and 'spirit'; yet welcome modern comforts in home living are undeniable and could never have independently come about without imports. Certain agendas may obscure this truth, but it remains so.

It must also not escape notice that whilst these modern settlement closures and gradual centralisation appear partially voluntary on the surface, they evoke emotions reminiscent of the worst days of colonialism – of forced relocations and residential schools to 'civilise the savages'. Even the best-intentioned and most popular early settlers found it hard to cast-off the mindset that their European virtues and lifestyles simply had to be adopted by natives, for their own good.

Something for every single person from a developed country to keep in mind if they visit a small, traditional society in a far-flung corner of the globe is: if this person was born through accident of circumstance in a place with trees or workable metal, or even with an already technologically-advanced platform, they may have invented the internal combustion engine, or the smartphone. The brain inside their head is no different in evolutionary terms than yours or an Ancient Greek philosopher's. It seems blindingly obvious in those terms, but is easily missed through skewed context when stood in front of a hunter wearing animal furs. Opportunity is a precursor to all, followed only then by inherent talent and ambition, and we do well to remember this.

Of course, if a hunting group or family wanted to reoccupy Etah, Anoritooq or even Qaqaitsut, which was recently discovered even further north, they could. However, they would receive no government assistance. Every single thing would be on their own backs – power, sanitation, supplies of food and medicines. This is how it was of course prior to the 'discovery' of the Polar Eskimos. At their heart, I'm sure the people could make it work once more. But, do they want to and what would the purpose be? Most likely no, and nothing.

There are two possible drivers of the Greenland government's Nuuk-based policy toward remote areas of the nation. One is that they have a fixed and limited budget, and they cannot make it stretch forever. Supporting tiny groups of hunters with large sums of money to give them facilities they're now accustomed to, purely because they fancy living somewhere culturally significant to them, is not logical. If someone decided to set up home on a small island off the shore of the UK and then asked the government for a school, shop, sewerage works, helicopter pad and so on, they would be laughed out of the room. This sort of subsidy for a region of Greenland that is already a loss-maker is understandably tough to justify. Subsidy in preference to investment can also be, in some cases, a precursor of cultural decline, apathy and a downward spiral. It is inversely correlated to local productivity, whether through cause or effect. From 1950 to 1970, Siorapaluk morphed from being self-sufficient to producing a mere quarter of what it consumed.

The other point of view is that token investment in one centralised location and then a policy of letting settlements, depleted of a significant population, disappear could be a strategy. If you wanted to move a dispersed population to a single, more controllable location, then you'd get your result in just a generation or two.

One trend accelerates the other. The more people that are attracted to the conveniences of Qaanaaq, the more likely that said investments will only be made in Qaanaaq. Inescapably, the contrast between hub and satellite becomes greater and the quality of life becomes even better in one and worse in the other. The same trend in native Canadian communities is an explosively political issue there, but at least it is being widely debated.

Is this a plot? My conclusion is that it is a convenient arrangement for the powers that be in Nuuk. Using the natural, trickle feed of families gravitating towards their extended families in Qaanaaq, there is both a demand for new improvements in Qaanaaq and an incentive for Nuuk to only invest there. One settlement is cheaper to subsidise then five. You end up with a bit of a chicken and egg situation. Did the Polar Eskimos start abandoning the smaller settlements and the government then reacted to this change in dynamic by investing in the home they've chosen, or did the people leave the hamlets because of a squeeze from the government making life untenable there? Either way, it has resulted in additional resentment from the population and has suited the politics of Nuuk's government.

The two long-term stated aims of the Polar Eskimos and government do not match their current trajectories. The people I spoke to want to continue as before, perhaps not fully appreciating that the way they live now does have significant benefits brought from the influence of the South and developed world. They do not live now as they did in 1800, or 1900, or 1950. So, at what point do they want modernisation to stop? I found no clear answer to that. Their community is modernising every year. A few years ago, they had almost no communications with the wider world. Now, there is very slow, but in the circumstances impressive, wireless internet and cell phone signal.

Their own rules – a legacy of Rasmussen's Thule Law – outlaw hunting or whaling directly from motor vehicles like skidoos in the winter and motorboats in the summer, but every year sees more vehicles driving on the sea ice for other purposes, and around town. Ahead of their time, the Polar Eskimos decided long ago that even having gained firearms, walrus must be harpooned at great risk to a hunter, and only then put down with a bullet. This would avoid over-harvesting with the balance so greatly swung in the favour of the hunter, even though game animals had become less tame after firearms appeared on the scene.

An outsider must act responsibly now and into the future, if a community has benefited from, and is accustomed to, new resources that are impossible to develop or assemble locally. Famously Robert Peary, once he had used the Polar Eskimos for his purposes in supposed North Pole glory, abandoned them. The supply of wood, metal and other bartered goods was abruptly halted and their reliance on them forced a shock re-adaptation to past ways. They even made bullets out of bone having exhausted their ammunition supply. To their credit once again, the Danish government was moved to replenish local supplies via Rasmussen even if their own commercial interests did not yet glance north of Upernavik, far south of Avanerriaq. This supply-addict-deprive cycle must not reoccur.

Whilst not explicitly published, governmental agenda to 'shut down' the North seems to correlate with consolidating a population in one place and creating increasingly dependence on the South, and what it provides. It wouldn't take long, once that is done, to pull the rug out from under those feet entirely. Through public relations rhetoric though, the government continues to champion the cultural importance of Greenlandic history and tradition. Their posters and websites are adorned with the polar bear, the kayak and the hunter.

It's perhaps inevitable that heritage means more to the remote outposts than to the people in the corridors of power. However, it does seem disingenuous to me for ministers to foster popularity, wear traditional costumes and champion unique history on one hand, whilst choking those very people who still live that heritage with the other.

I concede that a region with little industry and a cash-negative economy, and therefore a reliance on subsidy, cannot hold too much sway when arguing a cause to a treasury that needs to balance their books. The Polar Eskimos are a subsistence community historically, much like all other Arctic people. Trade and interaction did exist in the past, but sheer isolation made it difficult. This transformation from subsistence to needing support is a bit of a quandary – was the need thrust upon them, or demanded once accustomed to resources they couldn't self-generate? It's almost impossible to tell from observing how the land now lies. Regardless, the gap now exists.

The very connection of the North with the South is serviced by a part government-owned airline, Air Greenland. It's the only carrier active within Greenland and planes at times fly half full, with services often reduced. Weather and technical delays are daily frustrations, for which compensation must be paid to customers. It's a tough business model to operate. Helicopters and fixed-wing flights in the North are all 'service flights'. This means that all flights, full or empty, are loss-making with the shortfall made up for by other flights further south and to and from Denmark – or of course, by the government. The inefficiency of the North is evident here, perhaps fair reason for a cost-benefit analysis.

There is natural cynicism towards the domestic air policy. It's hard to confirm or refute, but more than one hunter felt that the monopoly of air travel is intentional. Demand to start an airline in Greenland cannot be high by simple commercial logic, but they don't believe another would be permitted to survive. This is a litmus paper to the public view of how business is done.

Ironically, sky-high prices for tickets to fly around Greenland have proven self-defeating. The airstrip near Qaanaaq was only built in 2001 for Air Greenland services, as part of a 47m Danish kroner compensation agreement. Prior to this, any air travel to and from the region had to arrive via the US airbase at Thule, then to be shuttled onwards by helicopter. It sounds convoluted but prices were keener on balance for visitors, scientists and so on. Is this infrastructure development really the action of a government hell-bent on its destruction? Perhaps it was actually due to pressure from the US military, who inflict strict rules on those transiting Thule, but Qaanaaq's minute tourist industry has been decimated by the rising costs. Hans lamented that after the airstrip arrived, his guesthouse makes a lot less than before and he considered closing it.

Qaanaaq does latterly host a real, modern industry. Aside from community employment like manning the airstrip, working on utilities or staffing the store, there is the produce that has always existed: food harvests. Not of the farming sort of course – there is no natural arable farming in Greenland. The limited seasonal activity in the Far South, below the Arctic Circle, is a result of imported plant species, grass for introduced sheep and some trees. Small berries and lichens are picked on a small scale in the short summer, but it's a tiny proportion of traditional diet. Early Norse settlers attempted from the tenth to fifteenth centuries to set up farmsteads, abruptly vanishing after having been overrun by Inuit ancestors. However, hunting and fishing has always been the mainstay of Inuit from all over Greenland. Indeed, it is the overwhelming reason for their and their ancestors' survival.

The bulk of animals hunted in Greenland, such as polar bear, walrus, narwhal and larger whales, cannot be exported due to CITES endangered animal legislation. Others – seal, caribou, auk and muskox – can be hunted and exported but with regulations. However, the international value of seal meat, for example, is low, although the skins do have some worth as souvenirs outside the Arctic. Narwhal tusks, some six feet long or more, hypothetically fetch over $10,000 US as ornaments in the south, but are almost entirely illegal to export from Greenland. This precludes using mammals as an industry to bolster the Greenlandic economy as a whole. Besides, there is very rarely a surplus due to the number of mouths, human and canine, to feed and the difficultly of the hunt itself. Fish are however another matter.

Avanerriaq is home to Arctic char in the freshwater lakes and streams of the summer, and with Greenland halibut, cod, shrimp, and other seafood in abundance. Nationally, fisheries employ over ten per cent of the population and dominate Greenland's exports – mostly to the USA, Japan, Norway, Thailand, Germany, Great Britain, Iceland and Denmark.

Whilst a small proportion of what Greenland can muster as a whole, Avanerriaq has potential to contribute alongside southern towns like Ilulissat hosting fully industrialised fishing ports and processing centres.

The fishing that we experienced on the sea ice out of Qaanaaq and the other settlements is productive and efficient. This is nothing new with evidence of ancient fishing operations across First Nations and Inuit lands occurring on an impressive scale. With the relatively meagre financial demands of the hamlets surely outweighed by current fishing rates or a gradual increase, perhaps it could be the solution to keep both Polar Eskimo and Nuuk happy. Alas, what transpired was alarming.

A decade ago optimism grew amongst hunters and fishermen of Qaanaaq as Royal Greenland, the national fishery, expressed interest and opened a small processing building near the beach. Their traditional freedom to fish was respected and prices made it worth their while.

The picture in 2014 was starkly different. A licence is needed to fish at all. Bait fish must be purchased from the fishing company and the quantities are recorded to compare to the catches coming back in. Any discrepancies can lead to fines or reduced quotas. Fish must be accounted for and local bartering is dissuaded. The most important issue, price, has become nigh on unworkable. With encouraging initial fees for catches meaning that some hunters fished in preference to hunting mammals, in just a year or so the price paid per kilo of halibut dropped from seventeen to twelve kroner. There was no explanation, negotiation or means to appeal. It's just how it is. The same fish are processed and then sold frozen for many times that price. I looked on in horror as I found fish available in the local store, clearly caught perhaps a mile or two away, for forty to sixty kroner per kilo. People were buying them. The customers could easily be the wives of the fishermen who caught those very fish. I couldn't believe that freedom to barter, exchange, sell and distribute fish locally as they have done for centuries wasn't encouraged. Sure, the odd fish was gifted under-the-counter here and there, but the exploitation by Royal Greenland is desperate. This is history repeating itself. Over half a century ago, a Polar Eskimo hunter might harvest furs sold for $330 in the south, and would be paid just the equivalent of $12. That, as prices of imported goods they then relied on were raised.

In a continuing story of despair and reduction in liberties amongst the hunters of Qaanaaq, just before this book was first submitted to press, I had a conversation with a friend in Avanerriaq. He told me that without warning, forty per cent of Polar Eskimo hunters had their licences revoked. Their crime? Making more than half of their income from other work, made necessary due to the cost of imported goods, such as fishing or casual labour at the school or building houses. I was speechless. These people simply cannot win.

We must find out more about this mysterious 'government' – the powers from the South. The South, by the way, both on the west and east of the southern ice sheet, is where I began my Greenland travels and a place I have no bias against whatsoever – quite the opposite in fact. It would be petulant to vilify anonymous administrators from Nuuk as they oversee controversial decisions.

In 1775, half a century after first arriving, and Hans Egede making initial trades, the Norwegian-Danish Kingdom claimed Greenland as a colony. In 1937 it officially took Avanerriaq out of Knud Rasmussen's hands, and in 1953 they modernised the terminology to brand the whole nation a province of Denmark. Rapidly, as education and ambitions improved, Greenlanders pressured the Danes for more control. In 1979, Greenland was granted Home Rule, making it autonomous but still part of the Danish Kingdom. Schooling and internal administration was a Greenlandic responsibility, but wider matters of funding, defence and international affairs still laid with Denmark. This, given that Greenland is geographically linked, and its people ethnically, to North America, not Europe, is an anomaly – an accident of history and somewhat artificial.

A strong modern independence movement has incubated in Greenland, punctuated by a 2008 referendum and with pro-independence politicians dominating today's Self Rule (an upgrade from Home Rule). Former Prime Ministers habitually centred on issues like compensation payments from the USA for use of Thule Air Base, with only one or two side-lining populist policies in order to tackle troubling and widespread alcohol abuse or domestic violence. Independence agendas are never too far buried. Neither are naïve alliances – the latest with President Trump until his awkward diplomatic faux pas in an apparently serious attempt to buy Greenland via Twitter. Scandals and claims of corruption are commonplace, perhaps inevitable in rapidly modernising nations with little history of centralised government, democracy and with small populations – lessons are being learned at an accelerated, compressed rate.

As a figurehead example, Prime Minister from 2013 until 2014, Aleqa Hammond, was even before election a convicted fraudster. She then stepped down from office due to a separate expenses misuse scandal. Hammond still sits on influential boards and committees regarding the Arctic's future.

Independence needs funding, serious funding, and it is no secret that even with significant fisheries exports and a small but stable tourism industry in the brief southern summers, Denmark picks up most of the large bills. Social welfare, for example, is still the backbone of Greenland's population's survival. That is not a criticism of the Greenlandic people. A small country with a growing population, a history of subsistence living and no Western-style expectation of employment, cannot create industry and employment from thin air. Modern amenities and demands were thrust upon them over a period of only a century or so, and these cost money, which they previously had no need for. It's the nature of the unique Greenlandic situation.

Indeed, many Danes do consider the independence movement as churlish or even ungrateful. This, even when taking into account the vested interest of a colonial power with territorial Arctic Ocean ambitions. Efforts from the very beginning were made to retain Inuit culture, they facilitated the EEC exit that solely benefitted Greenland through fishing freedoms, invested heavily in dog vaccinations, and provided security throughout the Second World War and Cold War, when the fledgling domestic government was in infancy. The latter has now led to bickering over who should pay to clean up military waste and abandoned equipment. Conversely, a nationalist might accuse the Danes of infecting Greenlanders with a Stockholm Syndrome.

For Avanerriaq, their view of belonging diverges from that of Greenland as a whole. Polar Eskimo isolation and their fiercely strong link of kinship to their closest cousins in Nunavut led to talk of independence from Greenland and becoming part of Canada. Indeed, today you need to have a specific Canadian Inuit heritage to be considered a true Polar Eskimo.

On a purely fiscal point of argument – it could be tabled that Denmark has invested hundreds of millions of dollars into Greenland at significant loss, and has yet to see a return on their investment that future mineral and oil exploration is likely to provide.

Greenland is an island rich in natural resources – of course, much of it hard or impossible to reach and shrouded in snow for most of the year. However, it is now common knowledge internationally that both its mountains and lowlands contain zinc, aluminium, rubies, uranium and more besides. Fjords offer access to inshore mines, offshore are significant oil possibilities, and there is an additional conflict of interest – a warming of global temperatures and consequential ice loss aids oil exploitation, but destroys traditional lifestyles. The former generates revenue and the latter costs money to support.

Successive national leaders have been notably pro-exploitation – the common narrative being that independence could be wrenched from the Danish colonists, towards whom acrimony was stirred up, by selling off resources. In a progression that many watch in horror, mining and drilling rights were sold off at an alarming and almost uncontrolled rate to American, Australian and British prospectors, and other exploitation companies. To an outsider, it seems as if Greenlandic governments had been blinded by dollar signs, and unleashed a monster in order to secure them at any cost. Local critics have offered a voice of reason and moderation, but Greenland's environment appears to regularly come second to the urge to patriotically decouple from Denmark.

The government and commercial businesses are almost impossible to separate. Ex-subsidiaries of the Royal Greenland Trade Depot, KNI (the national trading company), the Royal Arctic Line (the shipping link with Europe) and Royal Greenland are all wholly owned by the government. Air Greenland is owned by the government, SAS (the Scandinavian airline) and Denmark's government. Frequently, government-owned monopolies of vital national services are linked to corruption, nepotism and at least, lack of accountability. Regardless, you could reasonably argue with some precedent that the unique situation that Greenland finds itself with could necessitate this sort of central control. Simply to keep the ship afloat, so to speak. Greenland's geography does not make it easy to administrate or finance.

Nuuk is as modern as towns get in Greenland. A population of over 18,000 in 2020, vast by Greenlandic standards, with traffic lights, government buildings, and even some high(ish)-rise blocks. It's a world away from the majority of Greenlandic settlements, even though itself being nestled amongst beautiful western Greenlandic fjords and mountains.

Are traditional Greenlanders, be them hunters, fishermen, homemakers, the unemployed, and those cautiously embracing changes by working on airstrips and in guesthouses, even of interest to those in power in Nuuk? It's important to note that Nuuk doesn't directly control everything, despite the limited population. Greenland is divided into municipalities and larger settlements (dubbed towns despite their small size) have a mayor or leader of some sort, offering limited devolution to take account of local culture, even if the same few faces are circulated and these positions are out of reach for most.

Specifically, how do those in Nuuk feel about the Polar Eskimos of Avanerriaq, the most overtly traditional amongst a nation of already proud local people? Decisions are made behind closed doors and as with all politicians, public statements are carefully worded to not alienate the electorate. So, the question remains.

The only true test of their priorities are in the policies and regulations that manifestly affect the people living in Qaanaaq and the surrounding area. That, unfortunately, makes for grim reading indeed. Apart from the fishing regulations and price reductions for those caught, plus the encouragement for smaller settlements to close down and decamp to Qaanaaq, stories from the ground are unverified and circumstantial, but consistent. I heard much of the investment in Qaanaaq was part of American compensation for the 1953 Thule to Qaanaaq relocation (hearsay and almost impossible to verify), and that important workers are being coaxed to work in Iluissat (a larger town in the same political zone but a world away geographically and culturally). Also, that there will be a forced move to Ilulissat in 2020 after Qaanaaq is the final Avanerriaq settlement to lose government support – something that has not transpired. The controversial G60 plan half a century ago, to 'rescue the poor Polar Eskimos from their sorry existences' and bring them south never came to pass. Other predictions remain to be seen, but they represent a future many are resigned to. I heard again and again, "There is nothing we can do, but we must go on. We must go on."

My view is that there is, based on a mix of evidence, anecdotes and time to absorb the atmosphere and consensus of real people, a genuine disconnect between Greenlanders. This is despite a Danish court ruling that in the eyes of the law, in order to deny further compensation demands, all Greenlandic Inuit are deemed of the same 'tribe'. The political class in larger centres act with obliviousness of remote village life the further away they are. Nuuk is more insulated from 'real Greenland' than Ilulissat, which is more insulated than Tasiilaq, for example, and so on. In the same way that a central Londoner finds it hard to identify with a Shetland Islander, so it is for Inuit. It's more surprising though since the nation appears outwardly one of great cultural pride, small numbers and therefore a sense of togetherness.

Icons of the North and of Greenland; the dogs, the polar bear, narwhal, the ice, are all over government websites, leaflets and campaigns – especially those seeking investment or collaboration abroad. It could be considered manipulative.

You need not be a cynic to form the conclusion that one thing is being publicly broadcast and another pursued behind the doors of power. When it suits, the traditional Greenland is peddled. When it matters, the desire for independence, investment, cash and increased influence, all in suit and tie, wins out. It could even be said that certain individuals are embarrassed by true Greenland – those who see themselves more on the international stage than the local one. Perhaps a political appetite is lacking for standing as a traditionalist in a nation of hunters, fishermen, makers, menders, survivors and travellers. Consequent images of quaintness, and archaic and even primitive lifestyles are inevitable, and so shuffled to the rear. Speaking specifically about the Polar Eskimos of the Far North; they are no longer relevant to an independent Greenlandic state, are certainly not convenient or profitable, and so will surely become the future 'past' of Greenland. A tragedy.

At the core is what politicians are there to do. Are the elected representatives of a people, especially one catching up with the wider world, supposed to represent the needs and desires of their people, or lead them somewhere based on conviction and collective ambition? Whilst voting in Greenland is Western in its mechanics, the electorate are influenced by local hearsay, loyalty to families and places, and a lack of widespread education, especially in politics and governance. In the United Kingdom, an established and regulated democracy, the clamour prior to elections is invariably, 'they're all terrible, they're all the same, there's no real choice!' Imagine how much worse it is in what is essentially a brand new country finding its feet. Nuuk should act for the people and their interests, but the level of rural education presently doesn't enforce accountability amongst leaders, with the result that private agendas rule policy instead.

Referenda show overwhelming support for independence, but little knowledge or interest in how that might come about, or be funded. Patriotism and pride therefore work directly against the people. Take a typical professional subsistence hunter from a small village. Ask him about nationalism and independence. He will likely say that he is a proud Greenlander, that he doesn't want Denmark to control his country and his future, and wants Greenlanders to take full power. The same hunter may wish to continue his current-day way of life but not be forced to live a pseudo-western lifestyle. The issue is that the two goals are presently incompatible due to Greenland's industries and bank balance. It's not unique to Greenland. Voting preference and reality often mismatch for large proportions of electorates. That famed Polar Eskimo pragmatism badly needs to re-emerge.

This may lead you to surmise that Greenlanders are their own worst enemy. An inevitable lack of political awareness, a real mental disconnect from the corridors of power, a mistrust of outsiders and the Western world, a traditional, conservative pride and other factors make it seem a little hopeless. Should they even get to choose? Why should a group of people live in a time warp, with carefully cherry-picked parts of modernity world that suit, such as medevac for very ill people and mobile phones, and then have someone else foot the bill? Is there a place for a hunter dressed in animal skins in the twenty-first century? In most established nations, the population must live within the current framework of the place they happened to be born, enjoying its bonuses (a welfare safety net, for example) and enduring its inconveniences (tax, perhaps).

There is much amiss in these communities if they want to be compatible with the modern world. A minority, impossible to ignore, have palpable suspicion for Western terms of employment, have narrow worldviews, drink too much, and from that results endemic low-level crime and abuse of women and children. A great source of frustration for some of the most articulate and thoughtful Greenlanders and Polar Eskimos I spoke to, young and old, is the apathy of many – not trying to help themselves. A lack of hope, whether through laziness or a jaded resignation to today's reality. The cure to much of this is education. As we've heard though, improvement is plagued by school truancy and limited syllabus ambition. School lessons are more crowd control than anything else. Education, if achieved through a revolutionary fresh approach, could create new industry and also allow voters to make better choices. It could perhaps even open that sluice of cash and make independence prudent and not just about anti-colonialism.

I think there is a way forward, not bashing the government in an anti-establishment rant, and not mindlessly defending every demand of a minority. I believe that the government of Greenland has a long way to go before it gains credibility. Its job is mightily difficult – running a poor, sparsely populated, geographically barren ex-colony is a challenge. I think the people of Greenland, not least the Polar Eskimos, have to indulge in some introspection and need to end bad practices. Some need a reality check. They need to decide if they really want modernism and **everything** it entails, or if traditionalism is their goal deep down. Cherry-picking is not an option. We cannot rewind the world; borders and sovereignties, to an arbitrary date in the 1700s.

There is a gulf between what I suspect will happen and what I think should. Very little is going to change in the short term. In the first edition, I didn't believe the Far North and Qaanaaq would be abandoned by 2020, but I believed life there would be increasingly hostile and that many would migrate south. As I write this, Peter (to later return), Else and Marius have already done so, but births have kept the population stable. The earliest explorers of the Age of Contact sparked and oversaw the first great change for the Polar Eskimos. Jean Malaurie stumbled across the second: modernisation. I do hope that I am not one of the few to observe the third great change; the end.

I would still be surprised if both Qeqertat and Siorapaluk were populated in 2025. This is despite the general increase in local population, far from misleading headlines of Polar Eskimos 'dying out'. I think that over the next two or three generations hunting as a way of life will decrease dramatically as comfortable and indifferent teenagers fail to follow in their parents' footsteps. Politics will most likely make few attempts to abandon corruption, and won't really represent the remote areas of the island. I think that sooner or later, through revenue generated from resource exploitation, independence will be achieved against the wishes of the Danish, who covet their Arctic interests. They, the Greenlanders, will regret it. Foreign investment and its selfish interest, in my view, will leave Greenland far less 'theirs' than it is now with Danish oversight and Self Rule to balance. Much of the medium term is to be dominated by the changing climate. As sea ice reduces, hunting will need to adapt and tradition will give way to new techniques, as they have always done in the past.

My ideal future for Greenland and its people looks very different. To me, self-determination tempered by realism is a good middle ground. If the people, as a whole, truly wish to be hunters and hold on to traditional lifestyles, then that should be respected. It's not certainty the case though. Whilst existing hunters and the older generation are generally proponents of subsistence living and living off the land and ice, fewer children learn traditional skills. In the past, girls were also taught whip technique and boys went on their first committed bear hunt at around sixteen years of age. Interests are now more homed in on working as a chef, at the airport or just relying on social security. As far back as the 1960s, people noted that the limited earning potential and tough existence of a hunter made them second-choices in the dating scene, a far cry from the way just years before hunters would secure the villages' most desirable young women. The hunter was no longer king.

This inertia of tradition, 'we are hunters and must continue to be', may continue to ebb but we could even see a traditionalist resurgence. As it does, so must the direction of those making decisions locally and as outsiders. I see that the ancient culture of living off the Arctic environment in the rawest terms as part of what makes its people special. It should always exist in some form; not as a museum piece or condemnation to a third-world existence, but as a showpiece of how it can be sustainable and respectful to harvest food and integrate with the wild, instead of fighting it. Stewardship. But, can Avanerriaq's wildlife support over a thousand Polar Eskimos, when they numbered ten per cent of that originally?

I think the Danish have been, in general terms and I state this aware of the sensitivities and difficult political undulations, considerate settlers when placed relative to others in a historical context. A prominent early administrator, HJ Rink, led by example and extoled the virtues and moral need to affirm Greenlandic cultural identity, even at cost to Denmark. Certainly examples exist abroad where the relationship has been far more toxic, dictatorial and abusive. Having accepted how history led to our post-colonial era, the devolution to Home Rule was intelligently orchestrated to be gradual and not leaving either side all at sea. Perhaps this, as Greenland educates its children, standards improve and foreigners are less and less required to fill vital roles, will continue. Maybe one day this could result in total autonomy with a historic link, as Australia and Canada are to the

United Kingdom for example – recognising though their own indigenous rights issues. For now though, Danish money and expertise are needed.

Tourism will perhaps mature and grow, but it's unlikely to become a booming industry due to the costs, isolation and acquired taste needed to visit the Arctic. Fisheries and other exports are a vital source of independent income, pride and employment and so should expand but with a wisdom that doesn't betray sustainability or respect for the environment in pursuit of cash.

The precious metals, gems and oil that capture the headlines now are more controversial. You could argue to protect the mountains, the rock and the waters by banning or severely limiting foreign investment and exploitation, but that would prove self-defeating. Instead, the government must show restraint and turn down offers of quick cash that aren't in its long-term interests. Here again, as this book first went to press, and before the Twitter purchase fiasco, overtures were being made by Nuuk to the Trump administration. The resources of Greenland are for the Greenlanders to benefit from, but not at the cost of Greenland itself. As home-grown skilled workers swell in number and technical proficiency, fewer and fewer contractors from overseas will be needed and profits can flow through Greenlandic companies, not just licences sold and money siphoned away.

The youth of Greenland are connected with the world and each other through technology. Danish investment and cooperation by Nuuk and TeleGreenland have made internet surprisingly fast, reliable and nowhere near as expensive I remembered it to be in 2010. Facebook has the same enthusiastic crowd as I remember when it first appeared to the world when I was eighteen and at university. Web and technological skills in the young barely need input from governments – they grow naturally far faster than you could push them artificially. This, easily forgotten in discussions which centre around the famed aspects of an Arctic nation – the ice, the hunting and fishing, the history – could be key, I feel.

The Polar Eskimos also need a good doctor. One that cares about them, learns their language, and isn't merely a retired general practitioner attracted by a vast fee for a cursory fortnight's visit.

There is cause for optimism – education is without doubt improving at all levels, but not fast enough. There also needs to be more emphasis on teaching local skills for children whose parents can't or won't. Whilst there are no doubt naysayers and anchors holding some back, qualities of ambition and ingenuity are still at the core of many settlements. The unique characters that through the centuries made Inuit and in particular, the Polar Eskimos, such remarkable, adaptable survivors against near-unimaginable odds, are still evident. But, pragmatism is impotent without idealists fighting their corner from within allied with vision for the future. They must also be held to the same tests and benchmarks as everyone else, both positive and negative – equitability with the rest of the world.

The people of Greenland, and of Avanerriaq, need to decide what it is they really want – and seize it. Their opportunity to do so may not exist for much longer.

The race-winning team of *qimmit*

APPENDIX A: Early History

PERHAPS AS EARLY as 2500 BCE, a small group of humans had migrated north and east from Eastern Asia and in particular, the Russian Far East of Chukotka. These Asians were the first of what are now referred to as Paleo-Eskimo cultures, and they took advantage of more benign temperatures than today. Spreading across the Bering Strait into Alaska, Northern Canada and even as far as Greenland, they are collectively named Pre-Dorset, a simple relative term to contrast with those who followed, and they persisted for two millennia until 500 BCE. For those with a keen interest in human prehistory and migration, this appearance was long after the arrival of the ancestors of today's First Nations in North America – those misnamed by blundering colonial settlers as 'Indians'. Separating the migrations were vast glacial events that blocked the route, thereafter releasing the intrepid new migrants.

The origins and relationships between consecutive human inhabitation of a land which, although able to preserve objects well, is spectacularly barren, makes the art of piecing together their history difficult. It is likely that the Dorset Culture (named after artefacts found at Nunavut, Canada's Cape Dorset) was derived from the Pre-Dorset and perhaps another fresh migration of nomads, also giving rise to the Saqqaq of Greenland. But, the bow and arrow and drilling technology that the Pre-Dorset had enjoyed, appeared to have been lost throughout the Dorset's 'reign' from 500 BCE until the remarkably modern (by European technological standards) 1500 CE. The modern Eastern Canadian Inuit refer to these Dorset people as the Tuniit (meaning 'first inhabitants'), in their language Inuktitut.

In 2010 the first genome of an ancient human was sequenced, found in the Saqqaq area, and was that of a man unimaginatively dubbed 'Inuk'. This helped scientists begin to separate the different migration events from Asia to North America amidst the various glacial ebbs and flows.

In the confusing, interlocking territories of these tiny populations of mobile, partly nomadic people, modern Inuit legends tell of the Dorset people, their predecessors, being giants who were nonetheless easy to scare off or dominate. Others oddly told of 'dwarves', but what is for sure is that they spread far and wide, south to the eastern shores of Hudson Bay, across the Northwest of Greenland and to inhabit many of the islands of modern-day Nunavut. They were living unbeknownst to most at the time, although there are vague references to potential encounters; with the Norse explorers who had reached Iceland and the southern tip of Greenland approaching from the east.

From around 1000 CE, change was afoot – that which would define the human population and how we see indigenous Arctic people of North America today began. An entirely fresh migration, the Thule people or 'proto-Inuit', had crossed the Bering Straits into Alaska and quickly spread east across Canada and into Greenland, perhaps in search of new mineral deposits. You will have read the word Thule appearing throughout this book; as a description, as a place name, as a people. This is usually because one use borrows it from another. The word itself originated in Ancient Greece and means 'north', usually in reference to an unexplored or theoretical place.

There was Norse and Viking interaction, but it was the Dorset Culture who suffered most by this invasion of new people. Still tiny in number by modern human standards, resources were scarce and only the most successful communities could thrive. Although by no means known for certain, there appears to have been little or no interbreeding between Dorset and the rapidly expanding Thule, although evidence points to there having been some conflict, perhaps some trading and without doubt some appropriation of skills, for the Dorset technique of seal hole hunting was quickly adopted by the Thule.

By 1500 CE, the Dorset's last stronghold on Baffin Island and the shores to the south vanished and the Canadian Arctic and Greenland, now inhabited on both coastlines west and east of the vast icecap, belonged to the Thule. A rumour that the Sagdlermiut, a Hudson Bay culture whose last member died in 1903 from a settler-imported disease, were descended from the Dorset Culture was refuted by recent DNA evidence. The Norse, who became modern-day Icelanders, abruptly either died out or retreated to today's surviving Nordic territories.

It was these people, continuously occupying the prime Arctic territory of Alaska, Northern Canada (today's Northwest Territories and Nunavut) and Greenland, although now having retreated from the brutal north coast, who are the direct ancestors of modern-day Inuit.

Technology thrived, with marine mammals as their main hunting quarry, from great whales to seal, walrus and polar bear, and seal-skin kayaks and harpoons supplemented the bows and arrows used on and off in the region for thousands of years. Iron and copper deposits were discovered but wood was mostly absent and therefore proved valuable. Being far above the tree line meant only occasional driftwood washed up in the summer melt. Without any reference, it was believed that the wood grew on the bottom of the sea. Dog sleds, vital for their travel, were fashioned partly from scraps of driftwood but mostly from bowhead whalebones.

Through the Little Ice Age of c.1650-1850 and even beyond, towards the present day, the people were directly constrained by nature, and other disruptions and smaller migrations complicated the picture. Some people settled and became less nomadic, some were cut off and became isolated by the rugged terrain, languages diverged, communities died out (often numbering in single or double figures), and old hunting territories were rediscovered. The modern world of Inuit was born. Their range was limited mostly by the game (marine mammals, muskox, bear and so on), the tree line and Native Americans to the south, and the open expanse of the frozen ocean to the north.

Those First Nations who already had a long established territory and a patchwork of distinct nations across North America's tree line and southwards, acted as a de facto border to the ancestors of today's Inuit. The First Nations and indigenous Americans were on the whole more warlike than their Arctic neighbours, so emerged from almost all border disputes the victors. Despite this, a legacy of pride runs through Inuit of today regarding misty legends of past battles with 'Indians' and Vikings. It is highly likely that without this, Inuit would have adapted to the forested zones and with more elaborate resources, developed more rapidly than was the case as history played out.

It is notable in a time of debate over indigenous land rights and those of colonial settlers that the ancestors of today's Inuit were foreign settlers to a continent already inhabited for thousands of years. To the south, the First Nations made it clear they were in command of their territory and bison herds – might wins out, as they themselves found to their cost through subsequent European invasions – but the previous cultures of the North succumbed to Thule culture, partly through conflict. This must be a thinking point when tackling thorny issues of precedence and moral ownership. 'We were here first' is not always as clear-cut as it seems from the outset.

As they consolidated, there were territories certainly from where Inuit retreated, not due to clashes with other indigenous groups, but lack of game or impossible living conditions. Greenland's east coast, save a few pockets of survivors, and much of Canada's High Arctic Archipelago and Ellesmere Island are examples. As mostly maritime cultures, only a few nations of Inuit moved far inland, the latter supported by caribou herds and resorting to burning heather and twigs as they lacked blubber for fuel. Archaeologists must accept that the majority of ancient Inuit belongings were of natural materials and therefore biodegraded.

Populations of communities and wider groupings were comparatively low. Although it is common to describe most pre-contact Inuit as nomadic, that is a simplification and can be an unhelpful synonym for 'primitive'. The truth was very different. When it was prudent to move, they moved. When conditions and game dictated, the people settled, as historic cultures did the world round. Critically, for a variety of practical reasons, herding and farming animals for food and thereafter a division of labour, a prerequisite for almost all advanced civilisations, never took hold.

As the eighteenth century dawned, European mariner explorers had begun to make contact with some Inuit outposts, and the word Eskimo was first used, amongst other even less acceptable phrases, to refer to little-understood northern people en masse. This was the catalyst for rapid and fundamental change, the Age of Contact (in preference to Age of Discovery which demands a unidirectional point of view).

The ethnology of these people was completely unknown at the time, and the vast majority were not yet widely known of, so the very notion of a European or North American scholar being able to subdivide by language or culture at that stage was premature. Eskimos they were, clumsily lumped together as one.

I cannot leave this section without a nod to the other people of the Arctic, those not self-determined as Inuit. Some are only seasonal 'barrenlanders' who retreat back to the woodlands for winter.

It's perhaps easiest to deduce 'who is who' in the modern Arctic by looking at their languages. Languages diverge by cultural and geographical isolation over time, so it follows that the group identity of those people is linked. A good way to picture the current layout, although not exhaustive, is ethnolinguistically, all with their own cultures, traditions and challenges to face.

The Eskimo-Aleut or Eskaleut People
    Aleut (Western Alaska)
    (diverged c.4000 years ago from)
    Eskimo
        Yupik (Northeast Siberia) and Yup'ik (Central Alaska)
        (diverged c.1000 years ago from)
        Inuit (of Nunangat – the Inuit Homeland of Canada, and Greenland)
                Iñupiat (Northern Alaska)
                Inuvialuit (Western Canada)
                Central and Eastern Canadian Inuit Nations
                Kalaallit (Western Greenland)
                Tunumiit (Eastern Greenland)
                Inughuit (Northern Greenland) 'The Polar Eskimos'

Eastern Siberians
    Tungusic (Eastern Siberia)
    Chukotko-Kamchatkan (Extreme East Siberia)

Uralic
    Sami (Norway, Sweden, Finland and Kola, Russia)
    Northern Nenets (North and Central Siberia)
    Numerous additional small nation groups within Arctic Siberia

Turkic, including the Yukuts (North and East Siberia)

Note: Titles here are given in most commonly-used languages and with an attempt to exclude out-dated terms such as Samoyeds, now Nenets. Of course, most of these words have their own translations in each other's languages and in European languages. The Russian categories are heavily simplified, given the vast diversity of native groups there. As with Inuit, the majority of these ethnic group names mean 'people', 'numerous people', or 'real people' in their respective tongues – perhaps to promote unity or come to terms with a wider, far more populous world than first appreciated.

All modern Greenlanders, or Greenlandic Inuit, are obviously descendants of the Canadians, who are in turn descendants of people who made those early Thule migrations from Asia. The majority are Western and Eastern Greenlandic Inuit and after the first settlers found the best hunting grounds and least brutal areas to create communities, their numbers increased. The Far North, beyond today's Polar Eskimo homeland and widely navigated at first, was abandoned due to the total lack of winter daylight, the worst temperatures and poor hunting.

The extreme Northwest, the Melville Bay and Kap York region stretching four hundred miles north to Kane Basin, has had a succession of populations, ebbing and flowing due to migration and famines, as the main route from Canada to Greenland via the frozen Smith Sound. Confusingly, this area can be roughly described as the Thule Region, although the locals now use the Western Greenlandic name of Avanersuaq, or Avanerriaq in Inuktun, but this strictly covers the uninhabited north coast too.

As a stark illustration of the effects of isolation by hundreds of miles of perilous sea ice and mountainous coastline, small populaces, plus an inability to record skills and history, prior to the mid-nineteenth century the knowledge of how to construct a kayak (*qajaq* in Inuktun) from sealskin had been lost, as had the word itself. They numbered barely over one hundred. Instead, they had been locked into the annual cycle of hunting mammals only on the water edge, rafting out on precarious floes of ice, collecting birds and storing them for lean periods. They also wrongly believed that the plentiful caribou on the lowlands were inedible, becoming a taboo, and so turned their bows toward other fare. Regardless, Avanerriaq became a home territory, partly due to its proximity to the North Water polynya, an ocean zone where ice rarely forms, and the wildlife this supported.

To compound this, their generations of separation led to a now-unthinkable belief that they were the only humans in the world. Their self-description, Inughuit, Inugguit or Inughuaq, even means roughly 'great people' or 'the great and real human beings', great here meaning in number, not importance. Only first contact with 'white man', John Ross's expedition in 1818, ended that misbelief. At the time a name 'Arctic Highlanders' was given to the tiny outpost of Polar Eskimos – just thirty families in total across the whole region.

In the 1860s, a final native migration made its way along a treacherous route from the Canadian High Arctic east coast and settled in the area, sharing the vital kayak-making skill that once again allowed enhanced hunting of marine mammals for food, shelter and clothing. The Polar Eskimos were never the most fervent kayakers though compared to Southern Greenlandic Inuit, mainly through fear of walrus attack in open water, and the brief ice-free season. The legendary Qillarsuaq, a native of Baffin Island, led the phenomenal journey without maps, compasses (both of which Inuit have some disdain for) or guns, and cemented Inuit as amongst the world's greatest explorers. Some Polar Eskimo leaders, such as the shaman Hoqqaq in the absence of a 'tribal chief', first had reservations about their influence. Some Canadian Inuit left, many dying in their attempt to return to Canada, and others integrated into the community, eventually comprising fifteen per cent of the tiny population. They also encouraged the renewed hunting of caribou and were widely accepted. I suspect this may be a catalyst of the atypical tendency of the Polar Eskimos to welcome strangers.

The fortunes of these 'Thule People' improved as the decades passed. The term Thule People refers to modern people of the Thule Region/ Avanerriaq, and they are equally descended, no more and no less, from the previous Thule culture as all other modern Inuit. This broad overuse of the word Thule is why I have minimised its use.

The close of the eighteenth century loomed, beckoning the first in a sequence of dramatic changes in the lives of the Polar Eskimos. By that time, this ingenious community had reached the zenith of technological achievement that their climate and sparse natural resources allowed, something few human civilisations have ever attained. They had even escaped a true Stone Age limitation with the discovery of a ferrous meteorite near Kap York, but could not form it beyond basic shapes.

After the first encounter with southern explorers in 1818, a succession of wooden ships had appeared in Polar Eskimo territory throughout the century. Some were looking for fresh trade routes, some to search for shipwrecked or lost expeditions and others to exploit the seal and great whale populations for fur and oil. In almost all cases, though, the white pioneers also paid visits to the various semi-nomadic settlements along the coast (an ingenious rotation system across five zones kept people moving and halted small bands from becoming wealthier than others). The visits were through a variety of scientific and ethnographic interests, for removing meteorites and the like to end up in museums, and sadly as a sign of the times, an interest in using the locals for their skills and knowledge.

In a premonition of their new destiny, it is said on first contact with Ross one Polar Eskimo half lamented, half pleaded, "Don't destroy us – we are alive." It must have been quite a shock, initially believing the large wooden ships to be living things, and experiencing glass and mirrors for the first time – the glass understandably they expected to be formed of ice, yet it was warm and didn't melt.

It is interesting that the very few who took away negative views of the Polar Eskimo characters they encountered and oft-relied upon, were themselves often the scoundrels or magnets for calamity. Adolphus Greely considered them lazy and unreliable when his own 1882-4 expedition, which did admittedly collected vast scientific data, ended in death and disaster. Greely did not even get off to a good start – not on speaking terms with his second in command from Day One and so communicating via written notes. Hayes, a mutineer from Kane's 1854 expedition and sceptic of local prowess, drugged three Polar Eskimos with opiates and stole their furs as they attempted to help him.

Were these contacts with Polar Eskimos the start of a cultural corruption of sorts? The breakdown of what being Inuit really meant? There was now metal for traps, and wood for sleds – improvements, but how would the Polar Eskimos choose to balance history, identity, culture, progress and opportunity?

In the final decade of that exploration-rich century, American Robert E. Peary made his first visit in 1891. A great deal has been written about Robert Peary, Piulerriaq (or Piuli for short) to the locals, probably the most controversial of the early polar explorers; much of it negative regarding both character and actions. I feel that authors Herbert, Harper, Huntford and others have trodden that ground well enough in countless biographies. As such, I'll reflect not on his dubious 1909 North Pole claim, but instead on his significant impact on the lives of those in Avanerriaq and sum up my views on the man himself, mirrored by many.

Peary appeared to be (unmitigated by the apologist line of being a 'product of his time') and from the primary sources available, arrogant to the point of being abusive, and driven by a sense of his self-generated grand destiny. He ordered a barrel of biscuits to be poured out in front of villagers, laughing as they launched themselves in hunger. He even 'exported' a number of Polar Eskimos, only for one to die and have his skeleton displayed in a museum in full view of his son. A Polar Eskimo brought to New York to be 'exhibited' was returned to Greenland, only to be banished to an outlaw's camp for telling of high-rise buildings and telephones.

This unrelenting drive did admittedly lead to his considerable influence and success in some spheres. Critically, though, his obsession with personal triumph and condescension towards those he considered inferior led to deceit – most notably in the insistence of his priority to the North Pole and discovery of non-existent new territory, that he dubbed Crocker Land. He also fathered an extramarital child, Kaalipaluk or just Kaali, by a local Polar Eskimo, Aleqasina, who was aged just fourteen when they began a relationship.

Peary did appear to have an inconsistent paternal, albeit highly patronising, sense of affection for his 'faithful little tribe' though, writing that he hoped they'd escape white man's God, morality, vices and diseases. It was not to be, partly due to the fame he brought them.

From the 1910s onward the Danish, whether they were private explorers or representing the might of colonial Denmark and who I've written about previously, took their lasting position as central to the fate of the Polar Eskimos.

APPENDIX B: Detailed Report on the Viability of Dark Ice Project 2013/14

ONCE THE FOUR of us had digested the news and then checked the main meteorological sources to cross-check (some interpretations of the same ice can actually vary between experts); the Canadian Ice Service (CIS), Danish Meteorological Institute (DMI) and the Norwegian Met, I had to predict what this meant. Having spoken to some of the hunters and forming an average judgement of the inevitable variation in their advice, I came to three conclusions:

1.   Most importantly, the thin to medium ice already formed in the Robeson Channel is likely to disperse south of the huge bulged broken zone edge and then has to reform from scratch. This is likely to result in a highly fractured and rubble-strewn strait, especially the long Kennedy Channel and make it highly unlikely to consolidate or even end up with slow-moving navigable '9+/10' ice. We needed to get out of the straits and onto the Arctic Ocean by the first few days of January at the latest and having an epic drama in the straits would destroy our chances and could even lead to a career-ending, high-profile $5m+ rescue. An added suspicion would be that the instability and lack of thick ice would lead to 'arches', the upper and lower extents of immobile ice, not forming at all (this was later shown not to transpire, but was only an added concern).

2.   Due to the geography of this area of the Arctic, the main flow is uninterrupted from north to south along the western side, with a major 'bulb' of water to the east, north of Inglefield Land, and south of Washington Land. This, the dominant feature of the straits, the Kane Basin, was my second thinking point, but not due to the ice breaking. Because it is somewhat of a siding from the currents, ice is able to form, thicken and consolidate at ease there, not unlike how ice forms easily in narrow fjords, and is annually the first to do so. We were going to rely on this, using the

centre route (also the most direct route to the Kennedy Channel), to cross the basin on relatively good ice.

Why not go all the way over to the east, adding a few miles, to guarantee an even faster surface? Bears. For centuries, the Polar Eskimos of Kap York (Danish term for an area near Savissivik), and north of there to Qaanaaq and beyond, hunted polar bears for fur and meat. The concentrations in the southern extent and into Melville Bay are very high. To the north, the vast majority reside in the eastern coastline of Kane Basin, along the vast Humboldt Glacier. Here, the ice is often broken and the glacier edge provides myriad opportunities for hunting their quarry, seals. Polar bears will also congregate along newly forming ice edges (to the western side of Kane Basin) where seals haul out on the ice and come up to breathe. Our original plan therefore was to move through the consolidated centre route, directly to Washington Land, and minimise the chance of polar bear encounters in the dark. With open water (and highly mobile, super-thin ice) existing far, far north of Smith Sound and into the basin, plus only a thin band of consolidated ice in the east abutting the Humboldt Glacier, we would have to head far east.

We consulted with local hunters, finding that only some had ventured far north, past the most remote ruined huts that provided shelter, to that region. Although opinions varied, word of mouth and stories passed down the generations was very persuasive to the people and we listened to second hand stories with due care. I asked a few clear questions, via Anders in Danish or Hans in English, "if we were to be travelling on Kane Basin on the eastern route with the ice extent as low as it is now, with only a single bear-dog and not a team, would we have daily encounters with polar bears?" The answer was an emphatic yes. Polar bears are terrified of dog teams, and hunters actually have a job getting close enough to hunt them. A single dog though was for us purely an alarm and not a defence. We had expected occasional polar bear encounters, some aggressive, some predatory and some benign, if they were dispersed over a vast area and if away from their hunting territory. It dawned that with them likely to be concentrated into a smaller area, one we had to travel over

332

a hundred miles through, we would be constantly bothered by them.

In the dark during the working 'day' it would be arduous and demanding of our vigilance; at night it could end in tragedy. Heavily armed, I fancied our chances in most situations, but that was not really the point. We did not go there to kill polar bears, some of the most majestic, let alone IUCN Threatened, mammals on Earth. An Arctic expedition in the 1960s I will not name out of understanding for them behaving as was accepted at that time, killed so many polar bears that they had to call in an airdrop for more rifle ammunition. It would be tragedy; for the bears, for us, for expeditions, for everyone.

3.   Closer to Qaanaaq, the lack of snow even by local standards was very evident and the Polar Eskimo hunters had been complaining about it from day one. Sea ice is the preferred route, due to its hardness and it providing flatter routes, but occasionally overland shortcuts and rocky routes around headlands are needed. No snow means no sled travel on land and this could become a major issue for us.

APPENDIX C: The Attitude of the Visitor and the Visited

WHEN YOU CONSIDER a group of travellers from Europe, or a similarly developed region, appearing in a far-flung corner of the globe with an intention of writing of what they find, it can be a controversial can of worms that you unwittingly fling open. With centuries of conquest, war, slaughter, exploitation and outright racist abuse, most would flinch to become too heavily immersed in modern-day reportage. Outlooks are frequently emotive and deep-rooted, understandably, but they can also be outdated. Some nations have a particularly bad track record, mine included, and so to try and claim any moral authority or even a fair hearing is tough in some audiences. My team's cultural expedition gave rise to these concerns and challenges – very different to those I had anticipated for our winter alone on the ice of the Nares Strait and Arctic Ocean.

We could have decided to isolate ourselves and just get on with our journeys, not bothering nor integrating with *qaanaarmiut* (people of Qaanaaq). I couldn't resolve that though – it was counter to the goodwill we wanted to convey and knowledge we wished to absorb. I kept a mental code in my head – listen, never attempt to patronise or circumvent, work hard and importantly, don't be afraid to gently and constructively criticise. The first three in that list would afford us a pleasant time and would allow us to learn and accumulate new skills. The fourth is the one that needs explanation.

Balanced accountability is critical if bridges are ever to be genuinely built and old wounds soothed for good. I think that it applies to any reconciliation and trust-building process where old differences are being put to one side and a future striven towards – any situation where bigotry, discrimination, domination or even slavery existed. This is about our modern attitudes day to day and objective pragmatism must pervade.

There is an offence-phobic syndrome that many descended from historic perpetrators often display – automatic deferral and reverence to those who have suffered in the past, or now still. This can lead to an assumption of local superiority and good judgement by, in this case a small native Arctic community, and an assumption of bigotry and arrogance by any visitor. "They've lived here for centuries. It's their land. They'll always know best." To me, this appears to be an 'over-swung pendulum' in attitudes to make amends for years of hurt. In the same way that tokenism and artificial positive discrimination are an ineffective solution to inequality elsewhere, so it is in the remote corners of the globe. Some go a step further and advocate the self-flagellation of those with the audacity to be born into a community with historic links to shameful past behaviour. The counter-point is simple – it was not them, in the same way that a newborn German must not bear the mark of Cain for what some of their nation perpetrated in the name of National Socialism.

I would strongly advocate that those who have previously suffered the ills of colonisation and today occupy the less privileged rungs of an imperfect world, should not be made to be special cases. People do not respect special cases; they pity and tokenise them. These people should be held to the same scrutiny as all others, be valued for successes and called out for shortcomings. Then, in time, we might generate equality and decency from positions of mutual strength.

Some might decry my viewpoint as another example of a beneficiary occupying a demographic that has suffered little and has through modern history enjoyed opportunity. In fact, my own homeland has through the centuries been plundered, invaded and occupied multiple times by ancestors of our now European neighbours. My answer is that we need to treat people and their attitudes as individuals, not occupants of a generalised demographic pigeonhole unchanging through generations. I am not my ancestor, and neither are you yours.

If we seek historical recriminations, overcompensation and polarised bitter tribalism, we'll never find a solution. The pendulum of unfairness has existed for too long, held up to one side to benefit certain groups. We must together bring it to the central resting point, and not fling it violently over to the other side, only for it to swing back years later with equal ferocity.

I mulled over this sensitive, complex issue after reading a book by a jungle traveller and now television presenter. A British white, middle-class ex-Army officer, so in some minds undeserving of his platform, he decided to travel through the entire Amazon region over a period of several years on foot, albeit not in unbroken steps. Daily interactions with native communities were fundamental to success or failure, and even his survival.

One repeated viewpoint and spark of his modern sense of balance struck me. In an outdoor industry where every word by faux-humble Westerners speaking of native people is almost sycophantic, he saw them as no higher or lower than a person in the street at home. A real respect. There were good people, friends, but also scoundrels, idiots, drunks and incompetents. There were childish squabbles and reunions. The whole fabric of life was exposed and so was a true, realistic community. The key was he was comfortable to say all this without fear of attacks from the outside of colonial arrogance or racism – words carelessly doled out like bitter sweets in today's world of online article comments and anonymous, rage-blinded tweeters.

I would implore all those who encounter the Arctic, its people, its economics or its politics to reset their preconceptions. The wrongs of the past, as well as the myths, can be coaxed to remain there and not poison the future. Hold a person of the Arctic responsible for their actions and in the same regard as any other, or yourself. Not any higher, not any lower. Listen to, debate with, laugh with, criticise and praise. After all, why would you do otherwise? Only through this will they receive the platform and respect they may deserve – not pity, scorn or patronisation.

As someone who was going to speak, write and broadcast my experiences to a world with limited knowledge of the Far North, I had to remember: nothing is above derision if the evidence supports something contrary. There is no ring fence, only consistency – regardless of romanticism or faith. It's a 'tough love' route to an equal playing field. I had to tell the story of these remarkable people in a way a reader could trust as balanced, not as another awe-struck fan or one scared of reprisal from those with an axe to grind and without appetite for reconciliation.

The truth was the aim, and a phenomenal responsibility.

Second Edition Note
September 2020

QAANAAQ STILL EXISTS. This is good news. I didn't, and did not six years ago when I first starting writing this book, believe it would vanish. It's very hard for anything man-made to simply cease to exist in the High Arctic – such is the ability of the cold and dry air to preserve. But, neither have we been left with an abandoned ghost town. Indeed, the population is stable, even if not in all Avanerriaq's settlements. There is a retreat from the north that has progressed for centuries, as Siorapaluk's population is two-thirds of what I found on my last visit. Today this is driven predominantly by ice conditions, with more weeks of being cut off added each year, rather than a search for better game hunting or more amiable weather. Qeqertat stubbornly maintains its occupancy of two-dozen, but Savissivik is leaking families similarly to Siorapaluk – their destination? Qaanaaq. In turn, Qaanaaq is losing people to West Greenland, but birth rates are steadying any decline.

There has been some conspicuous investment, with the creation of a shingle quay perpendicular to the beach, allowing for easier unloading of shipped goods during the summer. I'm concerned that this is a multi-step plan. If Qaanaaq receives cursory investment, the tiny settlements will empty into it. Then, it's reasonably straightforward to use similar 'encouragement' to leave the Far North altogether.

But these are the statistics and the trends. Beneath these numbers are more nuanced lifestyle shifts – an unrelenting march toward something that still appears undefined. Each year I see more and more photos of my Polar Eskimo friends visiting family in the South, and in Denmark. Some have left altogether, although a handful returned. Poor Rasmus, with little other option, had to euthanise the majority of his dogs as the demands of alternative employment bit; the story even found its way onto online news portals outside of Greenland.

I don't see a people in command of their destiny, rather reacting to events as best they can. I again lay the blame in large part at the door of the government in Nuuk; through their lack of willingness to represent their people, and a void of long-term strategic thinking. The Polar Eskimos lack champions elsewhere; fifteen years ago the Danish courts absurdly ruled that they are no different culturally to other Greenlanders, and this attitude has stuck.

Film and television networks, with their eco-financiers and Hollywood A-listers, appear in the region for a week or so, get their clichéd visuals, and are never heard from again. The odd near-fetishisation of the 'noble savage' seems so hard to eradicate. My hope in the later section of this book that the people of Avanerriaq can be valued no lower and no higher than any other community, still seems distant. It requires compromise and realism from the inhabitants, but also decent behaviour from those who deal with the people, their leaders, and their institutions. I do not know if the North will close entirely in the medium term, but I cannot see how the current balance is viable into the future. Not enough people care about the maintenance of the culture, the language or the unique history, beyond casual attention throughout a ten-minute daytime news piece on CNN. That's the truth. The few that do care wield pitiful influence, and so we have this sad inevitability.

At the level of global leadership, there's simply no motivation to maintain isolated native populations. The people of Avanerriaq will continue to prove, like in the 1950s, a minor public relations irritation as the consolidation of military, mining, drilling and research interests enter a new era. Elsewhere one anomaly, the Sentinelese of a small Indian Ocean island, have rejected any outside integration, usually with a deadly volley of arrows. This wish has been latterly respected by their nominal government in India, and even photography of the tribe is banned. This will never apply to the Polar Eskimos. None of them wish for a return to pre-Contact conditions, and their admittance to the modern world is already apace.

Thule dogs are reducing in number proportionately to the decreasing freedom of the Polar Eskimo people to fish and hunt as a full time occupation. There are still hundreds, and breeding and maintaining their special attributes is not complex, so there is some cause for optimism. But, I worry that this spectacular variety of Arctic sled dog may end up having a handful of examples exported to the south, and then entered into the perverse breed-standard and kennel club system. Genetic variety and health will suffer, and descendants could end up a mere nostalgic reminder of what used to be; running and living with their Polar Eskimo companions in the Far North. This exotic provenance would no doubt be front and centre in how the pups would be marketed by breeders. Soon, their temperament as pets would be found lacking, and so cross-breeding would ensure the extinction of the Thule dog. Here is just one other reason why it should be politically toxic for the slow suffocation of Polar Eskimo life to continue unquestioned.

Inuktun, not even explicitly named as such by those who speak it natively, still lacks any formal definition or lexicon beyond some attempts at word lists by foreign linguists. When I showed these lists to friends as I asked for advice on spellings and meanings, their inaccuracy was told by the grimaces each time I turned a page. For a dialect with so few speakers, and so little consequent inertia, I think we will see the last speaker of what could be termed 'original' Inuktun pass away in the next decade or so. Some may react with a shrug. Language changes with time and cannot be halted for posterity.

I add this section amidst a strange year, in the second of no doubt many phases of the Covid-19 saga, and with a swathe of politically-charged social unrest combining to unsettle a world that previously seemed to be following a series of competing political and cultural avenues with unstoppable might. This may prove an anchor to small indigenous groups looking invitingly out, and often enviously, at the world they are irreversibly more a part of every day. Isolationism and fear may result. The same fallout may also install a new approach to race relations, rarely more evident in former colonies. The form that takes remains to be seen, but I can't imagine the matter of Greenland decoupling from Denmark will escape being drawn in, for good or for ill.

My solutions to what you could reasonably summarise as a gloomy outlook? A focus on investment in education, especially in small settlements. An immediate reversal of draconian rulings to penalise subsistence hunters and fishermen. Legal protection for Greenland dogs, and especially of each regional variety like the Thule dog. A ban on unneutered dogs being exported, and a continuation of restrictions for introducing other breeds to the region, except if under careful supervision to repopulate after a disease outbreak. Investment in an official written and oral record of Avanerriaq's dialect. Creation of protected areas around a broad zone where today's Polar Eskimos live and travel, with military and non-Greenlandic commercial activity banned within its borders. Improved subsidy for flights to and from Avanerriaq for residents, so life in the region is less of a financial penalty.

I recognise the imperfection inherent in my suggestions. They offer little certainty, and vary from the dispassionate and essential to the unashamedly subjective. I feel there should be space for both when you consider the future of a way of life. As for the certainty – well, none of us have a right to that.

To you, having read my contribution, I just ask for your thoughts, and for you to discuss them with those around you. Imagine the knock-on effects those thoughts could have if translated into action; whether subconscious and indirect, or as a concerted effort.

ACKNOWLEDGEMENTS

ANY WORK THAT tells a story of another people stands, at best, on brittle foundations if it is not written collaboratively. The four years of work that have concluded with the release of *Polar Eskimo* could have been compressed into a quarter of that time. However, this would have missed the point. The opinions (especially conflicting ones), advice and guidance of native people, travellers, linguists and other experts are why I believe this book can contribute to a snapshot of Avanerriaq in the early twenty-first century. These people offered their time generously and so I would like to extend my gratitude.

The people of Avanerriaq, including those we did not have a chance to meet, and in particular:

    Navarana K'avigak
    Aaqioq (who we knew as Peter Duneq)
    Marius Didriksen
    Else Nielsen
    Hans and Birthe Jensen
    Rasmus Avike
    Karen Pollas
    Mikael Jensen

Finn Hansen
Aleqatsiaq (Peter) Peary
David Qujaukitsoq
Mads Ole Kristiansen
Lars Jeremiassen

From the south:

My family
James Wheeldon
Anders Rasmussen
Anastasia Kim
Tilly Alcayna-Stevens and her support team
Merete Laubjerg
Troels Lund Brink
Robert Peroni
Admiral Sir Nigel Essenhigh RN
Captain Christopher Page RN
Dan Bernard *and the team at my publishers, distributors and printers*
Paul Cosgrove *from Montane*
Carolyn Dunn *from Bridgedale*
Eddie Bocquillon *from Aspen Fuels*
Mike Madylus *from Blackfriars*
Nick Farrell *from YB Tracking*
Tony Stephenson *from Tentipi*
Paresh Ruparelia *from Ledlenser*
Col Stocker *from Alpkit*
Dave Annandale *from BeWell*
Jenna Foster *from GTC*
Stephen Hoyt and Alex Stubbing
Mike Lunn
Trudy Wohlleben
Air Greenland Charters
Christian Fensbo
Dr Alexander Kumar
Kevin Pocklington
and many others, both home and overseas

FURTHER READING

Bown, Stephen R. *White Eskimo*, (Da Capo, 2015)

Breum, Martin. *The Greenland Dilemma: The Quest for Independence, the Underground Riches and the Troubled Relations with Denmark*, (Royal Danish Defence College, 2015)

Caulfield, Richard. *Greenlanders, Whales, and Whaling: Sustainability and Self-Determination in the Arctic*, (Dartmouth, 2000)

Cook, Frederick A. *My Attainment of the Pole*, (Mitchell and Kinnerley, 1913)

Dick, Lyle. *Muskox Land*, (UCP, 2001)

Dorais, Louis-Jacques. *The Language of the Inuit*, (McGill-Queen's UP, 2010)

Fortescue, Michael. *Inuktun. An Introduction to the Language of Qaanaaq*, (Institut for Eskimologi 15, Copenhagen University, 1991)

Freuchen, Peter. *Arctic Adventure; My Life in the Frozen North*, (Farrar and Rinehart, 1935)

*Freuchen, Peter. *Book of the Eskimos*, (Fawcett, 1973)

Galvin, Anthony. *The Great Polar Fraud: Cook, Peary, and Byrd*, (Skyhorse Publishing, 2014)

Gilberg, Rolf. *Changes in the Life of the Polar Eskimos Resulting From a Canadian Immigration into the Thule District, North Greenland, in the 1860s*, (Folk 16-17, 1974-75)

Grant, Shelaugh. *Inuit Relocations to the High Arctic, 1954-1960 "Errors Exposed"*, (Royal Commission on Aboriginal Peoples, 1993)

Greely, Adolphus W. *Three Years of Arctic Service*, (Charles Scribner's, 1886)

Harper, Kenn. *Give Me My Father's Body: The Life of Minik, The New York Eskimo*, (Blacklead Books, 1986)

Hauser, Michael. *Traditional Inuit Songs from the Thule Area*, (Museum Tusculanum Press 2010

Hendrik, Hans. *Memoirs of Hans Hendrik, the Arctic Traveller, Serving under Kane, Hayes, Hall and Nares, 1853-1876: Translated From The Eskimo Language*, (Cambridge University Press, 1878)

Herbert, Wally. *Hunters of the Polar North: The Eskimo*, (Time-Life Books, 1981)

Herbert, Wally. *The Noose of Laurels: The Discovery of the North Pole*, (Hodder and Stoughton, 1989)

Hibbert, Alex. *The Long Haul*, (Tricorn, 2010)

Hibbert, Alex. *Maybe*, (Tricorn, 2013)

Hingitaq 53, The American Journal of International Law Vol. 98, No. 3, Pages 572-578, (CUP, 2004)

Holtved, Erik. *Contributions to Polar Eskimo Ethnography*, (Meddelelser om Grønland, 1967)

Holtved, Erik. *The Polar Eskimos*, (International Polar Institute, 2011)

Jenkins, McKay. *Bloody Falls of the Coppermine: Madness, Murder and the Collision of Cultures in the Arctic, 1913*, (Random House, 2005)

Kroeber, A. L. *The Eskimo of Smith Sound*, (AMNH, 1899)

Lee, Hugh J. *Polar Eskimos – Houses and Tents, Igloos and Tupiks*, (Unpublished, 1894)

Malaurie, Jean. *Ultima Thule*, (Hachette, 2000)

*Malaurie, Jean. *The Last Kings of Thule*, (UoC Press, 1982)

Markham, Clements. *The Lands of Silence: A History of Arctic and Antarctic Exploration*, (CUP, 1921)

Final Report of the Truth and Reconciliation Commission of Canada, (McGill-Queen's UP, 2016)

Nuttall, Mark. *Arctic Homeland: Kinship, Community and Development in Northwest Greenland*, (University of Toronto, 1992)

Peary, Josephine. *My Arctic Journal: A Year Among Ice-field and Eskimos*, (Contemporary Publishing Co, 1893)

Peary, Robert E. *Greenland Diaries 1898-1902*

Peary, Robert E. *Secrets of Polar Travel*, (The Century Company, 1917)

*Rasmussen, Knud. *The People of the Polar North*, (Kegan Paul, Tenth, Trubner and co, 1908)

*Rasmussen, Knud. *Greenland by the Polar Sea*, (William Henemann, 1921)

RCAP. *The High Arctic Relocation: A Report on the 1953-55 Relocations*, (RCAP, 1994)

Riffenburgh, Beau. *The Myth of the Explorer: The Press, Sensationalism, and Geographical Discovery*, (SPRI, 1993)

Ross, John. *A Voyage of Discovery Vol. I*, (John Murray, 1819)

Schledermann, Peter. *Crossroads to Greenland*, (The Arctic Institute of North America, 1990)

Sonne, Birgitte. *Worldviews of the Greenlanders: An Inuit Arctic Perspective*, (UoA Press, 2018)

Steele, Harwood. *Policing the Arctic: The Story of the Conquest of the Arctic by the Royal Canadian Mounted Police*, (The Ryerson Press, 1935)

Steensby, H. P. *The Polar Eskimos and the Polar Expeditions*, (Fortnightly Review, 1909)

Sverdrup, Otto. *New Land: Four Years in the Arctic Regions Vol. I & II*, (Longmans, Green and Co, 1904)

Uvdloriaq, Inuuterssuaq. *The Narrative of Qitdlarssuaq*, (Translated by Kenn and Navarana Harper)

Vaughan, Richard. *Northwest Greenland: A History*, (UoM Press, 1991)

It is undeniable that oral histories and, latterly, a handful of films and other modern media created by Inuit, especially of Avanerriaq, do exist. But, it cannot escape notice that almost all written publications on this list are the work of outsiders. This was not for want of searching for relevant material. Encouragingly, there is a recent trend for improved representation across Arctic territories in artistic, music and literary works. I would be very pleased to see a work by an Arctic native (ideally from northern Greenland) on their history and from their own perspective. The need is urgent, so-as to not lose the accrued recollection of older generations. I, and those in positions of influence, should champion and facilitate this.